AF173474

Studies in Global Science Fiction

Series Editors
Anindita Banerjee
Department of Comparative Literature
Cornell University
Ithaca, NY, USA

Rachel Haywood Ferreira
Department of World Languages and Cultures
Iowa State University
Ames, IA, USA

Mark Bould
Department of Film and Literature
University of the West of England
Bristol, UK

Studies in Global Science Fiction (edited by Anindita Banerjee, Rachel Haywood Ferreira, and Mark Bould) is a brand-new and first-of-its-kind series that opens up a space for Science Fiction scholars across the globe, inviting fresh and cutting-edge studies of both non-Anglo-American and Anglo-American SF literature. Books in this series will put SF in conversation with postcolonial studies, critical race studies, comparative literature, transnational literary and cultural studies, among others, contributing to ongoing debates about the expanding global compass of the genre and the emergence of a more diverse, multinational, and multi-ethnic sense of SF's past, present, and future. Topics may include comparative studies of selected (trans)national traditions, SF of the African or Hispanic Diasporas, Indigenous SF, issues of translation and distribution of non-Anglophone SF, SF of the global south, SF and geographic/cultural borderlands, and how neglected traditions have developed in dialogue and disputation with the traditional SF canon.

Editors
Anindita Banerjee, Cornell University
Rachel Haywood Ferreira, Iowa State University
Mark Bould, University of the West of England

Advisory Board Members
Aimee Bahng, Dartmouth College
Ian Campbell, Georgia State University
Grace Dillon (Anishinaabe), Portland State University
Rob Latham, Independent Scholar
Andrew Milner, Monash University
Pablo Mukherjee, University of Warwick
Stephen Hong Sohn, University of California, Riverside
Mingwei Song, Wellesley College

More information about this series at
http://www.palgrave.com/gp/series/15335

Carol Margaret Davison
Marie Mulvey-Roberts
Editors

Global Frankenstein

Editors
Carol Margaret Davison
Department of English Language,
Literature and Creative Writing
University of Windsor
Windsor, ON, Canada

Marie Mulvey-Roberts
Department of Arts and Cultural
Industries
University of the West of England
Bristol, UK

ISSN 2569-8826   ISSN 2569-8834 (electronic)
Studies in Global Science Fiction
ISBN 978-3-030-08623-7   ISBN 978-3-319-78142-6 (eBook)
https://doi.org/10.1007/978-3-319-78142-6

© The Editor(s) (if applicable) and The Author(s) 2018
Softcover re-print of the Hardcover 1st edition 2018
This work is subject to copyright. All rights are solely and exclusively licensed by the Publisher, whether the whole or part of the material is concerned, specifically the rights of translation, reprinting, reuse of illustrations, recitation, broadcasting, reproduction on microfilms or in any other physical way, and transmission or information storage and retrieval, electronic adaptation, computer software, or by similar or dissimilar methodology now known or hereafter developed.
The use of general descriptive names, registered names, trademarks, service marks, etc. in this publication does not imply, even in the absence of a specific statement, that such names are exempt from the relevant protective laws and regulations and therefore free for general use.
The publisher, the authors and the editors are safe to assume that the advice and information in this book are believed to be true and accurate at the date of publication. Neither the publisher nor the authors or the editors give a warranty, express or implied, with respect to the material contained herein or for any errors or omissions that may have been made. The publisher remains neutral with regard to jurisdictional claims in published maps and institutional affiliations.

Cover credit: CSA Images/Getty

This Palgrave Macmillan imprint is published by the registered company Springer Nature Switzerland AG
The registered company address is: Gewerbestrasse 11, 6330 Cham, Switzerland

For Kestrel Zandra Davison, Charlotte and Emma Evans,
and girls and young women everywhere
and their waking dreams, wild and visionary.

Foreword

Many people have a story of how they first came across *Frankenstein*. Here's mine. I was about ten, and the books for adults in my parents' modest-sized living-room bookcase were beginning to interest me more than Enid Blyton's weekly magazine *Sunny Stories*. The bookcase contained a stout Casket-of-Literature kind of production called *The World's Best Books*, compiled in about 1934 by a literary man, Wilfred Whitten, who called himself John O'London. I have it still, its binding cracked by the tropic sun, its hinges loose. *The World's Best Books* went from Plato on the Death of Socrates to James Barrie's *The Little Minister*, taking in *Macbeth* and *Adam Bede* on the way—and *Frankenstein*. Of course, it did not contain the whole of the World's Best Books, only thrilling highlights from some of them, strung together with plot summaries and many, many fuzzy pictures, some taken from old British silent movies. This abridged *Frankenstein* was embellished with a portrait of Mary Wollstonecraft Shelley, her piercing, lashless eyes staring from the page. Her middle name was sinister to my ears, suggesting the craftiness of a wolf and a heart of stone. The James Whale film was not mentioned, but an illustration by an unknown artist showed the Creature, gaunt and bony, cackling with glee, bounding downhill with barefoot leaps, his black hair and tattered tunic streaming in the wind, casting a huge shadow on the opposite mountain slope. As a result, the lumbering fellow with the bolt through his neck has always struck me, I regret to say, as a bit of an imposter.

Frankenstein did not scare me out of my wits, but it did leave me with a recurrent waking dream in which a bony phantom hand would grab me by the throat and strangle me without leaving a mark. Retrospectively, I realised it also left me bothered by the sense of a world gone wrong for which there was no redress. Life was not fair, I knew, but books should be. The fairy tales that I had recently left behind me were full of outrageous creations and transformations, people being turned into asses, statues coming alive, and so on. But they usually ended in some kind of restorative justice. The good might not always prosper, but they would be vindicated in some way. The wise Socrates in *The World's Best Books* was made to drink hemlock, but the record of his calmness in death lived on to show that the good die bravely.

The Creature, however, had murdered innocent people, including a child. Having cheerfully led Frankenstein on to his death, he now declared that he was going to exult as he died in agony on his self-built funeral pyre, so ending up being even braver than Socrates. But as the story finished there, perhaps he was just boasting and had no intention of carrying out his promise. It was very perplexing. But if my moral world was rattled, John O'London's headnote was clear on a crucial point. It warned readers in no uncertain terms against the popular error that Frankenstein is the name of a monster. This was NOT TRUE, for "the only person who ever created a Frankenstein was Mary Shelley, the second wife of the poet." That, at least, was straightforward. A selection of famous poems by the poet in question was also included in *The World's Best Books*. So there they both were, Mary Wollstonecraft and Percy Bysshe, equals in John O'London's eyes.

As Mary Shelley would have said, it was that day that decided my destiny, or a good part of it. Which is how, in 1997, I found myself co-convening "Mary Shelley: Parents, Peers, and Progeny", a conference celebrating the bicentenary of Mary Shelley's birth, at the present Anglia Ruskin University in Cambridge. By this time, the perplexities that bothered my ten-year-old self had been reconfigured. Recuperating Mary Shelley's reputation as an author of many different kinds of writing, and situating her in the literary world of pre-Victorian Britain, was the work that (it seemed to me and others) most needed to be done at the time. It still continues. Twenty years ago, the emphasis was very much on "The Other Mary Shelley," "Mary Shelley in Her Times," and "Mary Shelley Beyond *Frankenstein*." It is a sign of those times that Marie Mulvey-Roberts, then best known for her groundbreaking study of Rosicrucian fiction, *Gothic Immortals*, contributed one of the only papers on *Frankenstein*, "The Corpse in the Corpus: *Frankenstein*, Rewriting Wollstonecraft and the Abject," splendid in title, original in content.

(Many of the conference papers, including Marie's, were later collected by Michael Eberle-Sinatra and published by Macmillan, just before it became Palgrave, in 2000 as *Mary Shelley's Fictions: From Frankenstein to Falkner.*) That was 20 years ago. But now, in 2018, the bicentenary of *Frankenstein* refocuses attention on Mary Shelley's first and best book. In his day, John O'London was unusual in valuing Mary Shelley's horror novel as a classic of literature, but he could not have predicted that it would become the most taught of all novels in the world. During the 1970s and 1980s, *Frankenstein* was revalorised as a feminist psychobiography, the first true science-fiction novel, a *chef-d'oeuvre* of female gothic, and a political allegory about the origins of the French Revolution. Attention was paid to close reading of *Frankenstein* as text; the first edition, out of print since 1818, was reprinted several times, and a debate ensued as to the degree to which Percy Shelley's interventions in the text had improved the writing or perverted Mary Shelley's intentions. Later, it turned out that Mary Shelley was not the first person to make a Frankenstein. In 2009, Julia Douthwaite discovered a precursor, Félix Nogaret's political allegory, *Le Miroir des événemens actuels* (1790), in which a scientist called Frankénsteïn makes a full-sized mechanical man who plays the flute. In the third millennium, it has become a commonplace to say that *Frankenstein* continues undiminished as a modern myth, speaking to many fears and burning issues of the twenty-first century. Elements within *Frankenstein* are found to anticipate modern ecocriticism, disability studies, transgender concerns, posthumanism, and anxieties about robotics. There has been a notable shift of scholarly interest towards the afterlives of *Frankenstein*. *Frankenstein* studies have fractured into disparate areas of expertise. The extraordinary proliferation of texts, contexts, and adaptations has surpassed the capacity of any single person to encompass them all. All the more reason to take the opportunity to mark *Frankenstein*'s bicentenary by opening up spaces where specialism can converse with specialism, as Marie Mulvey-Roberts and Carol Margaret Davison, globally known for their work on the Gothic, have done in assembling this collection. The contributors, established names and new ones, bring fresh insights to traditional areas such as Frankensteinian science, medicine, and monstrosity, or uncover fresh evidence of *Frankenstein*'s influence. It is hard to imagine a *Frankenstein* buff who will not learn something new—the sizable corpus of *Frankenstein* adaptations for children, for instance, or what happens to *Frankenstein* when it becomes a digital game. It is both a celebration and a guide to the cutting-edge areas in *Frankenstein* studies today.

Running through the collection is a thread of thought-provoking enquiry: are we approaching the limits to which *Frankenstein* can be adapted and still retain any meaningful relation to the original? The question is both pertinent and ironic: *Frankenstein* is itself a patchwork of other writings, an adaptation of (among other things) Greek myth, Shakespearean drama, the Godwinian novel, and perhaps even *Harlequin and Asmodeus*, the Covent Garden Christmas pantomime for 1810. William Godwin went to the Christmas show at Covent Garden theatre annually. It was his wont to take his family with him, including his daughter, Mary. In the 1810 season, they would have seen the master-clown Joseph Grimaldi beaten and chased off the stage by a pumpkin-headed man that he had created out of Covent Garden vegetables. It was a famous turn of Grimaldi; after *Frankenstein* was published, he began to be called Joe Frankenstein. Years later, people still remembered his fight with the Vegetable Man as one of the funniest things that they had ever seen. But if *Frankenstein* began with a pumpkin, the whirligig of Time has brought the pumpkin round again. Today, farmers looking for a seasonal novelty crop produce Pumpkinsteins for the Halloween trade, squashes grown in moulds in the shape of the head of Karloff's monster.

I am interrupted in these reveries. What do these sounds portend? I must arise and examine. What is this? It is an email about Frankenreads, a worldwide planned celebration of *Frankenstein*, sponsored by the Keats-Shelley Association of America, involving readings of the novel and other events worldwide on the model of the Joycean Bloomsday, to take place during Halloween 2018. Readers, teachers, and devotees of *Frankenstein* will be able to do more than put a scary Pumpkinstein in the window. As I write, 140 participant institutions in 30 countries are signed up to the project. A literalisation of the title of Mulvey-Roberts' and Davison's scintillating and timely collection—*Global Frankenstein* indeed!

Anglia Ruskin University   Nora Crook
Cambridge, UK
January, 2018

ACKNOWLEDGEMENTS

We would like to thank series editor Mark Bould for his encouragement and astute advice throughout the course of this project and Ryan Jenkins at Palgrave New York for his boundless enthusiasm at the onset. After he left the company, Ben Doyle at Palgrave, UK, proved to be a steady hand on the tiller during the transitional period before we were passed back to the New York office and into the safe hands of Allie Bochicchio who has been, along with her team, both helpful and efficient. Marie would like to thank the Department of Arts at the University of the West of England for their support and Angela Wright and Andrew Smith for creating some Frankenstein opportunities for her, which included judging a short story competition. Carol would like to thank generations of students over the years—undergraduate and graduate—who have brought *Frankenstein* to life for her in ways weird, sophisticated, and unimaginable. Thanks go to our loved ones for helping to see us through the Frankenstein years, especially Nigel Biggs, Marion Glastonbury, Maria Santamaria, William, Zandra, and Kestrel Davison. After 20 years of committed friendship and scholarly dialogue on vampires, monsters (especially female), dissection, medical nightmares, and all things Gothic, this is our first collaboratively birthed baby, born of a shared love of Mary Shelley. We hope we did her proud and look forward to other "hideous progeny" to come.

CONTENTS

NOTES ON CONTRIBUTORS

Emily Alder is Lecturer in Literature and Culture at Edinburgh Napier University, where she teaches nineteenth-century literature, popular culture, children's literature, and ecocriticism. Her research interests are interdisciplinary and lie in literature and science, environmental humanities, and weird, Gothic, and science fiction especially of the late nineteenth and early twentieth centuries. Recent publications include a special issue of *Gothic Studies* on Nautical Gothic, and she is at work on a monograph, *Weird Fiction and Science at the Fin de siècle*. She is an assistant editor for *Gothic Studies* and is a member of the Young Academy of Scotland.

Fred Botting is a professor in the School of Humanities, Kingston University, London. He has written extensively on Gothic fictions and literary theory and has published several books including *Making Monstrous: Frankenstein, Criticism, Theory* (1991), *Sex, Machines and Navels* (1999), and *Limits of Horror* (2008).

Scott Bukatman is a cultural theorist and Professor of Film and Media Studies at Stanford University. His research explores how such popular media as film, comics, and animation mediate between new technologies and human perceptual and bodily experience. His books include *Terminal Identity: The Virtual Subject in Postmodern Science Fiction* (1993), one of the earliest book-length studies of cyberculture; a monograph on the film *Blade Runner* (2012) commissioned by the British Film Institute; and a collection of essays, *Matters of Gravity: Special Effects and Supermen in the 20th Century*. *The Poetics of Slumberland:*

Animated Spirits and the Animating Spirit (2012) celebrates play, plasmatic possibility, and the life of images in cartoons, comics, and cinema. *Hellboy's World: Comics and Monsters on the Margins* (2016) investigates the "adventure of reading" that comics offer. Bukatman has been published in abundant journals and anthologies, including *October, Critical Inquiry, Camera Obscura,* and *Science Fiction Studies.*

Nora Crook Jamaican by birth and upbringing, is Professor Emerita of English Literature at Anglia Ruskin University, Cambridge. She has published widely on Romantic Period subjects and is best known for her editing of the Shelleys. She is a general editor of 12 volumes of the novels, biographical work, and miscellaneous writings of Mary Shelley (1996, 2002) and editor of Mary Shelley's *Frankenstein* and *Valperga.* She is co-general editor of the *Complete Poetry of Percy Bysshe Shelley* (three volumes published of eight planned), with special responsibility for poems that Mary Shelley published after Percy Shelley's death.

Carol Margaret Davison is Professor at the University of Windsor and a former Canada-US Fulbright Scholar. She is the author of *History of the Gothic: Gothic Literature, 1764–1824* (2009) and *Anti-Semitism and British Gothic Literature* (Palgrave Macmillan 2004). The editor of essay collections on *Dracula*, Marie Corelli, and the Gothic and addiction, her most recent edited collections are *The Gothic and Death* (2017) and *The Edinburgh Companion to the Scottish Gothic* (2017), co-edited with Monica Germanà. She is the author of dozens of articles and book chapters on the Gothic, Victorian literature, African-American literature, American literature, and cultural teratology, and remains the Director of the sickly taper website, the world's largest and most comprehensive website devoted to Gothic bibliography (www.thesicklytaper.ca). She is at work compiling a multi-volume collection devoted to the reception history of British and American Gothic literature.

Courtney A. Hoffman is a PhD candidate at the University of Georgia. Her dissertation project focuses on the interactions of temporality and affect in the exchange of letters in epistolary fiction of the eighteenth century, arguing that after *Pamela*, literary understandings of time passing become deeply entwined with expressions of feeling in epistolary novels. She is a past visiting fellow at the Chawton House Library and has an essay entitled "How to Be Woman in the Highlands: A Feminist Portrayal of Scotland in *Outlander*" to be published in a forthcoming volume, *The Cinematic Eighteenth Century.*

Jerrold E. Hogle is Professor of English and University Distinguished Professor Emeritus at the University of Arizona in USA. A past president of the International Gothic Association, he has been honoured with Guggenheim, Mellon, and other Fellowships for research, as well as the Distinguished Scholar Award from the Keats-Shelley Association of America, and has received several local and national awards for excellence in teaching as well. His books include *Shelley's Process, The Undergrounds of the Phantom of the Opera* (Palgrave), and (from Cambridge University Press) both *The Cambridge Companion to Gothic Fiction* (2002) and *The Cambridge Companion to the Modern Gothic* (2014).

Tanya Krzywinska holds the chair in Digital Economy at Falmouth University, Cornwall, and has a background in the computer industry, as well as in literature, film, and art. She has developed new methods and concepts designed to further our understanding of the formal uniqueness and potential of games. She is the author of a range of papers and books that sought to distinguish the formal and aesthetic differences of games from other media and has written extensively on the Gothic and Horror in games and other media. Since 2012, Krzywinska is editor-in-chief of the journal *Games and Culture* (Sage). She has designed and convened a range of games development courses in the UK. Krzywinska is Director of the Games Academy, which provides incubation-based and innovation-led game development, computing, and game art courses (www.falmouth.ac.uk/games). Given time, Krzywinska continues to practise as a fine artist.

Scott MacKenzie is Associate Professor of Film and Media, Queen's University. His books include *Cinema and Nation* (2000); *Purity and Provocation: Dogma 95* (2003); *Screening Québec: Québécois Moving Images, National Identity and the Public Sphere* (2004); *The Perils of Pedagogy: The Works of John Greyson* (2013); *Film Manifestos and Global Cinema Cultures* (2014); *Films on Ice: Cinemas of the Arctic* (2015); *Arctic Environmental Modernities* (Palgrave Macmillan, 2017); *Artic Cinemas and the Documentary Ethos* (Indiana University Press, forthcoming 2018); *The Cinema, Too, Must Be Destroyed: The Films of Guy Debord* (Manchester University Press, forthcoming 2018); and *Process Cinema: Handmade Film in the Digital Age* (McGill-Queen's University Press, forthcoming 2018).

Kirstin A. Mills specialises in Gothic, Romantic, and Victorian Literature, with a particular interest in the relationships between dreams, alternative states of consciousness, optics and vision, space, and the supernatural, and the ways in which these intersect at the borders of literature, psychology, and science. She has published on the literary and cultural representations of these ideas in authors from Horace Walpole to George MacDonald and Lewis Carroll, and is finalising her monograph on the ways that these ideas evolved across the nineteenth century in a context of speculative investigation into the spaces of the supernatural and the sciences of the mind. Mills' research also considers these concepts at work in broader contexts from medieval literature to twenty-first-century media. She teaches English Literature, Children's Literature, and the Gothic at Macquarie University in Sydney, Australia, where she also completed her doctoral thesis on Dreams, Space, and Victorian Fantastic Literature.

Beatriz González Moreno is a tenured professor at the University of Castilla-La Mancha, Spain, where she teaches English Literature. Her research interests focus on the nineteenth century, paying particular attention to the role of aesthetics. She has published a number of peer-reviewed articles and book chapters that address gender issues and aesthetic experience. Also, on that subject, she has published a book, exploring the categories of the beautiful and the sublime in Mary Shelley's *Frankenstein*. She has lectured widely on these topics and on how the aesthetic categories of the beautiful, sublime, and picturesque have permeated the Romantic period and evolved through time. Due to her interest in aesthetics, she analyses the relationship between text and image. She is part of the project LyA, which explores the relations among the different arts, and she is also part of the research project "Edgar A. Poe On-Line. Text and Image" (ref. HAR2015-64580-P) funded by the Spanish Ministry of Economy and Competitiveness.

Fernando González Moreno is a tenured professor at the University of Castilla-La Mancha (UCLM), Spain, where he teaches Art History, and is Associate Dean at the Facultad de Humanidades in Albacete (UCLM). His research interests focus on iconography and illustrated book history. In this sense, he has mainly studied the illustrated reception of two authors: Cervantes and E. A. Poe, about whom he has published several articles and book chapters and given several lectures. He is co-editor of the "Iconografía Textual del *Quijote*. Cervantes Project", Texas A&M University.

Nowadays, this project has become the most extensive online catalogue and archive of illustrated *Don Quixote* editions. He has published extensively regarding this subject and fully analysed the relationship between image and text. He co-directs the interdisciplinary research group LyA, which explores the relations among the different arts, and he also co-directs the research project "Edgar A. Poe On-Line. Text and Image" (ref. HAR2015-64580-P) funded by the Spanish Ministry of Economy and Competitiveness.

Marie Mulvey-Roberts is Professor of English Literature at the University of the West of England, Bristol. Her teaching and research interests include Gothic and gender. She is the co-founder and editor of *Women's Writing* on historical women writers for which she co-edited a special issue on Mary Shelley. Her single-authored publications are *British Poets and Secret Societies* (1986 rpt 2014), *Gothic Immortals: The Fiction of the Brotherhood of the Rosy Cross* (1990 rpt 2016), and *Dangerous Bodies: Historicising the Gothic Corporeal* (2016), winner of the Allan Lloyd Smith Memorial Prize. She has written numerous chapters and edited dozens of books including *The Handbook to the Gothic* (1998 rvd 2009) and *Literary Bristol: Writers and the City* (2015). Recently she made a film on *Frankenstein* and its links to Bristol and Bath for a Massive Open Online Course (MOOC) on the literary South-west.

David Punter is an academic, writer and poet, and Professor of Poetry at the University of Bristol. He has published extensively as a literary critic, much of his work being on the Gothic, including *The Literature of Terror* (1980), *Gothic Pathologies* (1998), and *The Gothic Condition* (2016) but also on other themes and areas—*Writing the Passions* (2000), *Rapture: Literature, Addiction, Secrecy* (2009), and *The Literature of Pity* (2014). He has also published six books of poetry, *China and Glass* (1985), *Lost in the Supermarket* (1987), *Asleep at the Wheel* (1996), *Selected Short Stories* (1999), *Foreign Ministry* (2011), and *Bristol: 21 Poems* (2017). In 2014, he released a CD of his poetry, *Flashes in the Dark*, and he maintains a blog at www.davidpunter.wordpress.com.

Xavier Aldana Reyes is Senior Lecturer in English Literature and Film at Manchester Metropolitan University and a founding member of the Manchester Centre for Gothic Studies. He specialises in Gothic and Horror film and fiction and has published widely in these areas, including the books *Spanish Gothic: National Identity, Collaboration and Cultural Adaptation* (2017), *Horror: A Literary History* (editor, 2016), *Horror Film and Affect: Towards a Corporeal Model of Viewership* (2016), *Digital Horror: Haunted Technologies, Network Panic and the Found Footage Phenomenon* (co-edited with Linnie Blake, 2015), and *Body Gothic: Corporeal Transgression in Contemporary Literature and Horror Film* (2014). Reyes is chief editor of the Horror Studies book series at the University of Wales Press.

Shannon Rollins is a fourth-year PhD candidate at the University of Edinburgh, Edinburgh College of Art, and has tutored Visual Culture Stages One and Two. With an undergraduate background in the History of Art and nineteenth-century Romanticism, she has worked extensively across disciplines to uncover the interstitial relationships between Romanticism and contemporary subcultures. Rollins is a founding member of PERCHANCE, a postgraduate and early career scholar seminar programme at the University of Edinburgh, which brings together nineteenth-century researchers across disciplines and institutions. Her thesis is titled '*The Steampunk Woman:* Inverse Ekphrastic Manifestations in Contemporary Steampunk Dress' and presents a study of the corset's resonances in Steampunk romance fiction as they impact community performances of gender and identity. Her other research interests include crafted bodies, digital humanities, memetics, monstrosity, and Mary Shelley's *Frankenstein*.

Victor Sage is Emeritus Professor of English Literature in the School of Literature, Drama, and Creative Writing at the University of East Anglia, Norwich. He has written extensively on the Gothic and Religion. He is the author of a collection of short stories, *Dividing Lines,* and two novels, *A Mirror for Larks* (1993) and *Black Shawl* (1995). He is the editor of Le Fanu's *Uncle Silas* (2001) and Maturin's *Melmoth the Wanderer* (2000) for Penguin Classics, and he is the author of Le Fanu's *Gothic: The Rhetoric of Darkness* (Palgrave Macmillan, 2004). Recent work has centred on the cultural transmission of the Gothic in Europe: he has an essay on Scott, Hoffmann, and the persistence of Gothic in *Popular Revenants* (2012); a study of 'European Gothic' in *Romantic Gothic: the Edinburgh Companion* (2016); and an essay on the 'Romantic Grotesque' in the bicentennial celebration Inspiring a *Mysterious Terror: 200 years of Joseph Sheridan Le Fanu* (2016).

Carolyn D. Williams is Associate Professor emerita in English Literature from the University of Reading. Her publications include *Pope, Homer and Manliness: Some Aspects of Eighteenth-Century Classical Learning* (1993, rpt 2014); *Boudica and Her Stories: Narrative Transformations of a Warrior Queen* (2009); '"Inhumanly brought back to Life and Misery": Mary Wollstonecraft, *Frankenstein,* and the Royal Humane Society', *Women's Writing,* and 'The Case of the Malnourished Vampyre: The Perils of Passion in John Cleland's *Memoirs of a Coxcomb'*, in *Demons of the Body and Mind: Essays on Disability in Gothic Literature,* ed. Ruth Bienstock Anolik (McFarland, 2010). A keen practitioner of amateur theatre, she has codirected John Gay's *The Beggar's Opera,* Aphra Behn's *The Rover,* and John Fletcher's *The Tamer Tamed.* Acting credits include Queen Margaret in Shakespeare's *Richard III.*

Bruce Wyse is an instructor in the Department of English and Film Studies at Wilfrid Laurier University. His research interests include the representation of mesmerism in nineteenth-century literature, Gothic fiction, the *fin de siècle* and neo-Victorianism. He has published articles on Bulwer-Lytton's *A Strange Story,* his "The Haunted and the Haunters," Conan Doyle's *The Parasite,* Horace Smith's *Mesmerism,* and du Maurier's *Trilby,* as well as articles on film (*Let the Devil Wear Black*), television (*Dr. Who*), contemporary drama, and crime fiction.

LIST OF FIGURES

CHAPTER 1

Introduction: Global Reanimations of *Frankenstein*

Carol Margaret Davison and Marie Mulvey-Roberts

A book is a dead man, a sort of mummy, embowelled and embalmed, but that once had flesh, and motion, and a boundless variety of determinations and actions. I am glad that I can, even upon these terms, converse with the dead, with the wise and the good of revolving centuries. (William Godwin, *Fleetwood*, 1805)

A global event brought *Frankenstein; or, The Modern Prometheus* into being. In 1815, Indonesia's Mount Tambora erupted with thunderous detonating sounds, its effects ricocheting on more distant coastlines with devastating tsunamis. It was, and remains, one of the largest eruptions in recorded history. The veil created by the spreading ash, in combination with the release of toxic gases infiltrating the stratosphere, had a worldwide effect, as would Mary Shelley's *Frankenstein*, the novel it

C. M. Davison (✉)
Department of English Language, Literature and Creative Writing, University of Windsor, Windsor, ON, Canada

M. Mulvey-Roberts
Department of Arts and Cultural Industries, University of the West of England, Bristol, UK

© The Author(s) 2018
C. M. Davison, M. Mulvey-Roberts (eds.), *Global Frankenstein*,
Studies in Global Science Fiction,
https://doi.org/10.1007/978-3-319-78142-6_1

1

helped to birth. The resulting extreme climate change had fortuitous literary aftershocks for it forced the visitors at Lord Byron's summer home, the Villa Diodati on the shores of Lake Geneva, to remain indoors and entertain themselves by recounting ghost stories. Thus were the seismic conditions that saw the genesis of Mary Shelley's *Frankenstein* set in motion.

In the same way as the volcanic eruption upset the eco-system, blasting human and geographical boundaries, so too did the novel upset religious sensibilities while unsettling assumptions about science and technology. As Muriel Spark argued over 70 years ago, Shelley's singular novel was pioneering. This first work of science fiction (1951: 133) paved the way for a new domain of literary speculation and adventure.[1] *Frankenstein* was also 'a new and hybrid fictional species' (128), Spark argued, that engendered distinctive and long-term literary aftershocks: marking 'the apex' of an old-school Gothic fiction, it signalled a new speculative species combining the supernatural and the scientific. This bold, innovative departure in Gothic literature conjured up a compelling narrative recipe: the traditional setting of feudal antiquity was rejected in favour of a more contemporary scene with its distinct fears and anxieties; the malevolent monk of earlier Gothic novels was supplanted by an overreaching scientist; the traditional villain's castle was replaced by a laboratory; the identification of the villain was confounded; and the putative 'monster' granted a sympathy-inducing sensibility and eloquence.

Perhaps most radically, Shelley's first novel reached back to such classics as Shakespeare's *Hamlet* and Milton's *Paradise Lost* whilst addressing contemporary Enlightenment debates about nature, human nature, being, scientific experimentation, socio-political institutions, and the psychological problem of evil to stake out new territory later classified by critic Robert Hume as 'metaphysical Gothic' (1969: 290). Like other works of Romanticism but in what Hume claims was a less coherent and articulate fashion, *Frankenstein* meditated on existential, ontological, and epistemological questions. In so doing, it inspired and paved the way for such meditative Gothic works as James Hogg's *The Private Memoirs and Confessions of a Justified Sinner* (1824), Emily Brontë's *Wuthering Heights* (1847), and Herman Melville's *Moby Dick* (1851). Despite Percy Bysshe Shelley's attempts in the Preface to the anonymously published first edition to disassociate *Frankenstein* from the Gothic, the work told a very different story,[2] its author later underscoring in the Preface to her 1831 edition her objective of crafting a ghost story that 'would speak to the mysterious fears of our nature and awaken thrilling horror—one that would make the reader dread to look round, to curdle the blood, and quicken the beatings of the heart' (1994b: 195).

Frankenstein certainly met its affective objectives, the predominant response to the novel highlighting its spine-tingling terror in combination with its evocation, particularly in the opening creation scenes, of the horrifyingly grotesque. Fittingly, given the spectacular and sublime creature at its centre, Shelley's novel, first published anonymously, received several mixed reviews whose rhetoric mirrored the composition of her 'hideous progeny' (1994b: 197). Assuming, like many, that the author was male, of the Godwinian school, and possibly Percy Bysshe Shelley, Sir Walter Scott described *Frankenstein* in his *Edinburgh Magazine* review as a 'new species of novel' at once 'unnatural, even impious' (qtd. in Wolfson 2006: 370) that was both 'wildly imaginative' and 'realistic' (371). Another contemporary reviewer in *The British Critic* deemed the novel a 'bizarre' production that monstrously combined 'horror' and 'absurdity' (qtd. in Wolfson 2006: 388–9), crafted by a writer 'with no common powers of mind' (389). Just a few years in advance of the publication of Thomas de Quincey's *The Confessions of an English Opium-Eater* (1821), the *British Critic* reviewer, as if still in the throes of distress, described the powerful effects of the tale developed from Mary Shelley's 'waking dream' (Shelley 1994b: 195) to be opiate-like: 'we feel ourselves as much harassed, after rising from the perusal of these three spirit-wearying volumes, as if we had been over-dosed with laudanum, or hag-ridden by the night-mare' (qtd. in Wolfson 2006: 387).

It is noteworthy that several positive critical assessments of *Frankenstein*—once the author's true identity was known to the public—such as that published in 1831 in the *London Literary Gazette* declaring the novel to be 'one of the most original works *that ever proceeded from a female pen*' (qtd. in Wolfson 2006: 398; emphasis added), included qualifying statements, for better or for worse, about the author's sex and age. 'It is a wonderful work,' Byron (obviously aware early on about the author's true identity) wrote to his publisher, '*for a girl of nineteen*' (Schoene-Harwood 2000: 27; emphasis added), an assessment Shelley herself echoed in her reference to her novel as a 'juvenile effort' in a thank-you letter to Sir Walter Scott (qtd. in Wolfson 2006: 378). Notably, and in keeping with the popular rhetoric deployed against Mary Shelley's parents—Mary Wollstonecraft and William Godwin—the response to Shelley as a *woman* writer also conjured up the trope of the monster.[3] Such commentary remained in evidence in the twentieth century after *Frankenstein* had suffered 130 years of critical neglect. Even Muriel Spark, whose critical biography *Child of Light: A Reassessment of Mary Wollstonecraft Shelley* (1951) is often credited with placing Shelley on the public and academic radar, deemed her not to be 'well acquainted with her own mind', something Spark says enhanced Shelley's story artistically because it tended towards 'the implicit utterance' as opposed to the explicit (1951: 129).

The idea of a monstrously mindless woman writer who, like her novel's protagonist, lacked control over her creation, took hold in the popular critical imagination. As Ellen Moers has noted, the tendency was to regard Shelley, based on both her 'extreme youth' and her sex, 'not so much as an author in her own right as a transparent medium through which passed the ideas of those around her' (1976: 94). In the words of Mario Praz, for example, in a passage hearkening back to traditional Victorian ideals about female passivity, '[a]ll Mrs. Shelley did was to provide *a passive reflection* of some of the wild fantasies which were living in the air about her' (1951: 114; emphasis added). Ironically, this passage disparagingly comparing *Frankenstein* with Percy Bysshe Shelley's *The Cenci* (1819) directly contradicts Percy's own assessment of Mary's novel, as published in the *Athenaeum* in 1818, as 'one of the most original and complete productions of its day' (qtd. in Wolfson 2006: 399). Even George Levine and U. C. Knoepflmacher, self-confessed 'closet aficionados of Mary Shelley's novel' and the editors of *The Endurance of Frankenstein: Essays on Mary Shelley's Novel* (1979) who offhandedly remark in their Introduction that they 'half-jokingly' (xi) undertook the first collection of scholarly essays devoted to *Frankenstein*, were motivated, they said, by such 'valid' questions as:

> How much of the book's complexity is actually the result of Mary Shelley's self-conscious art and how much is merely the product of the happy circumstances of subject, moment, milieu? The novel intimates that it knows little about its implications (although it seems clear enough about its literary sources in Milton, Gothic fiction, and Romantic poetry). Are not its energies, therefore, un-self-conscious and accidental? (1979: xii–xiii)

Thus has the author of *Frankenstein* often been infantilised and stripped of agency and authority, even by those who sought to resuscitate her literary works for serious scholarly attention. Any examination of the incredible appeal of *Frankenstein* over the past 200 years must take into account the long-standing sexist biases across history, different societies, and the academy in relation to 'Mrs Shelley'.

The fate of *Frankenstein* in the public domain was nevertheless positive and it fast assumed a life of its own. True to the nature of the monster at its heart, the novel proved immediately popular and immensely adaptable, being 'universally known and read' within eight months of its initial publication, according to one of Percy's friends (qtd. in Wolfson 2006: 372). The rapid move—and challenge—to render the monster more spectacularly visible by granting him fleshly, physical embodiment helped tighten his grasp on the public imagination. The novel's earliest adaptation, *Presumption; or the Fate of Frankenstein* (1823), was for the theatre and appeared only five years after *Frankenstein*'s initial publication. This move from page to stage was followed, in the twentieth century, by its move to the big screen. Producer, Thomas Edison, and Director, J. Searle Dawley, memorably introduced the creature to celluloid in 1910 in the very early days of cinema. This entrance was spellbinding indeed as Victor was presented more like a mad wizard-magician engaged in some sort of Satanic ritual than a scientific anatomist. The frightening, increasingly animated, and fiery skeleton-turned-monster who develops in a furnace-like vault in Victor's dorm-room in Ingolstadt and thereafter turns menacing wove a cinematic magic and terror all his own.

By far the most powerful and influential adaptation in the twentieth century, however, came in the form of James Whale's classic, pre-Code film for Universal Pictures in 1931, simply titled *Frankenstein*. A slew of Frankenstein-centred movies followed in its wake—*Bride of Frankenstein* (1935), *Son of Frankenstein* (1939), *Ghost of Frankenstein* (1942), *Frankenstein Meets the Wolfman* (1943), and *House of Frankenstein* (1944)—a cultural fixation that was continued in the six-part British Hammer Horror Series that began with *The Curse of Frankenstein* (1957), starring Christopher Lee and Peter Cushing, and ended with *Frankenstein and the Monster from Hell* (1974), the last film directed by Terence Fisher before his death. *Frankenstein* proved to be an equal opportunity, user-friendly narrative amenable to universal application. It could be readily reconfigured for Blaxploitation films (*Blackenstein*, 1972), commentary on racial engineering and hippie counter-culture (*Andy Warhol's Frankenstein*, 1973), comedy (*Young Frankenstein*, 1974), and camp (*The Rocky Horror Picture Show*, 1975). In terms of the global marketplace, the monster fast proliferated, leaving his mark—especially in the 1960s and beyond—on screens worldwide, from Italy, France, and West Germany to Mexico, Turkey, and Japan. While Mexican *Frankenstein* film adaptations were bizarre narrative mash-ups combining elements from Mexican film culture like Santo the wrestler with Hollywood zombies, vamps/vampires, and werewolves, Japanese films like *Frankenstein Conquers the World* (1965)—a Japanese-American co-production—incorporated the Kaijū genre, featuring giant monsters attacking each other, the military, and other urban centres.

From our twenty-first-century vantage point where Victor Frankenstein's monster exists as a cultural icon that has been given every artistic and generic treatment from the comic and the kitsch to science fiction and musical theatre, one might expect that the initial gruesome terror of Mary Shelley's production would have diminished in power by the twenty-first century. The cultural marketplace, however, tells a very different story. Theatre and cinema dovetailed in February 2011, for example, with the premiere of Danny Boyle's compelling National Theatre Company production based on Nick Dear's dramatisation that was screened live in cinemas around the world. In the same year, a live musical drama appeared called *Frankenstein's Wedding* that was televised in front of a live audience of 12,000 who, from nearby Kirkstall Abbey, Leeds, witnessed the marriage between Victor and Elizabeth. A recent ballet (2016) choreographed by Liam Scarlett and co-produced by London's The Royal Ballet and the San Francisco Ballet captivated thousands in audiences on both sides of the Atlantic.

More internationally, one of *Frankenstein*'s most successful, powerful, and innovative recent incarnations is set against the backdrop of the post-Iraq War. Ahmad Saadawi's *Frankenstein in Baghdad*, winner of the 2014 International Prize for Arabic Fiction (IPAF), translated into English in 2018, tells of Hadi Al-Attag, a rag-and-bone man who, striving to grant a decent burial to those blown apart in that civil war-torn city, stitches together an unnamed creature—the what's-its-name—from their various body parts. With the declaration of his divine mission to punish all earthly criminals and the discovery of his own need for spare parts to replace his decomposing ones, *Frankenstein in Baghdad* adheres to the intellectual recipe of Mary Shelley's original novel by taking up philosophically complex questions about moral absolutism and human nature. Drawing on the powerful Victor-monster doppelgänger dynamic, Saadawi asks, among other things, the vexed and provocative question: what distinguishes a criminal from a freedom fighter?

As these and hundreds of other cultural offshoots evidence, the extensive period of *Frankenstein*'s scholarly neglect failed to curtail its tremendous global impact. The afterlives of Mary Shelley's hideous progeny, a 'ghost story' that she directed to 'go forth and prosper' in her Introduction to the 1831 edition, have been many and multifarious. The novel has been translated into numerous languages beyond Europe—Japanese, Korean, and Indonesian,[4] the location, significantly, of the stratovolcano, Mount Tambora. It has been reconceptualised in different media, artistic forms, and material culture from Cuban rock opera and Japanese anime to the graphic novel, video games, Artificial Intelligence,[5] and a Lego kit. Despite his visceral origins in charnel houses, dissecting rooms and slaughter-houses (Shelley 1994a: 83), the monster has now entered cyberspace, a logical development given *Frankenstein*'s status as an early example of science fiction. Indeed, considering the seemingly endless stream of *Frankenstein* adaptations, the words of James Whale's inimitable mad scientist spoken as the monster comes to life—'It's alive!'—resonate meaningfully in relation to the novel and its far-reaching influence.

As so few literary works have delivered such a global impact, it is particularly timely to consider the broader significance of the novel in 2018, the bicentennial year of its initial publication. The question arises—how did a shambling eight-foot monster, assembled from corpses and rejected by humankind, manage to capture the world's imagination and continue that momentum across centuries, nations, and cultures with such consummate ease? While the literary abilities of its author may remain in dispute—David Punter contends, for example, that 'there would be critical reservation' about declaring *Frankenstein* a 'classic' as it is 'the work of a very young author, and the text is melodramatic, to an extent two-dimensional, [and] inexplicit about psychological complexity' (2016: 206)—the novel has proven to be remarkably multivalent, symbolically and ideologically, a fitting status given the monster's physical heterogeneity and the intertextual nature of Shelley's novel.

Interpretations have proliferated, varying greatly across the last 200 years. The creature has been identified—among other things—with the underdog, the disadvantaged, the outcast, Irish rebels, women, and the ungovernable masses. Shelley's monster has proven to be an extremely adaptable vehicle through which to engage diverse issues across a broad spectrum of historical periods and cultures. Responses to the author as a woman writer have prompted readings of psycho-biography, entangling birth myth with Mary Shelley's own childbirth traumas and familial bereavements, from which the monster, as a composite of corpses, has become a metonym for life and death. Readings of the creature as a member of the oppressed industrialised proletariat have positioned him at the core of class conflict. Attentive to racialised descriptions of the monster and race-inflected rhetoric in the novel, some critics have interpreted the creature in relation to British imperialism, African slavery, and even the 'yellow peril'. Others have considered him in relation to family dynamics, sexuality, and embodiment issues, invoking queerness and disability. Indeed, *Frankenstein* has become such an obsession with literary critics since the publication of Levine and Knoepflmacher's collection that, as one of our contributors, Fred Botting, provocatively commented in the Introduction to Palgrave/Macmillan's New Casebook devoted to Shelley's novel, the novel has become 'a product of criticism, not a work of literature' (1995: 1).

Perhaps one of the keys to the endurance of Mary Shelley's monsterpiece lies in the fact that it overreached its generic bounds. Drawing upon the popular Greek myth of Prometheus, *Frankenstein* has itself assumed mythic proportions, inviting and even requiring, according to George Levine and U. C. Knoepflmacher, 'alternative readings because *its mythical core* is so flexible, polymorphous and dependent on antithetical possibilities (1979: xiv; emphasis added). Indeed, this culturally iconic text that engages with what George Levine identifies as 'some of the fundamental dualisms, the social, moral, political and metaphysical crises of western history since the French Revolution' (1979: 3–4), has become what Berthold Schoene-Harwood rightly calls 'modernity's perhaps most compelling and ominous *myth*' (2000: 21; emphasis added). This classification was suggested some decades ago by Ellen Moers, who deemed *Frankenstein* a 'birth *myth*' (1976: 92, emphasis added) that expressed the fear of childbirth. As several of our contributors acknowledge, any critical examination of *Frankenstein* and its creative progeny must involve consideration of its 'mythic' aspects—the degree to which it lent, and continues to lend, expression to various culturally relevant natural or social phenomena.

Despite its title, this critical collection cannot fully convey the enormity and scope of *Frankenstein*'s worldwide influence or capture the extent of its continued popularity. As English-speaking scholars, we acknowledge the linguistic and cultural limitations of this collection and welcome other international interrogations of *Frankenstein*'s global reach and impact. What the present volume does strive to do is grant some sense of the novel's enormous influence across eras, genres, and artistic forms, reconsidering, where and when necessary, the original novel in the contexts of its historical and intellectual roots and its many reverberations—aesthetic, socio-political, religious, and philosophical. Some of our contributors mine what we might call the original '*Frankenstein* recipe' in terms of its narrative, ideological, aesthetic, and conceptual energies and elements in an attempt to understand and theorise about its longevity and significance in a broad spectrum of cultural productions. All of our contributors approach *Frankenstein* as a rich, socio-historically grounded, conceptual matrix out of which were spawned innumerable cultural offspring. They all think back matrilineally through to this mother-text as they consider its global reach and impact.

We are honoured to have Nora Crook, one of the world's most renowned Mary Shelley scholars, who is the General Editor of the 12-volume series, *The Novels and Selected Works of Mary Shelley* (Routledge), write the Preface for *Global Frankenstein*. The collection that follows is divided into five Parts comprising three essays each that are clustered thematically. We begin with an examination of the scientific developments taking place in Mary Shelley's lifetime, then move on in Part II to consider various engagements with the idea of the 'monstrous' body. Part III examines *Frankenstein* adaptations for stage and screen, followed in Part IV by an assessment of illustrations for, and literary adaptations of, Mary Shelley's novel. In our fifth and final Part, contributors consider *Frankenstein* in relation to the posthuman and its influence on futuristic digital technologies.

Part I, '*Frankenstein*: Science, Technology, and the Nature of Life', begins with Jerrold E. Hogle's attempt to account for why Mary Shelley adopted the Gothic mode for her explorations into the quandaries of science. He argues that it provided her with the most appropriate means of 'abjecting' into her novel and into its 'creature' (in Julia Kristeva's sense of that word) the unresolved divisions and indecisions Shelley saw in current debates about science, technology, and the nature of life. Furthermore, the tensions arising from older and emerging belief systems in Gothic texts she drew upon corresponded to the contentions within the scientific systems that she saw pervading the world around her.

Victor Sage's chapter seeks to put into context the vexed moral and political paradox of the relations between science and secrecy in *Frankenstein*. This paradox is presented through discussions between the parents of Mary Shelley and her critique of male romantic egotism in which a scientific revolution is tied to the withholding, not the dissemination, of knowledge, and Victor Frankenstein's ambivalence towards Paracelsus, the original man of secrets. Paracelsus stands for a revolutionary Neo-Platonic model of knowledge, which catapulted medical science from the Galenic tradition into modernity, but it remained (in the manner of the alchemical 'adepts') his personal possession, whereas post-Enlightenment, scientific knowledge must by definition be iterable and belong to the human race. This essay argues that Frankenstein was both right and wrong to choose Paracelsus as his master, and the inevitability of his fate, which is accentuated in the 1831 text, is intimately bound up with this original choice.

Marie Mulvey-Roberts explores another place of secrecy, the body's interior, as a site of blasphemy and taboo. She charts the history of anatomical dissection in relation to the novel, with references to the medical research being carried out by John Hunter, thought to have been a model for Victor Frankenstein, and Hunter's pupil John Abernethy, whose lectures were attended by Percy Shelley who trained as a medical student. The effect of seeing mutilated and dissected bodies was believed by Dr Robert Knox to have a detrimental effect on the artist by familiarising him with horrors. This can be seen in the case of Victor Frankenstein whose actions lead to death and destruction. The dissection of female corpses was regarded as especially problematic, exemplified by Victor's tearing apart of the monster's mate he had been creating. This 'Bride of Frankenstein' is re-membered by ORLAN, the French performance artist who reintegrates her in the surgeries carried out on her body in the name of performance art. ORLAN's digital hybridisations also celebrate the very hybridity and Otherness that had so repelled Victor Frankenstein.

Part II, '*Frankenstein* and Disabled, Indecorous, Mortal Bodies', continues the focus on bodies, considering, from a variety of critical perspectives, how the monster has been employed, sometimes as an evocation of the Other, to engage with issues of embodiment and hybridity within different cultures, disciplines, and artistic forms. Drawing on Richard Hengist Horne's reading of *Frankenstein* in *A New Spirit of the Age* (1844) as a creature of disability, and the insights of cultural critics who have noted *Frankenstein*'s concern with the aberrant body and the tyranny of normative embodiment, Bruce Wyse brings Disability Studies theory to bear on three revisions of Mary Shelley's novel: Edward Bulwer-Lytton's 'A Manuscript Found in a Madhouse' (1829), a short story published in the decade immediately following *Frankenstein*'s publication; Mel Brooks' film spoof, *Young Frankenstein* (1974); and 'The Crimson Horror' episode of the science-fiction television series, *Doctor Who* (2013). These *Frankenstein* adaptations clarify what is at stake in the creature's deplorable social exclusion as an anomalously embodied figure while rectifying and remedying the ethical derelictions of creator and society. According to Wyse, their romantic or sexual solutions maintain some residual ambivalence, their humanitarianism being shadowed by something problematic or perverse.

Carolyn D. Williams then turns her attention to the idea of the monstrous literary body by focusing on *Frankenstein* and the question of formal literary decorum. She builds upon evidence from the first surviving manuscript of *Frankenstein* to the 1831 edition suggesting that Mary and Percy Shelley tried to enforce literary decorum to maintain a mood of tragic seriousness. She also reaches back to both the association forged by Horace between variegated texts and abnormal bodies, and Samuel Johnson's definition of decorum as 'contrary to levity' to examine how the creature posed a threat to critical conventions. Considering contemporary reviews of *Frankenstein* that identified aspects of the work as comic and such later adaptations as *Young Frankenstein*, Williams asks the probing question: 'If a mixture of genres was monstrous, how could a story about a monster retain its generic purity?'

Carol Margaret Davison continues the consideration of *Frankenstein* and embodiment by examining various balletic and dance-theatre choreographies based on Mary Shelley's novel by Wayne Eagling, Rick Darnell, William Forsythe, Estefania Miranda, and Liam Scarlett. She claims that each engages with what she calls *corpsoreality*—the experience of our body as Other that is precipitated by our awareness, fear, and anxiety about being liable to disease and mortality despite major scientific, medical, and technological advancements and interventions. Davison examines how and why *Frankenstein* has been used over the past 40 years—an era characterised by intense death denial that has witnessed the traumatic AIDS crisis—to reflect on a broad variety of embodiment issues, including sex/gender-identification, the nature and development of the aesthetic, hetero-normative balletic body, and the uncontrollably 'monstrous', 'queer', and 'disabled' aspects of human corporeality/corpsoreality as culturally perceived and constructed. She claims that, in contrast to the Christian fixation on the other side of the grave in the eighteenth and nineteenth centuries and the 'good death', recent choreographers have used *Frankenstein* to focus on this side of the grave, the pains and the pleasures of embodiment, and 'good', successful mourning in the face of devastating loss.

Part III, 'Spectacular Frankensteins on Screen and Stage', considers how *Frankenstein* has been adapted theatrically and cinematically around the world. Courtney Hoffman starts this discussion off by assessing the British National Theatre's production of *Frankenstein* directed by Danny Boyle for which live performances were screened around Britain. Hoffman highlights the violence against women enacted on stage in that production, including Victor's necrophiliac acts used to taunt his creation/counterpart. Later, he and the audience watch as the creature rapes and then murders Elizabeth in a brutal simulacrum of sexual climax. Hoffman maintains that these scenes of violence against women, performed frankly, serve to undermine the text's possibility for the promotion of feminism. They subvert women's desire and agency, reinforce gender role stereotypes, and reflect the violence of assault and voyeurism back on to the audience, thus questioning the place from which violence emerges: audience or performers.

Scott MacKenzie then examines modern cinema as a technology of revivification, a Frankensteinian monster in its process of montage—the cutting and editing together of images of past events and deceased people. MacKenzie's two-part chapter begins by considering the allegorical and sometimes unconscious use of Shelley's monster to express anxieties in transnational, usually low-budget, cinema from such broad-ranging areas as the UK, Italy, West Germany, Mexico, Turkey, and Japan. He delineates how literal, censorious cutting was central to *Frankenstein* in popular cinema, citing the case of James Whale's *Frankenstein* for Swedish viewers where the process of censorious editing radically changed the text for non-American audiences. The second part of MacKenzie's chapter examines how iconic film footage of *Frankenstein* has been re-cut into found-footage films about *Frankenstein*, a process he nicely calls Eisensteinian/Frankensteinian montage that reveals much about the central role these images play in the imaginary of the cinema as a technology of revivification. The *metaphoric* cutting, across genres and national identities, and the *actual* cutting, within the film text itself, result, MacKenzie argues, in the creation of new cinematic life through transnational genre hybridity.

Xavier Aldana Reyes takes the Promethean myth in a different direction by seeking explanations for the entropy of the Frankenstein film adaptation that he sees as the corollary to the rise of the zombie movie. His chapter, which traces the cinematic developments of the *Frankenstein* myth in the twenty-first century, argues that the cultural work that Shelley's myth once carried out is now done by the figure of the zombie and/or rabid human, which has become enormously popular and undergone transformations in recent years. Zombies, as the sources of artificially engineered pandemics, now more readily channel contemporary anxieties regarding the dangers of unbridled scientific and technological advances. As zombies have gradually become sentient beings in films like *Warm Bodies* (2013), they also prod the boundaries between death and conscious life. Aldana Reyes demonstrates how contemporary zombies seem to have blended Shelley's Promethean concerns with a very modern microbiological fear in order to constitute a new form of twenty-first-century hybrid monster as featured in such films as *Army of Frankensteins* (2013).

Part IV, 'Frankensteinian Illustrations and Literary Adaptations', turns to an examination of illustrations for, and international literary adaptations of, *Frankenstein*. Scott Bukatman turns his attention to how the interiority of Frankenstein's monster is expressed in comics, which has implications, he argues, for the way readers engage with the story and the monster's place within it. The multiple modes of narration that comics offer—dialogue, 'voice-over' narrational captions, thought balloons, or the eschewal of any presentation of a character's thoughts—make it a particularly apropos medium for the adaptation (or continuation) of Mary Shelley's *Frankenstein*, a novel narrated by multiple figures, including both Victor Frankenstein and his misbegotten creation.

How *Frankenstein* has been retold for children in twenty-first-century picture books is a neglected area of analysis addressed here by Emily Alder. This oversight is surprising in view of the proliferation of picture books across the world. These include the Australian *Frankenstein* (2005) by Margrete Lamod and Drahos Zak, French author Marion Mousse's adaptation for Papercutz, *Frankenstein* (2009), and American texts such as Patrick McDonnell's *The Monsters' Monster* (2012) and Ludworst Bemonster's *Frankenstein: A Monstrous Parody* (2012). Despite their apparent simplicity, the best children's picture books are formally ingenious and offer absorbing, thoughtful narratives, sometimes hidden behind deceptively uncomplicated storylines, graphics, and characters, sometimes emerging through inventive interplay between artwork and written text. Even the most simplistic *Frankenstein* narratives exploit a pre-existing knowledge of the story and its iconography, while the most sophisticated examples mobilise for their young readers some surprisingly nuanced interpretations. Parody, visual jokes, and intertextuality are deployed to negotiate *Frankenstein*'s Gothic framework and structural complexity and to speak to child readers about social, familial, personal, or scientific issues in ways that reject binary narratives in favour of the ambiguities and multiple perspectives of a modern globalised world.

Beatriz González Moreno and Fernando González Moreno then take the reader on a fascinating journey chronicling and analysing the different iconographic interpretations of the monster since his first representation in Richard Brinsley Peake's play *Presumption; or, the Fate of Frankenstein* (1823) and the novel's first illustrations in Shelley's third edition of 1831. The González Morenos maintain that, since the creature's first visual representation on stage in the 1820s, and especially after his representations on screen, illustrators from varied backgrounds—French, American, Croatian, British, and Spanish—have resisted simple and reductive representations. Foregrounding the relationship between these illustrations and Shelley's text, this chapter dissects a cross-section of unique, sometimes poetic interpretations that enrich our reading experience, including those that, like *Frankenstein*, are intertextual in nature or reference such divergent issues as totalitarianism, Marxism, and feminism. The chapter concludes with an examination of some contemporary twenty-first-century neo-Victorian Steampunk and matricentric interpretations that even incorporate the figure of Mary Shelley.

The final Part of the collection, 'Futuristic Frankensteins/Frankensteinian Futures', offers chapters devoted to digital technologies and the posthuman. Kirstin Mills pursues *Frankenstein* into hyperspace, noting the significance of this novel's selection as the first digital book. Mills brings together the virtual digital realm and the multiple narrative pathways opened up by interactive fiction with the multi-layered and spatial construction of Mary Shelley's narrative world in *Frankenstein*. Her chapter is Janus-faced in looking backwards as well as forwards, summed up in her discussion of how Dave Morris' digital version of the novel paradoxically marks a return to some of its original preoccupations.

Tanya Krzywinska explores *Frankenstein*'s legacy for computer games, a lineage that lies buried under the legions of vampire and zombie games, from the 'stitched horrors' of *World of Warcraft* to the monsters of *Half-Life*. Krzywinska also discusses how the posthuman in games is often highly indebted to Shelley's novel. Her central thesis shows how games and Shelley's Frankenstein (the character and the novel) are predicated on a denial of death for the reason that this legacy is (pervasively) *implicit* rather than *explicit* in games. This is due to the fact that the denial of death in games is structural and crucially not thematic as it is in Shelley's novel. While the novel is tragic, therefore, the death-defying normative vocabularies of games render tragedy virtually impossible. For these reasons, games offer a very different form of catharsis from that offered by the novel.

Declaring *Frankenstein* to be drained of cultural resonance in the late twentieth century, Fred Botting advances a theoretically sophisticated assessment of the fate of Mary Shelley's text and her marginalised monster in relation to exploitative global capitalism. He argues that Frankenstein and his creature fail to resonate with the world of global posthumanism where monstrosity has become generalised—evidenced in the form of neoliberal vampires and nonhuman hordes of walking dead ('garbage humans')—and where life has become virtually indistinguishable from death. Noting that monstrosity radically shifted its focus from exclusion in the nineteenth century to the production of difference and identity in the twentieth, and piggybacking on Judith Halberstam's insight that *Frankenstein* is about 'the making of a human' (1995: 32), Botting argues that humanity barely plays a role in recent recastings of Shelley's novel. Instead, *Victor Frankenstein* (Paul McGuigan 2015), *The Frankenstein Chronicles* (ITV Encore, 2015), and *I, Frankenstein* (Stuart Beattie 2014) feature quasi-superhero monsters engaged in impossible crimes and adventures. In Bernard Rose's *Frankenstein* (2015), which recounts the tale of 'Monster', a character birthed into the extremely violent, supermodern, and hyper-technological world of Los Angeles by way of a large-scale 3D printer, Botting finds a singular updating of Shelley's novel that may hold out some hope for humanity, albeit from an unlikely source.

Our collection concludes, fittingly, by returning the reader to the imaginative domain of literature. David Punter's poem, 'Meditation on *Frankenstein*', begins at the end, with a lament uttered by the monster in archaic language prior to his being extinguished in a landscape of ice and flame. It tells a tale of personal anguish and suffering, of a monster created from scraps, but then broadens out to encompass the entire world. In Punter's masterful hands, the monster becomes a mouthpiece for the 'wounds of nations', a matrix of globalised suffering of war and terror. Like Shelley's novel, Punter's poem oscillates between different voices—that of monster and maker, creator and created, the piece becoming increasingly polyphonic. Even Mary Shelley has her say, intervening as a sort of mediator between her two creations, Victor and his creature, although to no avail. Mary Shelley's waking dream is ultimately and powerfully transmuted into a global vision of the fate of the human race—of hubris, war, death, and destruction though, like Pandora's Box, the poem contains a glimmer of hope for mankind.

In one of the most noted scholarly articles written about *Frankenstein*, Paul O'Flinn incisively states that '[t]here is no such thing as *Frankenstein*, there are only *Frankensteins*, as the text is ceaselessly rewritten, reproduced, refilmed and redesigned' (1983: 194). Indeed, Mary Shelley's 'hideous progeny' has been nothing if not prolific. *Global Frankenstein* aims to illuminate how, why, and to what divergent ends, a full 200 years after its initial publication, artists, authors, cinematographers, and game designers, among so many others, are still reconfiguring *Frankenstein* across nations, generations, media, and artistic forms, and why literary critics and other scholars keep returning to reread and reinterpret it. As we celebrate the bicentenary of *Frankenstein*, like the reader's last glimpse of Mary Shelley's creature who is 'borne away by the waves' at the novel's end, becoming 'lost in darkness and distance' (1994a: 191), we see no end in sight for such reanimations and re-examinations.

NOTES

1. See also the works of Brian Stableford, Judith A. Spector and the first chapter in Brian Aldiss.
2. See Angela Wright's recent assessment of the Female Gothic elements of *Frankenstein*, alongside the dozens of articles and book chapters situating it within that generic domain.
3. According to Horace Walpole, the grandfather of the Gothic, Wollstonecraft was a 'hyena in petticoats' and Godwin 'one of the greatest monsters exhibited by history' (qtd. in Sterrenburg 1974: 146). Ironically, Thomas de Quincey declared, looking back at the 1790s, that 'most people felt of Mr. Godwin with the same alienation and horror as of a ghoul, or a bloodless vampyre, or the monster created by Frankenstein' (qtd. in Sterrenburg 1974: 147).
4. See this link to the refereed, scholarly website 'Romantic Circles' for a fairly extensive catalogue of editions of Mary Shelley's *Frankenstein*: https://www.rc.umd.edu/editions/frankenstein/textual
5. MIT have developed a system of AI inspired by the work of Mary Shelley that writes stories in a collaborative way with human writers. It launches Halloween 2018 and is called Shelley: Human-AI Collaborated Horror Stories. See the following link for more information: https://www.media.mit.edu/projects/shelley/overview/

WORKS CITED

Aldiss, Brian. 1976. *Trillion Year Spree: The History of Science Fiction*. London: Paladin.
Botting, Fred. 1995. Introduction. In *Frankenstein*, ed. Fred Botting, 1–20. Basingstoke: Palgrave Macmillan.

Halberstam, Judith. 1995. *Skin Shows: Gothic Horror and the Technology of Monsters.* Durham/London: Duke University Press.

Hume, Robert D. 1969. Gothic Versus Romantic: A Re-evaluation of the Gothic Novel. *PMLA* 84: 282–290.

Levine, George. 1979. The Ambiguous Heritage of *Frankenstein.* In *The Endurance of Frankenstein: Essays on Mary Shelley's Novel*, ed. George Levine and U.C. Knoepflmacher, 3–30. Berkeley/Los Angeles/London: University of California Press.

Levine, George, and U.C. Knoepflmacher. 1979. Preface. In *The Endurance of Frankenstein: Essays on Mary Shelley's Novel*, ed. George Levine and U.C. Knoepflmacher, xi–xvi. Berkeley/Los Angeles/London: University of California Press.

Moers, Ellen. 1976. *Literary Women.* Garden City: Doubleday.

O'Flinn, Paul. 1983. Production and Re-production: The Case of *Frankenstein. Literature and History* 9: 194–213.

Praz, Mario. 1951. *The Romantic Agony*, 2nd ed. Trans. Angus Davidson. London: Oxford University Press.

Punter, David. 2016. Literature. In *The Cambridge Companion to Frankenstein*, ed. Andrew Smith, 205–218. Cambridge: Cambridge University Press.

Schoene-Harwood, B. 2000. *Mary Shelley: Frankenstein: Essays, Articles, Reviews.* New York: Columbia University Press.

Shelley, Mary. 1994a. *Frankenstein; or, The Modern Prometheus (The 1818 Text)*, ed. Marilyn Butler. Oxford/New York: Oxford University Press.

———. 1994b. The Author's Introduction to the Standard Novels Edition (1831). In *Frankenstein; or, The Modern Prometheus (The 1818 Text)*, ed. Marilyn Butler, 194–197. Oxford/New York: Oxford University Press.

Spark, Muriel. 1951. *Child of Light.* Hadleigh: Tower Bridge Publications.

Spector, Judith A. 1981. Science Fiction and the Sex War: A Womb of One's Own. *Literature and Psychology* 31 (1): 21–32.

Stableford, Brian. 1995. *Frankenstein* and the Origins of Science Fiction. In *Anticipations: Essays on Early Science Fiction and Its Precursors*, ed. David Seed, 46–57. Liverpool: Liverpool University Press.

Sterrenburg, Lee. 1974. Mary Shelley's Monster: Politics and Psyche in *Frankenstein.* In *The Endurance of Frankenstein*, ed. George Levine and U.C. Knoepflmacher, 143–171. Berkeley: University of California Press.

Wolfson, Susan J., ed. 2006. *Frankenstein, by Mary Shelley.* New York: Pearson.

Wright, Angela. 2016. The Female Gothic. In *The Cambridge Companion to Frankenstein*, ed. Andrew Smith, 101–115. Cambridge: Cambridge University Press.

PART I

Frankenstein: Science, Technology, and the Nature of Life

CHAPTER 2

The Gothic Image and the Quandaries of Science in Mary Shelley's *Frankenstein*

Jerrold E. Hogle

Perhaps in line with Percy Bysshe Shelley's Preface to Mary Shelley's original *Frankenstein* of 1818, which insists that the novel eschews 'supernatural terrors' (Shelley 2012: 5), some modern scholars see its use of the 'Gothic [as] just a façade' for an exploration of more serious issues (Knellwolf 2008: 64), including those raised at the time by the 'growing tensions between various kinds of science' throughout the Western world (Hunter 2008: 135). But I want to argue here, not only that the 1818 *Frankenstein* is quite thoroughly Gothic, but that it employs the kinds of figures initiated by Horace Walpole's *The Castle of Otranto* (1764), the first prose narrative to call itself *A Gothic Story* in its Second Edition of 1765 (see Walpole 1996: 3), precisely to articulate several specific 'tensions' troubling the burgeoning sciences of the West from the 1750s to the 1810s. Frankenstein's creature, after all, the young anatomist's principal display of science in action, looks back, not just to Erasmus Darwin's rumoured animation of dead matter recalled by Mary Shelley in the Introduction to her 1831 revision (Shelley 2012: 168) but also, she says

J. E. Hogle (✉)
University of Arizona, Tucson, AZ, USA

© The Author(s) 2018
C. M. Davison, M. Mulvey-Roberts (eds.), *Global Frankenstein*,
Studies in Global Science Fiction,
https://doi.org/10.1007/978-3-319-78142-6_2

21

herself, to 'some volumes of ghost stories' (166) that she, Shelley, Lord Byron, and Dr John Polidori read together at the Villa Diodati during the Summer of 1816 when Byron famously challenged each Diodati guest to write a new tale of terror. These were some French Gothic fictions translated from German and collected in 1812 under the title *Fantasmagoriana* by Jean-Baptiste Benoît Eyriès (see van Woudenberg 2014), from which Mary most remembers this image in 1831: 'a gigantic, shadowy form, clothed like the ghost in *Hamlet*, in complete armour', the animated spectre of a painting in a story entitled 'The Family Portraits' (see Apel 2005: 43–5), which is 'seen at midnight … to advance slowly along a gloomy avenue' and into its ancestral castle to bestow spectral 'kisses on the 'foreheads' of his sleeping grandchildren, 'who from that hour withered'' (Shelley 2012: 166–67), much as the oversized creature in *Frankenstein* kills the young people closest to his creator. Of all the *Fantasmagoriana* figures Mary Shelley could have recalled, this is the one most like the two principal spectres in *The Castle of Otranto*, the gigantic, armoured ghost of the effigy on the tomb of the Castle's original owner, Alfonso, that repeatedly appears in huge fragments (Walpole 1996: 19–21) and the shade of the current usurper's grandfather, Ricardo, that is suddenly reanimated and walks out of his portrait in the Castle (26), both of which allude to the Ghost of Hamlet's Father (120). If Shelley's creature is a demonstration of the sciences in deep conflict, he is cast in that role by being rooted in the Walpolean Gothic image, itself based on Shakespeare's most 'Gothic' spectre, in his Alfonso-esque enormity, his composition out of divisible pieces like those of Alfonso's ghost, his haunting of Victor Frankenstein with both the latter's and his culture's sins (such as grave robbing), his being the revenant both of the dead bodies that compose him and of an entirely artificial being (like Walpole's ancestral portrait or statue), and his abrupt and unsettling animation out of inanimation as he suddenly 'breathed hard', like Ricardo in *Otranto*, while 'a convulsive motion agitated his limbs' (Shelley 2012: 35).

In being this much of a quintessentially Gothic figure, moreover, Frankenstein's creature partakes of the fundamentally conflicted dynamic resident at the core of Gothic fiction from its inception. Walpole himself insisted on that conflict as the foundation of the 'Gothic Story' by writing in the 1765 Preface to his Second Edition of *Otranto* that his tale is an 'attempt to blend the two kinds of romance, the ancient and the modern' (Walpole 1996: 9), a deliberately Janus-faced construction that looks backwards to aristocratic and Catholic tales of supernatural medievalism from the 1100s to the 1590s and forward to the followers of the Protestant, middle-class, and more empirically oriented novels of Richardson, Fielding, and Smollett in the 1740s–50s. The belief-systems of the former, which the anti-Catholic 'translator' of *Otranto's* anonymous First Edition regards as 'exploded now' (Walpole 1996: 6), may attract Walpole's characters *and* readers because of their longings for the age-old reassurances of divine intervention (Walpole 1996: 17–18, 112–13). But the symbols of them in *Otranto*, in the face of rising Enlightenment empiricism, are all as hollowed out and fragmented as the pieces of its armoured ghost, so much so that the spectre that steps out of the picture comes only from a flat surface divorced from its historical groundings. The readers of the first 'Gothic Story' are thus symbolically caught, Janus-like, in a tug-of-war between still-attractive-but-crumbling and new-but-increasingly-dominant ideological schemes, manifestations of what E. J. Clery has revealed as 'a specific crisis in the experience of [Walpole and his] eighteenth-century audience': a 'contradiction' in British cultural attitudes of the 1760s between the 'traditional claims of landed property [mainly Catholic and aristocratic] and the new claims of the private family [largely Protestant and middle-class]' (Clery 1995: 77–79). Moreover, since Gothic figures in the wake of *Otranto* have continued this ancient-modern tug-of-war, albeit to both suggest and disguise different ideological *and* psychological conflicts at different times, several recent scholars, including myself, influenced by Julia Kristeva's *Powers of Horror* (1980), have seen the Janus-faced Gothic image as an especially apt repository for what she calls 'abjection', the pre-conscious act of 'throwing off' into a ghostly or monstrous Other the unresolvable contradictions in our beings and societies so that we can imagine the illusion of a consistent identity within ourselves, however much the resulting 'abject' is a fiction that conceals our underlying conflicts from us by ejecting them outside 'normal' humanity (see Kristeva 1982: 1–11; Hogle 2012). Gothic figures, it turns out, are inordinately well-suited, precisely by being so Janus-like from the start, to harbour abjected tensions between dying (retrogressive) and emerging (progressive) human inclinations, beliefs, and social structures that almost always co-exist—and that we always fear having to face—at nearly every stage of human history and many stages of individual growth.

Not surprisingly, therefore, Frankenstein's creature in Mary Shelley's novel, composed of fragments of dead bodies to demonstrate the newest science of life and hence a Gothic image *par excellence*, has come to be seen by several contemporary scholars as an 'abject' figure that incarnates

and half-conceals *numerous* unresolved conflicts of the 1810s and of
modernity thereafter—hence its lasting power in the many adaptations
since the 1820s. Profound tugs-of-war symbolised by 'the monster'—a
term Victor uses for the first time after he recovers from the fever that follows his creature's awakening (Shelley 2012: 39)—range from the strug-
gles between industrial entrepreneurs (like Frankenstein in his engineering
of a prototype) and the abject working classes they help to create (embodied by the impoverished creature) to the mechanisms of male technology
that subsume the female birth process (echoed by Victor's 'labour' in
making his 'child') and so extend the past subjugation of woman while
revealing modern advances as actually dependent on the women those
very advances ignore. Yet, all too little has been said about my subject
here: the several quandaries bedevilling the sciences of the Shelleys' time
that the making, development, and face of the creature symbolically suggest *precisely because* he is a supremely Gothic image. That relative inatten-
tion *is* surprising given what is immediately obvious in *Frankenstein*: the
creature is a Janus-faced combination of, on the one hand, Victor's regres-
sions to aspects of the medieval alchemy he has read about (Shelley 2012:
22–3), from the man of brass supposedly made by Albertus Magnus in the
thirteenth century to the elixir-infused homunculus associated with
Paracelsus in the sixteenth century, and, on the other hand, Frankenstein's
embrace of the post-Enlightenment science of 'the causes of life' (31) during which he echoes the very words of some of the best-known author-
scientists of Mary Shelley's era, recalling that both the alchemical and the
new sciences were interests of her father, William Godwin, to whom the
original *Frankenstein* is dedicated (see Ketterer 1979: 19–32, and
Vasbinder 1984: 47).

This interplay between the medieval and the modern, I would add,
however, is not simply unique to Victor any more than it was to Godwin.
In the novel, such a mixture is half-encouraged by the lecturer Victor most
admires, M. Waldman, at the University of Ingolstadt, in its own way a
Gothic contradiction of fourteenth-century buildings that came to house
a 'ferment of reformatory ideas' during the late 1700s when *Frankenstein*
takes place (Knellwolf and Goodall 2008: 4–5). For Waldman, the likes of
'Paracelsus' are 'men' to whom 'modern philosophers [are] indebted for
most of the foundations of their knowledge', even as these same modern-
ists have moved beyond old 'chimeras' to 'penetrate into the recesses of
nature', thereby extending the ambitions that most inspired Victor in
those now-ancient alchemists (Shelley 2012: 29). Such an accommodating,

non-polarised attitude, as Waldman in the novel often does, alludes to the words of Sir Humphry Davy, the most widely celebrated and published British chemist of the day, well known to Mary Shelley since Godwin took her to a Davy lecture in 1812 (Holmes 2008: 325–6). Davy himself writes in his *Elements of Chemical Philosophy* (also 1812), an item on Mary's reading list of 1816 (Shelley 1987: 96, 143), that, in the old 'heroic and fabulous stages of chemistry ... truths were discovered', even though 'another era was required to separate them from absurdities' (Davy 1972: 4.9–10). Such an account is clearly reminiscent of a Walpolean Gothic Story in its Janus-faced pulls towards the past and the future at the same time. By following Davy's lead, Shelley's *Frankenstein* makes its creature's formation one symptom of a wider cultural hesitation, also Janus-faced, between viewing the history of science as an uninterrupted development out of past endeavours—meaning the attractions of old alchemy should at least be acknowledged—and asserting, like the caustic professor Krempe, also at Ingolstadt, that modern science must be sharply separated from 'exploded' schemes (Shelley 2012: 27), Walpole's word for the ingredients of old romance in his Preface to *Otranto's* First Edition. As a conflicted Gothic figure of 1818, then, the creature of *Frankenstein* is, to begin with, a site of abjection for an ideological conflict enunciated by the best-known English chemist of that time, not just between and among particular sciences but about the history and progression of science itself.

Moreover, as I now want to argue in the rest of what follows, the creature as a Gothic image abjects, and thereby suggests *and* disguises in both his creation and his being, many other knots of contention in the West at the time of the novel within several rapidly emerging sciences. One of these conflicts goes to the heart of the fundamental 'concept of life' as it was then 'being contested across a range of developing disciplines' (Gigante 2009: 24). In recalling the process of working out his demonstration of life's 'principle', Victor remembers himself 'animated by an almost supernatural enthusiasm', especially when 'in the midst of [the] darkness' of tracking the 'change from life to death, and death to life ... a sudden light broke in upon me' (Shelley 2012: 31). This quasi-electric beam of ultimate knowledge leads him to think of himself as 'bestowing animation' on the body he is making entirely from outside it, much as the knowledge of the cause (which he never names) seems bestowed from outside him (32). During the very same 'circumstances', though, aided by 'chemical instruments' he has 'improved' himself and determined to feel 'no supernatural horrors' as he rifles through dead tissue from 'vaults and charnel houses', he sees his greater knowledge emerging only from 'examining and analyzing all the minutiae of causation' that lead from life to death and back, as though the cause can be found only in the relations of the minutiae to each other (31). Throughout this contradictory memory, Mary Shelley's title character is in fact replaying what Marilyn Butler was the first to explain in the 1990s: his author's knowledge of the 'publicly-staged debate of 1814–19' on the 'origins and nature of life' between 'two professors at London's Royal College of Surgeons', the largely traditional John Abernethy, who 'sought to unite religious and secular opinion', and the more 'boldly sceptical' William Lawrence, well known to the Shelleys as Percy's own physician and as Abernethy's now-rebellious protégé (Butler 2012: 406–7). Abernethy argued that life as both soul and electricity is a 'superadded force' infused from above as a 'mobile, invisible substance' external to any physical container (Abernethy 1814: 48, 52), the view echoed by Frankenstein in his invocation of the 'light bestowed' from beyond. Lawrence countered with the materialist argument that life is generated by how 'the particles of a living body are dependent on each other' from the time of any infant's conception, an understanding that can be achieved only by 'a close observation of the actions of living creatures' or the 'fabric' of bodies (Lawrence 1816: 126, 163) and thus by the very analysis of minutiae that Victor undertakes. By struggling to produce an artificial life-form that might accommodate each of these opposed philosophies, Frankenstein fashions a Gothic figure torn indecisively between them both, like much of Western Europe as it processed the Abernethy-Lawrence debates. He thereby makes his creature a fearsome site for embodying and abjecting that very irresolution in much of Mary Shelley's audience between life conceived of as a divinely-based 'preformation' and life understood as a self-shaping 'epigenesis' (Gigante 2009: 23–5).

Meanwhile, too, even if a scientist could somehow embody both these possibilities in an experiment, there remained great uncertainty in the 1810s about what the 'life principle' or *vis essentialis* actually consisted of and what it might lead to when it was goaded to accelerate its self-structuring drive, as it is in the creature. Numerous adaptations of *Frankenstein* have depicted that *vis* as predominantly electrical, licensed by that moment in Shelley's novel when the young Victor during a 'thunderstorm' sees 'a stream of fire issue from an old and beautiful oak'—another Gothic image that oscillates between taking in a bolt of lightning and pouring forth a flame the tree already contains—and learns that this force is called 'Electricity', which his father demonstrates further, à la

Benjamin Franklin, using 'a kite, with a wire and string' (Shelley 2012: 23–4). But when Frankenstein specifically details the later construction of the creature, even while still invoking the 'sudden light' of revelation, he makes no explicit mention of what Mary Shelley associates with Erasmus Darwin in 1831: a transmission of disembodied current into inanimate matter. Instead, Victor describes 'tortur[ing] the living animal to animate the lifeless clay' and then 'collect[ing] the instruments of life around me' (Shelley 2012: 33–5), which are never rendered as what we often see in *Frankenstein* films, apparatuses for transmitting electric current. As Denise Gigante has reminded us, electricity was identified from the 1770s through the 1810s as but one of several forces that *might* compose the often 'unspecified "vital principle"' (Gigante 2009: 8); for Lawrence, among others, the idea of 'organized bodies' being coalesced by 'electricity and galvanism, can only serve to perpetuate false notions' (Lawrence 1816: 131). Hence the making of Frankenstein's creature, while not dismissing the electricity of the thunderstorm, leaves the vital principle just as unnamed as Lawrence does, producing a Gothic image that, again, reflects and abjects the disagreement that remained unresolved in 1818 about the cause of life as electricity or something else.

Indeed, electricity in itself was a locus for ideological conflict, for many as much of an ominous threat as it was for some a promise of revolutionary insight. According to Joseph Priestley, quite familiar to the Shelleys as a proponent of electricity, Franklin himself admitted that his own kite experiment was both exhilarating and dangerous, since 'the clouds' that engulfed his kite could 'change from positive to negative electricity several times in the course of one thunder gust' (Priestley 1775: 1: 218). That caution is echoed in T. J. Hogg's memory of the electrical experiments he witnessed in 1810–11 in the young Percy Shelley's Oxford rooms: 'how many of the secrets of nature [c]ould such a force unlock', Hogg writes, yet 'what a terrible organ [might] the supernal shock prove!' (Hogg 1858: 1.51; see also Goodall 2008). In looking back to such contradictions in both Franklin's and the young Shelley's proclivities, as he certainly does, Victor in *Frankenstein* manifests them less in remembering his Ingolstadt cadaver table, where electricity is never explicitly invoked, and more in his sighting of the 'stream of fire' that produces the shattered oak. That Gothic image of sublime yet horrific power is most repeated in the novel when Frankenstein, in mourning for the death of his little brother William, recognises the creature for the first time since its awakening: 'While I watched [another electrical storm over Mont Blanc], so beautiful yet terrific … a flash of lightning illuminated … [a] shape [of] gigantic stature [in all] the deformity of its aspect … the filthy demon to whom I had given life' (Shelley 2012: 50). As with the oak, a fiery streak here exposes a powerful grandeur in the natural world and a horrible destructive force emerging from the same setting. It is as though electricity itself has produced both concurrently in one of this novel's most Gothic images, the sublime fulfilment of Victor's inspired labours and an ugly malformation that he knows, just by seeing it, to be the monstrous killer of his brother.

Mary Shelley is clearly aware that, in the public mind of her historic moment, electricity includes simultaneously one potential for solving and extending the secret of life *and* a terrifying capacity for generating an excess of energy that can produce deadly conflagrations. In some scientific theories that we know she read, the epigenetic life-force is so self-shaping, once it is seeded and fed, that it can carry out a rapid exfoliation of its relations among elements to the point of exceeding all known limits, producing, not just organic mutations, a quasi-evolution prophetic of Charles Darwin's *Descent of Man* (1871), but 'a monstrous vitality that [is] frightening in its assertion of unbounded purpose' (Gigante 2009: 210). Erasmus Darwin (Charles' grandfather) in *Zoonomia* (1794) confesses that an 'exuberance of nourishment to [a] fetus', perhaps like too many different ingredients combined in Frankenstein's creature, can lead to 'monstrous births with additional limbs', or perhaps abnormal size, rather than 'a new species of animal' (Darwin 1794: 1.501). The creature, among other things, is thus a manifestation of the widespread fear by the early 1800s that experimenting with the newly revealed 'exuberance' of vitality—which led to the public condemnation, alongside the adulation, of Franklin, Priestley, Erasmus Darwin, Lawrence, and even Davy, among others (see Butler 2012: 414–16, and Hunter 2008: 146–7)—can result in such an uncontrollable recombination of organic particles that the use of life science to bring about a better state of humanity, Victor Frankenstein's initial aim (Shelley 2012: 33), can ultimately produce monstrosities because of the largely unknown nature of vitality itself. That is why Shelley's creature, when he appears as a horror emerging from sublimity in a flash of lightning, parallels the Gothic image of the blasted tree to suggest a fearsome paradox—electricity as the bringer of death as much as new life, possibly to Europe's future (its children, here embodied by William)—that was eagerly pursued *and* greatly feared in the West from the later eighteenth into the early nineteenth century.

To be sure, as *Frankenstein* the novel proceeds, the creature's 'monstrosity' is complicated well beyond its roots in vitalism to become the product of his experiences, of the rejections he endures from the moment of his awakening, even as it may also result from his peculiar combination of physical ingredients. Added to the above conflicts of scientific belief abjected into this figure, it turns out, is a hesitation between nature and nurture as to which is most responsible for human behaviour as both were understood at Mary Shelley's time. Her raising of that issue, not surprisingly, involves her alluding to the contradictions in her era's sciences of the mind and arguments about the relationship of internal thought to sensory perceptions. The creature's account to his creator of his own growth, as a result, turns out to be as much of a Janus-faced Gothic figuration as he is, since it—and indeed the whole novel—is torn between competing conceptions of just this relationship. On the one hand, building on the Abbé de Condillac's 1754 'imagin[ing]' of a statue constructed internally like ourselves' to demonstrate how we learn through the five senses and Jean-Jacques Rousseau's hypothetical fiction in his educational treatise *Émile* (1762) 'that a child had at its birth the stature and strength of a grown man' so that he can model what 'natural' learning should be (Condillac 1930: xxx; Rousseau 1979: 61), the creature first remembers progressing from an initial sensory overload where 'no distinct ideas occupied ... [his] mind' (since he starts as a *tabula rasa* as per John Locke) into a separation of 'distinguish[ed] sensations' that produced ideas from them and then into 'distinguish[ing] the insect from the herb' without yet being able to name those differences (Shelley 2012: 71). To this point, his account seems neatly one-sided, tilting towards the theory of mind that gained considerable force from David Hartley's argument in his 1749 *Observations* that linked Lockean empiricism to emergent brain theory: that 'a material process of "vibrations" in the brain ... undergirded the workings of association' to such an extent that understanding, rooted solely in perceptions, was almost entirely 'passive' and 'mechanical' (Richardson 2001: 9–11). This approach to the science of mind gained a measure of endorsement in Godwin's empirical sense of learning in his *Enquiry Concerning Political Justice* (1793). There 'what is born into the world is an unfinished sketch', and while a capacity for 'understanding' does make decisions about the 'impulses of sense', what enters through those from outside them, which includes all forms of 'education', influences even the understanding, so much so that motivated 'actions and decisions' are inevitably the 'offspring of circumstances and events' (Godwin 1976: 97, 113)—nurture.

Hence, the many direct connections between how Mary Shelley's creature is treated, what he hears and reads once he learns language, and how he finally feels compelled to behave.

On the other hand, though, in recounting these developments, the creature has to admit that some objects and actions, even when observed for the first time, arouse in him 'sensations of a peculiar and overpowering nature' (*not* nurture) based on apparently pre-conscious proclivities (Shelley 2012: 75), on mysterious drives that even underlie his later rage against others and rise up, not simply in response to external stimuli, but sometimes to 'spectres' of remembered perceptions in 'my imagination' (79). Now the creature's recollections incline towards what Erasmus Darwin claims in another part of *Zoonomia*: that the human 'sensorium' includes, deeper than 'organs of sense', a 'spirit of animation, which resides throughout the body, without being cognisable to the senses, except by its effects' (Darwin 1794: 1.10). As Alan Richardson has shown, Darwin joined here with some other contemporaries in the 1790s to open up the conception of mind, albeit by way of a 'spirit' that many rejected, to both '*innate* desires' and '*unconscious* mental processes' that were 'not compatible with sensationalist psychology' (Richardson 2001: 14). The creature's account in *Frankenstein* remains hesitant throughout as to how much to accept this dimension alongside the Godwinian necessity of being determined by external stimuli, which the creature often uses to justify his destructiveness (Shelley 2012: 160), but the reader can hardly help linking the creature's 'overpowering' sensations back to Frankenstein's *very* unconscious response to the first sight of his finished creation. After recoiling from that horror and falling asleep exhausted in his bedroom, Victor famously dreams that he beholds his fiancé, Elizabeth, approaching him in Ingolstadt, and, as he tries to embrace her, she turns into the 'corpse of my dead mother', who had expired after catching scarlet fever from Elizabeth (Shelley 2012: 25), whereupon this entire vision dissolves into the visage of the creature looming over Frankenstein's bed (36). What seems to be suggested is that underlying the making of his 'child' is the absence of women in that process, alongside the suggestion that a pre-conscious desire *for* the mother really drives Frankenstein's foraging among the bodies of the dead. This dream, understandably, since it pre-figures Sigmund Freud's later grounding of psychoanalysis on the unconscious desire to return to the mother, has led to several Freudian readings of *Frankenstein* that see the creature as Victor's doppelgänger driven to carry through several of his creator's unconscious desires, such as the eventual strangling of Elizabeth (Shelley 2012: 140–1), seeing as she, in a sense, killed Victor's mother (as in Kaplan and Kloss 1973: 131–45). In being its own kind of Gothic image, this dream also advances the penchant in Gothic fictions from Walpole on both to employ empirically based associations of ideas and to intimate unconscious, archaic drives in people and whole societies, as when the princess Matilda in *Otranto* visually connects the apparent peasant Theodore to an old painting of the dead Alfonso and just feels 'somehow or other my destiny is ... related' to both (Walpole 1996: 41). Nonetheless, there remain disagreements among interpreters of *Frankenstein* over how much to explain the creature's actions with Victor's unconscious motivations and how much to accept the creature's empirical account of his motives as resulting from his perceptions, his miseducation, and the effects of social prejudices on his psyche. These divergent interpretations, I would argue, re-enact what is alluded to, debated, and left unresolved from science in the 1818 novel itself, given the Janus-faced Gothic it employs and the contentions over the roles of both experience and the unconscious in the still-developing theories of the brain at work noted above from Shelley's own time.

Meanwhile, too, the visage of the creature in *Frankenstein* raises other contentious issues from a very different science of that era. In Victor's first description of his completed man-child, he is shocked to behold its/his combination of 'yellow skin ... hair ... of a lustrous black, and flowing ... [all a] horrid contrast with his watery eyes ... the same colour as the dun white sockets in which they were set, his shriveled complexion, and straight black lips' (Shelley 2012: 35). Because he has attempted to create a composite new version of the whole human race, Frankenstein finds that the result (like humanity itself) is composed of several different 'colours' at once. While several scholars have rightly seen how this cross-racial 'otherness' reflects Shelley's awareness of the debates raging at her time over slavery (including slave revolts), colonisation, and British imperialism (see Fulford et al. 2004: 149–227; Mulvey-Roberts 2016: 52–91), only Anne Mellor has isolated how much this multi-coloured Gothic image invokes the explicitly racial *science* of the early nineteenth century. She has shown that the same William Lawrence, the Shelleys' physician and Abernethy's antagonist, was equally an ethnologist opposed, like the Shelleys, to the enslavement of any group—but was also insistent, following a German predecessor, on classifying the different races of humanity into five categories (while seeing humanity as one species), among them the white Caucasian, the yellow Mongolian, and the black Ethiopian (Mellor 2001:

7–8). The creature thus, according to this scheme, could well have been read in 1818 as combining the Mongolian (with his 'yellow skin') with some of the Ethiopian (his 'black lips'), particularly insofar as his composition from dead bodies and consequently 'shrivelled complexion' makes him resemble an Egyptian 'mummy' (Shelley 2012: 36), even as the different colours on his face remain distinct, as Lawrence would insist the different races should. That distinctiveness, sad to say, was vital to Lawrence because the different races for him had separate psychological attributes, with the Caucasian, he writes, boasting the highest 'moral feelings and mental endowment' and the Mongolian being notable, not just for 'inferiority' by comparison but also for 'docility', unless under the pressure of tyrants to commit what this same race seems also capable of, 'unrelenting slaughter', and 'universal destruction' (Lawrence 1819: 476, 483). Consequently, the creature's echoes of this description, which increase as the novel progresses, set him up for what he feels on overhearing the De Lacey family read aloud about the different races of the earth and their histories in the Comte de Volney's *Les Ruines* (1791): that, even if slavery and colonisation are wrong, the 'Asiatics' are 'slothful' compared to the 'stupendous genius' of the Caucasian 'Grecians' (Shelley 2012: 82). The creature therefore adopts some racist assumptions himself, quite common for subalterns, even while repeatedly being the victim of them, and the Western Caucasian worry about mistreated 'inferior' races rising up against them in the colonies and elsewhere leads his creator (even more prejudiced than Lawrence), not only to reject him as a monster at birth because he combines non-Caucasian colours, but to tear 'to pieces' a possible female creature because she and 'the monster' might reproduce in some distant land and, like Mongolians or any 'inferiors' aroused from their docility, might then become a rebellious 'race of devils', making 'the very existence of the species of man', pre-eminently Caucasian, 'precarious and full of terror' (Shelley 2012: 119).

To be sure, Mellor finally argues that the creature's understandable desire to be part of a family—even the De Laceys, who are already becoming interracial in the betrothal of 'Felix' to the Arabian 'Safie' (Shelley 2012: 85–6)—suggests that Mary Shelley, unlike Lawrence, her Victor Frankenstein, and most of the Europe she knew, was starting to believe that racial 'amalgamation' could 'represent a positive evolution of the human species' if prejudice did not stand in the way (Mellor 2001: 22). But, as I have been arguing here, among her larger aims in *Frankenstein*, and one reason for her concerted use of the Janus-faced Gothic image so good at symbolising conflicts among waning and ascending beliefs, is surely exposing her audience and culture to its own ambivalences, particularly in the several rising sciences that promise considerable social progress but are held back by counter-beliefs, often *within those very sciences*. The novel therefore leaves its readers much as its Gothic creature is left by his eavesdropping on the reading of Volney's *Ruines*. At that juncture, he recalls, he is poised between seeing, like Mary Shelley and her parents, the immorality of 'rank, descent, and [assumptions about] noble blood', as well as the discrimination against women and 'inferior' races bound up with such ideologies (Shelley 2012: 82–3), and accepting older, prejudicial, racist labels, such as the 'slothful Asiatics'; that latter choice leads him to see himself, in his final testament to Captain Walton over the body of Victor, as an 'abortion, to be spurned at, and kicked, and trampled on', even as he defiantly proclaims the 'injustice' of being made, like so many others around him, to see his very being as monstrous (Shelley 2012: 160). Such ambivalence in the world of this novel, barring major future changes in human civilisation, is ultimately inescapable, and that is certainly the case in the areas of scientific debate that *Frankenstein* brings forward and Gothicises to vividly suggest the divisions within them all and within the culture that viewed them, and views them still, with both excitement and suspicion. After all, there were sharp differences of opinion at Shelley's time, as there are in some circles today, over the use of dead bodies for science that Victor tries to further by making his creature. As Timothy Marshall has shown, the creature's combination of the medical advancements made possible by the study of cadavers and the revulsion he causes by being multi-coloured, proletarian, and a sacrilegious violation of sanctified burial-grounds reflects and abjects the great controversy in Britain from the 1790s through the 1830s over the frequent, if secret, dissection of many less-than-'respectable' dug-up corpses, often by highly respectable doctors and scientists (see Marshall 1995: 129–218). Mary Shelley did not imagine that such controversies would be completely eradicated, and we know they remain with us now, though some of them have changed their features and assumptions. Her main Gothic image finally recedes into 'darkness and distance' rather than dying before our eyes (Shelley 2012: 161) because it still haunts us, albeit at an abjected remove, with the unresolved quandaries of science—and civilisation as a whole—in our Enlightenment past, our present, and well into our future.

WORKS CITED

Abernethy, John. 1814. *An Enquiry into the Probability and Rationality of Mr. Hunter's 'Theory of Life'*. London: Longman.

Apel, August. 2005. The Family Portraits. In *Fantasmagoriana: Tales of the Dead*, ed. A. J. Day. Trans. Sarah Utterson, 37–61. St. Ives: Fantasmagoriana Press.

Butler, Marilyn. 2012. *Frankenstein* and Radical Science. In *Frankenstein: The 1818 Text*, ed. J. Paul Hunter, 404–416. New York: Norton.

Clery, E.J. 1995. *The Rise of Supernatural Fiction, 1762–1800*. Cambridge: Cambridge University Press.

Darwin, Erasmus. 1794. *Zoonomia; or the Laws of Organic Life*. London: J. Johnson.

Davy, Sir Humphry. 1972. *The Collected Works*, ed. John Davy. London: Smith, Elder, 1840; rpt. New York: Johnson Reprint.

de Condillac, Étienne Bonnot. 1930. *Treatise on the sensations*. Trans. Geraldine Carr. Los Angeles: University of Southern California.

Fulford, Tim, Debbie Lee, and Peter J. Kitson. 2004. *Literature, Science and Exploration in the Romantic Era: Bodies of Knowledge*. Cambridge: Cambridge University Press.

Gigante, Denise. 2009. *Life: Organic Form and Romanticism*. New Haven: Yale University Press.

Godwin, William. 1976. *Enquiry Concerning Political Justice*, ed. Isaac Kramnick. Harmondsworth: Penguin.

Goodall, Jane. 2008. Electrical Romanticism. In *Frankenstein's Science: Experimentation and Discovery in Romantic Culture, 1780–1830*, ed. Christa Knellwolf and Jane Goodall, 117–132. Aldershot: Ashgate.

Hogg, Thomas Jefferson. 1858. *The Life of Percy Bysshe Shelley*. London: J. M. Dent.

Hogle, Jerrold E. 2012. The Gothic Ghost of the Counterfeit and the Progress of Abjection. In *A New Companion to the Gothic*, ed. David Punter, 496–509. Oxford: Wiley-Blackwell.

Holmes, Richard. 2008. *The Age of Wonder: How the Romantic Generation Discovered the Beauty and Terror of Science*. London: Harper.

Hunter, Allan K. 2008. Evolution, Revolution and Frankenstein's Creature. In *Frankenstein's Science: Experimentation and Discovery in Romantic Culture, 1780–1830*, ed. Christa Knellwolf and Jane Goodall, 133–149. Aldershot: Ashgate.

Kaplan, Morton, and Robert Kloss. 1973. *The Unspoken Motive: A Guide to Psychoanalytic Literary Criticism*. New York: Free Press.

Ketterer, David. 1979. *Frankenstein's Creation: The Book, the Monster, and Human Reality*. Victoria: University of Victoria.

Knellwolf, Christa. 2008. Geographic Boundaries and Inner Space: *Frankenstein,* Scientific Explorations and the Quest for the Absolute. In *Frankenstein's Science: Experimentation and Discovery in Romantic Culture, 1780–1830,* ed. Christa Knellwolf and Jane Goodall, 49–69. Aldershot: Ashgate.

Knellwolf, Christa, and Jane Goodall, eds. 2008. *Frankenstein's Science: Experimentation and Discovery in Romantic Culture, 1780–1830.* Aldershot: Ashgate.

Kristeva, Julia. 1982. *Powers of Horror: An Essay on Abjection.* Trans. Leon S. Roudiez. New York: Columbia University Press.

Lawrence, William. 1816. *An Introduction to Comparative Anatomy and Physiology.* London: J. Callow.

———. 1819. *Lectures on Physiology, Zoology, and the Natural History of Man.* London: J. Callow.

Marshall, Timothy. 1995. *Murdering to Dissect: Grave-Robbing, Frankenstein and the Anatomy Literature.* Manchester: Manchester University Press.

Mellor, Anne K. 2001. *Frankenstein,* Racial Science, and the Yellow Peril. *Nineteenth-Century Contexts* 23: 7–8.

Mulvey-Roberts, Marie. 2016. *Dangerous Bodies: Historicising the Gothic Corporeal.* Manchester: Manchester University Press.

Priestley, Joseph. 1775. *The History and Present State of Electricity.* London: Bathurst and Lowndes.

Richardson, Alan. 2001. *British Romanticism and the Science of the Mind.* Cambridge: Cambridge University Press.

Rousseau, Jean-Jacques. 1979. *Émile, or On Education.* Trans. Allan Bloom. New York: Basic Books.

Shelley, Mary. 1987. *The Journals, 1814–1844,* ed. Paula R. Feldman, and Diana Scott-Kilvert. Oxford: Clarendon Press.

———. 2012. *Frankenstein: The 1818 Text,* ed. J. Paul Hunter. New York: Norton.

Vasbinder, Samuel Holmes. 1984. *Scientific Attitudes in Mary Shelley's Frankenstein.* Ann Arbor: UMI Research Press.

Walpole, Horace. 1996. *The Castle of Otranto,* ed. W. S. Lewis, and E. J. Clery. Oxford: Oxford University Press.

von Woudenberg, Maximiliaan. 2014. The Variants and Transformations of *Fantasmagoriana:* Tracing a Travelling Text to the Byron-Shelley Circle. *Romanticism* 20: 306–320.

CHAPTER 3

Paracelsus and 'P[r]etty Experimentalism': The Glass Prison of Science and Secrecy in *Frankenstein*

Victor Sage

'A Bird's Eye View of Your Heart': Godwin's Sentimental Education

Despite a certain wariness between them, at the end of June 1796, William Godwin seems to have written Mary Wollstonecraft a compliment, to which he received the following piquant reply:

> I send you the last volume of 'Héloise', because, if you have it not, you may chance to wish for it. You may perceive by this remark that I do not give you credit for as much philosophy as our friend, and I want besides to remind you, when you write to me in *verse*, not to choose the easiest task, my perfections, but to dwell on your own feelings – that is to say, give me a bird's eye view of your heart. Do not make me a desk 'to write upon', I humbly pray – unless you honestly acknowledge yourself *bewitched*.

V. Sage (✉)
School of Literature, Drama and Creative Writing, Faculty of Arts and Humanities, University of East Anglia, Norwich, UK

© The Author(s) 2018
C. M. Davison, M. Mulvey-Roberts (eds.), *Global Frankenstein*,
Studies in Global Science Fiction,
https://doi.org/10.1007/978-3-319-78142-6_3

> Of that I shall judge by the style in which the eulogisms flow, for I think
> I have observed that you compliment without rhyme or reason, when you
> are almost at a loss what to say. (Wardle 1967: 6–7)

Wollstonecraft begins by teasing him as a 'philosopher' (which seems in Socratic fashion to include 'lover') with a dose of his 'rival' ('our friend') Rousseau's *La Nouvelle Héloise*. This is a book which acts as a manual of emotional articulacy for both their generation and the next; it was to form the basis of the pilgrimage to the haunts of that novel made by Byron and Percy Shelley on the northern shore of Lac Leman in the Diodati summer of 1816, as reported in *History of a Six Weeks' Tour*, Mary and Percy Shelley's jointly written account of their journey to France and Switzerland (Shelley 1817: 117–30). Mary Shelley already mentions it in a letter in 1815, and she was reading it between June 27 and 2 July 1817. She read it again in early 1820 (Shelley 1987: Vol. 1, 174ff; Vol. 2, 670).

Wollstonecraft's tone here is that of an ironical instructor; she demands a different approach, not the evasive and 'polite' academic clichés she has received from him, mere signs of deferral and uncertainty, but the confidential revelation of all his actual emotional landscape, a confessional narrative, even if, or rather especially if, that involves 'bewitchment'. The emphasis on the term *bewitched* indicates her witty, challenging, prompting switch of voice: the challenge, to an Enlightened Philosopher, is to confess to a degree of superstitious credulity, if that's what it takes.

We can see from the revisions to his radical treatise, *Enquiry Concerning Political Justice* in that same year, 1796, that he was influenced by Mary Wollstonecraft's conversation and her emphasis on the necessity of domestic affections and human attachments. He begins to add to his account of the central role of 'private reason' as a motor of political and social change, his thoughts on the accompanying necessity of tempering human isolation: privacy of reasoned judgement was essential against Government, but openness was also essential between family and friends. There is a new emphasis, after the failure of the French Revolution, on communication as a necessity in the political process and a new stress on gradualism (Clemit 1993: 5–9).

By 1797, they were married and Wollstonecraft died in that same year, just after giving birth to their daughter, Mary. Devastated by grief, Godwin spent much of 1797 reading all her works and papers, and sat down to compose his frank and loving memoir of her which was published in 1798, which Godwin's editor Patricia Clemit refers to, interestingly, as also 'a defence of their experimental relationship' (Godwin 1994: xv). There is a crucial passage which made its first appearance in this memoir:

> True wisdom will recommend to us individual attachments; for with them our minds are more thoroughly maintained in activity and life than they can be under the privation of them; and it is better that man should be a living being, than a stock or a stone. True virtue will sanction this recommendation; *since it is the object of virtue to produce happiness,* and since the man who lives in the midst of domestic relations will have many opportunities of conferring pleasure, minute in the detail, yet not trivial in the amount, without interfering with the purposes of general benevolence. (Godwin 1994: xvi, emphasis added)

This passage then migrates verbatim into the 'Preface' to his novel *St. Leon* published in 1799. That novel is the fictional equivalent of his revision of *Political Justice*. But it also looks forward directly to the central conflict that runs throughout *Frankenstein* between the isolation caused by secrecy and the open exchange of ideas (including scientific knowledge) and feelings. In a memorable scene, Mary Shelley makes the Monster echo Godwin's ethical maxim: 'it is the object of virtue to produce happiness', in seeking to persuade Frankenstein to make him a mate:

> Remember, that I am thy creature; I ought to be thy Adam; but I am rather the fallen angel, whom thou drivest from joy for no misdeed. Every where [sic] I see bliss, from which I alone am irrevocably excluded. I was benevolent and good; misery made me a fiend. Make me happy, and I shall again be virtuous. (Shelley 1994: 520)

Frankenstein is persuaded, briefly, by this argument but, then, isolated in his laboratory in the Orkneys, without being able to speak to anyone, loses faith, becomes fearful for humanity, and destroys the half-built female in a fit of 'altruism'. Brought to the edge of an exchange, but each isolated from the other in his own story, he and his Creature fall progressively but at different speeds.

Godwin is famous for inventing in *Caleb Williams* (1794) a first-person narrative which was already reliant on the tradition of Rational Dissent; and he had already appropriated the arguments of Milton's Satan and Eve from *Paradise Lost* to discuss the question of the political liberty of the individual's 'private reason' from legislative restraint (i.e. more broadly, the Thirty-nine Articles and, more specifically in the 1790s, the Test and

Corporation Acts) before writing *St. Leon* (1799). In this, he anticipates Mary Shelley's use of Milton in *Frankenstein* (Clemit 1993: 5–6).

But it is in *St. Leon* (1799), whose first-person narrator is the immediate narrative model for *Frankenstein's* method of narration, that Godwin renders an ironic critique of the interventionism of his own generation, ten years after the French Revolution, and finds a way of directly articulating the theme of the Faustian fall into isolation of the individual who has mistaken himself for a moral singularity, matching this with a headlong, self-consciously confessional narrative, whose narrator is actually portrayed in the act of composing the text as we read it.

The novel tells the story of Reginald de St Leon, a sixteenth-century French knight, who as a young man was present at the legendary meeting in June 1520 at the field of the Cloth of Gold in Picardy between Francis I of France and Henry VIII of England. Events decline immediately after as the enlightened Francis is drawn into war against the Holy Roman Empire and St Leon sees action and distinguishes himself against the Spanish in the disastrous campaigns in the Northern plains of Italy, particularly in the siege of Pavia. Afterwards, St Leon retires in disillusionment to the splendours of the French Court and there wastes his entire patrimony at the gaming tables of Paris.

St. Leon's consolation lies in his marriage to Marguerite, Countess of Damville, a woman of wisdom, tenderness, and superior rationality, the model for whom, Godwin's friend Thomas Holcroft recognised, was the late Mary Wollstonecraft. He said his heart ached, as he read it. (Godwin 1994: xvi) Marguerite's father, the old Count de Damville, counsels St. Leon against ruinous gaming and the glittering world of the court, imploring him to rest in the bosom of the family he has now acquired.

The story tracks ruthlessly the shame and ruin, the death and separation, which St. Leon's perversely egotistical drive brings on that family. Gradually, he cuts himself off from his companion, the 'Mistress of his soul' as he calls Marguerite, while he is drawn irrevocably into guilt and isolation. They and their four children are compelled to retreat to a modest life on the land by the shores of Lake Constance in Protestant territory, where St Leon manages to make enough for them to live by working as a gardener to the Bishop as the health of his beloved wife begins to suffer. Yet despite their destitution and the hollowness that has come between them, they still manage some happiness. It is at this point that St. Leon takes in and gives shelter in a summer house to an old man, a destitute and ragged stranger who is an Alchemist. Eventually, he imparts his secret to

St. Leon, or rather his twin secrets, the elixir of life and the transmutation of base metals into gold.

St. Leon's new skills cannot be used, of course, to cure Marguerite who, before she dies, makes him a speech which translates the traditional theme of moral isolation to a new pitch of fallen and corrupted consciousness, which is strongly prophetic of the major theme of moral isolation in *Frankenstein:*

> An adept and an alchemist is a low character. When I married you, I supposed myself united to a nobleman, a knight, and a soldier, a man who would have revolted with disdain from every thing that was poor-spirited and base [...] Here is the end of all genuine dignity and the truest generosity of soul. You cannot be ingenuous; for all your dealings are secrecy and darkness. You cannot have a friend; for the mortal lives not that can sympathise with your thoughts and emotions [...] Equality is the soul of real and cordial society. A man of rank indeed does not live on equal terms with the whole of his species; but his heart also can exult, for he has his equals. How unhappy, the wretch, the monster rather let me say, who is without an equal; who looks through the world, and in the world cannot find a brother; who is endowed with attributes which no living being participates with him; and who is therefore cut off for ever from all cordiality and confidence, can never unbend himself but lives the solitary, joyless tenant of a prison, the materials of which are emeralds and rubies! How unhappy this wretch! How weak and ignoble the man that voluntarily accepts these laws of existence!
> (Godwin 1994: 210–11)

Godwin uses Wollstonecraft's frankness about equality in Marguerite's arguments here, as, resting her case on the aristocratic value of 'honour', she faces St Leon with his own 'monstrosity'—defined as the inability to have a friend, an equal—and the nightmare of his own fall. Implicit in this is the breach of the ethical, political, and scientific assumptions that truth must be communicable to others. St. Leon has doomed himself to become a wanderer and to the paradox of the secret that cannot be kept, indeed the secret that attracts opposition: everywhere he is to go, he is doomed to be driven out as a necromancer, because part of his secret—the fact that he *has* it—always seems to leak out via even the most trusted of servants. And Godwin pushes his narrative to the point of breakdown here: even when Marguerite is plainly ailing, St. Leon refuses to try to use his knowledge to help her and will not tolerate implicit readerly objections to his behaviour:

Some readers will perhaps ask me why, anxious as I was for the life of
Marguerite, and visible as was the decline of her health, I did not administer
to her of the elixir of immortality which was one of my peculiar endowments.
Such readers I have only to remind, that the pivot upon which the history
I am composing turns, is a mystery. If they will not accept of my communication upon my own terms, they must lay aside my book. I am engaged in
relating the incidents of my life; I have no intention to furnish the remotest
hint respecting the science of which I am the depository. That science affords
abundant reasons why the elixir in question might not, or rather could not,
be imbibed by any other than an adept. (Godwin 1994: 214)

Beyond the traditional ethical demand for 'candour' as the basis of 'benevolence' and the post-revolutionary political necessity of communication in
the late 1790s, the rhetorical bluff of Godwin's alchemist narrator to his
textually implied reader—his imposition of narrative silence—seems to
suggest, to the modern reader at least, that the secrecy of alchemy also
violates one of the principles of science in a modern sense, namely, the
iterative principle—that knowledge is only viewable as 'scientific knowledge' when it is 'iterable', or able to be repeated experimentally by another.
The step that follows—that such knowledge should become the property
of the human race, not of one individual—is also of course impossible to
make, if the first step cannot be taken.

Thus for Godwin, alchemy is already an equivocal metaphor: on the
one hand, it represents revolutionary vision as a form of intervention in
the world, and on the other hand, it incarcerates the subject in a species of
glass prison, a form of knowledge which is presented as ultimately incom-
municable to others. After this point, although he claims the authority of
his own experience, St Leon's authority as a narrator cannot be maintained
without question. The reader's relation to the narrative has changed; the
narrator has passed over to the other side.

My point here is that Godwin's particular tone focuses an urgent contemporary political theme—the cutting off of those human and domestic
ties which Godwin himself, partly through his relationship with Mary
Wollstonecraft, had come to value so highly, plus a political critique of his
own generation's interventional 'enthusiasm', a response he had begun to
distrust. The nature of St Leon's 'fall' is also strongly ethical: his narrator-
protagonist descends into a precisely repeated, but never quite predictable, series of moral perversities and political disasters, mistakes which he
alone commits, often against his will, through his self-imposed secrecy,
and from which he can never hope to absolve himself but only compound
and multiply over and over again.

VICTOR FRANKENSTEIN: VISION VERSUS EXPERIMENT

The main struggle in Victor Frankenstein's early life—the struggle between secrecy and the desire to communicate—begins very early. He was 11 years old (in the first draft, subsequently 14) when inclement weather drove a pleasure party at the baths at Thonon indoors, and they were obliged to remain for a whole day confined to the inn. He chanced to find on the shelves a book of Cornelius Agrippa, and he describes how a new light has dawned in his mind. He bounds up to his father to tell him:

> My father looked carelessly at the title page of my book, - and said Ah! Cornelius Agrippa! - My dear Victor, do not waste your time upon this - it is sad trash. If, instead of this remark or rather exclamation my father had taken the pains to explain to me that the principles of Agrippa had been entirely exploded[.] and that a modern system of science had been introduced which possessed much greater power than the ancient because the powers of the ancient were pretended and chimerical, while those of the moderns are real and practical; Under such circumstances I should certainly have thrown Agrippa aside, and with my imagination warmed as it was should probably have aplied myself to the more rational theory of chemistry which has at present the approbation of the learned. But the cursory glance my father had taken of my volume by no means assured me he was acquainted with its contents; and I continued to read with the greatest avidity. (Shelley 2008: 259–260)

I quote here from the first draft of the novel with its slightly eccentric punctuation to show how this theme was present for Mary Shelley from the beginning. Even at this early point, the dialectic of secrecy, in the face of paternal discipline, has installed itself. I quote again here from the first draft of the novel:

> When I returned home, my first care was to procure the works of this author and afterwards those of Paracelsus and Albertus Magnus. I read and studied the wild fancies of the authors with delight, they appeared to me treasures known to few besides myself; and although I often wished to discover these secret stores of knowledge to my father yet his definite censure of my favourite Agrippa, always withheld me. *I disclosed my secret to Elizabeth therefore, under a strict promise of secrecy*, but she did not interest herself in them and I was left by her to pursue my studies alone. (Shelley 2008: 260, emphasis added)

Secrecy extends from the inside to the outside; compare Blake's powerful 'Song of Experience', *A Poison Tree,* which he, another radical, engraved in 1794 (Blake 1961: 767). Secrecy flows from the content of what Frankenstein 'knows' to the fact that he knows it—we see it in the tautology of Shelley's early style—and it threatens to proliferate here as it does in *St. Leon*; ironically, Elizabeth is not interested. But Victor is already (retrospectively) reading the non-exchange with both his father and her as a narrative of his own destiny.

Victor Frankenstein's father wants to send him to Ingolstadt in Germany in order to get him to travel away from his native town, Geneva, the birthplace of Rousseau, which he seems never to have left, to broaden his mind.

Although Ingolstadt has a good reputation for science, it has also been a hotbed of political radicalism in its fairly recent past: in 1784, the Elector of Bavaria was moved to ban as seditious a notorious secret society called the 'Illuminati' led by one Adam Weishaupt, their name a deliberate parody of rational 'Enlightenment' ('Lumière'), an organisation which 'aimed at the destruction of all family ties' (Clemit 1993: 92; Voges 1987: 104–5). Godwin and the Shelleys were familiar with this history, probably through Volney (Clemit 1993: 162–3). As Richard Holmes reports, the bible of Percy Shelley in 1812 was the Abbé Barruel's *Memoirs, Illustrating the History of Jacobinism* (1797–8), a work which Godwin also records that he had read in his preparatory research for *St. Leon* in the late 1790s (Holmes 2005: 126–7, ftnote 127; Godwin 1994: xvii–xix). The ingenious Neoplatonist Percy Shelley read this paranoid counter-revolutionary tract, which includes lists of works and authors, and seeks to smear them by association, as a manual of Revolution and a bibliography of prosympathetic Revolutionary contacts, thus neatly turning upside down the writer's manifest intentions. It seems more than likely that either Godwin or Percy Shelley communicated this to Mary Shelley who has Victor Frankenstein encounter the decisive moment of his philosophical and scientific education at Ingolstadt at the alma mater of the 'Illuminati', the post-revolutionary European context adding to the ambivalence of values in the retrospective staging of Frankenstein's education in this section of the novel, particularly around the central questions of science, secrecy and the isolation of the individual. And secondly, we glimpse the significance of the Neoplatonic tradition, which Victor has strayed into, in his naïve reading of the 'magicians' Agrippa and Albertus Magnus, a tradition, which—in its tendency to heresy—has its own pressure for secrecy: what excites Victor about Agrippa is his claim to secret knowledge of the raising of the dead to life (Shelley 1994: 478–9; Empson 1994: 163).

When Victor gets to Ingolstadt, he is naively astonished to find two teachers, Herr Krempe, Professor of Natural Philosophy, 'a little squat man, with a gruff voice and a repulsive countenance', and the rather Rousseauistically named Herr Waldman, the magnanimous man of the woods, the Professor of Chemistry, who act respectively as the bad cop and the good cop of the history of science, with opposite points of view about the studies which the precocious young man has already been undertaking:

> The next morning I delivered my letters of introduction, and paid a visit to some of the principal professors. Chance – or rather the evil influence, the Angel of Destruction, which asserted omnipotent sway over me from the moment I turned my reluctant steps from my father's door – led me first to M. Krempe, professor of natural philosophy. He was an uncouth man, but deeply embued in the secrets of his science. He asked me several questions concerning my progress in the different branches of science appertaining to natural philosophy. I replied carelessly; and partly in contempt, mentioned the names of my alchymists as the principal authors I had studied. The professor stared: 'Have you', he said, 'really spent your time in studying such nonsense?'
>
> I replied in the affirmative. 'Every minute', continued M. Krempe with warmth, 'every instant that you have wasted on those books is utterly and entirely lost. You have burdened your memory with exploded systems and useless names. Good God! in what desert land have you lived, where no one was kind enough to inform you that these fancies, which you have so greedily imbibed, are a thousand years old, and as musty as they are ancient? I little expected, in this enlightened and scientific age, to find a disciple of Albertus Magnus and Paracelsus. My dear sir, you must begin your studies entirely anew'. (Shelley 1994: 482)

Not surprisingly, Frankenstein feels somewhat discouraged by this encounter. But like Godwin's St Leon, his perspective on it is entirely governed by notions of the vision and ambition of the alchemists he has been studying back home. He is encouraged by M. Krempe to think that the chances of becoming a *savant* or a Magus, like Paracelsus, or the other heroes of his father's books back in Geneva, whose reputations have historically disappeared with the advent of modernity and the restricting empiricism of Enlightenment, are nil:

> It was very different when the masters of the science sought immortality and power; such views, although futile, were grand: but now the scene was changed. The ambition of the enquirer seemed to limit itself to the annihilation of those visions on which my interest in science was chiefly founded. I was required to exchange chimeras of boundless grandeur for realities of little worth. (Shelley 1994: 483)

The last sentence here, added to the first draft in Percy Shelley's hand, compares the grandeur of the scientist as a 'visionary' or, perhaps more accurately, someone with a vision of what science can ultimately do, with the modern scepticism and empiricism which relies exclusively on experimental results—each version has its drawback—which reflects Frankenstein's sarcastic retrospective view of Krempe's idea of Natural Philosophy.

A complete reversal occurs in the second encounter with science's 'good cop', M. Waldman, the chemist. He too smiles 'at the names of Cornelius Agrippa and Paracelsus, but without the contempt that M. Krempe had exhibited'. (Shelley 1994: 484) M. Waldman displays magnanimity; he restores the grandeur and the vision to young Victor Frankenstein's idea of science as an ambition to change the world, and vindicates, in part at least, his study of the ancient alchemists, adopting as he speaks their Neoplatonic language and their notion of 'penetrating the secrets of nature':

> 'The ancient teachers of this science,' said he, 'promised impossibilities, and performed nothing. The modern masters promise very little; they know that metals cannot be transmuted, and that the elixir of life is a chimera. But these philosophers, whose hands seem only made to dabble in dirt, and their eyes to pore over the microscope or crucible, have indeed performed miracles. They penetrate into the recesses of nature, and show how she works in her hiding places. They ascend into the heavens: they have discovered how the blood circulates, and the nature of the air we breathe. They have acquired new and almost unlimited powers; they can command the thunders of heaven, mimic the earthquake, and even mock the invisible world with its own shadows.'
>
> Such were the professor's words – rather let me say such the words of fate, enounced to destroy me. (Shelley 1994: 483–4)

The phrase 'mock the invisible world with its own shadows', which was already in Mary Shelley's first draft (Shelley 2008: 268), recalls Plato's shadow play in the cave scene in the *Republic*. Waldman is making allusion in that phrase to a Neoplatonist language and tradition reminiscent of Percy Shelley's optimistic paradoxes in *Prometheus Unbound*.

Thus young Victor Frankenstein, a revolutionary tradition of 'science' in its Renaissance sense restored to him, is drawn back as a consequence into imagining himself a moral singularity, and from that will follow destruction and death.

Mary Shelley increased in the 1831 text the number of passages like the last sentence above in which Frankenstein implies that chance encounters were in reality a form of Fate, and that they had the effect of reducing, or even nullifying, his freedom of choice, supposedly increasing the tragic impact of his story. The isolation of its central figures is a form of inexorable self- and other-destruction. But against what happens on a thematic level, there is always a tension in the multiple retrospective (i.e. postlapsarian) testimonies themselves, just as there is in Shelley and Godwin's Miltonic model—they are ironic because they reveal an already inaccessible innocence. The tissue of interlocking first-person narratives that is Mary Shelley's text, time and time again brings characters and reader to the edge of an exchange—of knowledge or feeling—whose possibility has already been closed off by the Fall that their multiple testimonies confirm. The Romantic stereotype of the savant, the visionary who is utterly cut off from human society, is used in Mary Shelley's 1831 text to present the reader with an ironic post-revolutionary picture of the idealism of her own generation, the Romantic poet's Faustian idealism, symbolised in this desire to 'penetrate' and 'conquer' nature, which Frankenstein himself, speaking with hindsight to the young Captain Walton, another isolated male idealist, compares to the destructive progress of imperial conquest:

A human being in perfection ought always to preserve a calm and peaceful mind, and never to allow passion or transitory desire to disturb his tranquillity. I do not think that the pursuit of knowledge is an exception to this rule. If the study to which you apply yourself has a tendency to weaken your affections, and to destroy your taste for those simple pleasures in which no alloy can possibly mix, then that study is certainly unlawful, that is to say, not befitting the human mind. If this rule were always observed; if no man allowed any pursuit whatsoever to interfere with the tranquillity of his domestic affections, Greece had not been enslaved; Caesar would have spared his country; America would have been discovered more gradually; and the empires of Mexico and Peru had not been destroyed. (Shelley 1994: 489)

This is not the kind of thing that Captain Walton wants to hear. Like Frankenstein's creature, he wants a 'friend'—in effect, an 'other half', a demand which recalls Aristophanes' speech in Plato's *Symposium* (Plato 1961: 542–4)—who will vindicate his innermost desires to sail into the land of the mist and snow. From his point of view, this stoicism of Frankenstein's is a form of passivity and quietism. (The passage seems to derive, in fact, from Volney's anti-imperialism (Clemit 1993: 151–2).) But Frankenstein's point of view is profoundly unreliable, and his is not the only unreliable point of view, as we have seen already. The struggle of the text, as we can see from this example, is a Godwinian one, between knowledge as power, on the one hand, and, on the other hand, the moral and perhaps rational necessity for the scientist to make open contact with his fellow humans without the 'secrecy' of knowledge, a transparency that might indeed divert, restrain, or even nullify his own scientific activity.

At Ingolstadt, Frankenstein returns to M. Waldman's in the evening, and his feelings about this man's magnanimity are confirmed. He encourages him to open up his horizons:

> Chemistry is that branch of natural philosophy in which the greatest improvements have been and may be made: it is on that account that I have made it my peculiar study; but at the same time I have not neglected the other branches of science. A man would make but a very sorry chemist if he attended to that department of human knowledge alone. If your wish is to become really a man of science, and not merely a petty experimentalist, I should advise you to apply to every branch of natural philosophy, including mathematics. (Shelley 1994: 484–5)

I quote here from the 1831 text: in all the printed versions, 1818, 1823, and 1831, the phrase 'really a man of science and not merely a petty experimentalist' is identical, but in the first draft Mary Shelley wrote 'pretty experimentalist' (Shelley 2008: 73 and 246, Note 25) which is a quibble that suggests to me a slightly subtler relation between vision and experiment than the naïve reactions of young Frankenstein would suggest: rather than portraying empiricism as a confine, the phrase 'pretty experimentalist' suggests, from Waldman's point of view, an intellectually elegant but unambitious formalism, rather than the dismissal of mere pedantry implied in the term 'petty', unimportant to the history and progress of science. The original point for Waldman is to add to 'experiment' the power of vision. But the dramatic irony of Frankenstein's reaction to this speech is quite clear in Mary Shelley's text: he reads Waldman's words as yet another charter for secrecy and self-isolation.

PARACELSUS AND NEOPLATONIC TRADITION

Plato rewrote the myth of Prometheus in his *Protagoras* (Plato 1961: 318–20: Bloch 1986, Vol. 2, 627ff) in a way that seems a perfect charter for alchemists. In that dialogue, he has Protagoras the Sophist tell the story of the two brothers, Epimetheus and Prometheus, who were tasked by Zeus to furnish all the mortal creatures born of earth and fire, 'and the substances which are compounded from earth and fire', with suitable powers to be able to survive. Epimetheus insisted to his brother that he himself do it. But the foolish Epimetheus had used all the powers up by the time he reached humans and didn't know what to do with them. Prometheus then, to help his brother out, steals, not one thing, but two, 'from Hephaestus and Athena the gift of skill in the arts, together with fire'. Later, he has to stand his trial for theft.

To have him steal the technology of fire as well as fire itself makes complete sense; what use would fire be to man without the knowledge of how to work it? Mary Shelley, in the novel, gives room for that discussion in the Monster's story. But Hephaestus', or more familiarly to the Latin-speaking Middle Ages, Vulcan's knowledge, is necessary for survival. But men are still isolated in small groups. There were no cities, says Protagoras. Humans could not combine because they had no politics and couldn't make war on one another, which is a part of politics, says Protagoras, beginning to make room for himself. So Zeus had to send Hermes down and give them 'respect for others and a sense of justice' before their knowledge could be integrated into anything resembling a society. Protagoras, it turns out, will be the 'expert', the specialist, who will teach them. But Socrates rebels, claiming that virtue cannot be taught.

Albertus Magnus, Cornelius Agrippa, and Paracelsus are Frankenstein's chosen forerunners, heroes whom he calls (in contempt for Krempe's empiricist Natural Philosophy) 'my alchymists', heroes with one thing in common: they variously belong to the Neoplatonist tradition. This tradition rejected the tradition of Aristotle and the Scholastic Philosophy that was founded on him and which fed variously into the dominant orthodoxy of humours and Galenic medicine and the physical sciences of the Middle Ages. Paracelsus, for example, adamantly follows Pico della Mirandola, the Florentine thinker who helps liberate man from the guilt of original sin, and science from the Aristotelian tradition of the Middle Ages, by maintaining the notion of microcosm and macrocosm. In contrast to astrology, Pico favoured 'Natural Magic'—whose purport is 'to demonstrate the effects, virtues and limits of natural objects by adducing empirical evidence' (Pagel 1982: 287). Of course, this is not modern science, but it has an increased empirical input compared with the astrology employed by humoral pathology, for example.

Paracelsus also adopted Pico's Neoplatonic version of Imagination as an intervention, a force in the world, which Pico got from Plotinus: 'In Nature to contemplate is nothing but to be something and to do something' (Pagel 1982: 181). With characteristic ebullience, and undeniable originality, Paracelsus was able to use the Neoplatonic tradition as a gateway to empirical experiment and investigation into nature. Here is Walter Pagel:

> The supremacy of the spirit, the flow of action into matter from it through the power of imagination as a force distributed over the universe and all its parts—these ideas form the principle which Paracelsus follows up through all realms of nature. He thereby filled the conceptual framework of Neoplatonism with a wealth of naturalistic observations and allegorical interpretations of natural phenomena—and it is all this that gives his work its original flavour. (1982: 226)

This is Walter Pagel, Paracelsus' intellectual biographer who is very clear about what is 'modern' about his thinking. The notion of Imagination as a form of intervention sheds light on Frankenstein's fictional education at Ingolstadt and how it might contrast with the historical Paracelsus. Pagel shows in his book just how much Paracelsus was able to 'renovate' knowledge: for example, he completely reverses the relation between the disease and the patient: the theory of humours assumed that the patient was part of the disease, but Paracelsus regarded the disease itself as a dynamic with its own 'body'—that is, its own natural life—subject to the action of certain chemicals, and these chemical entities—salt, sulphur, and mercury—replace the humours. Disease exists in sites, or 'boxes', like a parasite or a live foreign microbody in the body of the individual.

So Paracelsus seems to have invented medical chemistry by reducing reactions in the body (wrongly, as it happens) to these three elements and substituting them for humours, a procedure which began a medical and scientific tradition in Central Europe. But as Pagel shows, this invention is inseparable from his adoption of a set of alchemical procedures, particularly those of the separation, rather than the 'compounding' of metals. Paracelsus was an expert on miners' diseases. He saw the presence of 'metals' in the human body, in the stone, which he called 'Tartarus'—and he regarded the organs as bodies in themselves, like stomachs accepting and rejecting the chemicals that were fed to them, a form of activity that he called 'the Archeus'. The Archeus, he said, was Vulcan 'operating inside objects' (*'der inwendig Vulcanus'*), its function being 'one of separation', a chemical operation in which, as he put it, 'all the arts are present in man as well as in alchemy outside' (Pagel 1982: 106). Nature imitates the alchemist, even in the human body. He was followed in the seventeenth century by his disciple, the experimental chemist J. B. Van Helmont, whose work translated some of the obscurities of Paracelsus into modified experiments that clearly result in chemical advances. Van Helmont in turn develops 'iatrochemistry'. Pagel also shows how Paracelsus began to experiment with poisons, with arsenic and mercury for syphilis, having understood from the bodies of his patients, the miners, that the poison can be a cure, if administered in certain doses. He understood that goitre was a chemical imbalance. He understood the homeopathic principle, which was foreign to humoral pathology, based as it was only on contraries (Pagel 1982: Note 59, 217).

However, despite these latter points, Pagel is insistent that the scientific work of Paracelsus is not that of the modern scientist:

> For it forms part of a personal revelation. This relates to the cosmos as a whole and the creator. Its aim is knowledge that enables the philosopher to ascend, to transcend and commune with the universe outside himself—a knowledge that liberates him from the fetters of passion and predestination. (Pagel 1982: 349)

Pagel states, '[I]t is personal wisdom rather than scientific, and indeed intellectual knowledge—a personal and not transferable possession' (1982: 349). If I may summarise here: part of Paracelsus' thinking, the obscure mantic and cosmological part, that is, remains outside the role of the 'petty experimentalist', always at a point prior to the transference and exchange of knowledge. Yet Pagel maintains Van Helmont managed to read his allegorical codes and translate them into chemical experiments.

Pagel's rather nuanced and apparently contradictory judgement here reinforces the role of the historical Paracelsus as another equivocal sign in Mary Shelley's text, because, although scientific knowledge is transferable, wisdom is not. Wisdom, like Socrates' notion of virtue in the *Protagoras*, needs a living dialogue, not merely technical instruction from a Sophist. Wisdom, like Socrates' virtue, cannot be taught. The historical Paracelsus is thus, to use the phrase which Mary Shelley originally gave to Professor Waldman in the first draft of her novel, a 'pretty experimentalist' who refused orthodoxy but not the possibility of communication. This makes him totally unlike Victor Frankenstein, who refuses both. It is a failure of imagination on Frankenstein's part, in its Paracelsian, Neoplatonic sense (Empson 1994, Vol. 2, 180ff and 229), that finally determines the narrative of his self-imprisonment.

WORKS CITED

Blake, William. 1961. *Poetry and Prose of William Blake*, ed. G. Keynes. London: Nonesuch Library.

Bloch, Ernst. 1986. *The Principle of Hope*, 3 Vols. Trans. Neville Plaice, Stephen Plaice, and Paul Knight. Oxford: Oxford University Press.

Clemit, Patricia. 1993. *The Godwinian Novel: The Rational Fictions of Godwin, Brocken Brown and Mary Shelley*. Oxford: Oxford University Press.

Empson, William. 1994. The Spirits of "the Dream". In *Essays on Renaissance Literature*, ed. John Haffenden, 2 Vols. Cambridge: Cambridge University Press.

Godwin, William. 1994. *St. Leon*, ed. P. Clemit. Oxford: Oxford University Press.

Holmes, Richard. 2005. *Shelley, the Pursuit*. London: Harper.

———. 2008. *The Age of Wonder*. London: Harper.

Pagel, Walter. 1982. *Paracelsus: An Introduction to Philosophical Medicine in the Era of the Renaissance*. Paris: Karger.

Plato. 1961. *The Collected Dialogues*, ed. E. Hamilton, and E. Cairns. New Jersey: Princeton University Press.

Shelley, Mary, with Shelley, Percy B. 1817. *History of a Six Weeks' Tour*. London: T. Hookham Junr and Paula C and J. Ollier.

———. 1987. *The Journals of Mary Shelley, 1812–1844*, ed. Paula R. Feldman, and Diana Scott Kilvert, 2 Vols. Oxford: Clarendon Press.

———. 1994. *Frankenstein*. In *Four Gothic Novels*. Oxford: Oxford University Press.

———. 2008. *The Original Frankenstein*, ed. Charles E. Robinson. Oxford: Bodleian Library.

Voges, Michael. 1987. *Aufklärung und Geheimnis*. Tubingen: Niemeyer.

Wardle, Ralph M. 1967. *Godwin and Mary: Letters of William Godwin and Mary Wollstonecraft*. London: Constable.

CHAPTER 4

Monstrous Dissections and Surgery as Performance: Gender, Race and the Bride of Frankenstein

Marie Mulvey-Roberts

I became acquainted with the science of anatomy.
Mary Shelley, *Frankenstein; or The Modern Prometheus*

The nineteenth-century surgeon and anatomist William Lawrence referred to dissection as a 'dirty source of knowledge' (Richardson 1988: 95). That the corpse continues to be a controversial site of learning is evident from the work of the contemporary German anatomist and corpse taxidermist, Gunther von Hagens, known as 'Dr Death' and 'Dr Frankenstein' (Castillo 2010: 1). Throughout history, anatomical dissection has been viewed as a particularly sordid violation of the body, though as the apologist Dr Southwood Smith pointed out in his article 'The Use of the Dead for the Living' in 1824: 'The basis of all medical and surgical knowledge is

M. Mulvey-Roberts (✉)
Department of Arts and Cultural Industries, University of the West of England, Bristol, UK

© The Author(s) 2018
C. M. Davison, M. Mulvey-Roberts (eds.), *Global Frankenstein*,
Studies in Global Science Fiction,
https://doi.org/10.1007/978-3-319-78142-6_4

anatomy' (Liggins 2000: 132). This would have been apparent to Percy Bysshe Shelley during his training as a surgeon at St. Bartholomew's hospital in London. Like the figure in Mary Shelley's dream in the 1831 edition of the novel, and her mad scientist, Victor, he too was a prospective 'student of unhallowed arts' (Shelley 1994: 196).

Theologically, the cutting up of the dead threatened to compromise the resurrection of the body on the Day of Judgement making the act of dissection both a blasphemous and intrinsically monstrous act.[1] In Mary Shelley's novel, Victor Frankenstein's illicit access to cadavers through body-snatching enables him to dismember and carve from dead flesh a male and female monster. But when Victor beholds in horror the male creature he has created, what actually repels him is the sight of a living corpse, whose shrivelled complexion bears the inscription of death, with 'yellow skin [which] scarcely covered the work of muscles and arteries beneath' (Shelley 1994: 39) (Fig. 4.1).

Fig. 4.1 *Frankie a.k.a. The Creature of Dr Frankenstein* by KLAT, the Genevan artists' collective, at the Plaine de Plainpalais, where the monster committed the first murder in the novel (© Marie Mulvey-Roberts, 2017)

This description, along with the frontispiece to the 1831 edition, resembles the muscular anatomical drawings contained in the highly influential, *De Humani Corporis Fabrica* (1543) (*On the Fabric of the Human Body*), written by the Renaissance anatomist and physician Andreas Vesalius.[2] The connection between anatomy and art is evident from the work of Leonardo da Vinci, who secretly dissected cadavers in order to understand the workings of the human body. Modern links between Frankenstein and art have been made by French performance artist ORLAN, who presents herself as a reincarnation of the Bride of Frankenstein and uses hybridity as a means of reconciling racial and sexual difference. Her surgeries have been filmed on video, broadcast in galleries and even transmitted to audiences around the globe via live satellite link-ups. In the novel, the making of the female monster goes beyond the criminality of grave-robbing and a distaste for anatomical dissection to taboos surrounding the anatomisation of the female body as an affront to female modesty or, worse still, as a form of sexual invasion by the male anatomist. Since Victor was creating a mate for his male creature, as well as a mother for their progeny, her monstrosity was also bound up with a threatening female sexuality, not least because he feared that she might prefer mating with mankind which could result in monstrous hybrid offspring.

Mary Shelley's scientist hero is generally thought to have been modelled in part on Percy Shelley, who had started training as a surgeon with his cousin, Charles Grove. It was following a conversation with his other cousin John Grove, who had already qualified, that 'The thought of anatomy [...] became quite delightful to Bysshe' (Hogg 1858: ii, 553). After he eloped with Harriet, he insisted to a friend in a letter: 'I still remain firm in my resolve to study surgery—you will see that I shall' (Ruston 2003: 3). Surgeons had been denigrated as part butcher and part barber-surgeon, in contrast to the other branch of the medical profession, the physician. In the second half of the eighteenth century, this difference in status was changing rapidly and surgery was becoming recognised as a profession for gentlemen. It seems to have had a particular appeal for another Romantic poet Samuel Taylor Coleridge who, as a schoolboy, was 'wild to be apprenticed to a surgeon' (Crook and Guiton 1986: 1). Shelley walked the wards with his cousin Charles while studying at St. Bartholomew's over three summer months, a time designated for medical courses. Dissections were usually reserved for the winter period, though techniques were being developed to preserve cadavers for teaching purposes in the warmer weather. It is not known if Shelley had the opportunity to observe or participate in a dissection, though his response to the sight of the flaying of Marsyas in a sculpture

Fig. 4.2 Antonio
Corradini, *Apollo Flaying
Marsyas* (1710–1750),
Victoria and Albert
Museum, London
(© Wikimedia Commons)

(see Fig. 4.2) does betray a certain 'insider' knowledge, when he insisted: 'If [the sculptor] knew as much as the moderns about anatomy, [then] I hope to God he did not' (Crook and Guiton 1986: 1).

It was feared by the Edinburgh anatomist, Dr Robert Knox, that exposing an artist to the 'mangled and dissected dead' could be detrimental to his art. He went on to declare that 'no artist' should enter 'a charnel-house, called a dissecting room' for in such a place, 'his mind may become accustomed, by frequent contemplation, to all that is detestable; familiar with horrors, with the emblems of destruction and death' (MacDonald 2005: 34). This process of desensitisation provides an insight into the moral and spiritual deterioration of Victor Frankenstein whose 'workshop of filthy creation' (Shelley 1994: 36) is where he forfeits his humanity, manifested by his revulsion towards his handiwork through his rejection of his creature and destruction of the female monster.

Getting enough cadavers for medical students was a grave concern in every sense. John Hunter, the first Professor of Anatomy at the Royal Academy of Arts, came up with a partial solution in 1775. With the assis-

tance of the Italian sculptor, Agostino Carlini, he positioned the fresh
corpse of an executed smuggler in the pose of the Ancient Roman statue,
the *Dying Gaul*. The skin was then stripped by Hunter's medical students
in order to make a wax mould from the cadaver for the purpose of demonstrating anatomy. The procedure had been pioneered in the fourteenth
century unusually by a woman, the early anatomist Alessandra Giliani.[3]
Nevertheless, for learning more about the mysteries of the body's interior,
cadavers, rather than waxen substitutes, were preferable. In Britain, the
Murder Act of 1752 allowed for a small number of bodies of executed
murderers to be requisitioned for dissection. Even with the addition of
relatively few private donors, this was still insufficient to meet a growing
demand, which allowed the trade in body-snatching to flourish. Grave
robbers were known as Resurrection Men, and Victor Frankenstein's
monster, as a composite of risen bodies, is an apt walking embodiment of
that collective. Only by raiding graves, charnel houses, and slaughter-
houses was Frankenstein able to obtain the raw materials for his monstrous
creations. These nefarious activities were undertaken at considerable risk.
So strong was public feeling against grave robbers that they were sometimes mobbed or even killed for disturbing and desecrating the dead.
Whilst the physician was emerging as a hero during the late eighteenth
century, the anatomist remained a more controversial figure, not only due
to associations with body-snatching and corpse mutilation but also with
murder, which had proved to be a means of supplying bodies for dissection. The notorious partnership of William Burke and William Hare provided Dr Robert Knox's anatomy school in the 1820s with over 15
murdered corpses.[4] As Tim Marshall notes in *Murdering to Dissect*, the
monster is a quasi-participant in this ghoulish industry by supplying
Frankenstein with the corpses of those close to him (1995: 11). It was not
until the Anatomy Act of 1832 that cadavers became more widely available
as a result of the unclaimed bodies of paupers being made available for
anatomical dissection. Marshall sees the 1831 third edition of Mary
Shelley's grave-robbing novel as an allegory of that legislation (330) which
led to 57,000 bodies during the nineteenth century being dissected in the
London anatomy schools alone (32). The idea of utilising dead paupers
was first proposed in 1819 to The Royal College of Surgeons in a speech
made by John Abernethy, whose lectures on anatomy had been attended
by Percy Shelley. Like Victor Frankenstein, Abernethy was a vitalist who
believed that life issued from some vital fluid or spark, rather like electricity.
His view was vehemently opposed by his former pupil, the anatomist and

surgeon, William Lawrence, a friend of both Mary and Percy, who became the latter's physician (Ruston 2005: 24–73). Lawrence was a dissenting sceptical materialist who regarded life as the product of an 'assemblage of all the functions' (Shelley 1994: xix). According to Marilyn Butler, it seems likely that his hotly contested and widely publicised debate with Abernethy was dramatised within the pages of the novel (xx). The dispute was signalled in Lawrence's Hunterian lecture of 1816, a period coinciding with the writing of *Frankenstein*.

The Hunterian Oration had been inaugurated in 1813 by the executors of the will of the pioneering surgeon John Hunter, regarded as the father of modern anatomy, whose lectures had been attended by Abernethy. Thus a direct line of pedagogical descent may be traced from Shelley back to Hunter, who can be seen as yet another model for Victor Frankenstein due to his interests in transplant surgery and the mysteries of creating life. Hunter's brother William had trained at the Edinburgh medical school where Byron's physician John Polidori qualified. Polidori had been present at Villa Diodati during the ghost-story telling entertainment that had spawned *Frankenstein* in the summer of 1816 and his conversations with Mary might have included the subject of anatomy. John Hunter, who studied anatomy at the London school of his brother, conducted maverick experiments including transplants on animals and supervising the first successful attempt at artificial insemination. Over the course of twelve years, he was present at the dissections of more than 2000 human bodies (Moore 2005: 96) and his payment for corpses to supply his anatomy school helped trigger the trade in body-snatching (Fig. 4.3).

There are grounds for supposing that Hunter joined clandestine expeditions to London graveyards on at least one moonless night (92). Even though he was never challenged by the authorities, Hunter did acknowledge that '[a]natomists have ever been engaged in contention' (Bynum and Porter 1985: 26). A particular 'contention' involved cutting up dead women for teaching purposes, with the unsettling possibility of one's wife, sister or mother being 'subjected to the gaze of lads learning to use the incision knife' (Jupp and Gittings 1999: 225). A variation on this occurs in the novel when Victor Frankenstein is in the process of creating the living from the dead in the form of a female creature as a mate for his monster and espies 'the daemon at the casement [… who] now came to mark my progress' (Shelley 1994: 138–9). The description is not unlike that of a medical student observing an autopsy or surgical procedure. Dissection on female cadavers was regarded in some quarters as a violation of female

Fig. 4.3 Thomas Rowlandson, *The Dissecting Room* (c.1840) is believed to represent William Hunter's dissecting room (© Wikimedia Commons)

modesty and, worse still, as a form of sexual assault. At St. Bartholomew's Hospital, there is the horrifying story of a porter who, in 1815, in front of medical students, committed necrophilia on the corpse of an attractive 15-year-old girl (MacDonald 2005: 33). During the mid-eighteenth century, it was uncommon for a woman to request autopsy, but an exception was the socialite Lady Caroline Holland as she was determined that the cause of her death be known. This taboo gradually changed as the century wore on. In many ways, dissection is a process of gradual desexualisation that has been particularly problematic for the female subject, who tends to be defined by her sex. The dissolution of human identity also involves degrees of dehumanisation. In *Frankenstein*, the opposite process takes place when Victor, after tearing apart 'the thing', or female monster, on which he had been engaged, sees in the fragmented remains the vestiges of coherent humanity: 'The remains of the half-finished creature, whom I had destroyed, lay scattered on the floor, and I almost felt as if I had mangled the living flesh of a human being' (Shelley 1994: 142). Victor's identification of himself as a quasi-murderer can be read as a kind of pre-emptive genocide that wipes out any prospect for his creations to propagate a 'new species' (36).

Hunter's brother and fellow anatomist, William, was especially keen on dissecting the corpses of pregnant women in order to penetrate the mysteries of procreation, the most secret of nature's hiding places. Female reproductive organs are body parts that Victor would have acquired as indicated by his concerns over the prospect of his monster's mate mothering a race of monsters. It was a rarity to dissect a pregnant cadaver especially in the later stages, so when Hunter got a lucky break in acquiring five pregnant bodies between 1750 and 1754, he was able to carry out pioneering research. This provided his brother with the necessary materials for his groundbreaking anatomical drawings of foetal development in *The Anatomy of the Human Gravid Uterus* (1774).

A famous dissection of a supposedly pregnant female corpse was witnessed in 1814 by William Harwood, a friend of Mary Shelley's father, William Godwin. This was conducted on the body of Joanna Southcott, the millenarian prophetess, who had a cult following of 10,000. Arguably the exponent of a kind of theological feminism, she was convinced that she had to struggle with Satan over banishing the guilt carried by women owing to Eve's role in bringing about the Fall. Her rehabilitation of the first mother of mankind aimed to restore every woman to her true role as 'help-mate' to their Adam. Similarly, Mary Shelley re-writes the story of Genesis, albeit mediated through John Milton's *Paradise Lost*, and Victor's scientific ambition to undo death and disease, the effects of the Fall, through his man-made Adam and Eve. God-like, he sees himself as the father of a new species, which has the capacity for reproduction. There are parallels with the bride Victor is creating and Joanna Southcott, the self-appointed bride of the Lamb, who proclaimed that she had been chosen by God to announce the Second Coming of Christ and, through an immaculate conception, would give birth to the divine Shiloh (a Biblical prophetic name for the Messiah). She even managed to persuade at least seventeen doctors of her pregnancy. In the event of her premature death, she left instructions about the delivery, insisting that no medical examination should proceed until at least four days after her death. *The Examiner* ran a report in early 1815 recounting how her disciples kept the body warm in order to 'preserve the vital spark' before the four days elapsed. The vitalists, including Victor Frankenstein in the creation scene of the novel, use similar language. Once the time had passed, surgeons were permitted 'to dissect her remains' and 'Mr Reece and Mr Want proceeded to perform their disgusting task' (Marshall 1995: 190–1), only to discover an empty shrunken womb. The dashed expectations of her followers correspond to the disappointment of the monster, devastated by the loss of a companion and mate for his monstrous progeny. Both the female monster and Joanna Southcott embodied the promise of apocalyptic change through the act of giving birth, whilst their bodies were subjected to scientific curiosity, epitomised by the medical gaze. In a cartoon by Thomas Rowlandson, *A Medical Inspection* subtitled *Miracles will never Cease* (1814) (Fig. 4.4), a gaggle of crouching physicians peer goggle-eyed under the skirt of Joanna Southcott as she exposes her nether regions, declaring: 'Behold the Naked Truth most Learned Doctors'. This is a satiric reminder of how the female body could be immodestly invaded through dissection and subject to the voyeurism of the anatomist. In his book, *The Body of Frankenstein's Monster*, physician Cecil Helman describes his own medical training in anatomy, pointing out that 'the dissecting room shows us the difference between erotic art and pornography, between human experience and the worship of parts. For the true parallel of dissection, as an esoteric form of performance art, is pornography' (1991: 121).

The preservation of female body parts, which normally found their way into pathology museums, could also give rise to romantic and erotic inferences. Thomas Hood's comic poem, 'Mary's Ghost, a Pathetic Ballad' (1827), resurrects the voice of a dead woman complaining to her fiancé about the robbing of her grave, which led to her remains being divided up amongst various doctors, including Sir Astley Cooper, a leading surgeon and anatomist during the first half of the nineteenth century (Hood 1827: 16–17):

> I vow'd that you should have my hand,
>   But fate gives us denial;
> You'll find it there, at Doctor Bell's
>   In spirits and a phial.
>
> As for my feet, the little feet,
>   You used to call so pretty,
> There's one, I know, in Bedford Row,
>   The t'other's in the City.
>
> I can't tell where my head has gone,
>   But Doctor Carpue can:

Fig. 4.4   Thomas Rowlandson, *A Medical Inspection or Miracles Will Never Cease* (1814) (© Wikimedia Commons, Wellcome Images)

> As for my trunk it's all packed up
>   To go by Pickford's van. [....]
>
> The cock it crows-I must be gone!
>   My William we must part!
> But I'll be yours in death, altho'
> Sir Astley has my heart.

A real-life example of the eroticisation of female body parts can be seen in the case of the African woman Saartjie or Sarah Baartman, exhibited in life as well as death. Particular attention was paid to her extreme steatopygia, or protruding buttocks, and prominent pudenda. Tellingly, she was known as the 'Hottentot Venus' and put on public display in Piccadilly London in the spring of 1811, not far from where Percy Shelley was living in Soho that year. Even though she was never an actual slave, her exploitation has been seen as a form of enslavement, which is relevant to readings of *Frankenstein* as a novel encoding the horror of slavery (see Malchow 1996: 9–40; Mulvey-Roberts 2016: 52–91). Indeed, her post-mortem dissection has been seen to parallel Victor Frankenstein's tearing apart of his female monster (see Kitson 2007: 83).

The reintegration of the Bride of Frankenstein is evident from the work of French performance artist, ORLAN, whose digital portrait, by Fabrice Lévêque in 1990 (see Fig. 4.5), is modelled on Elsa Lanchester's eponymous role in James Whale's film *Bride of Frankenstein* (1935). ORLAN uses the figure of the monster's mate as an empowering symbol of female monstrosity. It aptly expresses how she became the first artist to use surgery as an artistic medium, restructuring her face as a pastiche of other faces and thereafter digitally transforming it in line with racial hybridity.

Fig. 4.5 *ORLAN: The Digital Bride of Frankenstein: Official Portrait with Bride of Frankenstein Wig* (Photo: Fabrice Lévêque © Wikimedia Commons)

As a radical female artist, ORLAN uses her body as art to reclaim it from a patriarchal society that perpetuates gender inequalities. An instance of this may be seen in the way in which Shelley's female monster who, in spite of never materialising as a living body, serves as a bartering tool between her creator and his male monster, a fate linked to the death of Elizabeth Lavenza, Victor's fiancée who is murdered by the monster in retaliation for Victor's breaking his promise to make the creature a mate. In view of this, it is rather appropriate that in Kenneth Branagh's 1994 film, Elizabeth's doppelgänger is the female monster. In a parody of both anatomy and surgery, the male creator savagely tears out her heart. Victor restores Elizabeth to life by stitching a hideous, visibly sutured version of her former self. He attaches her head to the body of Justine Moritz, the family servant who, through the connivance of the creature, was wrongly blamed for the murder of Victor's brother William and subsequently exe- cuted. These female victims converge into one monstrous bride. In the novel, the monster's mate is the very epitome of female passivity, a series of body parts stitched together that are still in the process of construction. As an assemblage of multiple body parts, she is merely derivative and parodic of Eve who was created from a single body part—Adam's rib. ORLAN, as a reincarnation of the Bride of Frankenstein, however, retains agency by making decisions at every stage of her transformation to reap- propriate the female body from patriarchal myth and assumes the dual roles of creator and created in the surgical modification of her own body as art. Parallels can be seen in the interchangeability of Victor and his crea- ture and the commodification of the female monster as a made-to-order bride, a role that the eponymous heroine rejects in James Whale's *Bride of Frankenstein* (1935) through her revulsion towards the clunking bolted monster played by Boris Karloff.

Similarly, the 18-year-old ORLAN renounced the prospect of marriage by soiling the trousseau linens squirrelled away by her mother. Turning them into a canvas using sperm donated by lovers, she stitched deliber- ately bad embroidery over the stains, thereby rejecting her traditional female role and the custom of bridal sheets being used to denote the bride's state of virginity through the inscription, or not, of hymeneal blood. For her installation, *Medusa's Head* (1978), ORLAN hung up the sheets and cut a hole in them through which she displayed her own geni- tals as a protest against the Freudian phallic notion of female lack. This voluntary act of self-exposure contrasts with how the genitals of the

Hottentot Venus were exhibited after her death and without her consent at the Museum of Man in Paris.

ORLAN also used the trousseau fabric as a drape in the manner of religious iconography, along the lines of Gian Lorenzo Bernini's *St. Teresa in Ecstasy* and classical art work of the Virgin Mary exposing a breast, in imitation of the nursing Madonna. This statement pronounced that she had given birth to herself through art, thereby allowing for multiple rebirths, most notably through the cult of St. ORLAN. Thus did her personalised attack on religious belief and myth lead, ironically, to the creation of her own mythological and sanctified self. In this regard, ORLAN's identification with the Bride of Frankenstein ties in with Mary Shelley's creation of a new birth-myth. Like Victor, ORLAN makes use of dissection to create a monstrous composite, but instead of plundering graves and charnel houses, she harvests body parts from art galleries, her own face becoming a canvas for her art. During her surgery-performances, a surgeon carved and remodelled her flesh into a montage of the eternal feminine, derived from the canon of Western art in what can be seen as a parody of the Frankenstein project: her mouth was transformed into that of Boucher's *Europa*, her chin to Botticelli's *Venus*, her nose to Jean-Léon Gérôme's Psyche and her forehead brow to Leonardo's *Mona Lisa*. ORLAN's goal has never been one of beautification, but rather to deconstruct notions of female beauty and disrupt the codes of cosmetic surgery. A more recent demonstration of this is the surgical implants in her forehead, resembling horns. Like ORLAN, Victor selected beautiful individual parts for his creature, whom he refers to later as 'Devil' (Shelley 1994: 77), only he by contrast ends up rejecting the sum total as hideous.

Victor's reaction encapsulates the adverse effects of the gaze upon Otherness and likewise ORLAN sets out to critique the gaze in relation to the Other. She pronounces that she is both male and female, by reversing the gendered indefinite articles in French: 'Je suis un femme et une homme'. Concerning race, she strives to dissolve the kind of fear that prompted Victor Frankenstein to destroy his female monster, fearing that she would give birth to 'a race of devils' (Shelley 1994: 138) that might destroy mankind. He was also anxious she might prefer mating with man because of his 'superior beauty' to that of the monster, thus posing the spectre of a mixing of races, which had negative connotations at that time (see Mulvey-Roberts: 75–77). As an advocate of racial hybridity, ORLAN explains, 'The idea is to mix the differences in order to accept them. In order to coexist with OTHER and I, who is also "other"'.[5] Since 1998, she has been creating a digital photographic series called 'Self-Hybridisations', in which her face merges with those of different ethnicities taken from masks, sculptures and paintings from Africa, American-Indian and Pre-Columbian Mexican cultures. These amalgamations set out to challenge the gold-standard Europeanised aesthetic invariably replicated by the surgeon's knife and to demonstrate that ideals of beauty are not universal. ORLAN's mission has been to revolutionise notions of beauty in order to dispel the kind of horror Victor experienced when he gazed upon the face of his first creation with its 'yellow skin', a colour which some early ethnographers used to denote mixed race (see Mulvey-Roberts 75–76) and 'straight black lips' (Shelley 1994: 39). Indeed, ORLAN has even mused on how she might be affected if her skin colour changed from white to black.

A more material and biological mode of racial hybridity can be seen in her multi-media installation, *Harlequin Coat* (2009). Two years earlier, ORLAN collaborated with the SymbioticA laboratory in Australia, resulting in the bio-art installation *Harlequin Coat*, which involves creating a bio-technological organic coat from the live co-culturing of cells from her own body mixed with those of different species and races contained in a custom-built bio-reactor. By deploying this bio-art, she intends one day to merge her cells with those of animals and humans and grow a new hybrid skin to further break down the binary between self and Other. This is an even more integrated version of how Victor Frankenstein used animal and human parts in the creation of his monster, harvested from graveyards, charnel houses and slaughterhouses. For her fifth operation, ORLAN re-enacted an allegory of fabric and flesh through the symbolic racial melting pot of the *Harlequin Coat*, in a carnivalesque dismantling of the racialised body. This involved a black male dancer doing a striptease in the operating theatre. He sheds layers of a harlequin's costume, in which ORLAN is also dressed. Her inspiration was Michel's Serres' book, *The Troubadour of Knowledge* (1997), which conceptualises the cross-breeding of knowledge and tells the story of a harlequin king of the sun and the moon who removes layers of his clothes. When the last layer is removed, the king's flesh is revealed to be multi-coloured and covered in tattoos.

ORLAN's nine performance operations, taking place between 1990 and 1993, are forms of striptease, involving the removal of layers of her own skin. As an epigraph to her surgeries, she would read from *La Robe* (1983), written by Lacanian psychoanalyst Eugénie Lemoine-Luccioni, which explores the correlation between skin and clothes. In the

Harlequin Coat, ORLAN carries out a parody of burlesque while lying on the operating table by displaying her genitals. Near the start of her career as an artist, ORLAN subversively used wedding sheets from her trousseau for a striptease and also wore clothes resembling a naked female body for a piece of performance art entitled *To Dress Oneself in One's Own Nudity* (1977). She is deliberately provocative in her attitudes towards gender and race in the operating theatre where she kisses the surgeon and exposes her genitals in the presence of a stripper. That the stripper is black appears to be a deliberate way of confronting the stereotype of the sexualised black man. His name, Jimmy Blanche, resonates with Franz Fanon's *Black Skin and White Masks*, first written in French in 1952, about the divided self-perception of the black subject who has lost sight of his origins and adopts the culture of the mother country. His presence appears to be a commentary on cultural mimicry, reflecting race back on itself, or a reflection on how white women rather than black men are usually exploited as strippers. The surgery-performance raises questions about the relationship between coloniser and colonised and the inequalities of gender and race. When going under the knife, ORLAN refuses to represent the *passive* white female body, as opposed to the *active* black male body of Jimmy Blanche. While both participate in the striptease, ORLAN's performance goes beyond the removal of clothes to the epidermis, beneath which skin colour becomes immaterial. The troubling exchanges between the two mirror the interchangeability of Victor Frankenstein and his monster.

ORLAN's appropriation of the voyeuristic gaze is combined with a subversive eroticised medical gaze, which she turns on herself by peering into her own interior during an operation, made possible by local anaesthetic. In her Manifesto, which she calls *Carnal Art* (1989), ORLAN records how 'I can observe my own body cut open, without suffering! [....] I see myself all the way down to my entrails; a new mirror stage. I can see to the heart of my lover; his splendid design has nothing to do with sickly sentimentalities—Darling, I love your spleen; I love your liver; I adore your pancreas, and the line of your femur excites me' (ORLAN 2010: 29). Like Victor Frankenstein, she is in possession of a hidden prohibited knowledge and, like him, she 'pursued nature to her hiding places' (Shelley 1994: 36), only now the hiding places are under her control. Not only does she represent female nature, she also guides the hand of male science. The surgeon sculpting her body does so according to her wishes, even allowing her to direct the camera while the operation is being filmed. ORLAN's refusal to be a silent patient lying passively under the knife is evident from her reading aloud from French philosophic texts, including the following passage from Jean François Lyotard's *Libidinal Economy* (1974):

> Open the so-called body and spread out all its surfaces [...] as though your dress-maker's scissors were opening the leg of an old pair of trousers, go on, expose the small intestines' alleged interior, the jejunum, the ileum, the duodenum, or else, at the other end, undo the mouth at its corners, pull out the tongue at its most distant roots and split it, spread out the bats' wings of the palate and its damp basements, open the trachea. (2004: 1)

Eventually, the body is flattened out into an immense membrane as part of Lyotard's intention to destabilise the notion of the body as a stable signifier of identity, one into which libidinal energies have been channelled and subsequently subdued. Both he and ORLAN set out to disrupt the hegemony of the organic body so that its fragmentation can articulate a social transformation. They jointly question the social implications of embodiment. This is a process that has liberating potential for the categories of both gender and race. Furthermore, Lyotard figures theory itself as theatre and the theorist as viewing the representation of the world as if from a stage, in ways that chime with how ORLAN turns an operating theatre into a theatrical space.

During the Renaissance, the anatomical theatre, designed for teaching purposes, was a place of corporeal display or, in other words, a theatre of the body. More recently, Gunther von Hagens' first public dissection of a human body in 170 years was a sell-out to 500 people in a London theatre, for which he earned the media sobriquet of Dr Frankenstein. The event was denounced as a freak show, not least because the ticketed theatrical setting smacked of the exploitive commodification of the dead for the purposes of entertainment. The performative aspects of this were seen in von Hagens' approach as a showman, whose costume included, as always, a black fedora hat, which his critics interpreted as showing disrespect towards the corpse. His defence was that he wore it out of respect for his predecessors and in imitation of that worn by the anatomist in Rembrandt's *The Anatomy Lesson of*

Dr. Nicolaes Tulp (1632). The public dissection was televised in 2002 on the UK's Channel 4 and prompted complaints. The provisions of the Anatomy Act of 1984 rendered public autopsy a criminal act, hence the presence of police officers at the theatre, though they did not intervene. Von Hagens also aroused controversy as a modern-day Frankenstein by, allegedly, illicitly obtaining dead bodies for his travelling corpse-art and scientific exhibition, Body Worlds, which was visited by 40 million people in approximately 90 cities and countries. After flaying each corpse, he uses a process of 'plastination' for positioning animal and human cadavers plus body parts in performative poses, which are then exhibited in a number of public spaces including art galleries. This process involves skinning and then treating the corpses with a synthetic resin resolution for long-term preservation. To date, approximately 200 corpses are on display in von Hagens' macabre cadaver museum in Berlin. With their blood vessels and muscles exposed, this gruesome parody of a mass viva tableau is the ultimate striptease. Again, this points to the ambivalence surrounding the corpse, which throughout history has been deemed 'sacred', 'scientific' or 'saleable' (Richardson 1988: 79). Von Hagens won an injunction against the German newspaper *Der Spiegel*, which had alleged that he had exhibited, for the paying public, the bodies of executed Chinese prisoners without their permission. Indeed, there has been a long tradition of putting the bodies of murderers on public display. After committing murder, Frankenstein's 'monster' (with its telling Latin root 'monere' to warn) becomes a living embodiment of the walking criminal corpse. In James Whale's *Frankenstein* (1931), a rationale for this is provided by Igor, the scientist's assistant, who supplies a criminal brain for transplanting into the creature's cranium, with predictably catastrophic results.

Whilst Frankenstein's skills in anatomy were displayed through his creation of a living creature, so too does von Hagens display simulations of life by dissecting the dead bodies. As a modern recreation of Victor Frankenstein, von Hagens represents the horrors of monstrous dissections that, over the centuries, extended to the Judeo-Christian blasphemy of desecrating the human body made in the image of God. ORLAN, however, sees her work as a struggle against the God of the Catholic Church. Her surgical reconfiguring and transformation of her 'natural' female body through digital art form part of *The Reincarnation of St ORLAN*, a tongue-in-cheek act of self-canonisation. Victor

Frankenstein aspired to the divine by appropriating a God-like power over life and death through his skills in anatomy and surgery. For both Frankenstein and ORLAN, dissection opened up a route to transformation, which collapsed distinctions between self and Other. Nevertheless, for ORLAN, unlike Mary Shelley's scientist, surgery is used as a means of challenging inequalities of gender and race in a celebration of racial and sexual hybridity.

NOTES

1. This was not true of sixteenth- and seventeenth-century Calvinist theology in England where dissectors and theologians were not in conflict. See Sawday (1995: 106).
2. One edition was bound in golden brown human skin and presented to Brown University in the USA by an alumnus. This practice is known as anthropodermic bibliopegy and though a rarity is applied more commonly to medical books.
3. I am indebted to Anthony Mandal for drawing my attention to this connection.
4. The London 'Burkers' John Bishop, Thomas Williams, Michael Shields and James May provided even more with 500–1000 corpses.
5. Orlan, FAQ, on her official website http://www.orlan.eu/f-a-q/.

WORKS CITED

Bynum, W.F., and Roy Porter, eds. 1985. *William Hunter and the Eighteenth Century Medical-World*. Cambridge: Cambridge University Press.

Castillo, David R. 2010. *Baroque Horrors: Roots of the Fantastic in the Age of Curiosities*. Ann Arbor: University of Michigan Press.

Crook, Nora, and Derek Guiton. 1986. *Shelley's Venomed Melody*. Cambridge: Cambridge University Press.

Helman, Cecil. 1991. *The Body of Frankenstein's Monster: Essays in Myth and Medicine*. London: Chatto & Windus.

Hogg, Thomas Jefferson. 1858. *The Life of Percy Bysshe Shelley*, 2 Vols. London: Edward Moxon.

Hood, Thomas. 1827. *Whims and Oddities: In Prose and Verse, with Forty Original Designs*, Second Series. London: Charles Tilt.

Jupp, Peter C., and Clare Gittings, eds. 1999. *Death in England: An Illustrated History*. Manchester: Manchester University Press.

Kenneth Branagh (dir.). 1994. Mary Shelley's *Frankenstein*, film, USA, Japan, UK: TriStar Pictures, Japan Satellite Broadcasting, IndieProd Company.

Kitson, Peter. 2007. *Romantic Literature, Race, and Colonial Encounter.* Basingstoke: Palgrave Macmillan.

Liggins, Emma. 2000. The Medical Gaze and the Female Corpse: Looking at Bodies in Mary Shelley's *Frankenstein. Studies in the Novel* 32 (2): 129–146.

Lyotard, Jean-François. 2004. *Libidinal Economy.* Trans. Iain Hamilton Grant. London: Continuum.

MacDonald, Helen. 2005. *Human Remains: Dissection and Its Histories.* New Haven/London: Yale University Press.

Malchow, H.L. 1996. *Gothic Images of Race in Nineteenth-Century Britain.* Stanford: Stanford University Press.

Marshall, Tim. 1995. *Murdering to Dissect: Grave-Robbing, Frankenstein and the Anatomy Literature.* Manchester: Manchester University Press.

Moore, Wendy. 2005. *The Knife Man: Blood, Body-Snatching and the Birth of Modern Surgery.* London: Bantam Books.

Mulvey-Roberts, Marie. 2016. *Dangerous Bodies: Historicising the Gothic Corporeal.* Manchester: Manchester University Press.

ORLAN. 2010. Carnal Art Manifesto (1989). In *ORLAN: A Hybrid Body of* Art *Works*, ed. Simon Donger, Simon Shepherd, and ORLAN. Abingdon/Oxford: Routledge.

Richardson, Ruth. 1988. *Death, Dissection and the Destitute.* London: Phoenix Press.

Ruston, Sharon. 2003. One of the 'Modern Sceptics': Reappraising Shelley's Medical Education. *Romanticism* 9 (1): 1–19.

———. 2005. *Shelley and Vitality.* Basingstoke: Palgrave Macmillan.

Sawday, Jonathan. 1995. *The Body Emblazoned: Dissection and the Human Body in Renaissance Culture.* London/New York: Routledge.

Shelley, Mary. 1994. *Frankenstein or the Modern Prometheus*, ed. Marilyn Butler. New York: Oxford University Press.

Whale, James (dir.). 1931. *Frankenstein*, film, USA: Universal Pictures.

———. 1935. Bride of Frankenstein, film, USA: Universal Pictures.

PART II

Frankenstein and Disabled, Indecorous, Mortal Bodies

'The Human Senses Are Insurmountable Barriers': Deformity, Sympathy, and Monster Love in Three Variations on *Frankenstein*

Bruce Wyse

One of the recurrent motifs of *Frankenstein* is the human need for sympathy and its psychical and moral effects on the human subject. This is true of the Arctic explorer Walton, who admits to his sister his 'desire [for] the company of a man who could sympathize with me' (Shelley 1994: 53). It is also true of Frankenstein himself, who has the sympathetic support of his family circle but suffers estrangement from them when he complies with the monster's demand for a mate and feels 'as if I had no right to claim [their] sympathies' (Shelley 1980: 149). Sympathy, however, is at the very heart of the monster's predicament and narrative. Abandoned by his maker, the monster ventures into the strange terrain of existence with no familial or social support whatsoever. Spurned, abominated, and demonised at every turn, the monster becomes a case study in the debilitating effects of a deprivation of sympathy. Sympathising 'in [the] joys' of

B. Wyse (✉)
Department of English and Film Studies, Wilfrid Laurier University,
Waterloo, ON, Canada

© The Author(s) 2018
C. M. Davison, M. Mulvey-Roberts (eds.), *Global Frankenstein*,
Studies in Global Science Fiction,
https://doi.org/10.1007/978-3-319-78142-6_5

the De Laceys (Shelley 1994: 140), he is violently rebuffed in his carefully measured appeal for sympathy and finds '[him]self unsympathized with,' reacting with a will to 'spread havoc and destruction' (165). Eventually reaching a state of total interpersonal and social destitution, the creature, internalising heteronormativity, recognises that an engineered vehicle of sympathy—a mate—is his only recourse. He demands of his creator, 'You must create a female for me, with whom I can live in the interchange of those sympathies necessary for my being' (171). He presses this ethical appeal on the sole being that owes him any debt of care, Frankenstein, who begrudgingly admits, 'as I could not sympathize with him, I had no right to withhold from him the small portion of happiness which was yet in my power to bestow' (174). After Frankenstein reneges on his promise and the monster dedicates himself to systematically destroying the grounds of Frankenstein's happiness, the monster repudiates sympathy, telling Walton, 'No sympathy may I ever find' and asking rhetorically, 'But now, … that happiness and affection are turned into bitter and loathing despair, in what should I seek for sympathy?' (244).

The creature has one characteristic above all that precludes the sympathy of others and distinguishes his experiences from those of Walton and Frankenstein: his 'appalling hideousness' (242) and 'unearthly ugliness' (127). In their first tête-à-tête, the appalled Frankenstein cries out, 'Begone! Relieve me from the sight of your detested form,' and the acutely self-aware creature resourcefully complies: '"Thus I relieve thee, my creator," he said, and placed his hated hands before my eyes[,] … "thus I take from thee a sight which you abhor. Still thou canst listen to me, and grant me thy compassion"' (129). Only with the visual dimension suspended can the creature expect any hearing at all, let alone an impartial one. He has learned through painful experience that the 'human senses are insurmountable barriers' to any intercourse with humanity, and this is why he solicits from his maker 'a creature of another sex, but as hideous as myself.' '[W]e shall be monsters, cut off from all the world,' he asserts, hence 'more attached to one another' (172).

One persistently humanitarian strain in critical responses to *Frankenstein* is a concern with the aberrant body and the tyranny of normative embodiment. Richard Hengist Horne highlights this line of interpretation in his reflection on the novel's significance in *A New Spirit of the Age* (1844):

> The Monster ... is the type of a class deeply and cruelly aggrieved by nature—the Deformed or hideous in figure or countenance, whose sympathies and passions are as strong as their bodily deformity renders them repulsive. ...When the Monster pleads his cause against cruel man, ... he pleads the cause of all that class who have so strong a claim on the sympathy of the world, yet find little else but disgust or, at best, neglect. (227)

For Horne, the artificial deformity of Frankenstein's sui generis monster emblematises naturally occurring deformity. Setting aside the anomalous circumstances of the monster's very existence, his irreducible non- or para-humanity, the creature stands in for all those physically different human beings unjustly misrecognised, devalued, and excluded, subject to the social projection of dread and disgust, in short, dehumanised.

In writing about affective responses to disability, Bill Hughes observes that 'the basic aversive emotions [of] fear, hatred and disgust ... both inform the non-disabled imaginary and invalidate disabled bodies' (2012: 67–8). Disabled bodies are, he asserts, 'subjected to the subcutaneous violence of the intrusive, demeaning and disturbing non-disabled gaze.' Hence 'disability is a life lived before a looking glass that is cracked and distorted by the vandalism of normality' (68). Although Shelley's monster is an unearthly, transgressively fabricated, composite creature fundamentally like no other in existence, he is also a socially constituted pariah, an object of intense, reactive animosity, apprehended as, at best, a 'filthy type' (1994: 158) of the normative human image.

While the creature's appalling appearance is described at various points in the text, the moments in which he reluctantly assumes his visual identity and then finds his physicality inscribed and abominated in his creator-father's papers are particularly significant. In a grim variation on the Narcissus myth, the creature beholds his reflection in a pool of water and is terrified, the inimical image contradicting, if not nullifying, his nascent sense of a benevolent self. Although initially 'unable to believe that it was indeed I who was reflected in the mirror,' he becomes woefully 'convinced that I was in reality the monster that I am' (142). He subsequently reads Frankenstein's damning journal account of his 'accursed origin' in which 'the minutest description of my odious and loathsome person is given, in language which painted your own horrors, and rendered mine ineffaceable' (157–8). He internalises this crushingly definitive perspective and impotently protests, 'Why did you form a monster so hideous that even you turned from me in disgust?' (158).

Disgust, William Ian Miller argues, 'judges ugliness and deformity to be moral offences' for it 'knows no distinction between the moral and the aesthetic, collapsing failures in both into an undifferentiated revulsion' (1997: 21). Paul A. Cantor remarks that the 'monster's tragedy is that he is forced … to accept the opinion of the only beings he has ever known and they all think that he is hideously ugly'; in short, he is 'doomed to see himself as others see him' (1984: 126). But the visceral disgust and horror his unnatural Otherness provokes makes his plight much worse, for he is reflexively associated with evil. Only the blind can escape this association. As Anne Mellor observes, the assumption about the threat and the moral state of the creature becomes predictive or indeed causal: 'By consistently seeing the Creature as evil, the characters in the novel force him to become evil' (1990: 103). The tragic plot of *Frankenstein* helps readers realise the necessity of 'a love that sees all the products of nature—the old, the sick, the handicapped, the freaks—as sacred life-forms to be nurtured with care and compassion' (104).

Lawrence Lipking, in a bracingly dissenting review of the 'modern consensus' on the novel, decries 'the onesidedness and complacency of contemporary readings' (2012: 420), a consensus exemplified in Mellor's pedagogical strategies to advance the claim that the 'Creature is *not* innately evil, but forced to become so by the characters who deny him access to a human community' (2012: 421). Lipking argues that the corrective precept drawn from the novel, 'Love thy Creature,' 'reduces the novel to a late-twentieth-century platitude, giving readers a chance to feel good about their own superior wisdom' (421) and he highlights the 'extreme partiality' of this interpretative consensus by listing a series of antithetical details which undermine the selective advocacy-reading on the creature's behalf. He allows, however, that '[p]erhaps a novel that taught students to love the Other would be more instructive, or at least more acceptable to modern tastes' (422–3). Such an alternative novel, based on the 'modern consensus,' would sidestep or reduce 'the troubling power of the book itself' (423).

Adaptations, mutations, and appropriations of Shelley's *Frankenstein* are, of course, legion. The following discussion considers three of these that foreground the nexus of ugliness (or deformity/disability) and sympathy: Edward Bulwer-Lytton's short story 'A Manuscript Found in a Madhouse' (1829, 1836); the film spoof, *Young Frankenstein* (1974); and 'The Crimson Horror,' an episode of the science-fiction television series, *Doctor Who* (Series 7, Episode 11, 2013). These *Frankenstein* adaptations clarify what is at stake in the creature's deplorable social exclusion when the figure is construed as standing in for 'all that class who have so strong a claim on the … sympathy of the world, yet find little else but disgust' (Horne 1844: 227)—namely the disabled and the anomalously embodied. To varying extents, they also take the further step of rectifying the ethical derelictions of the improvident creator and the unwelcoming society in the original narrative. They imagine some alternative to or remedy for the monster's solitude, some device or vehicle for overcoming his Othering and degrading isolation, but their romantic or sexual solutions maintain at least some residual ambivalence, their humanitarianism shadowed by something off-kilter, problematic, or perverse.

'A MANUSCRIPT FOUND IN A MADHOUSE' (1829)

Edward Bulwer-Lytton's 'A Manuscript Found in a Madhouse' is quite possibly the first variation on *Frankenstein* to pick up on the representative status of the monster as an avatar of the deformed or physically anomalous. The story functions as a hermeneutic prism which concentrates and refracts Shelley's theme of the appeal for sympathy frustrated by the perception of deformity. Bulwer-Lytton replaces *Frankenstein*'s laboriously assembled and artificially animated creature with an entirely natural and human 'monster.' 'A Manuscript' dispenses with the science-fiction component of *Frankenstein* and shifts the presentation of extraordinarily anomalous embodiment and its consequence—radical social exclusion—towards a more recognisable social terrain.

The opening of the story has a folktale quality somewhat at odds with the autobiographical nature of the narration. The narrator is the eldest son of a noble and wealthy family who, like Frankenstein, is gifted with a remarkable intellectual capacity. His prospects should be enviable but, in stark contrast to his 'comely' siblings, he is singularly cursed with a horrific ugliness. His anguished complaints echo those of Shelley's monster: 'By what fatality was it that I alone was thrust into this glorious world distorted, and dwarf-like, and hideous,—my limbs a mockery, my countenance a horror, myself a blackness on the surface of creation,—a discord in the harmony of nature, a living misery, an animated curse?' (Bulwer-Lytton 1829, reprinted 1836: 197). The bleak perception—universal *and* personal—of his form ('limbs,' 'countenance') becomes a more encompassing stigmatisation of his 'self' as he takes on the abject status socially determined for him. The language then becomes figurative, histrionic, 'metaphysical,' and even quasi-sublime, the speaker's bitterly hyperbolic phrase 'blackness on the surface of creation' upping the rhetorical ante on the creature's awareness of himself as 'a blot upon the earth' in *Frankenstein* (Shelley 1994: 148). In a bit of intertextual wordplay, the phrase 'animated curse' affiliates the narrator with the animated corpse of *Frankenstein* and at the same time condenses both the monster's wretchedness and his destructive agency.

Like Shelley's creature who tells his creator that his 'soul glowed with love and humanity' (1994: 128), the narrator of 'A Manuscript' avows that he has 'the deepest sources of affection in [his] heart' and a surpassing 'benevolence which sheds itself in charity and love over a worm,' but like the creature he is 'shut out' from love and, for that matter, all 'social inter-course' (Bulwer-Lytton 1836: 197) because of his abominable appearance. While Shelley's monster is not of 'the same nature as man' (1994: 148), Bulwer-Lytton's protagonist is excluded from his own 'race' (1836: 197); he is not the product of a transgressive experiment but of some more inscru-table 'fatality.' While Shelley's monster can decry his maker's improvidence and demand an appropriate mate, Bulwer-Lytton's protagonist's Maker is divine and beyond reproach and, it seems, appeal. He cannot beseech his Maker for a companion, but instead finds what solace he can in 'Universal Nature' and in learning, cultivating the beauty of his soul. Yet his agonised question, 'For what—merciful God!—for what are these blessings of nature or of learning?' (197), echoes the monster's desperation in the face of the insurmountable and toxic antipathy of others.

Shelley's monster longed for sympathy and sought it out, but 'the human senses [proved to be] insurmountable barriers' (1994: 172) to any communion; so too Bulwer-Lytton's protagonist learns from painful experience that his physical state simply negates the human capacity to love. In his initial, pessimistic assessment of his place in creation, he even thinks of love as antipathetic to his being: 'I am its very loathing and abhorrence.' Hatred is his due and it clings to him like 'an atmosphere' (1836: 197). The passing account that he offers of his advent transposes Frankenstein's precipitous abandonment of his creation into a common-place familial context, although the reactions to his appearance and the effect on him are just as traumatic: 'At my birth the nurse refused me suck; my mother saw me and became delirious; my father ordered that I should be stifled as a monster.' He recalls his childhood love for 'every thing' from 'the living insect' to the 'dead stone' he walked upon, as well as his pathetic attempts to elicit love: 'I knelt to my mother, and besought her to love me—she shuddered. I fled to my father,—and he spurned me'

(198). His early relations with his family are thus curiously like the fiasco of the monster's abortive attempt to establish a reciprocal bond with the De Laceys, although devoid of the violent conclusion. He does have certain advantages the monster lacks—he is reared by a childless old woman—but his emotional development takes place within 'the eternal penthouse of a solitude' (198) mandated by his physical condition. He comes to rely on his own mental and emotional resources, delighting in nature and becoming a scholar and a poet.

Like Shelley's creature, he wanders the earth, until one day with the cued pertinence of a folktale he hears the voices of women from the other side of a hedge speaking of love. One young woman idealistically declares that physical beauty would play no part in her choice of a lover. She would be drawn to a 'mind which can command others,' asking only 'for genius and affection ... and nothing else.' Her interlocutor protests: 'But ... you could not love a monster in person, even if he were a miracle of intellect and of love!' (199). The high-minded maiden's reply references 'Beauty and the Beast': '*I* could have loved *that* monster.' The protagonist, of course, recognises himself in these hypothetical circumstances and is understandably thrilled by her principles and sentiments. He rapturously describes this fortuitous moment as 'a glimpse of Heaven' and 'the first glimmerings of hope' (200) in his life.

Just as Shelley's creature takes up secret residence next to the De Laceys' humble cottage, watching, learning, admiring, and sympathising, so Bulwer-Lytton's protagonist conceals himself in the nearby wood and at night steals 'unseen' to 'the shadow of her house' to 'listen to her voice' (200). Where Shelley's monster chops wood for the De Laceys, Bulwer-Lytton's hero leaves poems for the object of his affection, fills the air with music, and hopes to move her with his earnest passion. And just as Shelley's creature tells De Lacey that he is perceived as 'a detestable monster' (1994: 161), so Bulwer-Lytton's protagonist explains to his beloved that he is 'a thing which the daylight loathed to look upon' and 'more hideous than the demons which the imagination of a Northern savage had ever bodied forth' (1836: 201). She is, then, amply warned. But she reiterates her Platonic valuation of the beauty of the soul and tells him that anyone able to feel and write as he has 'could not be loathsome in her eyes'; indeed she could love him even if his 'form [were] more monstrous than [he has] portrayed it.' They arrange to meet under the cover of darkness with the protagonist wrapped 'from head to foot in a mantle' (201), artificially replicating De Lacey's opportune blindness. He awes her with his thought and learning, so much so that she enjoins him to 'gain the glory of fame' as an author, promising to be his once this condition is met. He insists that she seal this promise with an oath (201) that echoes the 'solemn oath' that Frankenstein exacts from the creature in return for his consent to make him a mate (Shelley 1994: 175). The unseen lover and hoodwinked beloved, like the creature and his creator, part with the understanding that once the agreed-upon task has been completed, they will meet again. Both meetings entail the long-desired, sympathetic union of 'monster' and mate.

Bulwer-Lytton's outcast retires to 'a lonely and far spot' and applies himself to the task of making his mark as a writer; it is here that the story conflates the driven, wonder-working scientist and the forlorn, misprised creature. While Frankenstein is a scientist, Bulwer-Lytton's hero is a polymath who both 'explore[s] … the arcana of science' *and* 'ransack[s] the starry regions of poetry,' transferring the 'treasures … stored within him' onto the page. He publishes his work anonymously and wins instant acclaim for his unprecedented 'discoveries' (Bulwer-Lytton 1829, 1836: 202). He returns triumphantly to his beloved who has guessed that he must be the revered but 'unknown' genius of the age, and he 'claim[s his] reward,' her love. Crossing the new archetype of *Frankenstein* with the classical myth of Psyche and Cupid, Bulwer-Lytton has his hero and his beloved consummate their relationship under cover of darkness, when the 'depth and deadness of night' (202) suspends the visual. Their strictly nocturnal relationship continues for months until the inevitable, pregnancy, occurs and they decide to marry. Just as the wedding day of Frankenstein and Elizabeth is the crisis point of the scientist's insupportable secret in that novel, so too it is in Bulwer-Lytton's story. The protagonist himself ironically causes the death of his bride and destroys his prospects of future happiness with the reluctant exposure of his monstrous aspect. While she has been warned about her lover's physical condition and has generously promised to transcend the visual bias that has poisoned his life, her moral triumph is notional and not experiential. The 'basic aversive emotions [of] fear, hatred and disgust' that 'invalidate disabled bodies' (Hughes 2012: 67–8) return with a vengeance.

The 'non-disabled gaze' (68) directed towards 'the filthy mass' of his creature may cause Frankenstein to feel 'horror and hatred' (Shelley 1994: 174), but while the creature is telling his life story in an appeal for sympathy, his visage tends to fade or recede in the reader's sustaining imagination, no longer the figure but rather the inescapable ground of the creature's experience. Spared the actual sight of the monster, readers are able to evade the involuntary, unreflective reaction of all but the blind De Lacey. By contrast, in Bulwer-Lytton's story, the young bride's indifference to appearances evaporates in an instant when she actually sees the narrator. Her physical intimacy with the human 'monster' was untainted by the toxic visuality of the 'non-disabled gaze' (Hughes 2012: 68) and nothing prepares her for the face-to-face encounter. All who *see* the 'monster' have this visceral reaction and the shock of the sight proves deadly. When she sees his 'countenance glare full upon her,' she utters a shriek and falls 'senseless on the floor' (Bulwer-Lytton 1829, 1836: 203). At the 'accustomed' (204) hour of their regular trysts, he returns to her chamber to find his bride a corpse. Bulwer-Lytton's story thus reworks the wedding-night scenario of *Frankenstein* with the protagonist occupying both the position of the bereaved spouse and the—here—unwitting murderer. Where Frankenstein experiences a 'sensation of horror not to be described' (Shelley 1994: 221) when he glimpses the grinning monster pointing at the body of Elizabeth, Bulwer-Lytton's human 'monster' laughs aloud, hysterical with despair at the sight of his wife's body. He then suffers an additionally cruel twist of fate when he unexpectedly beholds the body of their dead child, the 'beautiful likeness of myself!' (Bulwer-Lytton 1829, 1836: 204). Bulwer-Lytton's story here both realises and neutralises Frankenstein's fear of the propagation of 'a race of devils' (Shelley 1994: 192), for while the protagonist's self-identified 'monstrosity' is passed down to the next generation despite the 'normality' of his mate, his offspring is not viable. This is also the moment when he is traumatically compelled to recognise the inescapability of his own monstrous form mirrored in his progeny: 'A little infant monster!' (Bulwer-Lytton 1829, 1836: 204).

The most macabre section of Bulwer-Lytton's tale seems to rewind Shelley's narrative to the pivotal point at which the monster is created. The unhinged speaker perversely gloats over the corpses: 'it is a glorious mirth, to behold the only thing one loves, stiff, and white, … and food for the red, playful, creeping worm' (204), recalling Frankenstein's nightmare of Elizabeth transformed into 'the corpse of [his] dead mother' with 'the grave worms crawling' in her shroud (Shelley 1994: 86). Bulwer-Lytton's human 'monster' carries off his dead bride and child to a cavern where he 'watch[es] over' the process of their decomposition (1829, 1836: 204), the narrative regressing to Frankenstein's initial research where he scrutinises 'the corruption of death succeed[ing] to the blooming cheek of life' (Shelley 1994: 80).

As the story closes, it pulls back from its intensive, though selective, revisionist engagement with *Frankenstein*. In an informal epilogue, the protagonist returns home, taking 'possession of [his] titles and … wealth' (Bulwer-Lytton 1829, 1836: 203) and—in a fairy-tale formula of a happy ending—is able to state, 'And so I lived *happily* enough for a short time.' Unfortunately, he is eventually identified as 'the divine poet' (205); his sanctuary is invaded by his adoring readers whose esteem for his intellect and contribution to culture is supplanted by cruel delight in the spectacle of his physical deformity. He is reduced to the abject status of a monster on display, a spectacular 'freak' like the Victorian Elephant Man. This display is a vivid realisation of Hughes' 'subcutaneous violence of the intrusive, demeaning and disturbing non-disabled gaze' (2012: 68): 'And the crowd came—and the mob beset me—and my rooms were filled with eyes—large, staring eyes, all surveying me from head to foot—and peals of laughter and shrieks wandered about the air like disembodied and damned spirits—and I was never alone again!' (Bulwer-Lytton 1829, 1836: 205). The anomalous appearance of Bulwer-Lytton's hero does not just induce terror or revulsion but also provokes cruel laughter in those who approach him armed with expectations of a unique spectacle of bodily difference.

Young Frankenstein (1974)

Young Frankenstein, directed by Mel Brooks and co-written with Gene Wilder, is a good-natured parody of James Whale's *Frankenstein* films, but one that returns to this cinematic template with a curiously humane purposefulness. The opening credits proclaim that the script is 'Based on Characters in the Novel *Frankenstein* by Mary Shelley' (Brooks 1974) but the comedy pointedly diverts the tragic course of her plot. As a ludicrous enactment of Lipking's 'modern consensus,' the film rectifies the original Frankenstein's moral dereliction—his failure to love his creature and to be a responsible creator—and thus constitutes, perhaps improbably, a significant late twentieth-century reworking of some of the key problems of sympathy and disability from Shelley's novel. The film virtually cites Shelley's novel when Victor's young descendent Frederick discovers and devours the massive tome entitled 'How I Did It,' which includes lines directly taken from the text.

The film manifests an interest in non-monstrous disability and physical difference, admittedly in the service of visual, situational, and verbal jokes, implicitly situating the monster's unprecedented corporeality within this broader context of human experience. Although hardly commendable in its comic exploitation of the spectacle of the abnormal body, it does display a certain self-awareness about physical difference, particularly in its treatment of the figure of Igor, satirically highlighting this dimension of Whale's film. While the film treats disability and deformity facetiously, it also sets up some resistance to ableist presumptions. When the young Frankenstein first meets his future sidekick, he delicately says, 'I don't want to embarrass you ... but I'm a brilliant surgeon. Perhaps I could help you with that hump' and Igor deadpans, 'What hump?' This is a satiric subversion of Whale's film's depiction of the hunchback Fritz, rather than cavalier mockery of disability per se.

Although Brooks' creature (played by Peter Boyle) is a frank pastiche of the iconic cinematic depiction, Karloff's horrid appearance is invoked or referenced rather than fully reproduced; the monstrosity of the creature is attenuated. Boyle's creature is pale and has the requisite protuberant brows and stitched temples, but his bald, ordinary-shaped pate has no evidence of radical reconstruction. More importantly, while the dialogue of Whale's film sidesteps the conspicuous fact of the creature's appearance, *Young Frankenstein* tackles it head on in ways that respond to Shelley's novel. When his lab assistant, surveying the as yet lifeless body of the creature, says, 'He's hideous,' the young Frankenstein defiantly answers, 'He's beautiful and he is mine.'

The reparative motif of Brooks' film declares itself in a later scene. The young Frankenstein, in a display of compassion and courage, resolves to do right by the creature, declaring, 'Love is the only thing that can save this poor creature and I am going to convince him that he is loved even at the cost of my own life.' The new and improved Frankenstein, unlike his forebear, does not turn 'from [the monster] in disgust' (Shelley 1994: 158). Unlike Victor, Frederick acts in accordance with 'the duties of a creator towards his creature' (130) while also exhibiting paternal care. The ensuing scene resets the relation of maker and monster in Shelley's novel, redressing the original Frankenstein's abandonment and neglect of the monster. At the same time, the scene exemplifies and satirises the late twentieth- and early twenty-first century ethical critique of Frankenstein's role in Shelley's novel. Voluntarily locked in a room with the intimidating monster, Frederick gambles on flattery as a technique of persuasion. 'Hello handsome' (Brooks 1974), he ventures, and Boyle's monster does a double take. And so he improvises, with increasing conviction and fervency, a motivational, psychotherapeutic speech designed to give the wretch a shot of much-needed self-esteem: 'You're a good looking fellow, do you know that? People laugh at you, people hate you. But why do they hate you? Because they are jealous!' This hatred hasn't, however, been exhibited in the film narrative, but refers back to Shelley's novel and the subsequent adaptation tradition, while the supposed laughter gestures to phenomena beyond, though adumbrated in, *Frankenstein*—that is, the egregiously insensitive maltreatment of the disabled. The young Frankenstein affirmatively converts his creature's physical difference into the manifestation of the 'Olympian ideal' and likens the evidently flattered monster to 'a god.'

The humour of the scene is constructed on the discrepancy between Frankenstein's blandishments and the monster's anomalous appearance: 'Look at you, that boyish face; look at that sweet smile.' Young Frankenstein is the ideal, protective, loving father, the antithesis of Shelley's absent and antagonistic one. He comforts his unnatural progeny, cradling the sobbing monster-child in his arms, murmuring, 'This is a nice boy. This is a good boy. This is a mother's angel,' and then defiantly proclaiming in the face of prejudice, 'And I want the world to know once and for all and without any shame … that we love him.' Literally as well as figuratively embracing his 'child,' he arrests and reverses the process of moral deformation that Shelley's monster has undergone and, simultaneously and ironically, fervently embraces his inheritance and identity as a Frankenstein. Deviating from his literary precursor's course of neglect, 'Young Frankenstein' redeems the Frankenstein name.

Fittingly for a comedy, *Young Frankenstein*'s creature does not prove to be particularly violent; he exhibits neither the malicious vengefulness of Shelley's creature nor the reactive-instinctive violence of Whale's monster. However, in a burlesque of Whale's narrative, *Young Frankenstein*'s creature is purportedly defective since he has the 'rotten brain' of one 'Abby Normal.' Consequently, Frankenstein vows to teach him, to demonstrate that nurture can override nature. His public exhibition of the results of this educational programme, a song and a dance routine, comes very close to a joke at the expense of the disabled and ends in fiasco as the monster bungles his part. This failure leads Frankenstein to undertake a direct and risky transfusion of his own mentality to the monster. The monster rises from the operating table and, unprompted, launches into a lucid and rather formal monologue: 'I am the monster. As long as I can remember, people have hated me. They looked at my face and my body and they ran away in horror. In my loneliness I decided that if I could not inspire love which was my deepest hope, I would instead cause fear.' Since really none of this has occurred in the film, the speech is an intertextual recapitulation of the monster's perspective on his blighted life and his malice in Shelley's *Frankenstein*. This physical-psychic transmission of supplementary humanity completes young Frankenstein's work of rectification, seemingly at the cost of his life. But between the first rectification (by nurture) and the second (by transplant) there is yet another movement in the monster's redemption, which combines (however crudely) the affective and the physical, that is, the monster's sexual experience with Frankenstein's fiancée Elizabeth. This monster does not request a mate from his creator but takes matters into his own hands. Whereas Shelley's creature avenges himself for the destruction of his mate by murdering Elizabeth, this monster abducts his creator's Elizabeth. This leads to what is perhaps the most unsavoury and uncomfortable moment in the comedy when the monster seems on the verge of raping her, a scenario recuperated comically in the nick of time when the formerly frigid Elizabeth signals her transition from prospective victim to erotic partner. When she sees his prodigious genitalia, she—in keeping with a rather repugnant pornographic logic—responds, 'Oh my God! Woof!' In the cliché-drenched scene of their post-coital interactions, the now confident and cool monster hints at his insatiable sexual appetite and extraordinary sexual prowess and receives an enthusiastic response from his equally lascivious partner. This is the ribald solution to the problem of the 'insurmountable obstacle' of vision that sustains the bias against Frankenstein's creature. In a culmination of the salacious fantasy, it is revealed that, in the mutually beneficial experimental exchange between creator and creature, the young Doctor has acquired some measure of his creature's sexual endowments, just as the monster has attained a portion of young Frankenstein's intellect and sensitivity. The symmetry of the comic dénouement emphasises the reciprocal completion of creator and creature; they are equals, counterparts of each other, who have a share in each other's contentment.

'The Crimson Horror,' *Doctor Who* (2013)

Like Bulwer-Lytton's story and Brooks' film, 'The Crimson Horror' appropriates Shelley's archetypal creature as an emblem of atypical embodiment and, by extension, disability. Set in late-Victorian Britain, the episode relies on a double frame of reference: its caricature of the supposed narrow-mindedness of the Victorians is contrasted with the expansive perspective of the sci-fi series in which alien life and radically divergent embodiment are a given.

The Doctor investigates a projected utopian community called Sweetville, which only accepts 'the fittest and most beautiful' recruits (2013). The architect of the scheme is the fanatical Mrs Gillyflower, an apocalyptic eugenicist prepared to exterminate all but a small group of personally vetted, physically exemplary human beings worthy of preservation. When the Doctor is subjected to Gillyflower's process of purification-inoculation-preservation, he is instead transformed into a crimson-hued iteration of Boris Karloff's creature, but is clandestinely rescued and harboured by Gillyflower's blind daughter, Ada. Ada, Igor-like in her service to her mad-scientist mother, also combines the roles of the blind and tentatively sympathetic De Lacey and the monster's bespoken mate (one who, he hopes, will feel an affinity with him). However, although Ada saves, succours, and becomes attached to the Doctor-monster, this movement towards intertextual rectification (the provision of sympathy lacking in *Frankenstein*) is not unambiguous. Virtually petrified and rendered mute, the Doctor (far more even than Whale's creature) is unable to make any intelligible appeal to anyone. Ada acts on her own desire for companionship and, more disturbingly, keeps the Doctor-monster in chains in a cell—very much like Whale's monster after he has displayed erratic and dangerous behaviour—even though her 'dear monster' has not, as far as we know, exhibited any destructive tendencies. Although she feels sympathy and affection for him, she nonetheless regards him as a monster and seems to make (unwarranted) behavioural, if not moral, assumptions about him.

Ada, like the protagonist's lover in 'Madhouse,' knows full well that the Doctor-monster is physically anomalous and that she alone is capable of bestowing the compassion and perhaps the companionship that she assumes, transferentially, he craves. There is a certain suitability in the bond she establishes with him since he too is imperfect and she hopes to secure a place for them both in her mother's new Eden. However, her mother disdainfully tells her, 'I cannot bear to look at sick people…. There can be no place for people such as you' (2013). While the appearance and the ungainly movements of the Doctor-monster visually evoke the cinematic *Frankenstein* tradition, situationally Ada is more akin to Shelley's creature in being rejected by her unforgiving scientist mother for her imperfection, a resemblance only strengthened when we discover that it was her monomaniacal and callous mother that blinded and disfigured her in an earlier experiment. She is disdained and ultimately abandoned for being what her mother has made her.

The Crimson Horror directly repudiates the pernicious effects of disability-related disgust, particularly the conflation of physical difference with moral contamination. Abusively disowned by her mother, the distraught Ada elicits the sympathy of the Doctor, now restored to his ordinary state as an unimpaired and articulate subject. Lamenting that her mother 'doesn't want' her, she speculates that it was her 'own sin' which made her unworthy of acceptance into the engineered New Jerusalem, but the Doctor forcefully dispels this error, 'That's backwards, stupid backwards nonsense and you know it.'

In the episode's complex transposition of *Frankenstein*, there is a doubling of roles. The Doctor, formerly in the position of the monster, now speaks as the humane scientist and counteracts the noxious attitudes of the morally monstrous scientist-parent. Formerly the recipient of Ada's sympathy and care, he now shows sympathy as she, more isolated than ever before (more monster than monster's companion), abjectly internalises her mother's loathing. Although the Doctor speaks entirely in character, the shifts in their roles underscore a fellowship and regard arising out of similar experiences of disability, no matter how transitory in the Doctor's case.

Since only the physical-elect, the 'supermodels,' are remade to withstand the cataclysm to come, the category of the physical rejects and reprobates expands to encompass the majority of humankind. Ironically, Mrs Gillyflower, the self-proclaimed authority in this corporeal Calvinism, is herself physically anomalous, for a symbiotic parasite is concealed beneath her bodice. The parabolic amplification of science fiction here clarifies the untenable process of physical discrimination.

Like other variations on *Frankenstein*, 'A Manuscript Found in a Madhouse,' *Young Frankenstein*, and 'The Crimson Horror' subscribe to the 'modern consensus,' providing 'more instructive' alternatives or supplements to the original, in various ways contesting and circumventing the 'insurmountable barriers' to sympathy that bedevil the creature. They broaden the representational purview of *Frankenstein* to clarify its subtext of deformity and disability, and explore ways of setting things right for the stigmatised creature, rectifying the interpersonal and social derelictions in the novel. In response to Frankenstein's deficient, reluctant, and abortive sympathy, 'A Manuscript' and 'The Crimson Horror' imagine stand-ins for him, the genius and the scientist, directly experiencing the creature's misfortunes, while in *Young Frankenstein*, the physical exchange of mental and physical traits is the ultimate remediation. Finally, all three (tragic, comic, and tragicomic) narrative iterations find vehicles for the love denied Shelley's creature in companions indifferent to their surrogate creatures' fearsome physiognomies. Attuned to Shelley's creature's representative status, they not only deplore but invert the negative demonstration in *Frankenstein* of social monster making.

WORKS CITED

Brooks, Mel (dir.). 1974. *Young Frankenstein*, film, USA: Twentieth Century Fox.

Bulwer-Lytton, Edward. 1829 [1836]. A Manuscript Found in a Madhouse. In *The Student: A Series of Papers*, vol. 1, 197–205. New York: Harper and Brothers.

Cantor, Paul. 1984. *Creature and Creator: Myth-making and English Romanticism*. Cambridge: Cambridge University Press.

Horne, R.H. 1844. *A New Spirit of the Age*. Vol. 2. London: Smith, Elder and Co.

Hughes, Bill. 2012. Fear, Pity and Disgust: Emotions and the Non-disabled Imaginary. In *Routledge Handbook of Disability Studies*, ed. Nick Watson, Alan Roulstone, and Carol Thomas, 67–77. London: Routledge.

Lipking, Lawrence. 2012. *Frankenstein*, The True Story; or, Rousseau Judges Jean-Jacques. In *Frankenstein*, ed. Paul Hunter, 416–434. New York: W. W. Norton.

Mellor, Anne K. 1990. *Frankenstein* and the Sublime. In *Approaches to Teaching Shelley's Frankenstein*, ed. Stephen C. Behrendt, 99–104. New York: The Modern Language Association of America.

Metzstein, Saul (dir.). 2013. The Crimson Horror. *Doctor Who*, Series 7, Episode 11, television, UK: BBC.

Miller, William Ian. 1997. *The Anatomy of Disgust*. Cambridge: Harvard University Press.

Shelley, Mary. 1980. *Frankenstein (1831 text)*. Oxford: Oxford University Press.

———. 1994. *Frankenstein (1818 text)*. Peterborough: Broadview.

Whale, James (dir.). 1931. *Frankenstein*, film, USA: Universal Pictures.

CHAPTER 6

'We Sometimes Paused to Laugh Outright': *Frankenstein* and the Struggle for Decorum

Carolyn D. Williams

Many readers of *Frankenstein* have found its style excessively 'stilted' (Mellor 1989: 60). It appears that Mary Shelley, aided by Percy Bysshe Shelley (1792–1822), was trying to exclude all possibility of vulgarity, colloquialism, or anything else that might, by contemporary literary or social standards, be considered low; in the process, she eliminated nearly all humour. This is a risky business: like Gothic monsters, laughter, if banished, may return with devastating effect. Her dangerous strategy can be demonstrated by an examination of crucial instances in the 1818 edition, sometimes on their own, and sometimes alongside Charles E. Robinson's edition of the 1816/1817 manuscript draft, or adaptations in various media from 1823 to the present day. Contemporary reviews, however, provide the best starting point for this attempt to understand what Mary Shelley sought to achieve, and avoid.

Hostile critics insist that *Frankenstein* is funny. A particularly damaging attack suggests that, as 'one of the productions of the modern school in its highest style of caricature and exaggeration', it was meant to provoke laughter, but it has been only partially successful: 'for a *jeu d'esprit* it is

C. D. Williams (✉)
Department of English Literature, University of Reading, Reading, UK

© The Author(s) 2018
C. M. Davison, M. Mulvey-Roberts (eds.), *Global Frankenstein*,
Studies in Global Science Fiction,
https://doi.org/10.1007/978-3-319-78142-6_6

somewhat too long, grave, and laborious' (*Edinburgh Magazine* 1818: 249, 253). Others, with slightly greater charity, represent humour as the result of excessive ambition. For example, the *British Critic* declares, 'the horror which abounds in [these volumes] is too grotesque and *bizarre* ever to approach near the sublime, and when we did not hurry over the pages in disgust, we sometimes paused to laugh outright' (1818: 438). Both the *British Critic* and John Wilson Croker (1780–1857) of the *Quarterly Review* find similarities between *Frankenstein* and popular comic dramas. More sinister flaws are also connected with something inherently ridiculous: according to the *British Critic*, the author displays:

> [O]ccasional symptoms of no common powers of mind, struggling through a mass of absurdity, which well nigh overwhelms them; but it is a sort of absurdity that approaches so often the confines of what is wicked and immoral, that we dare hardly trust ourselves to bestow even this qualified praise. (1818: 438)

As condemnation extends from style to subject matter to ethics, accompanied by the hollow ring of contemptuous laughter, it becomes increasingly hard to find a single term to define the principle the author has transgressed. There is one, however, and the wide divergence between the critics' views and the author's is revealed by its ability to denote both their standard and her goal: decorum. Samuel Johnson (1709–1784) defines this complex word as 'Decency; behaviour contrary to licentiousness, contrary to levity; seemliness' (1785: sub 'Decorum'). Thinking about decorum vindicates, or at least explains, passages whose existence seems hard to justify and also casts fresh light on *Frankenstein* at its best, while critical and creative responses deplore, exploit, and celebrate its multi-faceted generic potential.

Potential links with *Frankenstein* appear in one of the most respected classical texts on literary decorum, the *Epistle to the Pisos* (19 BC), better known as *The Art of Poetry*, by Quintus Horatius Flaccus (65–8 BC). Mary's only written reference to this work before the publication of *Frankenstein* is an allusion to line 139, 'you would … be enclined say out of the mountain comes forth a mouse', in a letter to Percy dated December 5, 1816: this reveals more about Percy's use of a classical cliché than her direct contact with Horace (Shelley 1980–1988: I, 22). Nevertheless, she probably knew about it, since it was familiar to educated readers in general, and of great interest to Byron in particular.[1] Horace begins by comparing a muddled poem to a picture of a hybrid monstrosity assembled from different species, representing it as ludicrous:

Humano capiti cervicem pictor equinam
Jungere si velit, et varias inducere plumas
Undique collatis membris, ut turpiter atrum
Desinat in piscem mulier formosa supernè;
Spectatum admissi risum teneatis, amici? (Horace, lines 1–5, [2, B1v])

George Colman the Elder (1732–1794) provides this translation:

What if a Painter, in his art to shine,
A human head and horse's neck should join;
From various creatures put the limbs together,
Cover'd with plumes, from ev'ry bird a feather;
And in a filthy tail the figure drop,
A fish at bottom, a fair maid at top:
Viewing a picture of this strange condition,
Would you not laugh at such an exhibition? (Horace, lines 1–8, [2]B2r)

Horace then compares indiscriminate compositions to images conjured up by a sick man's delirium, '*ut nec pes, nec caput uni/Reddatur formæ*' (Horace, lines 8–9, 3[B2v]). A literal translation would be 'so that neither foot nor head is assigned to a single form', a conceit that acquires disturbing solidity when we think of Victor gathering materials for his creation. An explicit connection between *The Art of Poetry* and the narrative assemblage of a body had already been drawn by Horace Walpole (1717–1797). In the course of his novel, *The Castle of Otranto* (1764), huge pieces of armour and body parts of a ghostly ancestor begin to appear and finally coalesce into a single gigantic figure. A review condemned the supernatural episodes of *Otranto* as 'rotten materials', 'monstrosities', and 'absurdities' (*Critical Review* 1765: 51). On the title page of the second edition, Walpole retorts by reversing Horace's sentiment: '*tamen ut Pes, & Caput uni/Reddantur formæ*' ['nevertheless foot and head are returned to a single form'] (1765: [A1r]). His tale of supernatural horror may transgress classical literary conventions, but at least it restores integrity to one body rather than making a patchwork out of many.

Subsequently, a specific family resemblance between a badly made work of art and Frankenstein's creature appears when Horace compares a poet of limited range to a craftsman who can model fingernails and hair, but not a complete figure:

Non magis esse velim, quàm pravo vivere naso,
Spectandum nigris oculis, nigroque capillo. (Horace, lines 36–37, 5, [B4v])

To grasp the full force of this passage, it is necessary to understand that dark eyes and hair were, to Horace, supremely beautiful:

> To be this man, would I a work compose,
> No more I'd wish, than for a horrid nose,
> With hair as black as jet, and eyes as black as sloes. (Horace, lines 53–55, 5, C1r)

Frankenstein's description of his creature indicates that he shares Horace's preferences but, like the incompetent craftsman, is incapable of creating a harmonious whole:

> I had selected his features as beautiful. Beautiful!—Great God! His yellow skin scarcely covered the work of muscles and arteries beneath; his hair was of a lustrous black, and flowing; his teeth of a pearly whiteness; but these luxuriances only formed a more horrid contrast with his watery eyes, that seemed almost of the same colour as the dun white sockets in which they were set, his shrivelled complexion, and straight black lips. (Shelley 1818: I, 98)

Horace is particularly interested in writing for the stage; in his insistence on maintaining proper distinctions between tragedy and comedy, aesthetic values combine with social and even ethical discriminations:

> *Ne quicunque Deus, quicunque adhibebitur heros*
> *Regali conspectus in auro nuper et ostro,*
> *Migret in obscuras humili sermone tabernas*[.] (Horace, lines 227–229, 20[F3v])

Colman translates:

> That God or Heroe of the lofty scene,
> In royal gold and purple seen but late,
> May ne'er in cots obscure debase his state,
> Lost in low language[.] (Horace, lines 335–338, 20[F4r],)

The great and the good, then, must guard their status with a well-chosen vocabulary. Only high language, it seems, is suited to their important concerns. These are the business of tragedy, depicted by Horace as a great lady, conscious of her rank:

Effutire leves indigna tragœdia versus. (Horace, line 231, 20[F3v],)

Literally, she will not 'babble light verses'; as Colman puts it,

> With an indignant pride, and coy disdain,
> Stern Tragedy rejects too light a vein. (Horace, lines 340–341, 20[F4r],)

This recalls Johnson's definition of decorum as 'contrary to levity' (1785), a sense totally in keeping with Mary Shelley's approach to *Frankenstein.* The creature's nature, however, seems to pose a threat to critical conventions.[2] Horace's association of variegated texts with abnormal bodies was still influential. Colman himself described tragicomedy as a *'monster'* (1783: xxxix). If a mixture of genres was monstrous, how could a story about a monster retain its generic purity? Shelley tried, occasionally too hard, to keep order by enforcing decorum.

Mary Shelley's serious tone and choice of educated, even elevated, diction appears to have been motivated by reluctance to disrupt the mood of tragic seriousness. Percy's posthumously published review affirms that *Frankenstein* was intended to be 'a source of powerful and profound emotion', proceeding to its conclusion with 'an irresistible solemnity, and the magnificent energy and swiftness of a tempest', arousing pity as well as terror:

> The scene between the Being and the blind De Lacey in the cottage, is one of the most profound and extraordinary instances of pathos that we ever recollect. It is impossible to read this dialogue,—and indeed many others of a somewhat similar character,—without feeling the heart suspend its pulsations with wonder, and the 'tears stream down the cheeks.' (Shelley 1832: 730)

This account of the emotional high points is fully justified, but the book has little of the wit and informality that would have conducted the reader more comfortably through the intervening spaces. Sometimes the author's determination to keep her characters on their best behaviour seems counterproductive. Take Victor Frankenstein's first speech in the novel: '"Before I come on board your vessel," said he, "will you have the kindness to inform me whither you are bound?"' (Shelley 1818: I, 24). George Levine considers this 'drawing-room politeness' an example of 'uproarious camp'; although he adds that it was intended to provoke 'horrific intensity', hilarity is the more plausible reaction (1975: 208). As Philip Stevick observes, laughter at this point is 'a reaction that is as honest, as true to the text, and as deserving of respect as the accumulated reactions of the critical tradition' (1979: 239).

The knowledge that Percy Shelley 'oversaw his wife's manuscript at every stage' relieves Mary of sole responsibility for undue stylistic elevation (Shelley 1982: xviii). He produced 'much of the most inflated rhetoric in the text', by changing 'Anglo-Saxon diction and straightforward or colloquial sentence structures into their more refined, complex, and Latinate equivalents' (Mellor: 61, 60). The clearest confirmation is provided by comparing the 1818 edition with the 1816/1817 manuscript that Percy corrected. For example, Victor's determination to kill his creature was published in these terms: 'I resolved that I would sell my life dearly, and not relax the impending conflict until my own life, or that of my adversary, were extinguished' (Shelley 1818: III, 117). These balanced abstractions replaced Mary's earthier version: 'I resolved that I would sell my life dearly & not die until my adversary should lie senseless at my feet' (Shelley 2009: 402). Yet Mary chose to accept such revisions, which were in keeping with her practice of distancing her narrative from anything too familiar or low in tone. For example, the creature learns to speak by listening to the De Laceys, who are not only refined, but foreign to the area; consequently, he is unable to shock her readers' sensibilities by repeating the vulgar utterances of the peasantry: '"two countrymen passed by; but, pausing near the cottage, they entered into conversation, using violent gesticulations; but I did not understand what they said, as they spoke the language of the country, which differed from that of my protectors"' (Shelley 1818: II, 124–25). The 'gesticulations' are a contribution from Percy, replacing Mary's original 'gestures', but the rest is her own (Shelley 2009: 348). Mary's determination to keep light babblings to a minimum also appears in substantive developments. For example, the description of Victor and Clerval's sojourn in Oxford originally contained a witty account of the 'bigotry & devotion to established rules' of fashion that led to two students being threatened with expulsion for wearing 'light coloured pantaloons when it was the rule of the college to wear dark' (Shelley 2009: 368). There was also a satirical anecdote about their visit to a room once inhabited by Friar Bacon, 'which, as it was predicted, would fall in when a man wiser than that philosopher should enter it': 'A short, round faced prating professor who accompanied us refused to pass the threshold, although we ventured inside in perfect security' (Shelley 2009: 369). Percy, to his eternal credit, drove the point home by adding 'and probably he might have done the same' (Shelley 2009: 369). But by the time the episode is published, nothing is left of Oxford but historical associations and beautiful scenery.

Mary also casts baleful shadows on many of the signs of cheerfulness or amusement that appear in the novel. Smiles, even when expressing affection, may be problematic. The smile upon which the entire plot turns is directed to Victor by the creature: 'His jaws opened, and he muttered some inarticulate sounds, while a grin wrinkled his cheeks' (Shelley 1818: I, 100). Victor, too repelled by the creature's ugliness to respond to this attempt at bonding, runs away. A later smile is more ambiguous. Just as it has occurred to Victor that creating a mate for him might lead to the propagation of 'a race of devils', the creature appears at the window: 'A ghastly grin wrinkled his lips as he gazed on me, where I sat fulfilling the task which he had allotted to me' (Shelley 1818: III, 42, 43). He may simply be expressing affection for his future companion; Victor, however, detects 'the utmost extent of malice and treachery' on the creature's countenance, and this sight provokes him to destroy his handiwork (Shelley 1818: III, 43). After avenging this loss, the creature smiles again, in a display of indubitable hostility that includes an element of savage humour: 'A grin was on the face of the monster; he seemed to jeer, as with his fiendish finger he pointed towards the corpse of my wife' (Shelley 1818: III, 121). Laughter is even worse. Walton regards the prospect of his sister's mocking laughter with disgust: 'Will you laugh at the enthusiasm I express concerning this divine wanderer? If you do, you must have certainly lost that simplicity which was once your characteristic charm' (Shelley 1818: I, 34–35). Victor's expression of relief at the creature's disappearance in a peal of 'loud, unrestrained, heartless laughter' signals his mental, physical, and moral collapse (Shelley 1818: I, 109). The creature himself is responsible for the most sinister occurrence: when Victor swears vengeance at the family cemetery, he is 'answered through the stillness of the night by a loud and fiendish laugh' (Shelley 1818: III, 136). Mary Shelley does not just try to avoid provoking laughter: she demonises it. In the 1831 edition, she goes even further by making Victor exorcise it before telling his tale to Walton: 'Were we among the tamer scenes of nature, I might fear to encounter your unbelief, perhaps your ridicule; but many things will appear possible in these wild and mysterious regions, which would provoke the laughter of those unacquainted with the ever-varied powers of nature' (Shelley 1969: 30).

The banishment of laughter may have motivated Percy's insertion of a passage hitherto condemned as irrelevant. It appears in Elizabeth's letter to Victor, mentioning that Justine has been taken into service in the

Frankenstein household. At this point, Mary's manuscript says simply that Justine 'was taught all the duties of servant & was very kindly treated' (Shelley 2009: 284). In the published version, Elizabeth tells Victor, who must surely know already, that:

> The republican institutions of our country have produced simpler and happier manners than those which prevail in the great monarchies that surround it. Hence there is less distinction between the several classes of its inhabitants; and the lower orders being neither so poor nor so despised, their manners are more refined and moral. A servant in Geneva does not mean the same thing as a servant in France and England. Justine, thus received in our family, learned the duties of a servant; a condition which, in our fortunate country, does not include the idea of ignorance, and a sacrifice of the dignity of a human being. (Shelley 1818: I, 118)

Anne K. Mellor sees it simply as an opportunistic expression of Percy's 'revolutionary hostility to hierarchical institutions' (Mellor, 64). Nevertheless, it is a useful intimation that readers should not expect Justine to provide comic relief. This was important, since many would be familiar with the superstitious and garrulous Annette in *The Mysteries of Udolpho* (1794) by Ann Radcliffe (1764–1823), or the staff at Otranto, who respond to supernatural manifestations with panic, incoherence, and a threatened strike:

> … we heard the door of the great chamber clap behind us, but we did not dare turn back to see if the giant was following us—yet now I think on it, we must have heard him if he had pursued us—but for heaven's sake, good my Lord, send for the chaplain and have the castle exorcised, for, for certain, it is enchanted. Ay, pray do, my Lord, cried all the servants at once, or we must leave your Highness's service. (Walpole 1764: 40)

Literary decorum allows these characters to be the object of laughter: they are not only comic in being funny, but comedic in surviving the cataclysms that claim the lives of their social superiors. Justine, however, requires tragic 'dignity' to intensify the pity and indignation aroused by her unjust execution. This seems to have convinced the critics: in *La Belle Assemblée*, Justine is called 'interesting', indicating that she has engaged the reader's sympathy (1818: 140).

Although Percy's disquisition on Swiss society helps to preserve tragic decorum in the novel, *Frankenstein*'s transitions from page to stage and screen frequently require the inclusion of comic servants who enable the audience to get the laughter out of their system. The precedent is set by the first adaptation, *Presumption; or, the Fate of Frankenstein* (1823) by Richard Brinsley Peake (1792–1847). Fritz, Frankenstein's servant, opens the show: he engagingly confesses, 'Master only hired me because I looked so stupid' (Cox 1992: Act I, scene 1, 388). The provision of opportunities for laughter is not the least merit of Universal Pictures' *Frankenstein* (1931), directed by James Whale. These include the antics of Frankenstein's bumbling assistant (another Fritz), who stays alive until he alienates the audience by treating the creature with unmerited cruelty, and the mirth of medical students within the film when somebody brushes against an articulated skeleton, making it appear to dance. Even so, the atmosphere was initially volatile: according to Mordaunt Hall's *New York Times* review for December 5, 1931, 'many in the audience laughed to cover their true feelings'. Similar use is made of a servant in Whale's sequel, *The Bride of Frankenstein* (Universal, 1935); the housekeeper Minnie, played by the comic actress Una O'Connor, responds to the creature by shrieking like a banshee.

An indisputably brilliant passage reveals the operation of decorum in its more prosaic senses of 'decency' and 'seemliness'. The description of the moment when Victor's creature comes to life is fully worthy of its subject: 'It was on a dreary night of November, that I beheld the accomplishment of my toils. [....] It was already one in the morning; the rain pattered dismally against the panes, and my candle was nearly burnt out, when, by the glimmer of the half-extinguished light, I saw the dull yellow eye of the creature open; it breathed hard, and a convulsive motion agitated its limbs' (Shelley 1818: I, 97–98). The reviewer in *La Belle Assemblée* quoted it to 'shew the excellence of its style and language' (1818: 141). Walter Scott (1771–1832) also considered it 'an excellent specimen of the style and manner of the work' (1818: 615). Even *The British Critic* includes it, while Croker displays it as 'a very favourable specimen of the vigour of fancy and language with which this work is written' (*British Critic* 1818: 434; Croker 1818: 382). Mary Shelley later writes that when she started work on *Frankenstein*, she began with the words, '*It was on a dreary night of November*' (Shelley 1969: 10). There is no reason to contradict this claim, or to deny that the month and its concomitant cold, wet weather have superb atmospheric value. Yet her timing had other incidental advantages. It adds an element of probability to the preservation of the creature's decency. As he tells Victor, '"Before I had quitted your apartment, on a sensation of cold, I had covered myself with some clothes"' (Shelley 1818: II, 34). Mary Shelley clearly thought this through. However, she might not have consciously calculated that, since he acquires these clothes at the beginning of winter, the creature has time to become accustomed to wearing them before the coming of warmer weather renders them less necessary. An author who so rigorously expunges references to students' pantaloons might wish to avoid close consideration of the creature's attire—or what lies beneath.

People engaged in adapting *Frankenstein* for media involving visual representation do not have this luxury. In the earliest dramatisations, the counsel of perfection was to dress the creature, explain to the audience how he came to be dressed, and reassure the audience that he would be dressed on his first appearance. All three tasks are performed elegantly, while respecting Mary Shelley's choice of weather, in a Victorian edition of Peake's *Presumption:* the hero declares, 'I have clothed the inanimate mass, lest the chilly air should quench the spark of life newly infused' (Act I, scene 3) (Peake [1883?]: 6). The precedent of preserving the creature's modesty is still respected. In adaptations for media that permit prolonged and close-up views of the creature's construction in the laboratory, his genital area is generally covered or shadowed. In *Frankenstein: The Graphic Novel*, a publication designed for educational purposes, the creature, otherwise naked, is considerately provided with a black leather loincloth: a frontal view shows a small wedge between his thighs, enough to suggest normal masculinity without inviting further speculation (Shelley 2008: 22). Curiosity about the creature's physique has, nevertheless, been fuelled by the scale on which Victor worked: 'As the minuteness of the parts formed a great hindrance to my speed, I resolved, contrary to my first intention, to make the being of a gigantic stature; that is to say, about eight feet in height, and proportionably large' (Shelley 1818: I, 90). Increasing his size makes the creature more terrifying, but musing on anatomical details might lead to the comic 'grotesque' rather than the tragic and horrific 'sublime' (*British Critic* 1818: 438). An extreme instance is the 20th Century Fox film *Young Frankenstein* (1974), directed by Mel Brooks, where the creature (Peter Boyle) is seven feet tall: Elizabeth (Madeline Kahn) and Igor (Marty Feldman) conclude that, since everything is in proportion, he is qualified to have a successful social life. Experiential proof of this hypothesis impels the lady to break into song. Croker, on the other hand, uses a grotesque comic reference to support his contention that the creature's size prevented any union with a human woman: 'none of Eve's daughters, not even the enormous Charlotte of the Variétés herself, would have suited this stupendous fantoccino'; he elucidates this allusion in a note at the foot of the page: 'In a parody of Werter, at the Variétés in Paris, the Charlotte is ludicrously corpulent' (1818: 381).[3]

This is not the only time *Frankenstein* is brought into direct contact with comic drama. Apart from allusions to Shakespeare, two eighteenth-century comedies are referenced, to widely differing effect.[4] Croker refers to a comedy to express his disquiet at the texts from which the creature derived his education: Volney's *Ruins of Empires, Paradise Lost, Plutarch's Lives,* and *The Sorrows of Werther* (See Shelley 1818: II, 77 and 99). *The British Critic* castigates this selection as an 'extraordinary stock of poetical theology, pagan biography, adulterous sentimentality, and atheistical jacobinism' (1818: 436). Croker, with less overt hostility, calls it 'the Greco-Anglico-Germanico-Gallico-Arabic library of a Swabian hut, which, if not numerous, was at least miscellaneous, and reminds us, in this particular, of Lingo's famous combination of historic characters—"Mahomet, Heliogabalus, Wat Tyler, and Jack the Painter"' (1818: 380). Lingo, a former country schoolmaster employed as a butler, was a well-known character in his day, invented by John O'Keefe (1747–1833) for his comic opera, *The Agreeable Surprise*, which was first performed in 1781. Although Croker's list does not appear in the script, Lingo certainly has a habit of alluding to ill-assorted quartets. Classical myth combines with Scripture and history when he parades his learning before the dairymaid: 'O Cowslip, the great old heroes perhaps you have never heard of, Homer, Moses, Hercules, or Wat Tyler?' (O'Keefe 1783: Act I, scene 1, 17). Later on, a lament over his low social status reveals an odd addition to his classical syllabus: 'have I studied Syntax, Cordery, Juvenal, and Tristram Shandy, to serve wine on my knee to a mighty cheesemonger!' (O'Keefe 1783: Act II, scene 4, 47–48).[5] Finally, reconciled to his lot, Lingo plans to celebrate the two marriages that compose the happy ending by writing a 'latin epitaph' (probably 'epithalamium') 'wherein I'll provoke the patronage of Cupid, Thomas a Becket, Sir Godfrey Kneller, and Helley O'Gabalus' (O'Keefe 1783: Act II, scene 4, 50).

In the light of these lists, Croker's implication that he is attacking the creature's syllabus solely because of its random nature appears to be disingenuous. The two names Croker records accurately are associated with dangerous political instability: Walter Tyler (1341–1381) was a leader of the Peasants' Revolt in the reign of Richard II; the Roman Emperor

Elagabalus (AD c. 203–222) indulged in exhibitions of 'vices and follies' whose 'inexpressible infamy surpasses that of any other age or country', and provoked his assassination (Gibbon 1776: I, 210). Of Croker's two additions, Mahomet can be explained as a representative of the 'Arabic' component of the creature's education; Jack the Painter, one of the many aliases of James Aitken (1752–1777), was a sinister figure whose crimes were still remembered 40 years after his hanging. A Scot by birth, he espoused the American cause in the Revolutionary War, which he attempted to win single-handedly by destroying British ships and supplies in a series of arson attacks on naval facilities in Bristol and Portsmouth.[6] The panic his activities aroused turned him into a nightmarish figure. The lawyer who opened the prosecution at his trial drew 'a Picture of national Horror' that would have taken place had his plan succeeded (Anon 1777). Aitken acknowledged, but repudiated, his dehumanisation: 'they think it monstrous, and horrible, and I do not know what, to attempt to burn the Dock at Portsmouth, not considering how many docks, and towns, and ships of ours, have been burned by their soldiers in America' (Aitken 1777: 11). Like Frankenstein's creature, Aitken read books that supporters of the establishment found dangerously subversive: his favourite, by the Unitarian Dr Richard Price (1723–1791), argued that 'if licentiousness has destroyed its thousands, despotism has destroyed its millions' (1776: 14). Consequently, Croker's comic reference challenges the rejection of decorum at its highest political level.

Victor's journey on the Thames with Clerval provides a less threatening cue for comedy: 'We saw Tilbury Fort, and remembered the Spanish armada' (Shelley 1818: III, 20). The *British Critic,* with no apparent motive beyond a routine attempt to lower the tone, enquires, 'how came they to forget Whiskerandos?' (1818: 436). Readers familiar with *The Critic: or, a Tragedy Rehearsed* (1779) by Richard Brinsley Sheridan (1751–1816) would remember Don Ferolo Whiskerandos as the romantic hero of *The Spanish Armada,* rehearsed within the play. He is in love with Tilburina, daughter of the governor of Tilbury Fort; his death, when he is killed in a duel with a Beefeater, is indeed unforgettable:

Whiskerandos. And Whiskerandos quits this bustling scene
For all eter—
Beefeater. –nity—He would have added, but stern death
Cut short his being and the noun at once! (Sheridan 1781: Act III, scene 1, 92)

Since the actor playing the Beefeater is too slow to pick up his cue, the sequence is repeated, increasing the hilarity of the already enraptured audience. Puff, the author, asks for it to be done a third time but Whiskerandos protests, 'I can't stay dying here all night', and exits (Sheridan 1781: 93). When the Beefeater begins a lament for his fallen foe, Puff tells him, 'Dear Sir, you needn't speak that speech as the body has walked off' (93). Like *Frankenstein,* the play has brought us into a world where the boundary between life and death has dissolved, but decorum requires extreme levity. The fact that Victor and Clerval are in no mood to remember Whiskerandos emphasises their tragic plight.

The endurance and versatility of the *Frankenstein* legacy proved its worth in practical terms when I faced a generic quandary of my own. The problem arose when I was co-directing an amateur production of *The Tamer Tamed* (1611) by John Fletcher (1579–1625), performed November 20–29, 2008, at the Progress Theatre, Reading, Berkshire. This comedy, a sequel to *The Taming of the Shrew* (c. 1590), is based on the premise that Shakespeare's apparently happy ending turned sour: the hero Petruchio, now a widower, has remarried, but his new bride is even more intransigent than her predecessor. Finally Petruchio, pretending her behaviour has killed him, is brought on in an open coffin. Instead of displaying penitence, she weeps only to display her regret that such a foolish wretch should have existed and takes comfort from having refused to have sexual relations with a man so unfit to breed. At this point Petruchio, realising that nothing will tame this shrew, offers her total submission. The scene gets its effect from the audience's appreciation of the dramatic irony arising from their knowledge that Petruchio is alive, a fact unknown to most of the characters on stage. In our performance, there were only two exceptions: the wife's unruffled demeanour made it clear that she had seen through his deception from the first; his best friend, Sophocles, kneeling by the coffin, gave vent to exaggerated sobs to cover the crescendo of Petruchio's protesting cries. Fletcher's text, however, presents a problem: Petruchio never mentions his intention of feigning death. If the audience think he is 'really' dead, they will stop laughing. So Petruchio should make some movement, visible to them but not to the other characters, as soon as possible. In order to reassure the audience that this is not simply due to the actor's failure to keep still, a stylised signal is required: if it triggers metatheatrical associations, so much the better. The coffin was placed downstage right (i.e. to the left of the stage as seen by the audience), with Petruchio's right hand hanging over the edge where the audience could see it. Then he twitched his fingers, just as Boris Karloff twitched the fingers of his right hand in the 1931 film to indicate that Frankenstein's creature was coming to life. Sophocles drew the audience's attention to Petruchio by seizing the hand and laying it on Petruchio's breast: his abruptness indicated disapproval at his friend's lack of control rather than grief at his death. We sent the audience home happy on those dreary nights in November: by deflecting inappropriately tragic possibilities towards farce, an allusion to *Frankenstein* had extended Mary Shelley's quest for decorum, albeit in a rather unexpected direction.

References like these seldom rely on the audience having read *Frankenstein*. Whether in passing glimpses or full-scale performances, *Frankenstein* often appears as a combination of Mary Shelley's work with previous adaptations. For example, *Victor Frankenstein* (20th Century Fox, 2015) owes much to long-established traditions of stage and screen: the laboratory assistant Igor, played by Daniel Radcliffe, is far more important, in terms of screen time and emotional impact, than the creature. Nevertheless, Max Landis' screenplay provides sophisticated variations on Shelley's original themes, some of them generating dark irony: the disastrous career of Inspector Turpin, who correctly deduces Victor's activities but is considered insane when he imparts his theories to his colleagues, mirrors the tragic dilemma of Shelley's Victor, unable to clear Justine or himself of murder charges by accusing his creature, because nobody would believe him. Some of the most successful comic treatments focus on the fact that Frankenstein's creature, as created by Mary Shelley, was originally not only innocent but positively benevolent, needing nothing but reciprocated affection to make him completely happy. His achievement of this goal has been celebrated in various versions of Mel Brooks' *Young Frankenstein*, including the musical being performed at the time of writing at The Garrick Theatre, London, where it is creating much hilarity among its audiences. Two less direct imitations of Frankenstein's creature, who have both inherited toned-down versions of Boris Karloff's makeup, are Lurch, who first appeared in cartoons by Charles Addams (1912–1988), and Herman Munster: they graduated via television situation comedy, *The Addams Family* (ABS, 1964–1966) and *The Munsters* (CBS, 1964–1966), to film. They share some important characteristics: as butler and paterfamilias, respectively, each has a secure place in a warm and loving, albeit somewhat eccentric, family; above all, neither has ever realised that there is anything unusual about his appearance. The importance of this crucial difference from Shelley's creature is summed up by a moment in Carel

Struycken's performance as Lurch in Paramount and Orion's 1991 film, *The Addams Family*. Its closing section, when all is restored to happy normality (or what passes for it in the Addams household), begins with the arrival of some children at the door on their annual Halloween 'trick or treat' outing: as soon as Lurch opens it, they scream and run, leaving him peering into the darkness after them with a faintly bewildered smile. The sequence displays the excellent comic timing appropriate to a box office hit, but also provides a quietly eloquent commentary on the central pathos of Shelley's novel.

NOTES

1. On both points, see Stabler, Jane (1994), 'The Genesis of Byron's "Hints from Horace"', *Translation and Literature*, 3, 47–65.
2. For a similar threat to classical critical paradigms, and its relationship to *Frankenstein*, see Weiner, Jesse (2015), 'Lucretius, Lucan, and Mary Shelley's *Frankenstein*', in *Classical Traditions in Science Fiction*, ed. Brett M. Rogers and Benjamin Eldon Stevens, Oxford: Oxford University Press, 46–74.
3. Croker alludes to Duval, Georges and Rochefort-Luçay, Claude-Louis-Marie de, (1817), *Werther, ou les Égaremens d'un coeur sensible*, Paris: J.-N. Barba.
4. For Shakespeare's *Tempest*, see Scott, 617, and Croker, 380; for *The Taming of the Shrew*, see *British Critic*, 433.
5. 'Cordery' refers to Mathurin Cordier (1479–1564), author of a much-reprinted Latin textbook; see Cordier, Mathurin (1608), *Colloquiorum Scholasticorum Libri Quatuor*, London: [R. Braddock].
6. See Warner, Jessica (2004), *John the Painter: Terrorist of the American Revolution*, New York: Thunder's Mouth Press.

WORKS CITED

Aitken, James. 1777. *A Short Account of the Motives Which Determined the Man, Called John the Painter; and Justification of his Conduct; Written by Himself, and Sent to His Friend, Mr. A. Tomkins, with a Request to Publish it After His Execution*. London: John Williams.

Anon. 1777. *The Whole Trial of John the Painter, for Setting Fire to the Rope-House at Portsmouth, Which Came on at the Assizes Held at Winchester, on Thursday Last, the 6th of March, 1777*. (Broadside.)

Cordier, Mathurin. 1608. *Colloquiorum Scholasticorum Libri Quatuor*. London: R. Braddock.

Cox, Jeffrey N., ed. 1992. *Seven Gothic Dramas, 1789–1825*. Athens: Ohio University Press.

Croker, John Wilson. 1818. *Quarterly Review*, vol. 18, Anonymous review of *Frankenstein*, Art. V, 379–385.

Duval, Georges, and Claude-Louise-Marie de Rochefort-Luçay. 1817. *Werther, ou les Égaremens d'un coeur sensible*. Paris: J.-N. Barba.

Gibbon, Edward. 1776. *The History of the Decline and Fall of the Roman Empire*, 6 vols. Dublin: Hallhead.

Hall, Mordaunt. 1931. Review of *Frankenstein*, Directed by James Whale. *New York Times*, December 5. http://www.nytimes.com/movie/review?res=9901 E5D6143DEE32A25756C0A9649D946094D6CF

Horace. 1783. *Q. Horatii Flacci Epistola ad Pisones, De Arte Poetica. The Art of Poetry: An Epistle to the Pisos. Translated from Horace. With Notes. By George Colman*. London: T. Cadell.

Johnson, Samuel. 1785. *A Dictionary of the English Language*, 2 vols, London: J.F. and C. Rivington, L. Davis, T. Payne, T. Longman, B. Law and 21 others.

La Belle Assemblée 1818. 2nd Series, vol. 17 (March 1818), Anonymous Review of *Frankenstein*, 139–142.

Levine, George. 1975. Review of Christopher Small, *Mary Shelley's "Frankenstein": Tracing the Myth*, University of Pittsburgh Press, 1973, and James Rieger, ed., *Frankenstein* by Mary Shelley, Bobbs-Merill, 1974. *The Wordsworth Circle* 6(3): 208–212.

Mellor, Anne K. 1989. *Mary Shelley: Her Life, Her Fiction, Her Monsters*. New York/London: Routledge.

O'Keefe, John. 1783. *The Agreeable Surprise: A Comic Opera, in Two Acts*. Dublin: Sold by the Booksellers.

Peake, Richard Brinsley. 1883?. *Frankenstein. A Romantic Drama, in Three Acts*, Dicks' Standard Plays, No. 431. London: John Dicks.

Price, Richard. 1776. *Observations on the Nature of Civil Liberty, the Principles of Government, and the Justice and Policy of the War with America*. 3rd ed. London: T. Cadell.

Scott, Walter. 1818. Remarks on *Frankenstein, or the Modern Prometheus; A Novel*, *Blackwood's Edinburgh Magazine* 2(12): 613–620.

Shelley, Mary Wollstonecraft. 1818. *Frankenstein; or, the Modern Prometheus. In Three Volumes*. London: Lackington, Hughes, Harding, Mavor, & Jones.

———. 1969. *Frankenstein or The Modern Prometheus*, Edited with an Introduction by M. K. Joseph. London: Oxford University Press.

———. 1980–1988. *The Letters*, ed. Betty T. Bennett, 3 vols., 1980–1988, Baltimore/London: Johns Hopkins University Press.

———. 1982. *Frankenstein: Or the Modern Prometheus.* Edited with Variant Readings, an Introduction, and Notes, James Rieger. Chicago/London: Chicago University Press.

———. 2008. *Frankenstein: The Graphic Novel, Original Text Version,* Artists: Jason Cobley, Declan Shalvey, Jason Cardy, Kat Nicholson, Terry Wiley and Jon Howard, Litchborough, Towcester: Classical Comics Ltd.

———. (with Percy Bysshe Shelley). 2009. *Frankenstein or the Modern Prometheus, the Original Two-Volume Novel of 1816–1817 from the Bodleian Library Manuscripts,* ed. Charles E. Robinson. New York: Vintage Books.

Shelley, Percy Bysshe. 1832. Continuation of the Shelley Papers. On 'Frankenstein'. *The Athenaeum Journal of English and Foreign Literature, Science, and the Fine Arts.* London, No. 263, 730.

Sheridan, Richard Brinsley. 1781. *The Critic or a Tragedy Rehearsed.* London: T. Becket.

Stabler, Jane. 1994. The Genesis of Byron's "Hints from Horace". *Translation and Literature* 3: 47–65.

Stevick, Philip. 1979. *Frankenstein* and Comedy. In *The Endurance of 'Frankenstein': Essays on Mary Shelley's Novel,* ed. George Levine and U.C. Knoepflmacher, 221–239. Berkeley/Los Angeles/London: University of California Press.

The British Critic. 1818. New Series, vol. 9, Anonymous Review of *Frankenstein,* Art. XII, 432–438.

The Critical Review: Or, Annals of Literature. 1765. Vol. 19, Anonymous Review of *The Castle of Otranto,* Art. VII, 50–51.

The Edinburgh Magazine, and Literary Miscellany. 1818. 2nd series, vol. 2, Anonymous Review of *Frankenstein,* 249–253.

Walpole, Horace. 1764. *The Castle of Otranto, A Story.* London: Thomas Lownds.

———. 1765. *The Castle of Otranto, A Gothic Story.* 2nd ed. London: William Bathoe and Thomas Lownds.

Warner, Jessica. 2004. *John the Painter: Terrorist of the American Revolution.* New York: Thunder's Mouth Press.

Weiner, Jesse. 2015. Lucretius, Lucan, and Mary Shelley's *Frankenstein.* In *Classical Traditions in Science Fiction,* ed. Brett M. Rogers and Benjamin Eldon Stevens, 46–74. Oxford: Oxford University Press.

CHAPTER 7

Monstrous, Mortal Embodiment and Last Dances: *Frankenstein* and the Ballet

Carol Margaret Davison

> [T]he earth is a tomb, the gaudy sky a vault, we but walking corpses.
> *Mary Shelley*, 'On Ghosts' (1824)

Deep-seated anxieties about corporeality—the body's corruptibility given its vulnerability to disease and inevitable death and decay—drive Mary Shelley's *Frankenstein*. Indeed, we might label this novel's engine corpsoreality, which may be defined as experiencing one's own body as Other, an experience precipitated by our awareness, fear, and anxiety about being in a body that, despite major scientific, medical, and technological advancements and interventions, is always, and remains, subject to disease and mortality. As Todd May perceptively writes, '[o]ne is mortal not only at the end of one's life, but all throughout it' (2009: 7). The ultimate terror underpinning corpsoreality is that we are all, as Mary Shelley's opening epigraph to this chapter underscores, walking—or, in the case of the ballet,

C. M. Davison (✉)
Department of English Language, Literature and Creative Writing,
University of Windsor, Windsor, ON, Canada

© The Author(s) 2018
C. M. Davison, M. Mulvey-Roberts (eds.), *Global Frankenstein*,
Studies in Global Science Fiction,
https://doi.org/10.1007/978-3-319-78142-6_7

dancing—corpses, a terror exacerbated since Shelley's era by the fear that the corpse may mark a definitive end point to human existence, shutting down all possibilities of a spiritual afterlife. While this experience of one's mortal body as Other is projected onto a terrorising monstrous doppelgänger in *Frankenstein*, it is internalised in body-horror films of the late twentieth century—slasher, splatter, and 'torture porn'—where the *human* body is perceived as monstrous and alien, embodiment itself being perceived as terrorising, mortality writ in the flesh in gruesome and spectacular fashion. As this chapter examines at greater length and in relation to several provocative and contemporary dance choreographies of *Frankenstein*, this idea sits at the heart of Shelley's novel as Victor, despite marshalling and combining 'old' and 'new' scientific ideas and technologies with an eye to defeating the disease and death that claimed his mother's life, produces an emotionally bereft, uncanny neomort death machine, positioned between life and corpse who becomes, in Victor's own chilling, Gothically resonant words, 'my own vampire, my own spirit let loose from the grave, and forced to destroy all that was dear to me' (57). In a quintessentially Gothic text featuring a deftly manipulated monster-maker dynamic powered by the Freudian death drive, Victor learns that the horror of physical death may be reversed but only at tremendous cost and not, ultimately, with the desired result. Idealised immortality remains an elusive dream, with mortality and memento mori closing off the work.

Dance/balletic adaptations of *Frankenstein*—an animated body/corpse-centric and embodiment-aware novel—over the last few decades furnish fascinating material for cultural analysis given the centrality of that art form's primary medium, the body. *Frankenstein* and the ballet share much in common given that the dancer's sublime body may be said to be artificial and unnatural, usually non-self-selecting, like Frankenstein's, which is not formed at birth but painstakingly and 'mechanically' reproduced over years. One could argue further that the balletic body is also, similar to that of Frankenstein's monster, uncanny: while the latter is identifiably and familiarly human in terms of his component parts yet excessive/transgressive/sublime given his height and his embodiment of living death, the ballet dancer's body is identifiably and familiarly human yet sublime/uncanny in its ability to transgress the boundaries of natural, physical, human movement. *Frankenstein* and choreography are also a natural fit because corpsoreality is rendered particularly powerfully in dance/ballet where the body, classified by some dance theorists and feminists as deformed, is perceived by its audience as ideal and epitomising the height of health and athleticism.

Recent cultural studies (Turin 1994; Young 1999) have tangentially considered the connections between Mary Shelley's *Frankenstein* and dance. Gothic club dancing, for example, has been provocatively (and humorously) described by Tricia Henry Young as being 'automaton-like' (89), constituting a contemporary 'sort of *danse macabre*,[1] [whose practitioners] ... resemble the tormented or dying ... often bring[ing] to mind images of Frankenstein awakening, condemned prisoners being electrocuted, or victims of electroshock treatment' (82). A connection might not be readily in evidence between *Frankenstein* and more professional and/ or classical types of dance/ballet given the unwieldy awkwardness of Shelley's eight-foot-tall monster constructed of numerous disparate bodily appendages and organs. When one considers that narrative's focus on corpsoreality, however, it makes sense that Mary Shelley's thanatocentric, iconic novel has inspired numerous ballets over the past few decades: even those individuals possessing culturally idealised, sublime, and athletic bodies are subject to disease and death, the transformation being all the more poignant and tragic by the contrast.

It is especially noteworthy that choreographers have invoked the *Frankenstein*-monster motif and/or elected to stage adaptations of *Frankenstein* during an era characterised by intense death denial that has witnessed the traumatic AIDS crisis, alongside radical developments in choreographic theory relating to the dancing, hetero-normative body. From Wayne Eagling's one-act ballet with London's The Royal Ballet (1985), William Forsythe's *The Questioning of Robert Scott* created with Ballett Frankfurt (1986) and his *You made me a monster* undertaken with The Forsythe Company (2005), to Rick Darnell's 'Brides of Frankenstein' with the High-Risk Group in San Francisco (1991), Estefania Miranda's *Frankenstein* with the Konzert Theater Bern (2014), and Liam Scarlett's recent critically controversial three-act work co-produced by London's Royal Ballet and the San Francisco Ballet (2016), Frankenstein's monster, sitting at the crossroads of monster and corpse, the beautiful and the sublime, ability and disability, and male and female, has been used to engage a broad variety of embodiment issues, including sex/gender identification, the nature and development of the aesthetic balletic body, and the uncontrollably 'monstrous', 'queer', and 'disabled' aspects of human corporeality/corpsoreality as culturally perceived and constructed. As these varied choreographies evidence, probably because of rather than despite our extreme death-denying culture where we are witnessing the proliferation of medical/scientific/technological interventions to combat impending death, alongside our saturation in sensationalised body-horror and death-by-proxy entertainment, *Frankenstein* forces us to confront the fact that what our society considers monstrous about the body—disease, death, disability, decay, and many forms of desire, especially sexual—is but a defamiliarised and demonised form of that which is natural and quintessentially human. In the face of these phenomena and their related debates, *Frankenstein* has shown itself, at its bicentenary, to be extremely adaptable and socially relevant in the hands of adept, culturally aware, thought-provoking, and boundary-pushing choreographers who have crafted the popular medieval *danse macabre* anew.

*   *   *

Like the ghost and the monster, the corpse does cultural work that, tethered to the changing needs of the living, both challenges and reifies certain ideologies and belief systems. The corpses that litter the landscape in Mary Shelley's Enlightenment-grounded novel *Frankenstein* must be considered within their socio-historical, political, and cultural contexts. At the point of that work's production in 1818, the cultural terrain was extremely fertile: with the advent of secular modernity, the putative triumph of Reason, and the unsettling of religious certainties about the existence of God, the soul, and the afterlife, we became alienated from an earlier familiarity with death, more anxious and uncertain about mortality, loss, mourning, and memorialisation. Death became defamiliarised, a process that Elisabeth Bronfen describes as 'a retreat' that involved 'a double gesture of denial and mystification' (1992: 86). The resulting deeply entrenched cultural schizophrenia has been cogently theorised by renowned thanatologist Philippe Ariès: in tandem with the denial and deferral of the death of the self, we recognised and even celebrated the death of the Other.

Our mixed post-Enlightenment sentiments of denial, dread, and desire in relation to death were then projected onto the corpse, which came to serve, as Alan Bewell has noted, 'as the nexus of all spiritual imagery … [as] all narratives about life after death can be reduced to and derive their formal organisation from a primary confrontation, which every culture and every individual repeats, with the bodies of the dead' (1989: 190). Positioned at the threshold of the (possible) next world where it signalled the paradoxically dreaded-yet-desired annihilation of our individuality, subjectivity, and agency (Quigley 1996: 9) and signposted a (possible) secular cul-de-sac, the corpse became the 'supreme signifier for anything from human destiny and its redemption to life's meaninglessness' (Webster Goodwin and Bronfen 1993: 17). Bound up with the exercise and abuse of political power, the corpse also tapped the deep Romantic well of affect to different ends. It became crucial to the expression and exploration of subjectivity while also serving as a contested site and figurative battlefield for various ideas and debates, particularly those relating to medical science and religion and its moral authority.

In the pages of Gothic fiction, a novelistic sub-genre whose rise was concurrent with this cultural shift, readers engaged with death-related subject matter considered too macabre, controversial, or sensitive, and indulged dark death-related fantasies and fears. An intellectual collision was therein registered between pre-Enlightenment and Enlightenment belief systems and ideas relating, among other things, to death. Notably, the revered and reviled corpse—the uncanny subject/object often 'kept in remembrance' (Quigley 1996: 11)—refused to stay buried in the pages of Gothic literature where it was 'imbued with otherworldly powers' (18). Generally repressed anxieties and desires were also granted expression and projected in the Gothic—as exemplified by *Frankenstein*—onto the abjected *female* corpse (Bronfen 1992: 86) that served as a grotesque Bakhtinian reminder of physical human origins (birth) and endings (death). As Dale Townshend has argued, drawing on the work of Coral Ann Howells, the Gothic became 'a socially symbolic site of mourning' that permitted and promoted the expression of the 'more macabre realities of corporeal decomposition and religious insecurity'. It allowed for the expression of what Townshend has nicely characterised as a 'negated grief' that ranged beyond what tame neo-Classical proprieties dictated and allowed (2008: 89).

A culturally and historically transitional text that registers a collision between pre-Enlightenment and Enlightenment ideas about, and attitudes towards, death, mourning, and the afterlife, Mary Shelley's *Frankenstein* is an exemplary work of Gothic fiction that evidences the power and poignancy of the multivalent corpse. On the heels of his mother's sudden death from disease, a traumatised Victor Frankenstein, then a student of natural philosophy, declaring that he and his family should be done with grieving (1994: 27), turns his attention to freeing the world from death and disease. He is galvanised by thoughts of the tremendous gratitude of his new 'species' should he be successful in 'bestow[ing] animation upon lifeless matter, ... [and] in process of time ... renew[ing] life where death had apparently devoted the body to corruption' (36). To this end, using his 'profane fingers' to disturb 'the tremendous secrets of the human frame' in his 'workshop of filthy creation' (36), Victor fabricates a macabre, fleshly monster from a multitude of putrefying corpses collected from the charnel house, the dissecting room, and the slaughter house (83). Setting aside some key elements overlooked by critics—namely, the horrifying, Gothic aspects of the monster's inter-species physiology and Victor's experiments with torturing 'the living animal to animate the life-less clay' (36), acts that, literally, come back to haunt his dreams (123) and that influence later works like H. G. Wells' *The Island of Doctor Moreau* (1896)—it is important to note Victor's incredulity and conscious/ unconscious drives in response to the horror of the maternal corpse. Indeed, a paradox obtains with regard to the abjected maternal corpse given the mother's traditional and idealised associations with attachment, interdependence, and nurturance. In stark contrast to Edgar Allan Poe's sublimely configured beautiful female corpse, a figure fetishised by the male Anglo-Romantics who preceded him (Praz 1951: 209), the idealised, feminised, and submissive creature obsessively crafted while Elizabeth is ignored is radically transformed upon his birth and animation. Conception becomes misconception in what might be characterised as an uncanny encounter of the queerest kind. Victor's beautiful, feminised, and able creature morphs into a sublime, disabled, and disgustingly horrifying monster. While Victor may be initially blind to the grotesque realities of his monomaniacal, transgressive enterprise to reverse nature's and God's laws around corruptible corporeality, the awakening of his eight-foot-tall, abjected and uncanny monster issues a harrowing wake-up call.

Despite Victor's persistent myopia about the lessons of his own narra-tive, his flaunted lack of superstition and disbelief in the metaphysical and supernatural (Shelley 1994: 33), in combination with his disrespect for the dead—he considers the church yard as 'merely the receptacle of bodies deprived of life' (34)—resonate profoundly with the attentive reader. The same holds true for his mother's exemplary good, 'calm' (27), Christian death that evidences her lifelong 'fortitude and benignity' as she 'resign[s herself] cheerfully to death, and ... indulge[s] a hope of meeting [her fam-ily] in another world' (26). As this cataclysmic primal scene makes clear, the rational, empirically minded Victor Frankenstein and his Christian mother stand, figuratively speaking, at opposite ends of the grave in terms of their beliefs about death and the afterlife. In keeping with his father's worldview, Victor's homicidal monster fails to herald any liberating transcendence. He remains, instead, a physically grotesque and truly ter-rifying memento mori signpost who, ironically and tragically given his unique and unprecedented physiology and ontology (a subject upon which he meditates at great and anxiety-inducing length), epitomises the popular double-edged Gothic nightmare of fleshly, imprisoning, and ago-nising mortality/immortality—an uncanny monster of mortality who may, himself, be unable to die.

*   *   *

As Melanie Bales has noted, a tension—that some have called an antin-omy—has long existed between narrative and movement in ballet (2013: 180). The degree to which the *content* of a ballet—its storyline—should be prioritised by the choreographer has been the subject of much debate, especially in literary ballets like *Frankenstein*. The most accomplished and powerful choreographies of Shelley's novel in recent decades have not been straightforward plot-driven adaptations but those that select one or several of its psychological/philosophical aspect(s) or key motif(s) and develop them within a dance-theatre performance. Notably, the choreog-raphers I assess here who have successfully adapted *Frankenstein* have been considered mavericks in their own right. Like Shelley and her own scientist-protagonist, their works often constitute 'monstrous' formal hybrids that innovatively combine older and newer forms of dance while challenging traditional idea(l)s about the balletic/dance body, including notions about its gendering, perceived disability, and conventional range and style of movement. These daring choreographers have also used *Frankenstein* in a meta-balletic way to theorise about and push the bound-aries of dance-theatre to meditate on the pains and pleasures, freedoms and limitations, and abilities and disabilities, of embodiment.

Despite being separated by three decades, the works of Wayne Eagling and Liam Scarlett are narrative adaptations that achieve varying degrees of success as they strive to capitalise on Shelley's rich motifs and the psycho-logical complexities of Victor Frankenstein's relationship with his monster. While Scarlett's adaptation is vastly superior in terms of its critical under-standing and interpretation of *Frankenstein*, both works fail ultimately to capture and convey Shelley's foremost innovative contribution to the Gothic monster tale—namely, the monster's traumatic, emotionally pow-erful, and highly philosophical narrative. Eagling's representation of Victor Frankenstein's laboratory and scientific experiments is minimal to the point of comedy and unique in failing to capture or capitalise on the grotesque anatomical nature of his scientific enterprise. In adherence to George Balanchine's promotion of non-narrative ballets, Eagling produces a tame and lame, very low-budget ballet very loosely based on Shelley's novel that revolves around an unremarkable, quintessentially Romantic love triangle— expressed in the form of several equally unremarkable pas de deux (balletic duets)—involving Victor, his notably giant, looming white monster, and the diminutive Elizabeth, with Elizabeth at the centre. At ballet's end, after an increasingly frenzied pas de deux involving Elizabeth and the monster that results in her death, the monster lays her down and kisses her. When Victor intervenes, the monster weakly attempts to kill him before, in violation of Shelley's plot, committing suicide and being laid alongside Elizabeth. The ballet concludes with the unremorseful Victor, victorious and seemingly divine as he floats away over both corpses before briefly pausing beside the ballet's musician seated on a platform above the stage.

The subject of radically divergent reviews, Liam Scarlett's more recent co-produced adaptation of *Frankenstein* reproduces this triangulated relationship in a notably different format with the emphasis being placed on the unravelling of Victor's cherished domestic life following the animation of his monster. Scarlett has done his literary critical homework, incorporating several lovely touches into this meta-fictional, formally hybridised ballet. Alongside a more realistic rendering of Victor's scientific/medical experiments, the death of Mary Shelley's mother, Mary Wollstonecraft, is invoked in the death in childbirth of Victor's mother who goes into labour during the dance sequence celebrating Victor's engagement to Elizabeth. Similarly, the novel's representation of Victor's mother's death as the catalyst for the animation of the monster is underscored in this ballet as a guilt- and grief-stricken Victor, prior to undertaking his act of skilfully re-sectioning a sheet-draped corpse, removes his mother's cameo from his pocket, tenderly pressing it to his chest. Signifying and celebrating the enduring power of Shelley's novel and the written word, Scarlett cleverly weaves a resonant book motif into each of the major scenes. The book circulates from scene to scene, and reader to reader, transmuting from an intimate diary shared between Victor and Elizabeth (with echoes of the romance between Mary and Percy Shelley who exchanged books and kept detailed reading lists), to the anatomy students' notebooks and Victor's scientific journal. In this manner does Scarlett suggest that the novel, *Frankenstein*, has been widely circulated, assuming an afterlife of its own that spans and defies time.

It is in his objectification and Othering of the monster, however, that Scarlett rejects Mary Shelley's portrait, electing not to explore the ambivalent, dysfunctional relationship between the monster and his maker. He also subverts a crucial aspect of that paternal relationship by portraying the monster—rather than Victor—fleeing the birth room on the heels of Victor's rejection of the monster's embrace in a problematically hurried and confusing scene. Zero sympathy is generated for the monster who is, instead, manipulated to emblematise—significantly and symbolically— both queer desire and the merciless inevitability of death. The triangulated relationship between Victor, his monster, and Elizabeth casts Victor and his creature in a secret, monstrous, and homosexual relationship in Ingolstadt that literally shadows and threatens Victor's heterosexual bond and marital engagement back home. In an anguished and impassioned solo performance following Victor's passionate return to Elizabeth, the monster emerges from out of the shadows. He revels in his body and physicality throughout this sequence, his hand reaching downwards to clasp his groin whilst clutching Victor's notebook. Thus does Scarlett render explicit the idea of a homosexual union.

This taboo relationship is fittingly portrayed in combination with the Christian medieval *danse macabre* (dance with death), whereby Death becomes a personified, class-levelling reminder of our ultimate fate prior to divine judgement. This image of Death—notably played by the monster—as a dancing memento mori is suggested and enacted in various pas de deux during the atmospheric *Schauerroman*-infused bloody wedding celebration of Victor and Elizabeth that follows. With the newlyweds bathed in white light while darkness enshrouds the guests and stage, the ghosts of Justine and William quickly but forebodingly enter and exit the scene in a brief *danse des ombres* (dance of the shades). A series of deaths ensue: on the heels of Victor's father's stress-related death subsequent to the marriage ceremony, the monster strangles Henry Clerval, thereafter seductively inviting the horrified Elizabeth to dance. The initial intimacy rapidly transforms into a violent and frenzied pas de deux that concludes with her murder.

Thus does Scarlett's rendition of *Frankenstein* piggyback on what some critics have described as the quintessential queerness of *Frankenstein* where two obsessive masculine figures engage in 'a debilitating and self-destructive form of narcissism' (Haggerty 2016: 117) while advancing Lee Edelman's controversial claim (2004) that queerness, in its non-reproductive aspect, is often a popular cultural figuration of the death

drive of the social order. Following Elizabeth's murder, an enraged, grieving Victor faces off in a tormented pas de deux with his vengeful monster.
Briefly pointing the gun at his creature, Victor turns it upon himself after
spying Elizabeth's corpse, signalling his inability and unwillingness to live
without her. The monster's subsequent violent raptures involve him sitting atop Victor's corpse, manipulating his maker's hands to stroke his
face in imagined paternal/queer fondness. In a loaded, final symbolic gesture, the monster returns the book to the stage, the pages falling on to the
floor signalling, simultaneously, the end of the tale and the imminent end
of the monster. With the backdrop transformed into a distant volcano, the
ballet concludes as the monster walks suicidally towards it.

Scarlett's intriguing but problematic representation of a conjunction
between homosexuality and death in *Frankenstein* dates back at least a
quarter century to Rick Darnell's 'Brides of Frankenstein' (1991), a social
activist adaptation of *Frankenstein* with the High-Risk Group in San
Francisco. Darnell, noted for his innovative artistry and activism, 'descended
from the Judson choreographers who challenged assumptions of dance
theatre in the '60s, expanding dance possibilities to include pedestrian
movement, theatrical gesture, and political commentary' (Kaplan 1989).
His dance company, whose name 'declared openly the status of its members as gay and, physically or metaphorically, HIV positive' (Gere 2004:
148), debuted in San Francisco in 1986 in an atmosphere of AIDS anxiety
and fear. To openly identify as gay in the 1980s and in such a manner, 'was
a radical act in theatrical dance performance, even several years into the
official epidemic, especially in light of the company's equally radical performance of gayness and effeminacy, so long proscribed from the U.S.
theatrical stage' (152). Darnell's highly acrobatic, gender-subversive, and
insurgent 'Brides of Frankenstein' featured five men garbed solely in tutus,
prom dresses, and high tops, their genitals bared. This ballet simultaneously challenged notions of the traditional balletic body, movement, and
performance while offering a singular and provocative response to the dev-
astations of the 1980s' AIDS epidemic and the tremendous vulnerability of
the marginalised and demonised LGBTQ+ community who became, in
Darnell's arresting words, 'married to death' (Wright 1991). In such a
manner during such an era was corpsoreality queered, emblematised by the
potentially fatally diseased homosexual body as figured by the feminised
bride(s) of Frankenstein, this identification being notably in keeping with
the idea of the traditionally abjected, socially marginalised female body.
Defying the Othering of that queer body and in their own manic, campy

playful *danse macabre*, the High-Risk group members raged and revelled in their physicality. Darnell's statement was, like those of other gay dancer/choreographer-activists of the 1980s who responded to the AIDS crisis and a society that demonised homosexuals, profound and powerful.

As Gerald Siegmund (2011) has noted, the unique, post-structuralist works of maverick American dancer-choreographer William Forsythe, long-term Director of the Frankfurt Ballet (1984–2004) and The Forsythe Company (2005–2015)—considered the anti-Christ of ballet by at least one detractor—offer what is arguably the most intensive, extensive, and experimental engagement with the Frankenstein-monster trope in the canon of dance choreography. Forsythe's engagement with corpsoreality ranges across his oeuvre, from his initial conception of the Frankenstein monster in *Die Befragung des Robert Scott* [*The Questioning of Robert Scott*] (1986) where the explorer Robert Scott freezes to death in the Arctic ice and Victor Frankenstein's monster appears, through to his representation of the distorted and diseased body in his poignant dance performance-installation, *You made me a monster* (2005), an elegy in dance form for his dancer-wife Tracey-Kai Maier who died of ovarian cancer in the early 1990s.

Notably resonant with Victor Frankenstein's role as a revolutionary engaged in the revitalisation of dead bodies, Forsythe has been hailed by many as a visionary choreographer 'celebrated for revitalizing what many had dismissed as the dead idiom of ballet' (Groves 2012: 118), for 'rejuvenating an art form that had become ossified' (Spier 2011: 2). In his post-structuralist approach to ballet as a type of language, Forsythe rendered it less sacrosanct, a subject of interrogation. His formally hybrid choreographic experiments essentially combine multi-media with the styles of two maverick women dancer-choreographers: the contact improvisation of Trisha Brown (one of the founders of the Judson Dance Theatre and the postmodern ballet movement) and the Tanztheater (dance-theatre) of Pina Bausch. Although considered the heir to George Balanchine in the development of the *danse d'école*, Forsythe undermines Balanchine's rigid, straitjacketing ideas around ballet and the idealisation of certain aesthetic, putatively hetero-normative, and gendered body types. In the astute words of Melanie Bales, Forsythe 'celebrates the grotesque' (2013: 190). As Deborah Jowitt has reiterated in *The Village Voice*, Forsythe 'knocks the classically trained body off its Apollonian verticality' (Jowitt 2003), 'disorienting the [traditional balletic body's] classical line' in order 'to convey imperfection, disconnectedness, and alienation' (Jowitt 2010).

Forsythe's fascinating and broad-ranging use of the monster trope in relation to the process of choreography and the conception of the balletic body involves what might be called the expression and performance of the Gothic body. This entails exploring the liminalities of the body as it expresses and gestures towards the uncanny transitional state between life and death, being and non-being, ability and disability, and male and female as conceptualised and restricted in traditional ballet. Gothic body performance also involves probing the body's limits, especially the body in extremis, at the point of death or, in equivalent balletic terms, as it strives, even to the point of its own destruction, towards an unrealisable balletic ideal. This last aspect is especially in evidence in *The Questioning of Robert Scott* (1986), a conceptually innovative improvisational piece painstakingly developed over 15 years that served as the blueprint for the Forsythe style. In a Frankensteinian manner of studying the anatomy and physical coordination of the balletic body, Forsythe brilliantly 'connects the race to the South Pole in 1911–12 with the choreographer's quest for ideal forms, perfection, and new steps' (Siegmund 2011: 24), in the process experimenting with the traditional principles of ballet—movements, positions, and alignment of the limbs—that he pushes to their limits, segments, and rearranges. According to Siegmund, Forsythe portrays 'this newly devised body of the ballet dancer to be a Frankenstein's monster, … an entirely artificially assembled body' whose ultimate realisation proves impossible (25–6). Siegmund fails to note that the appearance of the monster in the Arctic ice also conjures up the image of the Promethean scientist, Victor Frankenstein, who likewise aims at unrealisable ideals.

On the heels of various choreographies of grief and fantasised resurrection after his wife's death, including *Of Any If And* (1995), the figure of Frankenstein resurfaces again in *You made me a monster* (2005), a dance performance-installation that integrates Forsythe's deep personal loss with the political issue of xenophobia, a subject about which the Ballett Frankfurt was simultaneously choreographing a ballet, *Alien/a(c)tion*, while his wife was undergoing cancer treatment in the early 1990s. At that time, as Forsythe explained in a *New York Times* interview, 'political refugees in Germany' from Turkey and elsewhere 'were being burned alive in their houses by gangs of ultranationalists' (Solway 2007). Thus does Forsythe, drawing parallels between a country's xenophobia and his wife's cancer, engage with the question of vulnerable bodies—bodies at risk—connecting real and imaginary monsters in the form of the actual terrors of cancer and cancer treatment with the imaginary terror of invaded and infected national space. With the aim of destabilising his audience by making them experience their own bodies, they are brought to a semi-lit stage occupied by a dozen tables laden with cardboard bone constructions, where they are directed, Frankenstein-like, to create a human skeleton by adding other bones to the sculptures and sketching the results. In a type of visuo-sonic choreography, dancers emerge who undertake contorted movements while creating tortured, computer-generated soundscapes, including howls of despair and anguish, contingent on the placement of the sculptures. They thereafter move to the front of the stage as agonising graphic text written by Forsythe detailing his wife's medical treatment and demise is projected onto the screen behind. In such manner does Forsythe bring his audience into a type of *danse macabre* performance piece, erasing the boundary between the living audience and dancers, and the once suffering, now deceased but inspirational love object.

Firmly in the dance-theatre tradition and following on from the grief work undertaken in Forsythe's *You made me a monster*, Estefania Miranda's *Frankenstein* with the Konzert Theater Bern (2014) is a quintessentially twenty-first-century choreography in that it extends Victor Frankenstein's thanatophobia and bereavement to a broader cultural level. In Miranda's more distilled, focused type of psychomachia chronicling the Frankenstein-monster relationship, Victor becomes a grieving Everyman. Victor's scientific study is engendered by the primal scene/Ur-trauma of his mother's death, his obsessive interest becoming, as the voice-over describes it, 'habit forming'. The ballet's opening image of Victor holding his dead mother, her body and head wrapped in a black lace veil, tenderly and powerfully captures Mary Shelley's suggestion about the catalyst for Victor's anatomical experimentation. This image is highlighted in a large circular mirror at centre stage that shatters, after which the music commences. Thus does Miranda subvert Jacques Lacan's conception of the mirror stage as a child's first realisation of his/her status as an individual distinct from the mother? The image of Victor maternally cradling his black-veiled mother highlights a different, more symbiotic sense of self-identity, one that inextricably links the child to the mother in a notably inter-generational bond. This idea is reinforced by Victor's physical entry up and along the diagonal platform on the left hand side of the stage, dragging the corpse of his mother behind him, before pulling her down onto the stage proper. Victor is thereafter showcased as a melancholic man in mourning, dancing with manic grief.

In response to this loss, Victor resists bereavement, as he does in the novel, trying instead to gain control over death by way of knowledge and medical science. His manic voice-over betrays the true nature of his desperate, anxious, monomaniacal pursuit. His painstakingly rational and scientific observations about the physical processes that occur just before and after the moment of death—the body loses oxygen while the brain shuts down, bacteria attacks the cells, and the process of decomposition commences—fail to reveal anything about death that might alleviate his sense of loss and bereavement. This clinical description conflicts with his agitated and agonised movement. Indeed, his detailed descriptions of the unnatural world created by his experiments sound like the ravings of a madman and are inflected with the supernatural:

> But now, nothing is at is was before. It's as if the order of things has gone into reverse. The sun no longer goes down. Night is no longer dark. An apple that used to fall to the earth now flies upwards. When uttering a phrase, you hear yourself talking in a strange, foreign language. Houses, living people, rivers climb up mountains and trees, roots move skywards. Birds are chewing in the basement like rats and rats are circling high above the city.

The *danse macabre* in Miranda's choreography is thus centred on Victor's dance with grief and debilitating loss, which transmogrifies into a type of physical and scientific struggle to gain mastery over the forces of life and death. This is beautifully suggested in the form of the mother figure who, following on Victor's afore-cited words about everything moving into reverse, casts off her black winding sheet to emerge in a white spandex costume of mummy-like gauze. She then moves behind Victor, animating—essentially ghosting—his actions as he works to resurrect the dead who likewise emerge onto the stage in similar mummy-like outfits (see Fig. 7.1). Victor expends some time marshalling these energies prior to the birth of his monster who is clothed—perhaps reflecting the catalysing forces of death and madness that motivate him—in a white spandex outfit resembling both a winding sheet and a straitjacket.

By way of a multi-functional mirror that serves as both a pendulum denoting the passage of time and a portal between the realms of life and death, Miranda shows Victor's concerted efforts at wresting control over these forces prior to the monster's emergence through the birth-canal portal. His immediate response following the creature's birth is one of surprise and fascination: he revels in the monster's embodiment, examin-

Fig. 7.1   Creating a monster. Estefania Miranda's *Frankenstein* with the Konzert Theater Bern (Photo credit: Philipp Zinniker)

ing him closely and marvelling at his hands and spine as one would a newborn. All changes suddenly to terror, however, when he embraces this newborn creation who exhibits agency and care by hugging him in response. Victor detaches himself and flees.

Thus does the central narrative dynamic shift—as it does in the novel— from Victor trying to wrest control over the forces of life and death, to the monster gaining power through agency. In a manner befitting a dance choreography with its focus on embodiment, Miranda chronicles in movement the monster's developing control and mastery over his limbs (see Fig. 7.2). Mothered by a female dancer who plays both the role of Victor's dead mother and Elizabeth, a significant association given their yoking in Victor's sexually perverse dream in Shelley's novel immediately after the creature's 'birth' (1994: 39), the monster is shown growing into, embracing, and revelling in his embodiment. In keeping with Shelley's representation of the creature as possessing a feminine/female sensibility, a commentating female voice expresses his feelings. Thus does a female choreographer, unlike her male counterparts yet in keeping with Mary

Fig. 7.2 The creature (Norikazu Aoki) revelling in embodiment. Estefania Miranda's *Frankenstein* with the Konzert Theater Bern (Photo credit: Philipp Zinniker)

Shelley's novel, lend some sympathy to the creature. Through the female commentator, he insists that he is a thinking and feeling human being. If he is a murderer, he says, it is because Victor made him one. The choreography bears this out: when Victor presents the monster with a female counterpart, the new couple commence an awkward but tender pas de deux that fast transforms into a tug of war once Victor comes between them. As she reaches out to the monster, Frankenstein twists her head and kills her, an action reproduced in the monster's subsequent murder of Elizabeth. If a telling difference exists between these two grotesque acts of violence it is that the creature, unlike Victor, experiences remorse.

In keeping with the novel, women in this dance-theatre choreography, like those in Eagling's and Scarlett's choreographies, function solely as objects of exchange. This motif is consistent throughout with women literally pushed or pulled between men. And they are always veiled—either in a wedding veil or in a winding sheet—as if never individuated, self-actualised, or seen/understood by the men who objectify, abuse, and exchange them. In this manner, Victor's veiled, dead mother is reduced to a symbol, transformed from a relational creature—*Victor's* mother—to death personified, a memento mori of our inescapable fate. But Miranda's broader message, echoing Mary Shelley's, is clear: in this world of patriarchal and paternal struggle, there is no place for women as individual agents, or for the maternal and an ethic of care. Instead, women remain slaves/dolls/puppets throughout, deprived of their nurturing maternal powers by usurping, power-hungry, and brutal men who reject and carelessly destroy their emotional, sensitive selves. Where the character of Elizabeth is employed by Eagling as an object of desire in a battle between Victor and his creature, and Scarlett uses her to mediate their taboo same-sex relationship, Miranda portrays her as the female force of love, fertility, nurturance, and healing who is ruthlessly sacrificed by a brutal male world, to the tremendous detriment of that world. Given Elizabeth's association with Victor's mother in Miranda's choreography where the same dancer plays both roles whilst in the same costume, Victor is ultimately revealed, tragically and ironically, to be a conflicted, divided man who both yearns for and brutally sacrifices love and maternal care.

In this unnatural world where the order of things has gone into reverse, death finally defeats Victor in the form of his own paternal creation, a force—like death—that he can neither control nor escape. As Miranda's choreography suggests, the natural cycles of life and death overcome Victor, the monster/son ultimately usurping the place of the Master/father. An unnatural, inter-generational Gothic cycle prevails as the son kills the father before being overwhelmed with grief. In this manner is a damnable cycle perpetuated. As Shakespeare's *Hamlet* and other Christian consolation manuals make clear, excessive grief, while impeding one's ability to move through and beyond the death of a loved one, catapults one into a mentally unhealthy state of melancholy. According to Sigmund Freud in his 1917 essay, 'Mourning and Melancholia', which was written as the world witnessed the staggering carnage of the First World War, the work of mourning, when successful, should relieve the symptoms of melancholia. As painful a process as it may be, the subject's decathexis from the love object should occur with the assistance of memory. Erich Lindemann, extrapolating from Freud on what Lindemann terms 'grief work', describes the 'emancipation from the bondage to the deceased' (1944: 190) that occurs when a person successfully undertakes the grieving process.

Just as Victor Frankenstein essentially denies his mother's death and does not enact good, successful mourning, so too does the grieving creature who closes Miranda's ballet seem likewise doomed to melancholia by way of failed mourning. Bad future cycles are prophesied as the creature's cradling of his dead father's corpse mirrors Victor's cradling of his mother's corpse at the ballet's commencement. By way of this motif of cradling, Miranda highlights the interdependent parent-child mirror stage of identity while highlighting our childlike nature and needs throughout life. Victor's creature, neither cradled nor parented, is unlikely to experience successful mourning due to his unfulfilled desire for parental love. This eight-foot-tall symbol of memento mori whose true meaning in relation to death is entirely overlooked by his creator serves as Victor's doppelgänger who signals and mirrors Victor's failed grief work. Just as the tormented creature haunts the creator to whom he remains spiritually and emotionally enslaved, so too does Victor remain in bondage to his deceased mother, a figure he resurrects in his abjected monster.

* * *

While, over the past half century, *Frankenstein* provided the perfect narrative ingredients and dynamics for the rapidly evolving forms of ballet and modern dance-theatre to reflect on their own practices and theories about movement and embodiment, it has also served to mediate larger cultural concerns about disease, dying, living, artistic expression, death, mourning, and memorialisation. In place of the Christian fixation on the other side of the grave and what became known as the 'good death'—a driving force in Shelley's novel that was the focus of the *ars moriendi*, manuals popular from the fifteenth to the eighteenth centuries that promoted prescribed prayers, actions, and attitudes to secure spiritual salvation—recent choreographers engaging with *Frankenstein* have focused on *this* side of the grave. In compelling works fixated on embodiment, they have highlighted, echoing Shelley's novel, an ethic of care alongside the phenomenon of corpsoreality—the experience of our bodies becoming Other in their vulnerability to debilitating disease and death. In the face of suffering and our ultimate demise, choreographers have promoted the creation of expressive and meaningful art and the fostering of 'good'—fulfilled and loving—lives. Only thus, when faced with devastating loss, may we experience a 'successful' mourning and stave off 'bad', debilitating haunting. Either explicitly or implicitly, these contemporary works of *danse macabre* promote the traditional message that death is a leveller we all must eventually face and embrace. They do so, however, not with an eye to eschatological concerns about the next world, but to living and loving relationally and ethically in this one. While being haunted is portrayed as intrinsic to the human condition for which the phrase, *I am haunted, therefore I am*, may serve as the mantra, these choreographies urge us, despite the tremendous, crippling pain of loss, to cultivate and embrace our cherished ghosts. Only thus may we avoid engendering needy, gnawing ghosts of regrets past. We should dance, these choreographers suggest, *because* we will die. We should dance, they remind us, like no one is watching, revelling in living and loving, embracing the joys of embodiment and even of loss, always recognising that our next dance may be our last.

NOTE

1. Originally a spectacular type of cautionary play about eschatological inevitability involving the four last things—Death, Judgement, Heaven, and Hell—the *danse macabre* featured skeletons leading individuals from all walks of life, including both ecclesiastics and laypeople, to the grave.

WORKS CITED

Bales, Melanie. 2013. Touchstones of Tradition and Innovation: Pas de deux by Petipa, Balanchine and Forsythe. In *Dance on Its Own Terms: Histories and Methodologies*, ed. Melanie Bales and Karen Eliot, 175–205. Oxford: Oxford University Press.

Bewell, Alan. 1989. *Wordsworth and the Enlightenment*. New Haven: Yale University Press.

Bronfen, Elisabeth. 1992. *Over Her Dead Body: Death, Femininity and the Aesthetic*. Manchester: Manchester University Press.

Darnell, Rick. 1991. *Brides of Frankenstein*. San Francisco: The High-Risk Group.

Edelman, Lee. 2004. *No Future: Queer Theory and the Death Drive*. Durham: Duke University Press.

Eagling, Wayne. 1985. *Frankenstein*. London: The Royal Ballet.

Forsythe, William. 1986. *Die Befragung des Robert Scott [The Questioning of Robert Scott]*. Frankfurt: Ballett Frankfurt.

———. 2005. *You Made Me a Monster.* Frankfurt: The Forsythe Company.

Gere, David. 2004. *How to Make Dances in an Epidemic: Tracking Choreography in the Age of AIDS.* Madison: The University of Wisconsin Press.

Goodwin, Sarah Webster, and Elisabeth Bronfen, eds. 1993. *Death and Representation.* Baltimore/London: John Hopkins UP.

Groves, Rebecca M. 2012. *Dance Review Journal,* 44(2): 117–120. Rev. of *William Forsythe and the Practice of Choreography: It Starts from Any Point,* ed. Stephen, Spier, 2011, London/New York: Routledge.

Haggerty, George E. 2016. What Is Queer About *Frankenstein?* In *The Cambridge Companion to Frankenstein,* ed. Andrew Smith, 116–127. Cambridge: Cambridge University Press.

Jowitt, Deborah. 2003. How Many Ways to Twist it? *The Village Voice,* October. https://www.villagevoice.com/2003/10/07/how-many-ways-to-twist-it/

———. 2010. The Beauty and Limits of the Dance World's Ongoing Love of Virtuosity. *The Village Voice,* August 11. http://www.villagevoice.com/2010/08/11/dance/the-beauty-and-limits-of-the-dance-worlds-ongoing-love-of-virtuosity/

Kaplan, Rachel. 1989. Eat That Idiom Spit It Back: The High Risk Group, Julian Theatre at New College, Apr. 23. *San Francisco Bay Times,* May.

Lindemann, Erich. 1944. Symptomatology and Management of Acute Grief. *The American Journal of Psychiatry* 101 (2): 141–148.

May, Todd. 2009. *Death.* Stocksfield: Acumen.

Miranda, Estefania. 2014. *Frankenstein,* Konzert Theater Bern. https://vimeo.com/129354518

Praz, Mario. 1951. *The Romantic Agony.* Trans. Davidson, A. London/New York/Toronto: Oxford University Press.

Quigley, Christine. 1996. *The Corpse: A History.* Jefferson: McFarland and Company.

Scarlett, Liam. 2016. *Frankenstein,* The Royal Ballet (London) and the San Francisco Ballet.

Shelley, M. 1990. On Ghosts. In *The Mary Shelley Reader,* ed. B.T. Bennett and C.E. Robinson, 334–340. Oxford: Oxford University Press.

Shelley, Mary. 1994. *Frankenstein; Or, the Modern Prometheus.* Oxford: Oxford University Press.

Siegmund, Gerald. 2011. Of monsters and Puppets: William Forsythe's Work After the "Robert Scott Complex". In *William Forsythe and the Practice of Choreography: It Starts from Any Point,* ed. Steven Spier, 20–37. New York/Oxford: Routledge.

Solway, Diane. 2007. Is It Dance? Maybe. Political? Sure. *The New York Times,* February 18. http://www.nytimes.com/2007/02/18/arts/dance/18solw.html?pagewanted=2

Spier, Steven. 2011. Introduction: The Practice of Choreography. In *William Forsythe and the Practice of Choreography: It Starts from Any Point*, ed. Steven Spier, 1–3. New York/Oxford: Routledge.

Townshend, Dale. 2008. Gothic and the Ghost of *Hamlet*. In *Gothic Shakespeares*, ed. John Drakakis and Dale Townshend, 60–97. London/New York: Routledge.

Turin, David. 1994. Why Death Rock Won't Die. *L.A. Weekly*, January 14–20, pp. 35–36. Database on-line. http://www.vamp.org/Gothic/Text/hsreport.html. August 2016.

Wright, Frankie. 1991. The High Risk Dancers Live Up to Name: San Francisco-based Troupe That Will Be at the Sushi Aims to 'Explode' Oppression and Exclusion. *Los Angeles Times*, September 25. http://articles.latimes.com/1991-09-25/entertainment/ca-2635_1_high-risk

Young, Tricia Henry. 1999. Dancing on Béla Lugosi's Grave: The Politics and Aesthetics of Gothic Club Dancing. *Dance Research: The Journal of the Society for Dance Research* 17: 75–97.

PART III

Spectacular Frankensteins on Screen and Stage

'Now I Am a Man!': Performing Sexual Violence in the National Theatre Production of *Frankenstein*

Courtney A. Hoffman

Theatrical adaptations of Mary Shelley's *Frankenstein* appeared on the stage only five years after the novel's publication and have continued to be produced across a variety of genres into the twenty-first century.[1] The leading actors of the last few decades have taken on roles in these productions, including, most recently, James McEvoy and Daniel Radcliffe, while Kenneth Branagh, Robert DeNiro, and Helena Bonham Carter starred in a film directed by Branagh in 1994. Significantly, Bonham Carter's Elizabeth is subjected to physical violence as DeNiro's Creature rips out her heart, as well as when Branagh's Victor reanimates her body after having sewn her head onto another woman's body, and she chooses self-immolation. The tortured female body appears multiple times in Branagh's film, leading to Elizabeth's burning body literally setting the world aflame around her. Yet, while Elizabeth is threatened with sexual

C. A. Hoffman (✉)
School of Literature, Media, and Communication, Georgia Institute of Technology, Atlanta, GA, USA

© The Author(s) 2018
C. M. Davison, M. Mulvey-Roberts (eds.), *Global Frankenstein*,
Studies in Global Science Fiction,
https://doi.org/10.1007/978-3-319-78142-6_8

violence by the Creature in Branagh's text—the Creature finds her in bed and lays atop her before shoving his fist into her chest—she does not undergo the trauma of rape. Such is not the case for the Elizabeth in the 2011 National Theatre Production of Nick Dear's stage adaptation of the novel, directed by Danny Boyle and starring Benedict Cumberbatch and Jonny Lee Miller in alternating roles of Victor and the Creature. For their performance, they jointly won both the Olivier Award and *Evening Standard* Theatre Award (Porter 2013: 1). Claudia Capancioni and Sibylle Erle have argued that the doubling of the actors, as well as the echo of ethical questions asked first by De Lacey and later by Elizabeth, 'pushes the *Doppelgänger* motif beyond its limits to the point where we can no longer distinguish between Creature and creator' (134). This is, I think, indicative of an important and extremely fraught question: what creates monstrosity, and how do we, as individuals and as a society, deal with those who commit monstrous acts? Answers to this question lay along well-trodden ground, but my intent, rather than revisiting familiar arguments, is to examine the performance of such monstrous acts—displays of sexual violence, specifically—by both Victor and the Creature during this production and to question the effects of these acts. Violence is a characteristic associated with the creature given the number of people he kills in Shelley's text, including William Frankenstein, Henry Clerval, Elizabeth, and, indirectly, Justine Moritz. But those murders occur off-stage, and the reader is told about them, rather than shown. Despite the fact that Dear's adaptation eliminates Henry and Justine, the other two deaths remain, and the play includes performances of sexual violence. While William's death occurs off-stage and Victor disassembles the Female Creature behind a curtain, her bloody corpse revealed in the aftermath, the violence perpetrated against Elizabeth is explicitly performed. Showing Elizabeth's death renders it different, drawing the spectator into complicity in normalising the connection between rape and death that becomes part of the Creature's own performance of masculinity.

Shelley's text limits Elizabeth's participation in the narrative to a brief recital of her place within the Frankenstein family structure, a few letters written to Victor, and a scream heard at a distance by Victor as the creature takes her life. The narrative revolves around Victor's voice, conveyed through his recital to Walton about the horror he has brought to life and the consequences of that action.[2] But Victor's focus consistently returns to how his choices have affected him. Elizabeth is only important insofar as Victor sees a reflection of himself in her—she had been 'given' to him by his mother when they were both young:

> On the evening previous to her being brought to my home, my mother had said playfully, "I have a pretty present for my Victor—tomorrow he shall have it." And when, on the morrow, she presented Elizabeth to me as her promised gift, I, with a childish seriousness, interpreted her words literally and looked upon Elizabeth as mine—mine to protect, love, and cherish. All praises bestowed on her I received as made to a possession of my own.... [T]ill death she was to be mine only. (Shelley 1992: 37)

Shelley juxtaposes multiple definitions of 'present' here, conflating Elizabeth with a 'gift' bestowed upon Victor and firmly positioning her as an object: a 'pretty present' that was 'presented' to him. And just as a child may set aside a toy when it does not interest them, no matter its beauty, Victor ignores Elizabeth throughout much of the novel. Despite the fact that she steps in to take the place of Victor's mother for the younger children when Caroline Frankenstein dies, running the household and writing to Victor when he is away at university, having 'interpreted [Caroline's] words literally,' Victor treats Elizabeth as an object, a 'possession of [his] own.' Even Shelley's repeated use of the word 'mine' in this short excerpt reinforces Victor's sense of ownership over Elizabeth. The repetition of 'mine—mine … mine' is reminiscent of a child's demands for and claims of ownership over whatever object they desire. In Shelley's text, Elizabeth is thus merely an extension of Victor, there for his creature to destroy. Dear, however, takes Elizabeth as a character and expands her role, focusing much of the play's sexual tension, and ultimately sexual violence, around her.

Most of the history between Victor and Elizabeth is omitted from the stage production. Elizabeth appears on stage as an adult, not a child, this introduction corresponding with the Creature's murder of William Frankenstein. She first plays a game of hide-and-seek with the child, but after he disappears, she informs the searchers of the circumstances leading up to his disappearance. It is in this scene, 45 minutes into the performance, that we also get our first glimpse of Victor since his rejection of the Creature in the first ten minutes of the play. When Victor accuses Elizabeth of irresponsibility regarding William, she asks, 'So you have responsibility for—what, exactly?' (Dear 2011: xxiii).[3] She questions his actions, suggesting that his obsession with science and his work has led him to neglect his family: 'I haven't seen you for a week. You're always up in your room' (xxiii). Rather than acquiescing to his need for solitude, and his implicit rejection of her company and person, she insists that he be an active participant in their relationship and reminds him that he is supposed to 'talk to [her] occasionally' (xxiii). When Victor later informs her that he must leave Geneva to go to Scotland and that their wedding must be postponed, she demands to go with him. He attempts to dissuade her, suggesting both that it will be very boring while he is involved with library research and that Scotland is not very pleasant. Eliciting a chuckle from the audience, Victor describes the land as 'barren rocks in a barren ocean. It is, I am told, an awful place' (xxv).

This brief moment of humour intercedes into what is, for the most part, a grim and despairing production, reflective of the nature of Victor's character, and presenting the audience with the picture of a man who cares little for the woman who is meant to be his wife. To Elizabeth's question of whether he has any interest in her, he replies, 'You are beautiful. ... You will make a beautiful wife' (xxv). He holds her arm out to the side, posing her like a doll, inspecting her form and figure as if, as she accuses him, she was 'a specimen' (xxv). To Victor, Elizabeth's only value is in her body, not even as the potential mother of his future children, since, after all, Victor has succeeded in circumventing the natural processes of procreation. Instead, in his eyes, she merely functions as the model for the female companion he has just promised to make for his creation. Victor's lack of interest in the 'usual way' is further demonstrated as Elizabeth attempts to entice him with her body (xxix). When she asks him to 'show [her] how [he'll] give [her] children,' he backs away (xxv). She follows him, stretching up to kiss him herself when he will not initiate the embrace, bringing his hands to her breasts, asking him to 'touch [her],' to 'feel [her] heartbeat,' her intent to use her body to keep him by her side evident as she asks, 'Must you go? Can't you stay?' (xxv).[4] Of course, he does not.

This performance of Elizabeth's character is intricately tied to the physical: on the one hand, she is simply a body to be admired or ignored as the moment necessitates, as her lack of education places her on a much different level than Victor intellectually, and he dismisses her interest in his work as 'well beyond a woman's scope' (xxv). Her worth stems purely from her presentation as a body of physical perfection, on whose pattern Victor can mould another of his creations, one of his 'specimens.' On the other hand, however, Elizabeth uses her physicality and sexuality to attract Victor. She employs her body as a lure, promoting a sense of sexual freedom, in order to get what she wants. Her desire for children allows her to see her sexuality as something useful and productive, and she, unlike Victor, views human sexual reproduction as something to be exercised and celebrated. In contrast to Shelley's portrayal of the relationship between Elizabeth and Victor, which always seems to be conducted at a distance, either through letters or due to mourning the death of Justine Moritz, Dear's adaptation emphasises the potential sexuality of their connection as a couple engaged to be married. Instead of rejecting sexual contact, of insisting on virginal behaviour before marriage, Elizabeth initiates sexually charged caresses, her sexuality becoming a potential locus for power. Though Victor resists her attempts at seduction, his reluctance to leave is obvious as he lingers long enough in their embrace to demonstrate that he feels some desire for her. His imperative to appease his Creature is greater than his wish to remain with his betrothed, however, and he leaves with her blessing. 'Then go,' she tells him, 'and do your work. And be brilliant. And after that, come home to me and be my husband. Give me a dozen children. Go' (xxv). To be her husband is not to support her financially or to share conversation over the dinner table; to be her husband is to give her children, to participate in passionate embraces, and to impregnate her in 'the usual way' (xxix). Elizabeth performs a certain kind of powerful femininity here, one that moves beyond a Darwinian drive to perpetuate the species to one that embraces her sexuality and physicality. Rather than hiding or being ashamed of her desire, she anticipates pleasure in sex. Though Elizabeth's ultimate goal for intercourse is conception and not just the fulfilment of desire, this particular production of *Frankenstein* is able to promote a feminism that is unafraid of the body and overturns a dynamic of male-initiated sexuality. Elizabeth can have power in her relationship with Victor, not because he allows it but because she takes it.

These feminist undertones in the play become fraught, however, as Victor works on the Female Creature immediately after the scene in which he chooses to leave Elizabeth. Isolated in the isles of Scotland—that 'awful place'—he imagines a conversation with his now-deceased brother William, in which they discuss the process of his reanimation of the dead. 'Will they reproduce?' William asks with childlike curiosity after expressing disgust over Victor's utilisation of cadaver parts, 'Will they have wombs, the females? Will they breed? How quickly will they breed? How fast is a cycle? How many in a litter? Fifty? A hundred? A thousand?' (xviii). Again, the science of reproduction enters the conversation in relation to the female body. The use of terms like 'breed' and 'litter' reduces the possibility of intercourse between Victor's Creatures to an animalistic act, while the word 'females,' rather than 'women,' further reduces the body in Victor's lab to mere biology. The exaggerated number of potential offspring in a 'litter' further distances the Female from identification with the human and pushes her into the realm of non-human; no human female, after all, has produced a thousand offspring and certainly not in a single gestational cycle. The irony of Dear's phrasing here is that, although the Creature begs Victor for a companion, 'a mate ... the possibility of love,' and not for the ability to create a family of his own, it is Elizabeth who asks Victor to engage in procreation, for what is essentially the ability to 'breed' (xxiv). It is Elizabeth who spurs the rejection of femininity and the celebration of reproduction. And, significantly, it is Elizabeth on whom the Female is modelled, thus tying Elizabeth firmly to the realm of the material body and, by extension, to the non-human, since, if the Female is a non-human body, Elizabeth can be so as well.

The Creature's perusal of his companion continues to emphasise the physical and, furthermore, the spectacular nature of the body on stage. Joining Victor in his Orkneys workshop, he demands to be shown the work in progress. Victor obligingly brings his newest creation into full view, out from behind the curtain obscuring the womb-like structure that serves as the mechanism for his process. He slowly walks her forward, posing her limbs as if she were a mannequin, one leg slightly in front of the other, her arms graceful in a classic ballet posture, as the actress embodying the inanimate, yet complete, figure of the Female maintains a blank expression. 'Isn't she fine?' Victor asks the Creature, who is panting with visible excitement. 'She is ... beautiful,' he answers. 'Your work is so detailed! The cuts are so fine! The lustre of her skin!' (xxviii). The Creature brushes his fingers over her hair, her arm, lifting her hand a fraction, in which position she now remains. The body on display—and it is definitely a sense of display, both to the Creature and to the audience, that is performed here—is not limp, simply immobile. But it is *only* a body; there is no mind, no personality in this character.

Rather, the Female Creature is a prop with which Victor tortures the Creature. First, Victor denies him the Female, asking how dangerous she might be. When the Creature promises to teach her morality, as he learnt it, and to go with her to Argentina, Victor retorts that she might refuse: 'Come on! *Use* your brain! She might reject you. She might abhor the sight of you. She might take one look at you and run. She might say that she prefers to live with a man, not a monster' (xxviii; emphasis added). While saying this, he drapes his arm around the Female's shoulders, leaning her up against him—the man—in a pose of intimacy and desire. Contemptuous of the Creature—the monster—Victor directs his counterpart's gaze upon specific elements of the Female's body, constituting her once again as only a collection of parts, as to him, she undoubtedly is. 'Look at her. Look! Exquisitely constructed, wouldn't you agree?' Victor taunts him, stroking the body in full view of his audience—both on stage and in the theatre—conflating the Creature's gaze with that of the people in the seats (xxviii).⁵ In the broadcast edition of the play, the camera frames Victor and the Female in the shot, cutting the Creature out of the scene and highlighting the connection between the audience's and the Creature's gazes. We are meant to see what he sees, to assume his position, to watch as Victor touches the displayed female body. In a scene much more explicitly sexual than Shelley writes of Victor's Orkneys workshop, the Creature learns that sexuality is inherently violent.

The Creature makes incoherent sounds of distress as Victor continues, leaning in as if to kiss the Female, saying, 'Look at those cheeks, those lips, those breasts. Who would not desire those breasts?' (xxviii). She is truly a specimen in Victor's eyes, one whose value inheres only in the physical perfection she represents. Here is a female body that does belong—at this point—only to Victor; whereas Shelley's narrating scientist claims Elizabeth as his possession, on stage, Elizabeth has a warm, living, breathing body, a voice, and a mind that is capable of acting as an agent separate from Victor. This inanimate female body can be displayed and fondled when and if he chooses; she cannot contradict or tempt him, as she has no capacity for thinking at all, let alone in a manner that is different from his. This female body also has the potential for reproduction, however, so that control of her future no longer remains within Victor's hands—the very stipulation of her creation and then gaining the spark of life is in fact that that body and the possession of it be given to the Creature, then removed from the same hemisphere as that in which Victor resides. That loss of control cannot be tolerated, as the power and potential product of female sexuality, to which Victor seems to have been awakened by Elizabeth's plea for him to stay with her, threaten to escape the bounds in which Victor had imagined it contained—as he appears not to have imagined it at all prior to this—and thus must be destroyed. Eerily, as Victor chops his Female to pieces behind the backlit curtain that covers his false womb, a shrill noise reminiscent of a woman's scream is heard, perhaps an echo of the potential life that he might have created. Distraught, the Creature promises Victor that '[He] may expect [him] again!' but gives no specifics as to when or where (xxviii).

That vengeance comes almost immediately, as the scene shifts from Scotland to the bridal bedchamber in the Frankensteins' Geneva home. Here, we again see Elizabeth, whose sexuality, like that of the Female Creature, must be contained. While she eagerly awaits her wedding night, Victor is concerned only with security. He confesses to her what he has done, telling her that he has lured the Creature to Geneva with their wedding in the hopes of killing him. Victor indicates that his purpose for having the wedding at this particular moment, despite having delayed and avoided it for as long as he had, is because he has something to offer up as bait for the Creature: Elizabeth herself. She is merely a vessel to him—not for producing his children but for his vengeance. This, as Capancioni and Erle argue, presents another conflation between the creator and creation: the female body, whether the potential life of the inanimate Female or the animated, desiring Elizabeth, is merely a tool for the men's reciprocal plans to destroy the other (142–3). In focusing on the similarities between Victor and the Creature, however, Capancioni and Erle neglect the ways in which Elizabeth and the Female also become paired beyond their uses as the means to vengeance for their male counterparts. They are both dangerous beings: Victor scoffs at Elizabeth's request to accompany him to Scotland, though he admits that the fault is not in her intellect but her education. 'I can learn,' she tells him, 'I want to talk to you about your work, about the world, about music, politics, everything!' (xxv). But once Elizabeth learns, about his work, the world, everything, she might—just as the Female Creature might in the case of her union to the Creature—choose not to remain with Victor. Both Elizabeth and the Female modelled on her form are 'perfect ... the perfect wife,' as Victor defines the idea (xxviii). Because she serves as the original upon which Victor designed his Female, the desire for children is inherent to that perfection. Although he imagines the Female may not wish to live with the Creature, he cannot similarly imagine that she may not want children, nor even that he, as the literal architect of her physical body, could eliminate that possibility by electing not to include a uterus in her fabrication. Yet, such a deliberate choice to restrict the Female's reproductive ability by neglecting to complete her anatomy in and of itself would be a kind of violence perpetrated by Victor against the Female. Thus, she must die, even before she lives, the only appropriate fate for such a dangerous being, at least in Victor's mind.

Elizabeth too then, constructed on stage as an equally perilous creature, will suffer a similar fate. Her sexuality is turned against her as, in an interchange that mirrors her earlier attempts to seduce Victor, she is drawn to feel the Creature's 'heat' and 'heartbeat' before he grabs her breast in a perverse imitation of her positioning Victor's hand in the same place (xxix).

In Shelley's novel, Victor narrates Elizabeth's death after the fact, since he confesses that he had been on the lookout for his nemesis on his wedding night, given his belief that the creature will wish to kill him, rather than his bride. 'I discovered no trace of him,' Victor tells Walton:

> [W]hen suddenly I heard a shrill and dreadful scream. It came from the room into which Elizabeth had retired. As I heard it, the whole truth rushed into my mind, my arms dropped, the motion of every muscle and fibre was suspended; I could feel the blood trickling in my veins, and tingling in the extremities of my limbs. This state lasted but for an instant; the scream was repeated, and I rushed into the room. She was there, lifeless and inanimate, thrown across the bed, her head hanging down, and her pale and distorted features half covered by her hair ... her bloodless arms and relaxed form flung by the murderer across its bridal bier. (199)

Although it is possible that Shelley implies the creature's rape of Elizabeth, the text does not specifically state that he does so. Very little time passes between when Victor hears her screams and when he finds her dead: 'This state lasted but for an instant.' Her position on the bed could be interpreted as indicating sexual assault, but Shelley's choice of the words, 'thrown across the bed' and 'flung by the murderer,' to discuss the body's arrangement equally imply contempt and disregard from the creature, as though she were the thing Victor's language proclaims her, ready to be tossed away. Victor does not witness the interaction, if any occurs, between Elizabeth and the creature in her chamber. He is left with the aftermath and a 'lifeless and inanimate' corpse, recalling the body of the female creature he had created and subsequently destroyed.

The play, in contrast, further cements the connection between the two females as Dear's script brings Elizabeth's death into the forefront of the action and pairs it with spectacular violence witnessed by Victor and the audience. On stage, Elizabeth's death is preceded by the performance of the Creature's rape of her first struggling and then passive body, while Victor, having burst into the room to find his wife being sexually assaulted, watches helplessly, unable to even aim the pistol he holds. Victor's location as slightly downstage and right brings him closer to the audience, while his own body appears smaller as he falls to his knees almost in the foetal position. As when the Creature's gaze is projected onto the audience as Victor molested the female, again, the audience's gaze is conflated with Victor's as he is unable to stop the assault on Elizabeth being performed before their eyes. Dear's script includes a stage direction where '*Victor hangs back in appalled fascination as he watches his Creature mating*' (xix). Yet, the choice to edit the footage from the camera above the stage into the broadcasted film focuses attention onto the rape occurring on the bed. Victor is cut out of the scene, just as the Creature had been removed from view when, earlier, Victor assaulted the female. Now, he seems not to exist, the audience's gaze forced to remain on the rape, even should they wish to look away.

Because the camera angle is above the bed, the audience is not asked to assume Victor's gaze here but a voyeuristic bird's eye view that mimics an outside perspective; the broken fourth wall is three dimensional when the camera is added to the theatrical equation. Where a live audience would never be able to assume a viewpoint from above, the film audience becomes more fully immersed in viewing the violent spectacle before them. The Creature's cries of sexual pleasure crescendo to indicate orgasm as he ravishes Elizabeth unimpeded, before collapsing on top of her. He gently strokes and kisses her cheek as she remains unresponsive, then sits up, and, pulling her with him, breaks her neck. Kneeling on the bed over her dead body, he cries, 'Now I am a *man!*' (xxix).[6] It has taken, it seems, not only sexual activity—and rape, no less—but femicide for the Creature to fully assume the mantle of manhood. Capancioni and Erle argue that here, 'the Creature is turned into a parody of a creator because he too violates human beings in order to use their bodies for his own intent' (143). And while I agree that the conflation of Victor and the Creature is most poignantly and horrifically demonstrated in this moment, I must challenge their argument that Elizabeth's rape gives the Creature pleasure, as does the way he taunts Victor, thus demonstrating 'the actively evil side of his human nature' (144). To attribute these actions to evil seems simplistic and suggests that the underlying morality of the narrative on stage is black and white. Certainly, neither Victor's nor the Creature's actions are good or right. But rape is not about mere pleasure. It is about power, about controlling the body of another person. The interactions between the male and female characters on stage are much more nuanced and intricately developed than can simply be termed evil or not evil.

I want to suggest instead that this scene and that in which Victor violates the Female Creature highlight the construction of gender on a larger scale. I think it is important to emphasise the role of this text *as* a theatrical performance. Sarah Kane, a proponent of creating new traditions in twentieth-century British theatre, often utilises violence on stage as a method by which to provoke the impetus for social change in her audiences. In doing so, she intends to shock those watching the performance; her use of violence is thus purposefully crafted and not simply a device for astonishment (Biçer 2011). Instead, her plays 'focus on violence as the single most significant aspect of history' (Biçer 2011: 82). In doing so, Kane emphasises that violence, and particularly violence against women, is a specifically political act. To perform violence on stage brings what is too often an incident experienced by others at a distance into the physical sphere of the audience members in an environment where they cannot deny its reality.[7] As such, there is the potential for affective revision of an audience's position in regard to violence and particularly violence against women.

Similarly, Ketu Katrak suggests, in analysing two plays that engage with the effects of sexual violence on victims of assault, that '[v]iolence on women's bodies in live performance can elicit profound emotional responses from spectators' (Katrak 2014: 31). In the two plays Katrak examines specifically, '[a]ffective responses such as hope, social consciousness of injustice and outrage, among other emotions, are elicited by the transformative potential of powerful theatrical representation of violence on female bodies and the latter's resistances' (32). The power of resistance and of overcoming the trauma of such assaults, and the performances of such empowerments, may indeed be the result of witnessing violence on the stage. Indeed, theatre has been used in sexual assault prevention programmes for just this reason, though such performances can run the risk of reinforcing prevailing stereotypes of gender performance (Iverson 2006).

The two bodies on which such assaults are committed in this performance of *Frankenstein* are allowed no resistance, no recovery, as both are rendered lifeless by their molesters. There can be power in silence, when it is performed as the result of a deliberate choice. Silence cannot be a form of power for Elizabeth or the Female Creature in this production, however, as neither are granted the ability to choose it. Instead, silence is forced upon them by the men who seek to control them, whose violence against them is considered a normative part of the performance of their own identities, their own sexualities. Just prior to raping Elizabeth, the Creature tells her:

> I am good at the art of assimilation. I have watched, and listened, and learnt. At first I knew nothing at all. But I studied the ways of men, and slowly I learnt: how to ruin, how to hate, how to debase, how to humiliate. And at the feet of my master, I learnt the highest of human skills, the skill no other creature owns: I finally learnt how to lie. (xxix)

He has mastered the arts of 'men': lying, hating, debasing, humiliating. The Creature associates masculinity with these traits; to him, he is correctly performing 'man' by coming to Elizabeth's room 'to debase' and 'to humiliate.' Victor has taught him that violence against women is, pointedly, intertwined with the desire and need to hurt other men. It is not enough to simply kill Elizabeth as recompense for Victor's refusal to reanimate the Female Creature; as Victor himself demonstrated, sexual contact without consent (since the female could not agree, the Creature learns it is unnecessary) precedes death. Shelley's text does much the same: Elizabeth and the female Victor creates serve as representatives of how patriarchy objectifies and violates women because of their relationships to other men. Yet, where Shelley's women seem to escape sexual violence committed by the men who perish as punishment for their actions, Dear's are blatantly and cruelly assaulted in full view of the audience by men who end the play by continuing their journey together into the Arctic sunset, relatively hale and unharmed.

Indeed, the enactment of sexual violence on women's bodies in Dear's *Frankenstein* closely resembles the 'narratology of rape' that Sanchayita Paul Chakraborty and Anindya Sekhar Purakayastha suggest functions as part of the ways in which gender is socially constructed:

> The assimilation of violence into the identity-formation of woman is becoming a norm, reinforced by multiple patriarchal strategies and ideologies. Invasion on the woman's body is taken as natural. This violence imposed on the woman's body becomes part of the language and lifestyle of a culture. (1–2)

In this narratology of rape, they argue, 'the voyeuristic structure of knowledge based on the conventions, symbols and representations of rape is enjoyed as a spectacle and within this process, it is normalized by the spectator/reader' (Chakraborty and Purakayastha 2013: 3). When this voyeurism is used as a method to subvert patriarchal representation of women through stage performance, as Chakraborty and Purakayastha suggest, there may be potential for resistance (2). However, because neither Elizabeth nor her creature counterpart has the opportunity for resistance or recovery, because rape is normalised as part of manhood by the Creature's learnt performance, rather than finding some catharsis or social rage over the injustice of sexual violence as it is performed here, I want to suggest that Danny Boyle's production of Nick Dear's *Frankenstein* adaptation provokes questions about how we construct masculinity, as well as femininity, in our society.

As spectators whose voyeurism permits and thus normalises the violence performed on the stage, audiences must face the possibility that our willingness to watch such violence makes us complicit. When the female characters suffer abuse as pawns in a conflict between men that is not about their own plight as women oppressed within patriarchal structures, rather than suffering as a specific tool through which social change might be inspired, the violence enacted on stage meets no true objective. Violent masculinity, the type that accepts rape as simply a means to harm the man to whom the woman supposedly belongs, is perpetuated through performances such as this one. This production of *Frankenstein* and the performance of sexual violence on stage within it reinforce a cultural acceptance and narratology of rape as both a method of control and the construction of gender.

NOTES

1. Lester D. Friedman and Allison B. Kavey examine the various ways by which *Frankenstein* has been adapted throughout the centuries in their work, *Monstrous Progeny: A History of the Frankenstein Narratives.*
2. For considerations of narrative structure in Shelley's novel, see Aguirre, Benford, Clark, Joshua, and Newman.
3. The published script is slightly different from the actors' performances in a few places, as can be the case with stage performances. I indicate where the discrepancies affect my argument in the body of the chapter but otherwise indicate any alterations in the dialogue in the notes.
4. Dear's script indicates that '*she fondles him*,' but on stage, she places Victor's hands on her breast. In the script, she asks him to 'Feel my heat!' a phrase that will be echoed later, when the Creature surprises her in her bedroom.
5. The text reads, 'wouldn't you say.'

6. Emphasis added to reflect the actor's performance.
7. Randy Gener argues that the value in Lynn Nottage's play *Ruined* lies in its ability to bring the realities of wars occurring in Africa, of which many in the United States are ignorant, home to audiences. Similarly, Elizabeth W. Son argues that plays examining the use of Korean comfort women during World War II can aid in the healing on a cultural level.

Works Cited

Aguirre, Manuel. 2013. Gothic Fiction and Folk-Narrative Structure: The Case of Mary Shelley's *Frankenstein*. *Gothic Studies* 12 (5): 1–18.

Benford, Criscillia. 2010. "Listen to my tale": Multilevel Structure, Narrative Sense Making, and the Inassimilable in Mary Shelley's *Frankenstein*. *Narrative* 18 (3): 324–346.

Biçer, Ahmet Gökhan. 2011. Depictions of Violence Onstage: Physical, Sexual and Verbal Dimensions of Violence in Sarah Kane's Experiential Theatre. *Journal of International Social Research* 4 (16): 81–88.

Boyle, Danny. (dir.). 2011. *Frankenstein*, National Theatre Live Broadcast, Landmark's Midtown Art Cinema, Atlanta. October 30, 2016.

Branagh, Kenneth. (dir.). 1994. *Mary Shelley's Frankenstein*. USA: TriStar Pictures.

Capancioni, Claudia, and Sibylle Erle. 2012. "Have You no Compassion?": Danny Boyle's and Nick Dear's Re-examination of Monstrosity in *Frankenstein*. *English Studies in Italian* 25 (3): 133–145.

Chakraborty, Sanchayita Paul, and Anindya Sekhar Purakayastha. 2013. Resistance Through Theatrical Communication: Two Women's Texts and Critiques of Violence. *Global Media Journal-Indian Edition* 4 (2): 1–14.

Clark, Anna E. 2014. *Frankenstein*; or, the Modern Protagonist. *ELH* 81 (1): 245–268.

Dear, Nick. 2011. *Frankenstein*. London: Faber and Faber.

Friedman, Lester D., and Allison B. Kavey. 2016. *Monstrous Progeny: A History of the Frankenstein Narratives*. New Brunswick: Rutgers University Press.

Gener, Randy. 2010. In Defense of *Ruined*: 5 Elements That Shape Lynn Nottage's Masterwork. *American Theatre* 27 (8): 118–122.

Iverson, Susan V. 2006. Performing Gender: A Discourse Analysis of Theatre-Based Sexual Violence Prevention Programs. *NASPA Journal* 43 (3): 547–577.

Joshua, Essaka. 2001. "Marking the Dates with Accuracy": The Time Problem in Mary Shelley's *Frankenstein*. *Gothic Studies* 3 (3): 279–308.

Katrak, Kethu H. 2014. "Stripping Women of Their Wombs": Active Witnessing of Performances of Violence. *Theatre Research International* 39 (1): 31–46.

McGuin, Paul (dir.) 2015. *Victor Frankenstein*, film. USA: Davis Entertainment.

Newman, Beth. 1986. Narratives of Seduction and the Seductions of Narrative: The Frame Structure of *Frankenstein*. *ELH* 53 (1): 141–163.

Porter, Lynnette. 2013. It's Alive! But What Kind of Creature Is National Theatre Live's "Frankenstein"? *Studies in Popular Culture* 35 (2): 1–21.

Shelley, Mary. (1992). *Frankenstein; or, The Modern Prometheus*, ed. Maurice Hindle. London: Penguin Books.

Son, Elizabeth W. 2016. Korean Trojan Women: Performing Wartime Sexual Violence. *Asian Theatre Journal* 33 (2): 369–394.

CHAPTER 9

The Cadaver's Pulse: Cinema and the Modern Prometheus

Scott MacKenzie

With the invention of the edit, or the cut, at the end of the nineteenth century, the cinema became a Frankensteinian monster. The cut, or montage, allowed the cinema to take shots of dead things, of events past and people recently or long demised, and cut them together into new undead images, replicating the illusion of life. The cinema, in this light, can be seen as a technology of revivification. In this process of revivification, the re-telling of Mary Shelley's *Frankenstein; or, The Modern Prometheus* (1818) has played a reoccurring role, re-animated and brought back to life across historical periods, national cinemas, and a wide array of genres. As Stephen King notes, with only some hyperbole, '*Frankenstein* has probably been the subject of more films than any other work in history, including the Bible' (1981: 62).

This chapter focuses on two aspects of revivification as it pertains to the image of *Frankenstein* on film: the transnational use of *Frankenstein* in cinema and the re-cutting of *Frankenstein* in avant-garde and experimental films. The first part of the chapter addresses the ways in which the story of

S. MacKenzie (✉)
Department of Film and Media, Queen's University,
Kingston, ON, Canada

© The Author(s) 2018
C. M. Davison, M. Mulvey-Roberts (eds.), *Global Frankenstein*,
Studies in Global Science Fiction,
https://doi.org/10.1007/978-3-319-78142-6_9

149

Frankenstein's monster has been 'cut into' and 'cut up by' national and transnational cinemas, and the ways in which the monster has been used in allegories to mediate and articulate anxieties in various national contexts, in films such as *Frankenstein* (J. Searle Dawley, USA, Edison, 1910), *Life Without Soul* (Joseph W. Smiley, USA, Ocean Productions, 1915), *Frankenstein* (James Whale, USA, Universal, 1931), *Bride of Frankenstein* (James Whale, USA, Universal, 1935), *The Curse of Frankenstein* (Terence Fisher, UK, Hammer, 1957), *Frankenstein Conquers the World* (*Furankenshutain Tai Chitei Kaijū Baragon*, Ishirō Honda, Japan/USA, Toho, 1965), and *Frankenstein '80* (*Mosaico*, Mario Mancini, Italy/West Germany, 1972). In these often low-budget films, the re-telling of the *Frankenstein* tale implicitly or explicitly addresses cultural and political tensions of their contemporaneous constituent nation-states. Cutting *Frankenstein* into these anxieties sheds light on the popularity of the Monster as an image of the unconscious tensions surrounding various nations, historical periods, and film genres and movements in the popular consciousness.

The second part of the chapter tells another related tale, focusing on the various ways the iconic filmic images of *Frankenstein* from Whale's films and a wide variety of footage not from the *Frankenstein* cinematic canon have been re-cut in experimental found footage films such as *Frank Stein* (Iván Zulueta, Spain, 1972) and *Spark of Being* (Bill Morrison, USA, 2010) to examine the central role that these images play in the imaginary of the cinema as a technology of revivification. In the case of both 'transnational Frankenstein' and 'found footage Frankenstein', the chapter considers the ways in which forms of metaphoric cutting (across genres and national identities) and actual cutting (within the film text itself) lead to the creation of new 'cinematic life' through transnational genre hybridity and the making of new films out of old, dead ones. These processes of revivification are central tropes in a wide range of Frankensteinian cinema and indeed to the cinema writ large.

MONTAGE AND THE CREATION OF NEW LIFE

Lest one thinks that the notion of cutting dead images into new life is a torturous metaphor, it is important to note that the kind of editing that dominates classical and contemporary Hollywood cinema—the seamless sewing together of shots which functions to erase the cut, often defined as 'suturing', that positions the audience as a passive, ideologically interpolated viewer (see Oudart 1977/78)—elides the creation of new life that is central to montage as it has been understood by filmmakers and theorists alike. This form of cutting—or montage—that foregrounds the constructed nature of the cinema, placing images in dialectical juxtaposition, has a long history. The first principles of montage were developed through an experiment by Soviet filmmaker Lev Kuleshov in 1921. Interested in exploring the ways in which cutting created meaning for audiences, he wrote the following about his experiment: '[…] I created a montage experiment which became known abroad as the "Kuleshov effect." I alternated the same shot of Mozhukhin with various other shots (a plate of soup, a girl, and child's coffin), and these shots acquired different meaning. The discovery stunned me—so I was convinced of the enormous power of montage' (1974: 200). It is curious to note that this creation of new meaning out of dead images is described by Kuleshov in the quotation earlier as an 'experiment'. He worked with raw, dead material to create new meanings where none previously existed. Because of this, as Ronald Levaco notes, for Kuleshov, the cinema '[…] was quintessentially the ordering of strips of film' (1974: 7). This ordering, and re-ordering, became a central tenet not only of Soviet montage but also in the formal and transnational re-iterations of the *Frankenstein* narrative across the cinema's first century. Building on Kuleshov's experiment, Sergei Eisenstein, director of Soviet classics that foregrounded the practice of montage such as *The Battleship Potemkin* (*Bronenosets Potyomkin*, USSR, 1925), *October* (*Oktyabr'*, USSR, 1928), and *Ivan the Terrible* (*Ivan Grozniy*, USSR, 1944/1958), argued that film's ability, through dialectical montage, to create mental images was of the utmost importance. Film was therefore structured dialectically in order to generate meaning in the spectator, meaning not embedded in the image-text itself but in the collision of images. Indeed, Eisenstein argued that cinematic images—constituent parts of the larger cinematic whole body—carried no meaning outside of their function to bring to life a theme extending throughout a cinematic work, which was greater than the sum of its parts. He defined this process as follows:

> What is essentially involved in such an understanding of montage? In such a case, each montage piece exists no longer as something unrelated, but as a given particular representation of the general theme that in equal measure penetrates all the shot-pieces. The juxtaposition of these partial details, in a given montage construction calls to life and forces into the light that general quality in which each detail has participated and which binds together all the details into a whole, namely, into that generalized image, wherein the creator, followed by the spectator, experiences the theme. (1947: 11)

Eisenstein's theory of montage posited that the cinematic image was of no value as a sign related to a referent in the real world; in his eyes, the cinema could only signify meaning through the juxtaposition of one image in collision with the next. These collisions begat a new life through the cinema, for meaning and through the realisation of this meaning, for the audience itself. The power of the cut to create new and different meanings through juxtaposition was not only a practice engaged in by Soviet formalists; these lessons played a key role in early cinema and in the emergence of the *Frankenstein* narrative as reoccurring and often re-cut.

EARLY *FRANKENSTEIN*: CUTTING THE NARRATIVE AND RE-CUTTING THE FILM

J. Searle Dawley's *Frankenstein*, like many of its later cinematic progeny, caused a stir upon its release by the Edison Corporation in 1910, despite the fact that the promotional material surrounding the film explicitly de-emphasised horror and violence. Edison, to avoid the potential censorship issues that were pervasive in early cinema, decided to rely on literary adaptations as source material, as these works could be publicised as 'respectable' (see Laird 2015: 116). In Edison's in-house magazine *Edison Kinetogram*, *Frankenstein* is framed in the following manner:

> In making the film the Edison Co. has carefully tried to eliminate all actual repulsive situations and to concentrate its endeavors upon the mystic and psychological problems that are to be found in this weird tale. Whenever, therefore, the film differs from the original story it is purely with the idea of elimination what would be repulsive to a moving picture audience. (1910: 3–4)

This is the first of many examples of the re-cutting of *Frankenstein*, in this case, on a narrative level, removing what an audience might find 'repulsive'. Despite these efforts, the film still caused shock and consternation. As Carlos Clarens notes: '[…] trade publications of the period comment on the reaction of certain exhibitors who found *Frankenstein* a bit too weird for their patrons' (1967: 39). This did give pause to filmmakers who made subsequent adaptations, with producers again playing down the horror—the exact element that would attract audiences—to avoid the moral probity of censor boards and religious organisations. A case in point is *Life Without Soul* (Joseph W. Smiley, USA, 1915), a 70-minute film also based on Shelley's book. While lost, some press accounts do exist, which include the comment that the monster was 'awe-inspiring but never gro-tesque' (Clarens 1967: 39) as the actor Percy Darrell Standing played the role with little make-up. This second *Frankenstein* film was therefore looked upon as slightly more tame, particularly as it had not generated the furore surrounding Edison's version. However, there were some controversies surrounding this version too, and *Life Without Soul*'s rights were sold by Ocean Pictures, the film's production company, to Raven Productions a year after its release. Once Raven acquired the film, it initiated the long tradition of literally re-cutting Frankensteinian cinema. An article in the trade publication *Moving Picture World* outlines the changes Raven made:

> In its new form, *Life Without Soul* […] will tell a slightly different story. While the theme has not been tampered with, a new interest has been added to the production in its re-editing. […] In the revision of this picture, Mr. Raven […] had some scientific scenes inserted […]. These scientific films show blood coursing through veins and arteries, the conjugation of cells and the reproduction of life in the fish world. They lend a more convincing atmo-sphere to the laboratory scenes and cause the final results of the scientist to appear logical. […] In its new form, *Life Without Soul*, besides its entertaining value also has an educational worth. (*Moving Picture World* 6 May 1916: 996)

While this version of the film is also lost, the edits outlined earlier tell a striking tale. It is hard to believe that the inclusion of the reproductive life of fish and the circulation of blood make this into an 'educational film', let alone one that would appear to make 'the scientist appear logical'. Indeed, here we see another instantiation of Eisensteinian/Frankensteinian mon-tage where cutting new work into an older cinematic body revivifies it, creating logic and meaning that did not previously exist. Science is mobil-ised to give *Life Without Soul* the veneer of empiricism and therefore respectability. Most likely, Raven did this to alleviate exhibitioners' fears that the film would be horrific and therefore exploitative after the contro-versy surrounding the first cinematic version of *Frankenstein*. This was only the first of many *Frankenstein* films to be cut up to create new mean-ings and new lives for the story.

WHALE's *FRANKENSTEIN* AND *BRIDE OF FRANKENSTEIN*

The Monster in James Whale's *Frankenstein* has become the iconic image of Shelley's creation, replacing the high intelligence found in the creature's depiction in the novel with that of a mute, dim monster and changing its appearance drastically. One reason for this shift is yet another form of cutting to create new life: the film was as much, if not more so, an adaptation of Peggy Webling's 1930 London stage play as it was an adaptation of the novel proper. (In this manner, *Frankenstein* followed *Dracula* in its transition from page to stage to screen, the first stage version of *Frankenstein* being produced several years after its initial publication). Moreover, four different writers at Universal (including the uncredited French writer and director Robert Florey) worked on the script as it made its way through to production.

On a metaphoric level, throughout production, *Frankenstein* and *Bride of Frankenstein* were works stitched together from a variety of parts from national traditions. The transnational—mostly Anglo-American—background of the work was magnified once Whale, a British expat, came on board as the director. Many of the other key players in the films were also British expats (playwright Peggy Webling; Editor Maurice Pivar; and actors Boris Karloff, Colin Clive, Frederick Kerr, Lionel Belmore, Elsa Lanchester, and Ernest Thesiger). As Peter Hutchings notes, '[…] *Bride of Frankenstein* can to a certain extent be seen as a British horror film in exile […]' (2001: 117). The Monster also takes on other characteristics that were in no way central to the original narrative yet function as a reflection of both American and British fetishes and sensibilities. As Robin Wood notes in his classic study of American horror cinema, Whale's *Frankenstein* was also a film about class and the proletariat, a claim he based 'partly on the strength of its pervasive class references, more on the strength of Karloff's costume: Frankenstein could have dressed his creature in top hat, white tie and tails, but in fact chose labourer's clothes' (Wood and Lippe 1979: 11) (Fig. 9.1).

That *Frankenstein* became a class allegory at the height of the Great Depression speaks to the ways in which popular narratives are re-cut and re-cast through various historical and political moments, becoming texts embedded with heretofore unknown fears. Increasing the transnational aspect of the work was the influence that German Expressionist films such as *The Cabinet of Dr. Caligari* (*Das Cabinet des Dr. Caligari*, Robert Wiene, Germany, 1920) had on the director, which Whale screened repeatedly for the cast and crew (Curtis 1998: 149). *Bride of Frankenstein*, through its use of low and high angles, drastic juxtapositions of light and dark, and the characters of Doctor Septimus Pretorius (Ernest Thesiger)— who resembles both Dr. Caligari and Dr. Mabuse—and the Bride herself

Fig. 9.1 The proletarian creature. From James Whale's *Frankenstein*. Frame grab (© Universal Studios)

Fig. 9.2 The Expressionist creature. From James Whale's *Bride of Frankenstein*. Frame grab (© Universal Studios)

(Elsa Lanchester), resonates with German Expressionist cinema, especially the 'false' Maria robot in Fritz Lang's *Metropolis* (Germany, 1927) (Fig. 9.2).

For all of these reasons, Whale's two films speak as much to the tensions and transformations of the early 1930s (class politics, the fear of migration as embodied by the 'Other', the effects of émigré transnationalism, and the fear of European sexual decadence) as they do to those of the nineteenth century (such as the role of repression and deformity). Whale's two *Frankenstein* films stitch together the aforementioned transnational anxieties about war and migration central to European and American politics of the era.

Because Whale's films brought these fears to the surface, they had to be cut. The two Universal films faced a myriad of forms of censorious editing in order to tame the tales as horror films could not address the actual terrors of society. If *Life Without Soul* cut in new footage to create an acceptable form of cinematic life (including images of the creation of life itself), *Frankenstein* and *Bride of Frankenstein* were cut, at times drastically, creating what were virtually new films in the process, leaving these new versions as vivisected shells of their former selves.

In the pre-Code Hollywood era (1929–1934), film censorship was undertaken at local and state levels in the USA. Many jurisdictions wished to cut Whale's film; some jurisdictions did, others negotiated with Universal. As Gerald Gardner notes, 'The movie's gruesomeness and irreverence were attacked by censorship boards in many states and all parts of the world' (1987: 65). Perhaps the most extreme example was in Kansas where 32 cuts were proposed, which would have cut the film in half (Doherty 1999: 297). Eventually, it was agreed that the film could be released with only half the cuts. Put another way, cutting one-quarter of the film would suffice.

Numerous other nations also called for cuts, which led to literal cutting in the form of what might be called censorious montage. These quite literal cuts drastically changed the text and its viewing experience for non-American audiences. The British Board of Film Classification (BBFC) mandated cuts to the film prior to its release in the UK in 1931. James Curtis notes that *Frankenstein* was cut drastically (1998: 159). Tom Dewe Mathews, in his study of British film censorship, points to the fact that a new rating category was created for the film: 'H' for 'Horror' (1994: 78). Perhaps the most extreme case of cutting took place in Sweden, where films such as *Public Enemy* (William Wellman, USA, Warner Bros., 1931) and *Freaks* (Tod Browning, USA, MGM, 1932) were banned because of violence and horror (see Holmberg 2010: 36). Whale's *Frankenstein* was cut from 76 to 51 minutes (or by one-third) on its release in Sweden in 1932, a ban only removed in 1976. When *Bride of Frankenstein* was released, the cuts in Sweden were also extensive:

> Sweden eliminated two solid pages of dialogue and shots from the film, including the scene of Frankenstein stealing the coffin, the scene of the hangman, the father with child in his arms, the monster drowning Hans and killing his wife, the scene of the monster throwing rocks down on his pursuers, the scene of the monster tied to a tree and being stoned, the monster breaking open a coffin. The deletions of the Swedish censors were so numerous that the film seemed destined to be released as a short subject. (Gardner 1987: 71)

Other countries followed suit: Trinidad, Palestine, and Hungary banned *Bride of Frankenstein*, and China, Singapore, and Japan called for extensive cuts. In a move that broke with its typical practice, the Motion Picture Production Code censor forewarned Universal's producer (and son of the studio head Carl Laemmle) Carl Laemmle Jr what was about to happen when they issued their Seal of Approval: '[...] As I have informed you verbally, however, it is more than likely that this picture will meet with considerable difficulty at the hands of censor boards both in this country and abroad [....] you may well expect difficulty with it wherever the picture is shown' (Gardner 1987: 71). The amount and diversity of cuts to which *Frankenstein* and *Bride of Frankenstein* were subjected meant that different localities, states, and, indeed, nations saw different films; some versions were nearly unintelligible. The continuous re-cutting and reassembling of Whale's two monstrous works were attempts to eradicate the cultural fears and taboos which the works represented in each constituency. Cutting the narrative and cutting the films themselves were both attempts to make a better Monster, yet ironically, these cuts only scarred the films and, in doing so, made the scars all the more visible. This incessant re-cutting was not only the providence of censors but also used as a means by which to continue the cycle of films. In *Frankenstein*, given the strictures of the Production Code (launched in 1930, but only coming into full force in 1934) that stated murder must be avenged, the Creature dies at the film's conclusion. Yet there was a need to revive the Monster to perpetuate the series and produce a sequel. To this extent, *Bride of Frankenstein* is yet another iteration of the cinema bringing the dead back to life through montage, in this case the Monster itself. Because of the popularity of the first film, early scenes in *Bride of Frankenstein* were made by re-cutting the conclusion of *Frankenstein*, allowing the creature to escape a return to death through immolation by falling into the windmill's well. The cutting of *Frankenstein*, in this instance, is used to bring the Creature and the film cycle back to life.

TRANSNATIONAL *FRANKENSTEIN*

It is probably clear by now that, as Paul O'Flinn argues, 'There is no such thing as *Frankenstein*, there are only *Frankensteins*, as the text is ceaselessly rewritten, reproduced, refilmed and redesigned. The fact that many people call the monster Frankenstein and thus confuse the pair betrays the extent of that restructuring' (2001: 105). Susan Tyler Hitchcock also notes, 'By the 1950s the story was so familiar it could be retold with little or no reference back to Mary Shelley' (2007: 211). The use of the Frankenstein monster in transnational cinemas represents an under-analysed aspect of the histories of global *Frankenstein*: films deploy narrative and stylistic devices hybridised from the different film movements and national cultures in which the story of the Monster circulated. To this extent, these works represent a trend in European cinema—and world cinema writ large—that has often been marginalised, precisely because it is seen as a threat. As Tim Bergfelder notes:

> Discourses on European cinema have traditionally focused less on the inclusive or cross-cultural aspects the term "European" might imply, but on notions of national specificities, cultural authenticity and indigenous production contexts. In order to establish a national identity for a particular film culture, features that transcend or contradict these identity formations have been either neglected or marginalised, but also viewed as threatening. (2000: 139)

A case in point is the British film industry in the 1940s and 1950s. The rise of genre films in the UK, most notably melodramas and horror films—and films that crossed both genres—functioned as attempts to carve out a properly British popular cinema in a country whose screens were dominated by Hollywood productions. This problem—present throughout Europe after World War II and the implementation of the Marshall Plan (the American plan that paid to rebuild post-War Europe but also turned the continent into a new market for US domestic products)—was exacerbated by the fact the UK and the USA share a common language. British producers, then, turned to English literary traditions to carve out a properly national form of film production, yet these very productions also relied on popular Hollywood genres. Companies such as Ealing, Gainsborough and Hammer all vied for this market, and while all successful, the Hammer cycle of horror films was the one international success to arise from this strategy (see Pirie 1980; Petley 1986).

It then dawned on Hammer Films, after the unexpected success of *The Quatermass Xperiment* (Val Guest, UK, 1955), that films made in Britain which drew on the tradition of the Gothic found a market in both the UK and the USA. They began this series with a new adaptation of *Frankenstein*. As in the case of Whale, the studio faced a great deal of resistance from the BBFC, especially because the film was to be shot in colour. The BBFC censor wrote, upon reviewing the script, 'We are concerned about the flavour of this script, which, in its preoccupation with horror and gruesome detail, goes far beyond what we are accustomed to allow even for the "X" category. I am afraid we can give no assurance that we should be able to pass a film based on the present script and a revised script should be sent us for our comments, in which the overall unpleasantness should be mitigated' (Kinsey 2005: 60). Hammer, however, decided to proceed with the script as it was. The resultant film, *The Curse of Frankenstein,* was widely popular though reviews at the time were unkind, with Fisher's work being compared unfavourably to Whale's earlier iteration. Yet, *The Curse of Frankenstein* spawned a new form of properly British Gothic Horror, though one linked to transnational processes of exchange. This spoke to a larger cultural interchange that was in process. As Brian Wilson notes:

> During this period Britain struggled with its national identity as it experienced an influx of alternative artistic and ideological patterns from America. As its youth culture became introduced to the ideals of Hollywood cinema and rock-and-roll, British cinema began to reflect the anxieties of this cultural transition through the established structures of the horror and science fiction genres [...] it seems appropriate that Hammer's most successful series of films drew upon defining aspects of a long repressed national cultural tradition [and its] emphasis upon the redefinition of the horror genre represented a revival of the Gothic British cultural tradition [...]. (2007: 55)

Therefore, the film was not simply a return to the British tradition of the Gothic. *The Curse of Frankenstein* paralleled (though in reverse) the transnational foundations of rock music: Shelley's novel was re-imagined in the USA by Universal and then the Whale film was re-imagined yet again as it migrated back to the UK, the changes undertaken being as much about copyright infringement as they were about making a properly British Gothic tale. As Peter Hutchings notes:

> British horror films do not merely reflect or reproduce socially specific trends and issues but instead imaginatively transformed whatever they incorporated. For example, in the case of Hammer in the 1950s, its work can be seen to have involved seizing upon aspects of a contemporaneous social reality that were not naturally connected—in particular, shifts in gender definition and changing notions of professionalism—and weaving these into an aesthetic unity in the interests of making horror relevant to the British market. (2001: 122)

This transnational cutting, not of narrative per se but of differing national anxieties through the use of specific nation-state's genres, meant Hammer horror, and *The Curse of Frankenstein* in particular, allowed the story to be re-animated through contemporaneous fears. Yet there were nevertheless linkages between Whale's *Frankenstein* and Fisher's *The Curse of Frankenstein*. Stephen King, for instance, sees a pertinent link between Whale's Monster and the one found in Hammer: '[…] although in both cases the monster is horrible to look at, there is also something so sad, so miserable there that our hearts actually go out to the creature even as they are shrinking away from it in fear and disgust' (1981: 69). Another trope which is implicitly present in both Whale's (who was as open as one could be about his homosexuality in 1930s Hollywood) and Fisher's films is a seething undercurrent of homoeroticism (Fig. 9.3).

The use of the *Frankenstein* story as a cauldron into which national fears and anxieties could be poured and then recombined into something new, beyond the sum of its parts, quickly became a global phenomenon. *Frankenstein Conquers the World* (*Furankenshutain Tai Chitei Kaijū Baragon*, Ishirō Honda, Japan/USA, Toho, 1965) functions as an allegory for the lingering effects of World War II, combining Nazis, the bombing of Hiroshima, and *Kaijū*, the then-popular Japanese genre of gigantic monsters (the cinematic progeny of Godzilla (Gojira), a cycle of films originated by Honda in 1954). Like many Japanese giant monster films, *Frankenstein Conquers the World* has a convoluted plot: the Nazis have the Monster's heart and transport it to the Japanese for research during World War II. The heart arrives in Hiroshima just before the first atomic bomb is dropped. Fifteen years later, a wild child is found in the streets; it is determined that he is Caucasian and has grown from the now irradiated heart. He starts to grow exponentially. Once he escapes the lab in which he is

Fig. 9.3 The creature as figure of pity. From Terence Fisher's *The Curse of Frankenstein*. Frame grab (© Hammer Studios)

imprisoned, he makes his way from Tokyo to Mount Fuji, where he battles Baragon, a more 'traditional' gargantuan monster in the Gojira tradition. The Frankenstein creature, as is often the case, is misunderstood, and while he defeats Baragon, both of them plummet to their demise, although the human characters note that the monster will be back as, in this iteration, he is immortal. As Tyler Hitchcock notes, 'In a low-budget hour and a half and at many different levels, the film re-enacted the past twenty years of world history and its cultural consequences. The secret force of Germany, possessed by the Japanese, then irradiated, takes on the form of a Caucasian giant and grapples with the ancient dragon of the East' (239–40).

At this point, parts of the *Frankenstein* narrative had been recombined so many times as to be nearly unrecognisable, continuously coming back from the dead in a transmogrified form, cut up with new national parts added to the narrative creature. Other national cinemas continued in this vein. *Killing Frankestayna Karsi* (Nuri Akinci, Turkey, 1967)—now lost—placed the Creature in battle with Kilink, a Turkish superhero/anti-hero from a popular series of films, cutting a globally known character into battle with a nationally known one. *Dracula* vs. *Frankenstein* (*El Hombre que vino del ummo*, Tulio Demicheli, Spain/West Germany/Italy, 1969) was a subset of the then popular genre of alien invasion films; here, the aliens revive the Universal monsters, which then do battle. *Frankenstein '80* (*Mosaico*, Mario Mancini, Italy/West Germany, 1972) combines elements of the Italian Gothic film genre, the *giallo*, and the emergent tradition of the slasher film. In each of these cases, the Monster is cut into national genres and movements, creating transnational cinema so far removed from Shelley's original tale that they are unrecognisable. But the figure of the Creature nonetheless lives on.

Found Footage *Frankenstein*

If transnational versions of *Frankenstein* are both cut in various national traditions and lead to censorious cutting, then the avant-garde tradition of re-telling the *Frankenstein* story relies on the actual re-cutting of found footage film to tell the tale, foregrounding the materiality of the cinematic process of building new life from dead images. Describing the epistemological function of found footage filmmaking, and the ways in which the process builds new works, William C. Wees writes, 'Whether they preserve the footage in its original form or present it in new and different ways, they invite us to recognize it as found footage, as recycled images, and due to that self-referentiality, they encourage a more analytical reading [...] than the footage originally received' (1993: 11). This form of found footage filmmaking is a descendant of the works of Eisenstein and Kuleshov. Two avant-garde works in particular take *Frankenstein*, and the Frankensteinian found footage filmmaking legacy, as both the form and the subject of their works. Spanish experimental filmmaker Iván Zulueta's three-minute *Frank Stein* (Spain, 1972) tells the tale through the re-cutting and re-purposing of Whale's film, focusing on faces as the locus of horror. In this film, the narrative and its Gothic/German Expressionist setting are reduced to a play of light and dark; the juxtaposition of these images, the faces contained therein, and the soundtrack turn the horror into a highly affect-riddled experience. What Zulueta's work demonstrates is that the images of the *Frankenstein* mythos can be stripped out of their national or transnational frames—and from their narrative contexts—and still be terrifying (Fig. 9.4).

As Matt Losada notes, *Frank Stein*, made with '[...] leftover pieces of 35 mm film [...] distills the original 1931 James Whale feature down to three minutes, mixing fast-motion with freeze-frames on moments of high emotion, often close-ups of agitated faces' (2010).

If Zulueta's work functions as a means to create a new horrific cinematic body out of old materials, Bill Morrison's *Spark of Being* draws on the entire history of cinema's detritus to revivify *Frankenstein*. *Spark of Being* is entirely made up of found footage film, none of it from any of the previous iterations of filmic *Frankenstein*. Yet the film was still inspired by Frankensteinian cinema, as Morrison states, 'I was [...] inspired by other free adaptations of *Frankenstein*: Thomas Edison (1910), James Whale

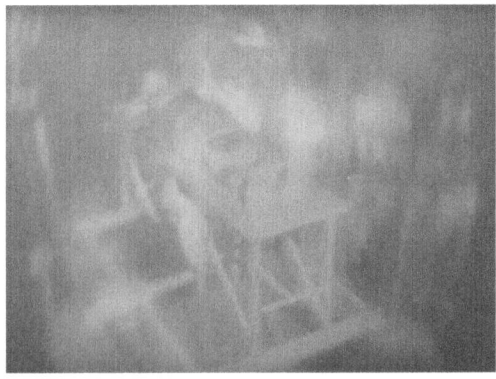

Fig. 9.4 Revivifying Frankensteinian cinema. From Iván Zulueta's *Frank Stein*. Frame grab (© Iván Zulueta)

(1931), Andy Warhol (1973), and Mel Brooks (1974), as well as Peter Ackroyd's 2008 novel *The Casebook of Victor Frankenstein* (2016: 59). *Spark of Being* is divided into 12 chapters, all with different found footage aesthetics and all using forms of decayed film: archival, mouldy, over-exposed, chemically stained, tinted, and scratched (all parts of analogue cinema that are typically thrown aside as useless and dead, the bits that are cut away to build the perfect beast). Opening the film in the Arctic, as so few cinematic versions of *Frankenstein* do, Morrison draws on Frank Hurley's original 1911–1914 footage of Ernest Shackleton's fated Antarctic expedition, arguing that, 'Shelley's original narrative begins in the Arctic, and I imagined an image of a boat stuck in a frozen ocean, then realized, I've seen that!—in the famous Shackleton 16 mm footage, shot by men who were abandoned for two years in Antarctica' (2016: 58). Yet cutting together to build a new work is also central here as Antarctica stands in for the Arctic. Morrison's building of his Frankensteinian cinema body goes beyond the use of Shackleton's film, as he deploys a range of found footage from other sources, including soft-core porn, old Movietone newsreels, educational films, and other remnants of detritus cinema. Here is the clearest elucidation of building a new work and bringing it to life through discarded parts of other cinematic bodies. Morrison nevertheless hews close to the original novel, in many ways more so than any of the other Frankenstein cinematic works. He states:

> To my mind, *Spark of Being* can be thought of as a loop. You have these three men—the ship's captain, the doctor, and the creature—and they change roles. The captain of the ship welcomes the passenger who starts telling the story that the captain then relays. The passenger is a doctor, who tells how he created a living creature with his own hands. The story is then told from the perspective of this creature, who describes his education and his ultimately fruitless quest for love. The creature ultimately confronts his creator, and, in my twist on the original story, the doctor flees the monster, ultimately captaining a boat to the polar region seen at the beginning of the film. (MacDonald 2016: 59)

Spark of Being is also a work that materially replicates the cinema itself as a cadaverous monstrosity. As Morrison notes in an interview with Scott MacDonald, 'So I re-read *Frankenstein*, and [...] started thinking about a film made out of found-footage-spare-parts, like the monster is made out of "found" body parts' (MacDonald 2016: 58). He goes on to note, 'The film itself is the Creature' (2016: 60).

The fact that Morrison's film *is* the Creature perhaps makes *Spark of Being* the purest adaptation of *Frankenstein*. Yet, what perhaps becomes clear is that no filmmaker has truly adapted Shelley's influential novel for the cinema; each iteration reconstructs the narrative, and in some cases the materiality of film itself, to its own ends. From the re-cutting of *Life Without Soul* into an 'educational' work, to the numerous censorious cuts to Whale's film, to the transnational cutting of the *Frankenstein* narrative into various national cinema contexts and anxieties, or even monstrous mutilation or dissections brought on by censorship, to the literal cutting of film in avant-garde works, each iteration creates a new form and life for the narrative. Each filmmaker, and censor board, then, is his or her own Victor Frankenstein. The profound, global influence of the novel, then, can be seen not only through the continual viability of aspects of the narrative that captured a global imagination but also in the philosophical issues about what life and death means as raised in *Frankenstein; or, The Modern Prometheus*. Shelley's work is a pre-cinematic model for film and its ability to continuously raise images from the dead, giving them new life.

WORKS CITED

Akinci, Nuri. (dir.). 1967. *Killing Frankestayna Karsi*, film. Turkey: Omur Film.

Anon. 1910. '*Frankenstein' Edison Kinetogram*, 15 March: 3–4.

———. 1916. '*Life Without Soul* (Ocean)' *Moving Picture World*, 6 May: 996.

Bergfelder, Tim. 2000. The Nation Vanishes: European Co-productions and Popular Genre Formula in the 1950s and 1960s. In *Cinema and Nation*, ed. Mette Hjort and Scott MacKenzie, 139–152. London: Routledge.

Browning, Tod. (dir.). 1932. *Freaks*, film. USA: MGM.

Clarens, Carlos. 1967. *An Illustrated History of the Horror Film*. New York: Capricorn Books.

Curtis, James. 1998. *James Whale: A New World of Gods and Monsters*. London: Faber.

Dawley, J. Searle. (dir.). 1910. *Frankenstein*, film. USA: Edison.

Demicheli, Tulio. (dir.). 1969. *Dracula* vs. *Frankenstein* (*El Hombre que vino del ummo*), film. Spain/West Germany/Italy: Eichberg-Film/International Jaguar Cinematografica/Producciones Jaime Prades.

Doherty, Thomas Patrick. 1999. *Pre-code Hollywood: Sex, Immorality, and Insurrection in American Cinema 1930–1934*. New York: Columbia University Press.

Eisenstein, Sergei. (dir.). 1925. *The Battleship Potemkin* (*Bronenosets Potyomkin*), film. USSR: Mosfilm.

———. (dir.). 1928. *October* (*Oktyabr*), film. USSR: Mosfilm.

———. (dir.). 1944/1958. *Ivan the Terrible* (*Ivan Grozniy*), film. USSR: Mosfilm.

———. 1947. Word and Image. In *The Film Sense*, Jay Leyda (ed. and trans.), 3–68. New York: Harcourt.

Fisher, Terence. (dir.). 1957. *The Curse of Frankenstein*, film. UK: Hammer.

Gardner, Gerald. 1987. *The Censorship Papers: Movie Censorship Letters from the Hays Office 1934 to 1968*. New York: Dodd and Mead.

Guest, Val. (dir.). 1955. *The Quatermass Xperiment*, film. UK: Hammer.

Hitchcock, Susan Tyler. 2007. *Frankenstein: A Cultural History*. New York: W. W. Norton.

Holmberg, Jan. 2010. Censorship in Sweden. In *Swedish Film: An Introduction and Reader*, ed. Mariah Larsson and Andres Marklund, 34–42. Lund: Nordic Academic Press.

Hondo, Ishirō. (dir.). 1965. Film, *Frankenstein Conquers the World* (*Furankenshutain Tai Chitei Kaijū Baragon*). Japan/USA: Toho/American International Pictures.

Hutchings, Peter. 2001. The Problem of British Horror. In *Horror: The Film Reader*, ed. Mark Jancovich, 115–123. London: Routledge.

King, Stephen. 1981. *Danse Macabre*. Berkeley: New York.

Kinsey, Wayne. 2005. *Hammer Films: The Bray Studios Years*. Richmond: Reynolds & Hearn.

Kuleshov, Lev. 1974. In Maloi Gnezdnikovsky Lane. In *Kuleshov on Film: Writings of Lev Kuleshov*, ed. Ronald Levaco, 196–207. Berkeley: University of California Press.

Laird, Karen E. 2015. *The Art of Adapting Victorian Literature, 1848–1920: Dramatizing Jane Eyre, David Copperfield, and The Woman in White*. London: Routledge.

Lang, Fritz (dir.). 1927. *Metropolis*, film. Germany: UFA.

Levaco, Ronald. 1974. Introduction. In *Kuleshov on Film: Writings of Lev Kuleshov*, ed. Ronald Levaco, 1–40. Berkeley: University of California Press.

Losada, Matt. 2010. Iván Zulueta's Cinephilia of Ecstasy and Experiment. *Senses of Cinema* 56. http://sensesofcinema.com/2010/feature-articles/ivan-zulueta's-cinephilia-of-ecstasy-and-experiment. Accessed 15 Nov 2017.

MacDonald, Scott. 2016. Interview with Bill Morrison: 6 Recent Films (for Dan Streible). *Millennium Film Journal* 64: 56–75.

Mancini, Mario. (dir.). 1972. *Frankenstein '80* (*Mosaico*), film. Italy/West Germany: M.G.D. Film.

Mathews, Tom Dewe. 1994. *Censored: The Story of Film Censorship in Britain*. London: Chatto & Windus.

Morrison, Bill. (dir.). 2010. *Spark of Being*, film. USA. Bill Morrison, USA: Hypnotic Pictures.

O'Flinn, Paul. 2001. Production and Reproduction: The Case of *Frankenstein*. In *Horror: The Film Reader*, ed. Mark Jancovich, 105–113. London: Routledge.

Oudart, Jean-Pierre. 1977–8. Cinema and Suture. *Screen* 18: 4, 35–47.

Petley, Julian. 1986. The Lost Continent. In *All Our Yesterdays: 90 Years of British Cinema*, ed. Charles Barr, 98–119. London: BFI.

Pirie, David. 1980. *Hammer: A Cinema Case Study*. London: BFI.

Smiley, Joseph W. (dir.). 1915. *Life Without Soul*, film. USA: Ocean Productions.

Wees, William C. 1993. *Recycled Images: The Art and Politics of Found Footage Films*. New York: Anthology Film Archives.

Wellman, William. (dir.). 1931. *Public Enemy*, film. USA: Warner Bros.

Whale, James. (dir.). 1931. *Frankenstein*, film. USA, Universal.

———. (dir.). 1935. *Bride of Frankenstein*, film. USA, Universal.

Wiene, Robert. (dir.). 1920. *The Cabinet of Dr. Caligari* (*Das Cabinet des Dr. Caligari*), film. Germany: Decla-Bioscop AG.

Wilson, Brian. 2007. Notes on a Radical Tradition: Subversive Ideological Applications in the Hammer Horror Films. *CinéAction* 72: 53–57.

Wood, Robin, and Richard Lippe, eds. 1979. *American Nightmare: Essays on the Horror Film*. Toronto: Festival of Festivals.

Zulueta, Iván. (dir.). 1972. *Frank Stein*, film. Spain: Iván Zulueta.

CHAPTER 10

Promethean Myths of the Twenty-First Century: Contemporary *Frankenstein* Film Adaptations and the Rise of the Viral Zombie

Xavier Aldana Reyes

To trace the state of the Frankenstein myth in post-millennial films is not an easy task. On the one hand, the various themes and archetypes that have coalesced into the Frankenstein myth—from Promethean references to Greek mythology and the creation of mankind to the configuration of the notion of 'monstrosity' in the Romantic period and its coalescence into a physically 'othered' and metaphorically complex creature (Botting 2009: 204)—have come into play and merged in ways that make any notion of purity unthinkable.[1] This complicates clear-cut definitions of Frankenstein cinema and makes an exhaustive account a titanic endeavour. Even narrowing down the body of films to adaptations of the 1818 *Frankenstein* is of little help for, as Mark Jancovich notes:

X. Aldana Reyes (✉)
Department of English, Manchester Metropolitan University, Manchester, UK

© The Author(s) 2018
C. M. Davison, M. Mulvey-Roberts (eds.), *Global Frankenstein*,
Studies in Global Science Fiction,
https://doi.org/10.1007/978-3-319-78142-6_10

167

[f]ew, if any, of the films that are associated with Mary Shelley's novel were actually an adaptation of this source text. Many are actually adaptations of other sources, such as plays, other films and comic books. They are also rarely even simply adaptations of these other sources but are rather produced in relation to a range of different intertexts. [...] Adaptations of the Frankenstein story are inevitably a response to a range of other trends within the period within which they were made, trends that not only motivate an interest in materials culled from Mary Shelley's novel but also shape what materials are deemed to be of interest and how they are interpreted and hybridized with other elements from elsewhere. (2016: 191)

To illustrate Jancovich's point, in the case of a film such as *Victor Frankenstein* (Paul McGuigan 2016), the Igor character (Daniel Radcliffe) is obviously drawn from cinematic sources: it evokes characters from *The Hunchback of Notre Dame* (Wallace Worsley 1923), *Freaks* (Tod Browning 1932) and, most importantly, James Whale's *Frankenstein* (1931). Yet, Frankenstein's companion in the latter film is called 'Fritz', for the film itself was adapted, in part, from the stage adaptation of 1823, *Presumption; or, the Fate of Frankenstein*, by Richard Brinsley Peake.[2] As Esther Schor has pointed out, the role of cinema in the creation of the Frankenstein myth is of particular importance, for it has helped visualise the body of a creature whose physique remains rather vague in the novel.[3]

While I acknowledge that it is impossible to trace a legitimate line of what we could term 'Frankencinema', I want to focus in this chapter on the type of referential films that Jancovich flags up precisely because they might help us distinguish what is (or is not) at stake in the current return to *Frankenstein* in contemporary cinema. While it is perfectly possible to argue that 'those films that explicitly establish a relationship [to Shelley's novel] often do so in an uninspired bid for respectability or a simple exercise in branding' (Jancovich 2016: 203), examining these patterns enables an assessment of the state of the Frankenstein myth today (its potential relevance or decline) and the identification of significant strands in the horror genre and the cinematic Gothic mode more widely. I support the position that cinema of any kind, but especially genre cinema, is not produced in a cultural vacuum; much more often, it responds to market flows of supply and demand. In a sense, then, I am less interested in what makes contemporary adaptations of *Frankenstein* 'good' adaptations (whatever our criterion for judging this may be), what specific sources they rely upon or how faithful they are to them. More crucial to me are what ideas, derived from the palimpsest that is the Frankenstein myth, continue to be explored and expanded today.

My tracing of the cinematic developments of the Frankenstein myth in the twenty-first century aims to reach two main conclusions. First, I want to argue that the quality and box-office performance of post-millennial 'referential adaptations'—my term for the adaptations that create a direct link to other Frankenstein texts, especially by name—show clear signs of creative exhaustion and simultaneously reveal larger shifts that have seen Gothic monsters (vampires, ghosts, werewolves, zombies) recast as sympathetic characters with complex psychologies. Mainstream adaptations have persisted in turning Frankenstein's creature into a hero (*Frankenstein* (Marcus Nispel 2004)), superhero (*I, Frankenstein* (Stuart Beattie 2014)) or victim (*Frankenstein* (Bernard Rose 2015), stylised as *FRANKENSTEIN*), with little critical or financial success. Even the attempt to give Igor a voice in *Victor Frankenstein* received a lukewarm response from audiences and reviewers. These films are therefore interesting because they epitomise various popular cinematic approaches to the Gothic in recent years (superhero Gothic, in particular) and because they show that Gothic period films may be on the wane, whichever their generic allegiance.

Second, following the work of Lester D. Friedman and Allison B. Kavey, I speculate that one possible reason for the current lack of interest in referential Frankencinema is that the cultural work that Shelley's myth once carried out has, in recent years, shifted towards the figure of the viral zombie. Zombies, as the source of artificially engineered pandemics, now channel more readily anxieties regarding the dangers of unbridled scientific, medical and technological advances, especially their impact on the human subject and the environment. They also prod the boundaries between life and consciousness, especially as zombies have gradually become sentient beings. I show that, to a certain extent, contemporary zombies have blended with Shelley's Promethean monster to the point where the two have become virtually indistinguishable. I cannot do much more than gesture towards these changes and developments in the space of this chapter, but a greater focus on the use, value and reception of the Frankenstein myth should paint a clear picture of what role the text and its allegorical potential have yet to play for post-millennial film audiences.

Contemporary *Frankenstein* Film Adaptations

The influence of Kenneth Branagh's adaptation of *Mary Shelley's Frankenstein* (1994), patently as indebted to Francis Ford Coppola's *Bram Stoker's Dracula* (1992) and its empathetic monster as it was to Shelley's text, could be felt in the 2004 television three-hour film directed by Kevin Connor. This sober adaptation followed the novel closely, thus echoing another television film, the well-remembered *Frankenstein: The True Story* (Jack Smight 1973). Correct and stylistically accomplished, Connor's film is perhaps the most faithful to Shelley's text yet, but it did not, however, do anything radically different with the myth: the period setting was maintained, as were the main characters and elements in the story. More daring was another television film, broadcast that same year, which was originally intended as a pilot for a series—Marcus Nispel's *Frankenstein* (2004). If Connor's adaptation may be seen as a homage to Shelley, Nispel's film transplanted the story into the present and expanded it. In it, Frankenstein, or rather Victor Helios (Thomas Kretschmann), is a villain whose second experiment, an unhappy serial killer incapable of suicide, is eventually hunted down and murdered by the main monster figure, 'Deucalion' (Vincent Perez). This choice is indicative, as is the Branagh film, of a contemporary tendency to rethink the monster as a tragic hero, a tendency on the rise after the successful spate of Hollywood superhero productions that has characterised twenty-first-century American cinema.[4] This decision had two obvious effects on the film. First, the monster does not generate fear, or indeed pity, as he does in the novel; he is composed, educated and gentle, and moral principles move him to revenge. Second, despite it being directed by Nispel, the man who became famous for *The Texas Chainsaw Massacre* remake (2003), the film plays very much like a dark thriller, with significant screen time devoted to the working relationship between two detectives studying a number of interconnected deaths.[5] Apart from a brief mention of stem-cell research, there is little of the modern or the original in this film. In many respects, the appearance of the monster is superficial and even ancillary to the action.

The trend for contemporary settings was continued in *I, Frankenstein*, where the superhero treatment of the creature also became most evident and central. The film appears to borrow from, and expand upon, the novel—beginning with the death of Frankenstein in the North Pole, an opening scene recounts key plot elements, including the death of Frankenstein's wife at the hands of the monster.[6] However, the film very soon turns into a fantasy action adventure more reminiscent of *Thor* (Branagh 2011), and possesses an aesthetic look that echoes that of the *Underworld* franchise (2003–17), with whom it shares its producer. The inclusion of a new mythology exploring the wars waged between gargoyles, who were created by the archangel Michael to protect humanity, and demons in search of soulless bodies they may use to bring back the hordes of the 'descended' (those who have been sent to Hell) gives the story a very different spin. Although the film tries very hard to inject references into the plot that may resonate with the Frankenstein myth—experiments to reanimate corpses being carried out in the twenty-first century, the soulless bodies waiting to be inhabited—and is, to some extent, truthful to the spirit of the creature, who is doomed to incomprehension and loneliness, the result is confused at best, both in generic and narrative terms. 'Adam' (Aaron Eckhart), a super-hero capable of destroying a whole demon army with just a few swords, would feel more at home in an action video game, and the introduction of Christian folklore (belief in souls, demons, angels) seems at odds with the myth's materialist ethos. Unsurprisingly, the film was a commercial disappointment and received unanimously poor reviews.[7]

One of the last mainstream attempts to adapt the Frankenstein story opted for a change of focal point. In *Victor Frankenstein*, the backbone of the Frankenstein myth remains, but the Igor character becomes much more—he is, in fact, the narrator—in a bid for innovation. The opening scene includes his voice-over, one that warns viewers of their potential over-familiarity with events: '[y]ou know this story. The crack of lightning. A mad genius. An unholy creation. The world [...] remembers the monster, not the man. But sometimes, when you look closely, there is more to a tale. Sometimes the monster is the man'. The scene serves to introduce the circus where Igor, as a hunchback, performs in a nod to other well-known Gothic texts such as *The Hunchback of Notre Dame* and *Freaks*. But it also serves to identify humankind's detrimental behaviour to those who deviate from normative anatomies (the so-called freak body, in this context), thus creating an obvious link between Igor and the creature. If this sequence runs the risk of stating the obvious, the common saying that 'knowledge is knowing Frankenstein is not the monster. Wisdom is knowing Frankenstein *is* the monster' belies the general melodramatic aspects of the story. Like Shelley's novel, *Victor Frankenstein* is more of a tragedy with Gothic horror elements than a straightforward 'horror story'. The film's apparent interest in exploring the tensions between religious faith and a more empirical understanding of life (albeit a fantastic one, where death can be reversed) makes it anachronistic, a feeling reinforced by behaviours and exchanges between the characters that seem completely out of place in the film's Victorian London setting. *Victor Frankenstein* was critically panned, among other things, for its lack of originality.[8]

Much more interesting is the independent film *Frankenstein* (Bernard Rose 2015), which, despite going largely unnoticed (it premiered in a few film festivals and was then released on home video), offers an interesting reinterpretation of the story in modern times. Monster centred, like its predecessors, the creature here is the love child of two scientists who turn on him after he begins to develop a deforming skin disease, a result of abnormal cell replication and bad circuitry. The brain of an infant has been used, so when Adam (Xavier Samuel) awakens he has to be taught to eat and speak again. This innovative twist on the 'abnormal brain' motif of James Whale's adaptation leads to an unusual rendering of the 'it's alive!' moment, reframed here as a birth scene rather than as a strict reanimation. The scientists' attempt to kill off their faulty creation fails, as they discover that he has the 'strength of ten men'. His reawakening, after what appears to be his death, sees him become homicidal, although whether Adam understands the effects of his actions is unclear. The question arises: is he a born killer or merely reacting to a hostile environment that tries to abort him? In this sense, the film does a very good job of capturing some of the myth's (I would even suggest of Shelley's text's) pervasive themes, while managing to relocate the story to a contemporary setting. The monster's biological needs (thirst, hunger, cold) also paint a complex picture of the human predicament, of how life involves pain and misery. The relevance of the myth is thus reinvigorated, the hubristic fall of the scientist is dropped in favour of the trauma of existence the monster represents. Rose's film also cites memorable moments from previous adaptations: the drowning girl scene is replayed, a flash mob attacks Adam and calls him a 'monster', Adam becomes friends with a blind man, Adam improves his capacity to express himself by copying others, fire is kept as a symbol of life and its destruction. Monstrosity, physical (Adam is referred to as the 'elephant man' at one point) and social (he behaves in ways that break the law), is also explored. Nevertheless, these similarities mean that a case could be made that Rose's *Frankenstein* does little more than modernise the myth at the level of setting. The film seems on the cusp of merging anxieties about robotics with Frankenstein's delusional creationism, especially towards the end when the doctor's new creature is shown in an upright metallic case with an automated device apparently welding the visceral insides of his head together. However, this idea is left underdeveloped, with Frankenstein merely referring to his experiment as an effort to discover God's 'formula of life'.

Aside from monster mash-ups like the supernatural action films *Van Helsing* (Stephen Sommers 2004) and *Frankenstein* vs. *the Mummy* (Damien Leone 2015), the Frankenstein myth has also been borrowed by children's films. Universal's design was revived in Genndy Tartakovsky's happy Gothic homage parodies *Hotel Transylvania* (2012) and *Hotel Transylvania 2* (2015), where the monster is played very much for his referential appeal as a well-known icon in the Gothic horror canon, alongside Count Dracula and the Wolf Man. The 2012 remake of Tim Burton's short film *Frankenweenie* (1984) also made referential use in its story of a child who learns how to revive his dead dog. Various decisions, from shooting the film in black and white to the sprinkling of many references to previous *Frankenstein* adaptations, especially to those by James Whale, make the *Frankenweenie* remake an unusual children's film that may also be enjoyed by horror and Gothic cinema connoisseurs. The plot, however, simply merges themes and motifs from other reanimation films, such as *Re-Animator* (Stuart Gordon 1985) and *Pet Sematary* (Mary Lambert 1989), with those of other monster films like *Godzilla* (Ishirō Honda 1954). The interest lies, as it does in *ParaNorman* (Sam Fell and Chris Butler 2012), in the relocation of adult narratives involving such unsavoury topics as the living-dead and stitched-up corpses into children's territory. Some scares may be carried over, but the horrific aspects are inevitably reworked into comedy, or else quickly dispelled.

It is important to note that, for all of the innovations to, and expansions of, the Frankenstein myth, the aforementioned adaptations and expansions covered earlier have not proven critically or commercially successful.[9] Even *Victor Frankenstein*, which appeared to aim high in its casting of well-known and celebrated actors (especially Daniel Radcliffe, who is perhaps still expected to command a sizable young audience following his *Harry Potter* fame), was a major flop, not managing to recoup its costs and having 'the worst opening [week] ever for a movie opening on more than 2,500 screens' (McAloon 2015). This does not necessarily signal that the adaptive potential of the myth is completely exhausted, as the very successful 2011 stage adaptation by Nick Dear and the TV series *Penny Dreadful* (2014–16) demonstrate. Either we must accept that the twenty-first-century *Frankenstein* films have been inadequate in various ways or else entertain the possibility that the Frankenstein myth is migrating elsewhere.

Since *Frankenstein* has been given more than one treatment (Gothic melodrama, but also adventure story, superhero films and art-house horror), it is perhaps true to say that it is not resonating with contemporary film audiences when too many of the 'original' elements are kept in adaptations. As Jancovich (2016) warns, however, it is also important to avoid a simplistic 'narrative of decline'. Instead, it would appear that 'the most interesting appropriations [of the Frankenstein myth] are by films that do not explicitly invoke the novel' (203) or, indeed, that simply seize on key crucial themes and motifs.

Changes in cinematic trends are also worth noting. With the exception of *The Others* (Alejandro Amenábar 2001), *The Woman in Black* (James Watkins 2012), *Crimson Peak* (Guillermo del Toro 2015) and *The Witch* (Robert Eggers 2015), twenty-first-century horror has not thus far been known for its Gothic period films, developing instead a new subgenre, the realistic and explicit torture porn, and the digital ghost in the machine trope, and returning to the possession film popularised in the 1970s by William Friedkin's *The Exorcist* (1973). It is, therefore, not surprising that cinematic adaptations of *Frankenstein*, which, together with Bram Stoker's *Dracula* (1897), have in the past constituted the backbone of Gothic cycles like those of Universal Studios in the 1930s/1940s or Hammer Horror in the 1950/1960s, have not become a noteworthy staple of contemporary Gothic cinema or led to the development of popular franchises. In what remains, I want to argue that contemporary viewers are still interested in the Frankenstein myth, if not necessarily exactly as derived from Shelley's novel or its referential adaptations. As the concerns and anxieties raised by the myth are picked up by other horror subgenres, the figure of the mad creationist doctor and the monster brought back from the dead fragment and disperse to the point where they may even spark filmic traditions of their own.

VIRAL ZOMBIES AS FRANKENSTEINIAN DISPERSIONS

Whether the main guiding principle be an adherence to narrative principles or simply an interest in the creation of artificial life, what makes a film part of the *Frankenstein* canon has been a source of scholarly debate. For *Frankenstein* adaptation expert Caroline Joan S. Picart, reflecting on the generic mobility of a 'cinemyth' that appears in comedies, horror and science-fiction narratives, let alone in hybrid combinations of these genres, the net is cast wide. At the heart of *Frankenstein* films lie two main concerns:

(1) the emphasis on parthenogenetic births (male self-births, such as Frankenstein's birthing of his creature), and (2) the focus on the third shadow, or representations of the female monster and the feminine-as-monstrous, as a crucial site of ambivalence revelatory of tensions regarding gender, power, and technology. (Picart 2003: 2)

This means that films as disparate as *The Rocky Horror Picture Show* (Jim Sharman 1975), which parodies *Frankenstein* and even includes analogous characters in Dr Frank N. Furter (Tim Curry) and his creature, Rocky Horror (Peter Hinwood), and *Alien* (Ridley Scott 1979), which also contains 'monstrous rebirths' (Picart 2003, 80) that could be read as inverting the parthenogenetic myth, are both considered modern remakes of *Frankenstein*. Picart is not oblivious to the fact that the *Alien* series (1979–97) may not be immediately recognised as a Frankenstein myth and makes two significant points regarding the inclusion of this film in her study. First, many directors of *Frankenstein* adaptations only keep 'superficial elements of the original narrative' (Picart 2003: 79) so that they can be just as conspicuously identified with the original. Their overt referential allegiance to the source text or myth, however, seems to provide them with a modicum of legitimacy. Second, Picart acknowledges, following the work of Janice Rushing and Thomas Frentz, that if we are to posit *Frankenstein* as an evolving myth, then it should be as a 'narrative concerning our ambivalences concerning power, gender, and technology' (2003: 79).[10] The focus on technology and the position of human experience and feeling has, in fact, been the subject of critical interest (see Denson 2014).

Picart's position is a valid one, especially if we are to escape taxonomic constraints of what constitutes an adaptation and the extent to which a myth may mutate and develop from its original context. At the same time, such a theoretical manoeuvre could remove the Frankenstein myth too much from recognisable scenarios. This is precisely the point raised by Lester D. Friedman and Allison B. Kavey (2016: 147), who claim that amalgamating approaches ignore 'the structural and thematic guidelines' of Shelley's novel. They ask, 'where is the Frankenstein figure who constructs the monster out of dead tissue in the *Alien* series?' Their redefinition of *Frankenstein* films according to three broad categories shares the elasticity of Picart's evolving myth while limiting its potential spillover. These are:

1. Transitions, featuring narratives about organisms that were never alive being given life, in purported adaptations of the novel and in comedies humorously incorporating Shelley's basic narrative;
2. Translations, incorporating tales about hybrid creations and once-dead organisms brought back to life resulting in biological mutations, in films that do not use Shelley's characters or settings;
3. Transformations, exploring artificially created beings in cyborgs and robot movies, a logical evolution of Shelley's novel. (Friedman and Kavey 2016: 147)

The first category basically adheres to adaptations of the novel, whatever the treatment, and includes parodies such as the aforementioned *Rocky Horror* and *Young Frankenstein* (Mel Brooks 1974). The second distinguishes between biological mutations and reanimations, adding films such as *Re-Animator*, *The Fly* (David Cronenberg 1986), *Pet Sematary*, *Jurassic Park* (Steven Spielberg 1993) and *Splice* (Vincenzo Natali 2009) to the list. The third category, the one that interests me the most, identifies cyborg and robot films as 'two Frankenstein film clusters that contain few if any, direct allusions to Shelley's novel or Whale's film but that incorporate their narrative, thematic, and/or iconographic elements, often situating their characters and plots in futuristic settings with resemblances to the present' (Friedman and Kavey 2016: 185). Films such as *RoboCop* (José Padilha 2014) and *Ex Machina* (Alex Garland 2015) pose prescient questions about the distinction between humans and machines in an age of bionic prosthetics and artificial intelligence. Exactly where the line should be drawn between the creators and the created is a pertinent issue persistently probed by these new techno-Gothics.

To this last category of transformations, I want to add a tentative third one: viral zombies. These modern monsters, born technically in the 1954 novel *I Am Legend*, by Richard Matheson, and then expanded in the first *Resident Evil* video game in 1996, have blossomed in the twenty-first century, particularly in film (see Abbott 2016). Although the zombie film has a long tradition that dates back to *White Zombie* (Victor Halperin 1932), if not to the 1916 film *The Man without a Soul* (George Loane Tucker 1916), the brain-eating zombie is a product of 1968's George A. Romero's *Night of the Living Dead*. There are good reasons why most zombie films are not considered part of the *Frankenstein* film canon. Zombies have traditionally been the result of nuclear or radiation catastrophes and 'produce' one another via contagious bite; they, therefore, lack an obvious creator. However, things begin to blur by the time such zombie films as *28 Days Later* (Danny Boyle 2002) and *Resident Evil* (Paul W. S. Anderson 2002) enter the picture. In them, viruses have been engineered in laboratories, often by mad scientists now connected to larger hierarchised bodies, such as countries or corporations. As zombies become experiments for biological warfare, explicitly in *Planet Terror* (Robert Rodriguez 2007) and implicitly in *World War Z* (Marc Forster 2013), they also get closer to the built-for-purpose Frankenstein monster.

More importantly, as the Frankenstein myth has done since Shelley, the viral zombie challenges the boundaries between the living and the dead, as well as the ontological grounding of both. This is particularly obvious in the medicalisation of zombies. In a crucial episode of the TV series *The Walking Dead* (2010–present) entitled 'TS-19' (S1 E6), where the MRI video of the titular test subject reveals the reanimating specifics of 'walkers', zombies are presented as an infectious disease that kills the body but reactivates the brain stem and thus a subject's basic vital functions. These are not magical zombies, the possessed zombies of Haitian lore. They are far more human than fantastic, an aspect that has allowed them to resonate with contemporary scares surrounding outbreaks of avian flu, Ebola and, more recently, the Zika virus.[11] Viral zombies—a term used here irrespectively of the specific sources of contagion—force us to rethink what humans deem 'life', especially where consciousness is concerned.[12] Nowhere is the distance between the living and the undead most succinctly explored than in 'Vatos' (S1 E4), another episode from *The Walking Dead*, where Amy (Emma Bell), a likable character, 'returns' while being held by her loving sister, Andrea (Laurie Holden). The point at which Amy goes from living to living-dead is the same at which she becomes a threat and thus 'non-human'. Yet the TV series is known for its ontological ambiguity. As it is revealed that all of the characters are already infected and waiting to become walkers upon their inevitable deaths ('we are the walking dead'), the distinction between categories of being and non-being (even 'being' while apparently already 'dead') and between 'normality' and 'monstrosity' begins to disappear. Since most characters eventually act out of desperation or survival instinct, the series seem to ask whether there are any stark differences between zombies and humans. The indistinction is such that, even in a film such as *28 Days Later*, often described as a zombie film, the zombies are rabid humans.

Films such as *Warm Bodies* (Jonathan Levine 2013), *Wasting Away* (Matthew Kohnen 2007) and *Otto; or Up with Dead People* (Bruce LaBruce 2008) have further shortened the distance between the human and the zombie through the notion of zombie consciousness. In *Warm Bodies*, for example, zombie 'R' (Nicholas Hoult) learns to love Julie (Teresa Palmer), and this leads to his eventual cure and de-zombification. Importantly, however, the film starts with 'R' having thoughts and explaining his condition, a sign that these zombies are not simply a brainless mass that may stand in for the neoliberal subjects of, say, *Dawn of the Dead* (George A. Romero 1978), hordes caught in their aimless capitalist wanders around a shopping mall. In *Wasting Away*, viewers are aligned with the consciousness of zombies through colour point-of-view shots that reveal how these creatures see themselves as 'normal' humans. Significantly, they are likeable, empathetic characters. In *Otto*, the hero may or may not be a real zombie, with zombiedom becoming a proxy state for sadness and alienation. TV series like *In the Flesh* (2013–14) and *iZombie* (2014–present) have developed this trend, positioning the zombie as a minority and, in the case of the former, even as a victim of pharmaceutical—and thus, state—control. Like Frankenstein's creature, the zombie becomes a figure through which to examine normative discourses and the plight of those who do not fit the social straitjackets imposed by the status quo, those who are 'monstered' or 'othered' and whose lives become unliveable as a result.

As zombies have been read metaphorically—they now are '*the* metaphorical monster', according to zombie scholar Kyle William Bishop (2010: 17)—they have channelled anxieties about racial oppression and slavery; the effects and failures of neoliberalism; the fear of apocalyptic end days for contemporary and future generations; and the negative aspects of the viral quality of communication technology.[13] The one thing guiding all these allegorical readings and usages, the same one that underpins the Frankenstein myth, is that humans continue to be seduced by creationist delusions of grandeur and power, abusing technology and pushing it in 'unnatural' ways. The main difference—perhaps the one that has allowed the viral zombie's Frankensteinian ethos to thrive where referential adaptations have failed—is a focus on the irredeemably fraught or evil heart of humankind. In viral zombie films, salvation is rarely an option. We have gone too far and all that remains are the vast wastelands of a post-human (in the sense of 'after the human') world. The highly articulate monster of

Mary Shelley's novel is speech impaired in the cinematic version played by Boris Karloff, which in turn has been supplanted by the nameless, groaning, relentless and anonymous bodies of viral zombies.[14] In *The Girl with All the Gifts* (McCarthy 2016), zombies (in this case, fungal but equally contagious) actually become the next evolutionary step, closing the gap between humans, their monstrous creations and zombies. The future is one where we do not only get our just deserts for our reckless behaviour towards, and interventions against, 'nature' and biology (climate change, nuclear apocalypses or genetically driven hierarchies), we quite literally become our very own experiments. There is hope in *The Girl with All the Gifts*, but it is not premised on life as we know it. At no other point in cultural history have we imagined the extinction of the human race as actively as in the twenty-first century. Viral zombies are the quintessential Frankenstein myth for self-diagnosed terminal societies whose citizens are 'living in the end times' (Žižek 2011).

To summarise, this chapter has suggested that the *Frankenstein* myth has experienced some changes in the twenty-first century, maybe as a result of adaptive fatigue, because adaptations have been poor or because the period coordinates of the myth have grown somewhat obsolete. The direct and more faithful adaptations of the novel, those that still hark back to it in either name or characters, have experienced a noticeable decline and, importantly, have struggled in a market saturated with horror films. Even those films, like *Victor Frankenstein*, which have chosen angles more melodramatic than horrific, have not managed to captivate the attention of viewers and critics. My second suggestion has been that the new viral zombie films, with their lumbering creatures who walk the line between life and death, may now be embodying the most relevant aspects of the myth. In other words, what can appear as the thematic irrelevance of the Frankenstein myth can be recast as part of a process of dispersion that has seen other horror subgenres subsuming and developing the core thematic concerns of Shelley's novel: man-made monstrosities, freedom of will and the border between life and death in an increasingly secularist and materialist society. *Frankenstein* is alive and well but, like the Gothic more generally, it is now found in individual motifs and characters in other films and hybrid genres (science-fiction horror, most notably). This is not to say that the Frankenstein myth is dead but rather that it has been broken down and assimilated by an entertainment industry eager to cash in on timely anxieties such as genetically modified foods, in vitro fertilisation and cloning. It is to Shelley's credit that the themes and motifs in her 1818 novel remain pertinent. Like all enduring myths (the vampire, the mummy, the werewolf, the ghost), the mad scientist and his ill-fated creation have become part and parcel of the Gothic canon, iconographic and capable of articulating meaning outside of their original historical and cultural contexts.

NOTES

1. For the plurality of interpretations of the Frankenstein monster in the twentieth century, see Svehla and Svehla (1997).
2. The film acknowledges Shelley's novel as source text.
3. Hence, cinema's focus on the reanimation scene, which does not feature as significantly in the novel. See Schor (2003).
4. The reboot of Universal's horror films as superhero films from 2017 onwards is indicative of this move towards action and adventure. For more on the superhero phenomenon, see Hassler-Forest (2012).
5. This can be explained by the fact that Nispel's *Frankenstein* started as a pilot for a television series. The project did not take off.
6. It should be noted that not all elements are kept intact, even in the film's brief summary scenes: the monster is thrown into a river, something that does not happen in the novel, and Victor is the one to pursue the monster, a scenario that reverses the one found at the end of Shelley's text.
7. The film made $71 million on a production budget of $65 million. It currently holds a score of 3% in Rotten Tomatoes (averaged from 89 reviews), which indicates a very poor reception. BoxOfficeMojo.com. Accessed October 13, 2016. http://www.boxofficemojo.com/movies/? id=ifrankenstein.htm; RottenTomatoes.com. Accessed October 13, 2016. https://www.rottentomatoes.com/m/i_frankenstein/#contentReviews
8. The critical consensus in Rotten Tomatoes is that the film 'ultimately offers little of interest that viewers haven't already seen in superior Frankenstein films'. RottenTomatoes.com. Accessed October 13, 2016. https://www. rottentomatoes.com/m/victor_frankenstein_2015/
9. Even the most successful of these, *Frankenweenie*, only made a modest profit. The film is listed in the website *Box Office Flops: A Database of Films that Failed at the Box Office*, where its ticket sales are described as 'c[oming] in far below expectations'. BoxOfficeFlops.com. Accessed October 13, 2016. http://www.boxofficeflops.com/yearly-breakdowns/2012-2/ frankenweenie
10. See also Rushing and Frentz (1995).

11. From a microbiological point of view, these films also engage with debates on whether viruses themselves are forms of life. See Woodard (2012: 18).
12. In this respect, they also echo work carried out in the area of philosophical zombies and identity politics. See, for example, Kirk (2005) and Aldana Reyes (2014).
13. See Luckhurst (2015).
14. In films like *Frankenstein's Army* (Richard Raaphorst 2013) and *Army of Frankenstein* (Ryan Bellgardt 2014), it is actually quite difficult to separate Frankenstein monsters from traditional zombies.

Works Cited

Abbott, Stacey. 2016. *Undead Apocalypse: Vampires and Zombies in the 21st Century*. Edinburgh: Edinburgh University Press.
Aldana Reyes, Xavier. 2014. Nothing but the Meat: Posthuman Bodies and the Dying Undead. In *We're All Infected': Essays on AMC's The Walking Dead and The Fate of the Human*, ed. Dawn Keetley, 142–155. Jefferson: McFarland.
Beattie, Stuart. (dir.). 2014. *I, Frankenstein*, film. USA/Australia: Hopscotch Pictures, Lakeshore Entertainment, Lionsgate and SKE Films.
Bellgardt, Ryan. (dir.). 2014. *Army of Frankensteins*, film. USA: Six Stitches Entertainment and Boiling Point.
Bishop, Kyle William. 2010. *How Zombies Conquered Popular Culture: The Multifarious Walking Dead in the 21st Century*. Jefferson: McFarland.
Botting, Fred. 2009. Monstrosity. In *The Handbook of the Gothic*, ed. Marie Mulvey-Roberts, 204–205. Basingstoke: Palgrave.
Branagh, Kenneth. (dir.). 1994. *Mary Shelley's Frankenstein*, film. USA/Japan: The IndieProd Company, American Zoetrope and Japan Satellite Broadcasting Inc.
———. 2011. *Thor*, film. USA: Marvel Studios.
Burton, Tim. (dir.). 2012. *Frankenweenie*, film. USA: Walt Disney Studios Motion Pictures.
Coppola, Francis Ford. (dir.). 1992. *Bram Stoker's Dracula*, film. USA: American Zoetrope and Osiris Films.
Denson, Shane. 2014. *Postnaturalism: Frankenstein, Film, and the Anthropotechnical Interface*. Bielefeld: Transcript-Verlag.
Ferland, Guy. (dir.). 2010. 'TS-19', *The Walking Dead*, television. USA: AMC.
Friedman, Lester D., and Allison B. Kavey. 2016. *Monstrous Progeny: A History of the Frankenstein Narratives*. London/Piscataway: Rutgers University Press.
Hassler-Forest, Dan. 2012. *Capitalist Superheroes: Caped Crusaders in the Neoliberal Age*. Alresford: Zero Books.
Jancovich, Mark. 2016. *Frankenstein* and Film. In *The Cambridge Companion to Frankenstein*, ed. Andrew Smith, 190–204. Cambridge: Cambridge University Press.

Kirk, Robert. 2005. *Zombies and Consciousness*. Oxford: Oxford University Press.
Kohnen, Matthew. (dir.). 2007. *Wasting Away*, aka *Aaah! Zombies!!*, film. USA: Shadowpark Pictures and Wasted Pictures.
LaBruce, Bruce. (dir.). 2008. *Otto; or Up with Dead People*, film. Germany/ Canada: Jürgen Brüning Filmproduktion, Existential Crisis Productions and New Real Films.
Levine, Jonathan. (dir.). 2013. *Warm Bodies*, film. USA: Mandeville Films.
Luckhurst, Roger. 2015. *Zombies: A Cultural History*. London: Reaktion.
McAloon, Jonathan. 2015. 2015's Biggest Box Office Flops. *The Telegraph*, November 12. http://www.telegraph.co.uk/film/what-to-watch/2015-box-office-flops. Accessed 10 Oct 2016.
McCarthy, Colm. (dir.). 2016. *The Girl with All the Gifts*, film. UK: Altitude Film Sales, BFI Film Fund and Poison Chef.
McGuigan, Paul. (dir.). 2016. *Victor Frankenstein*, film. USA: Davis Entertainment Company and TSG Entertainment.
Nispel, Marcus. (dir.). 2003. *The Texas Chainsaw Massacre*, film. USA: Next Entertainment, Platinum Dunes and Radar Pictures.
———. 2004. *Frankenstein*, film. USA: Flame TV, Flame Ventures, L.I.F.T. Production and USA Cable Network.
Picart, Caroline Joan S. 2003. *Remaking the Frankenstein Myth on Film: Between Laughter and Horror*. New York: State University of New York Press.
Raaphorst, Richard. (dir.). 2013. *Frankenstein's Army*, film. USA/Czech Republic/the Netherlands: Dark Sky Films, Pellicola and XYZ Films.
Renck, Johan. (dir.). 2010. 'Vatos', *The Walking Dead*, television. USA: AMC.
Rose, Bernard. (dir.). 2015. *Frankenstein*, aka *FRANKEN5TE1N*, film, USA: Bad Badger, Eclectic Pictures and Summerstorm Entertainment.
Rushing, Janice H., and Thomas S. Frentz. 1995. *Projecting the Shadow: The Cyborg Hero in American Film*. Chicago: University of Chicago Press.
Schor, Esther. 2003. *Frankenstein* and Film. In *The Cambridge Companion to Mary Shelley*, ed. Esther Schor, 63–83. Cambridge: Cambridge University Press.
Smight, Jack. (dir.). 1973. *Frankenstein: The True Story*, film. USA/UK: Universal Studios.
Svehla, Susan, and Gary J. Svehla. 1997. *We Belong Dead: Frankenstein on Film*. Baltimore: Midnight Marquee Press.
Woodard, Ben. 2012. *Slime Dynamics*. Winchester/Washington, DC: Zero Books.
Žižek, Slavoj. 2011. *Living in the End Times*. London: Verso Books.

PART IV

Frankensteinian Illustrations and Literary Adaptations

CHAPTER 11

Frankenstein and the Peculiar Power of the Comics

Scott Bukatman

I've written about monster comics, but inspired by the writing of Allen Weiss, I've also written about comics *as* monsters. 'Monsters exist in margins,' Weiss declares, and are 'avatars' of such things as 'chance, impurity, heterodoxy; abomination, mutation, metamorphosis; prodigy, mystery, marvel' (Weiss 2004: 125). They pose a threat, he argues, to the established order of the world and to the very idea of orderliness itself. This is true of Frankenstein's monster of course but also of the marginalised, heterodox, and hybrid form of comics. For much of their history in America, comics were relegated to the margins: comic strips on the margins of the newspaper or comic books on the margins of respectability. They are impure in their profligate mixture of words and images, and they have been viewed as abominations more than once in their history. I believe that comics have an affinity for monsters and a particular affinity for generating monsters that arouse a reader's empathy.

Horror fiction's primary affect arises through some admixture of fright and disgust, but the genre has long sought to awaken compassion

S. Bukatman (✉)
Department of Art and Art History, Stanford University, Stanford, CA, USA

© The Author(s) 2018
C. M. Davison, M. Mulvey-Roberts (eds.), *Global Frankenstein*,
Studies in Global Science Fiction,
https://doi.org/10.1007/978-3-319-78142-6_11

for the monster and its plight. This surely began with Mary Shelley's *Frankenstein*. The novel is a web of embedded and framed narratives— Captain Walton's letters frame the text, and Victor Frankenstein's story is stunningly interrupted by the personal narrative related across five chapters by his misbegotten creation. This narration brings us, perhaps for the first time, into the mind of a monster. Previously, the genre was content to objectify and observe—or avoid—its monstrosities or horrors. In contrast, Shelley imbues Victor's creation with an interior life, a personal history and, consequently, a tragic dimension. This is far from the greatest of the novel's myriad accomplishments, but it still warrants attention: horror fiction was unalterably changed by the introduction of a monster's subjectivity, and comics, since the 1950s, turned out to be especially good at granting readers intimate knowledge of what goes on in the mind of their monsters.

The literary world took notice when John Gardner published *Grendel* in 1971, retelling the saga of *Beowulf* from the monster's perspective, but managed to overlook the first appearances of both *Swamp Thing* (DC) and *Man-Thing* (Marvel) that same year. These two 'things' went on to become the first monsters to star in ongoing comic book series. But Marvel's superhero line was already peppered with monsters, including the polymorphously monstrous Hulk (who managed to be simultaneously Frankensteinian, Jekyllesque and werewolfish), the misshapen X-Man known as the Beast, and, the ur-hero-monster that was *the Thing* of the Fantastic Four. Weiss writes that monsters 'manifest the plasticity of the imagination and the catastrophes of the flesh,' which speaks to me loudly and clearly of the deep fantasies that comic books have offered (Weiss: 125). Superhero comics are fundamentally about the plasticity of both imagination and body, and 'catastrophes of the flesh' are abundant, undergirding nearly all the origin stories of heroes and villains. The superhero genre, with its pseudo-rational explanations of its wonders, may edge up on science fiction, but its fantasies have a darker component that brings it to (or beyond) the edge of horror. The Marvel monster-heroes were particularly grounded in vicissitudes of the flesh that were transparent metaphors for the vicissitudes of puberty; like misunderstood teenagers (the very ones reading these comic books?), they were all empathetic figures, though adults in the stories feared them to greater and lesser degrees.[1]

The Monsters of Literature and Cinema

To probe the specific ability of comics to get us into the mind of the monster, it's worth reviewing, in broad strokes, the related media of literature and cinema and their methods of presenting monsters. *Frankenstein* is a perfect case study; it began 'life' as a novel before spawning multitudinous adaptations and continuations across a host of media.

The horror genre has its genesis in oral traditions, but printed prose has proven amenable to its gruesome charms throughout its history. Prose is rich in descriptive power, whether of empirical phenomena or psychological states, and first-person narration brings the reader closer to the experience of the characters, whether that of Victor Frankenstein or the nameless monster who would come to inherit his name. But what fiction cannot do is keep the image of the monster before us. Peter Mendelsund argues that, in reading, we visualise far less than might be supposed. 'Description,' he proposes, 'is not additive' (Mendelsund 2014: 146). Authors orchestrate their imagery sequentially, but, as with music, we don't hold all the notes together in our minds and experience them synchronically. Prose is diachronic. Details are recalled to mind as they are highlighted, while the entirety lurks in the background.

Consider the world's introduction to Frankenstein's newly animated monster, in Shelley's novel:

> How can I describe my emotions at this catastrophe, or how delineate the wretch whom with such infinite pains and care I had endeavoured to form? His limbs were in proportion, and I had selected his features as beautiful. Beautiful! Great God! His yellow skin scarcely covered the work of muscles and arteries beneath; his hair was of a lustrous black, and flowing; his teeth of a pearly whiteness; but these luxuriances only formed a more horrid contrast with his watery eyes, that seemed almost of the same colour as the dun-white sockets in which they were set, his shriveled complexion and straight black lips. (Shelley and Moser 1983: 51)

The reader of *Frankenstein* will likely keep the monster's monstrousness in mind without difficulty, but will watery eyes and black lips always accompany the general sense of a gaunt, discoloured wretch? Another salient detail of the monster's appearance is his huge stature, about which readers had already been informed, but this is absent from Victor's recorded impressions here. (Further, Shelley's description conflicts with the iconic form of the movie monster incarnated by Boris Karloff in 1931 with make-up by

Jack Pierce. How do subsequent readers juggle this familiar image with the description in the novel?)

The selectivity and nonadditive nature of details can aid in the empathetic exploration of a monster's interiority. The reader need not envision that 'yellow skin' that 'scarcely covered the work of muscles and arteries beneath' when processing the creature's own description of its coming into the world:

> A strange multiplicity of sensations seized me, and I saw, felt, heard, and smelt at the same time; and it was, indeed, a long time before I learned to distinguish between the operations of my various senses. By degrees, I remember, a stronger light pressed upon my nerves, so that I was obliged to shut my eyes. Darkness then came over me and troubled me, but hardly had I felt this when, by opening my eyes, as I now suppose, the light poured in upon me again. (Shelley and Moser 1983: 106)

Here, the monster's description of 'a multiplicity of sensations' replaces the earlier description of his external appearance. While Victor's description gives us a measurably monstrous man, the creature provides what could well be the inchoate experience of an ordinary infant. Prose permits the reader to perceive the monster from without or within, and while there will be times when those perceptions will overlap, there are many where they don't. The creation really only feels monstrous to the reader in those moments when he is perceived as such by others. Judith Halberstam writes, 'We are disposed as readers to sympathize with the monster because, unlike the characters in the novel, we cannot see him' (Halberstam 1995: 39).[2]

So, prose withholds, even when it seems not to, but if prose description is not additive, Mendelsund continues, '[v]ision … is additive, and simultaneous.' (Mendelsund 2014: 146). Comics and cinema are unlike literature because they can keep the monster's monstrousness in continual view—they must, conversely, work to *hide*, rather than reveal, details. Frankenstein's monster has a matter-of-fact, visible *thereness* in comics and cinema, but further differences distinguish these media from one another.

Cinema has fewer narrators than literature (voice-overs are common but not typical). But there is what Tom Gunning has called a 'narrator-function': the filmmaker's editorial interventions—emergent across the medium's first 15 or so years—that reveal particular details to viewers at specific moments. But crucial to this narrator function is the invisibility of that directorial presence: the spectator experiences the cut, not the hand with the scissors. Narrative cinema presents stories that often seem to tell themselves (Gunning 1999).

This narrative mode is supported by the medium's indexicality. Cinema, throughout most of its history, has been a recording medium (despite the presence of post-production manipulation and effects work). The external world imprints itself upon both light- and sound-sensitive materials, providing a record of *something* that seems to have occurred before the camera's lens. It's a medium that excels at the reproduction of a seemingly objective reality, regardless of how studio-bound that production may be. And that objectivity is in the service of a story that seems to tell itself. Or in more banal terms, cinema shows more than it (evidently) tells.

Cinema, then, typically keeps us on the outside, and in the case of monster movies, that has typically meant monsters (whether giant ant, vampire, zombie, or, yes, Frankenstein's monster) seen more from without than within. They become objects of vision. Writing of James Whale's 1931 *Frankenstein*, Marc Redfield writes that 'of all the changes Whale and his writers made, arguably the most significant was their reimagination of the creature as seeable, and the making of the creature as a visual experience' (Redfield 2003). This becomes more emphatic in correlation with the other profound shift from Shelley's novel to Whale's film (by way of Richard Brinsley Peake's 1823 stage production, *Presumption; or, The Fate of Frankenstein*): the muteness of the monster. Gone is the eloquent voice of the monster/narrator that informs both Victor and the reader of his thinking as well as his sensational and emotional processes. In its place are the expressive growls and gestural delicacy of Boris Karloff, signifying interiority without permitting the spectator direct access. This muteness will remain a constant until *Young Frankenstein* (Mel Brooks 1974), in which Frankenstein transfers some of his intellect to his creation, giving him, as the monster puts it, 'a somewhat more sophisticated way of expressing myself.'

Redfield explicitly links the muteness of cinema's Frankenstein to the cinematic medium itself, pointing to the 'silent-film theatricality' of Whale's film and Karloff's performance. Shane Denson discusses several silent film adaptations of *Frankenstein*, the earliest being Edison's film of 1910, and he finds in the 1931 film's wordless monster an engagement with the 'technological revolution' represented by 'the shift from silent film to talkies' (Denson 2014: 138). Eyes and the vitalising power of light and electricity are prominent motifs, and Redfield finds 'seeing and the seeing of seeing' to be a prominent theme of the first film. William Nestrick has also seen *Frankenstein* as a film about another cinematic technique: 'Editing reassembles separate shots into an illusion of continuity. It is a mechanical stitchwork, a piecing together that becomes another cinematic equivalent of the Frankenstein Monster' (Nestrick 1979: 303). The con-tinuing visuality of the monster insists on his monstrosity. Viewers can neither avoid nor forget his grotesque visage, the bolts in his neck or his unnatural lurching; they are more sporadically allowed to see the pain in his eyes or the imploring gestures of his hands.

The muteness of the monster stages a transfer from the subjective (the novel's eloquent monster with a rich internal life in which we participate) to the objective (a mute cinematic monster we observe from without). Denson observes that there are two brief shots from the monster's per-spective in the film, but they serve more to rupture the viewer's experience without fully engaging with the monster's subjectivity and this marks a difference between literature and cinema (although it acknowledges, importantly, that the monster *has* subjectivity). (Denson 2014: 94).

Emma Raub argues, however, that the muteness of the monster in the earlier 1823 stage production (the earliest adaptation), far from rendering the monster unsympathetic and bestial, aligned him instead with a longer tradition of the mute in stage melodrama who was 'almost always a sym-pathetic figure with a terrible and mysterious past … meant to evoke great pity,' and who was often 'the centre of pathos and distress' (Raub 2012: 443). Pantomimic gesture was both natural and universally understood, while words (and the characters who use them) could prevaricate and dis-tance. When the monster makes his first appearance on the stage, he looks at Frankenstein and 'approaches him with gestures of conciliation' (Peake 1823). The play even includes the moment, recreated in *The Bride of Frankenstein* (Whale 1935) when the monster, enchanted by music, seeks to pluck the notes he hears from the air around him.

The play also created a disconnect between the horrifying make-up of the monster and the lithe, athletic body of the actor who portrayed him. The monster was visually less monstrous than Karloff's later incarnation, and there was more expressive pantomime to his role. Further, Christian Metz and other film theorists have argued that the physical presence of the actor in a play arguably prevents a complete immersion in the fiction being presented. 'Because the theater is so real, theatrical fictions yield only a weak impression of reality' (Metz 1974: 10). Conversely, the absence of the real in the cinema 'produces a strong impression of reality because it corresponds to a "vacuum," which dreams readily fill.' The stage monster, then, can't *ever* be as monstrous as the movie monster.

I am neither arguing that film cannot be subjective, nor that prose lacks monsters with interiority, just that these media tend to tilt in different directions, each generating its own affect: Shelley's *Frankenstein* engenders a complicated empathy for the monster, whom we come to understand so deeply, while Whale's more objectified film provokes something more like a profound sympathy.

THE MONSTER IN PICTURES

Before turning to the specific potentials and limits of the comics, I need to broach a more general question: Are comics scary? By rights, they shouldn't be—the reader has too much control. Literary horror hides its surprises within the symbolic system of prose, with no visual spoilers telegraphing the action. Cinematic horror depends upon the medium's complete control over the viewer's experience of time and space—the spectator, seated in the dark, can turn away, but by then it's too late (and squishy/sinister sounds retain their power). And reveals become very predictable—like the abrupt cut signalled by a surge of music and the protagonist's eyes widening at the sight of something offscreen. Comics' horror presents horrific visuals, but—except for the reveal that comes with the turn of a page— two pages of horrors are evident to the reader's eye well before the brain has progressed through the narrative explanations or descriptions. The reader controls, to a great degree, the pace of reading and can thereby control the experience of shock.

But this works the other way, too. A picture can fascinate—the reader encounters a particularly striking, startling or even shocking image or image sequence in the course of reading, and moves on. Until she doesn't. The page that is turned can also be turned back, *to look again*. And again. And, tomorrow, again. A picture can be very haunting (especially for a kid who isn't yet allowed to watch horror movies, or in the days before home and streaming video made cinema perhaps *overly* accessible). Ostensibly depictive, a picture can play with shadows and light, hiding and revelation. An image might even *dare* a reader/viewer to confront it again, the challenge being to somehow master the feelings it stimulates. One could say that images in books and comics do more than haunt, they *lurk* between the pages, waiting to emerge and re-emerge.

This applies not only to comics but also to book illustration. The first illustrated edition of *Frankenstein* dates from 1831, or eight years *after* the first theatrical adaptation. The need to *see* the monster seems irresistible.[3] The woodcut illustrations of Lynd Ward, a prolific illustrator of both adult and children's literature, adorned a 1934 edition, in the wake not only of Whale's *Frankenstein* but also of four of Ward's wordless woodcut novels. Grant F. Scott finds in Ward's creature some of the pantomimic quality that also marked the 1823 stage production and the 1931 film (Scott 2012: 208). Ward's emphasis is on the monster's body, not his face; he is a hulking figure that dwarfs those around him. According to Scott, 'Ward repeatedly depicts him covering or shielding his face from the viewer and other characters' (Scott 2012: 216). Yet when he sees his own face reflected in the water, that face is hardly monstrous. 'Rather than the ravaged outer mask Victor constructs and describes,' Scott states, 'this image invites us to bear witness to the vital innocence of the creature's soul' (Scott 2012: 218). Woodcut lends itself to the allegorical, and in the body of Ward's monster, Scott recognises a nearly identical treatment of the heroicised, and somewhat homoerotic, bodies of the working-class protagonists of his 1932 woodcut novel, *Wild Pilgrimage*.

Barry Moser also uses woodcuts in the 1984 Pennyroyal edition, which he designed and illustrated. His images, true to his general style, are quiet and undramatic; his cuts are finer, more delicate than Ward's, and that delicacy serves *Frankenstein* surprisingly well. Little is dramatised or staged; instead, portraits, settings and objects dominate. Most images take up a full page; others are smaller and more ambient. There are few scenes of discovery or reaction (no aghast creators or villagers). The first time the reader sees the face of the creature is when he approaches Victor, who has fled to the sublimity of the mountains for solace. Moser only shows us part of the face; the rest is lost in shadows. What we see is something both cadaverous and rotting. Wisps of hair emphasise a sunken, skull-like physiognomy: only one eye is visible, and there is no nose. The skin is mottled and shrivelled. It is an unrelentingly horrific visage, a truly haunting image.

Book illustration does not keep images constantly before the reader's or viewer's eye as do comics and cinema. Illustrations punctuate books, appearing at intervals, playing their game of hide-and-seek in both their placement and their strategies of depiction. It should be noted, though, that some images in comics also lurk, whether nesting among more innocuous images or hidden behind the turn of a page.

The multiple narrators of Shelley's *Frankenstein* exemplify some of the strategies of the early nineteenth-century novel, just as the mute visibility of the monster in Whale's films exemplifies the technological vision that undergirds the cinema. If there is as perfect an equivalent in comics, one that exemplifies something fundamental about the medium, I have yet to find it. But perhaps that's the point: perhaps no single text speaks to the uncontainable variation of comics. The medium not only combines word and image but pictorialised words and legible images. The use of language varies, as does the style of drawing. Further variety arises from the treatments of panel, page, story length (from single panels or pages to the 100-year continuing saga that is *Gasoline Alley*), the dimensions of the physical book, the paper choices and the presence or absence of colour. Comics are difficult to encompass and define; they are best understood in their multiplicity.

The plurality of *Frankenstein* comics' adaptations and continuations begins to suggest the range of strategies that characterise the medium. Comics offer multiple modes of narration (descriptive captions, speech balloons, wordless comics) that make it particularly appropriate for the adaptation (or continuation) of Shelley's *Frankenstein*, with its multiple narrators. Comics also have a unique capacity to depict thought, whether through dialogue, 'voice-over' narrative captions or thought balloons. Dialogue and narration, though not their visualisation, are also characteristic of prose and cinema, but thought balloons are unique to comics. Michael Marrinan finds in these the epitome of literature's 'free indirect discourse.'[4] In this rhetorical mode, 'certain material configurations of language generate representations of another person's thoughts without positing a fictive, all-knowing character or narrator' (Bender and Marrinan 2010: 72–3). In the service of modernist experimentation, some authors further devised complicated sets of shifters to allude, on the written page, to the non-linguistic nature of thought. In the thought balloon, comics have 'a very specific and graphic way of marking this phenomenon without all the difficulties presented to writers' (Bender and Marrinan 2010: 72–3).

Not only is a thought balloon anchored to the thinking character in the panel, but its cloud-like, amorphous outlines mark this as something 'other' than speech. With typical meta-textual playfulness, Grant Morrison gives us a character whose thought balloons have a physical presence in the world: 'I even have my own **superpowers**, see?... A consciousness so focused and so disciplined, it can actually manifest words in a **cloud** above my head.... That's right, visible thought' (Morrison and Weston 2004). While they don't actually manifest in the real world, comics, uniquely, give us visible thought. And by doing so, the medium combines the externality and visuality of the cinema with the easy access to interior thought and experience that characterises prose.[5] The presentation or elision of the interiority of Frankenstein's monster—the presence or absence of speech or language, the use or absence of first-person narration and thought balloons—has implications for the ways that readers engage with, or relate to, the monster.

Denson has explored several Marvel Comics stories that tie into both Shelley's novel and the Whale films, some of which go so far as to reflexively incorporate those works as mere iterations of the larger story of Frankenstein's monster. By assimilating, or swallowing, these earlier versions, he writes, 'the comic book is able to claim its own superiority as a medium, one which combines literature and cinema—word and image—and is thus able to subject them to a synthesis unimaginable in either medium in isolation' (Denson 2011: 540). Denson is noting the ability of the comic book narrative to contain other narratives—drawing upon both literature's articulate monster and cinema's mute one—but it also speaks to the medium's ability to combine written word (as description, as dialogue and as sound effect) with an insistent visuality.

The Monster of Frankenstein (Marvel, 1973–75) is a good place to start; the first four issues constitute what may be the best adaptation of the novel to comics. Not only do writer Gary Friedrich and artist Mike Ploog retain the nested narrations of the novel, they go it one better by introducing yet another narrative frame, this from the great-grandson of Captain Walton. The comic thus 'contains' the novel, which consequently becomes just another iteration, or episode, of an even larger story, and it advances that story into the present (circa 1973).

The narrative 'voice' of the monster is fascinatingly unstable across the 18 issues of the series. Early on, when the monster relates his story, he possesses the eloquence of Shelley's original, even if the language is necessarily simplified: 'You constructed me piece by piece … endowed me with a brain devoid of all knowledge … created me against all the laws of god and man … gave me life … only to desert me … leave me alone and helpless …' Just a few more issues in, though, he just sounds like a comic book villain: 'Fools! Do you not know how strong I truly am? And now you will pay for your ignorance—pay with your very lives!' This could as easily be the voice of the highly melodramatic Dr Doom.

The monster's verbal degeneration continues. In a later issue, he goes mute in the *completely* logical way the monster hypothesises in a series of thought balloons: 'Her ripping at my throat—her vampire blood mingling with mine—it seems to have done something to me! [...] My vocal cords have been paralyzed somehow!' This quasi-explicable phenomenon is followed by another which goes entirely unexplained: the creature's *thought* balloons cease. The reader will never again have access to the mind of this monster. Instead, captions provide a third-person narration that describes both the character's actions and emotions so thoroughly that the images are sometimes rendered superfluous. Denson is right to find in this muting of the monster 'a cross-medial nod' to its cinematic forebears (2011: 550–1).

But to return to my question: does the shift from first- to third-person perspective, and from direct to indirect discourse, affect the affect of the monster? It actually doesn't. Leaving aside the issue of better and worse writing in the series, what characterises the entirety of *The Monster of Frankenstein* is the proliferation of written text. In the 1970s, the 'Marvel Method' of collaboration, where writers provided story outlines to artists (who thus had more control over the pacing and design of the comic), yielded to a period of full, and often overfull, scripting. This new emphasis on script was a sign that comic books were, rather self-consciously, 'growing up:' becoming more literate, more psychologically driven and more engaged with the real world. The two writers on the series, Gary Friedrich and Doug Moench, provide abundant narrative captions, speech balloons and thought balloons. Panels tend to be small, and words sometimes crowd the art. Silent panels are rare. The result of this textual logorrhoea is that we are never far from the monster: if he isn't telling us his story, then the narration is. We remain privy to the monster's emotional life, even as the narrative returns him to the mute, shambling, inchoate creature of the movies. By the end, the narration reveals the monster in ways that exceed his own self-understanding.

The narrative possibilities of comics are dwarfed by the unquantifiable range of visual styles offered up by comics' art, and these, too, have implications for a reader's empathetic response. Three artists produced multiple issues of *Monster of Frankenstein*. Early issues were illustrated by Mike Ploog, whose art is cartoonishly exaggerated but not overly so: faces are individuated, detailed and modelled. Tear ducts and the marks of age are visible, and the monster has a suitably shrivelled complexion, in keeping with the novel (Fig. 11.1).[6] Denson demonstrates the ways that Ploog uses the monster as a framing device: as the monster begins to tell his story, his face becomes something of a permeable panel boundary—his greenish pallor becomes the ground from which the recalled narrative

Fig. 11.1 *Monster of Frankenstein* #1 (Marvel Comics, 1973) Gary Friedrich (w), Mike Ploog (a), John Costanza (l)

events emerge. Ploog is also adventurous with his page layouts; it is no surprise that he left comics for animation since his work is so dedicated to a world-building aesthetic that encompasses figures and faces as well as panels and pages. All of Ploog's technique brings us into a more empathetic relation with his monster, even as that monster remains a frightening figure.

Later issues were pencilled by John Buscema, whose art is more recognisably connected to what could be called Marvel's house style: panel boundaries adhere more clearly to a grid, even as some askew angles provide a destabilising dynamism. And while Buscema's work spanned genres—superhero, romance, horror, barbarian, science fiction—he essentially drew the same way in each. Figures are lithe or hulking, faces stern or malevolent (or, if female, sultry), and motion and impact lines emphasise the kineticism of bodies in motion. The last issues were pencilled by Val Mayerik, whose stylised art hearkens back to Ploog's but is somewhat more realistic—extensive feathering gives clothes texture, landscapes detail and faces depth.

Ploog and Mayerik limn a more monstrous monster, while there is not much differentiating Buscema's monster from his Conan the Barbarian (Conan has a sword. And a tan). Their monsters are also the most empathetic. These grotesques are rendered with what can only be called loving care, and they stand out, proudly individuated. Buscema's issues are more action oriented (Frankenstein fights Dracula!), and the monster is at once the least introspective and the least visually distinctive. He is no more monstrous, and is arguably considerably less monstrous, than any of a number of Marvel heroes of the time. These examples hardly begin to encompass the range of styles available to comic artists, but given that this all happened across 18 issues of a single title, it is suggestive. And all of these concatenations of narrative and visual modes combine cinema's visible monster with literature's richly subjective one, a hybridity that comics generate with ease.

Before comic books grew up in the 1970s, they grew up in the 1950s. The soon-to-be-notorious EC Comics was producing work geared, at least ostensibly, to an older audience of comics readers. EC's 'New Trend' produced comics across a range of genres: horror, science fiction, pirate stories, war and humour. One sign of the new maturity of the New Trend was that the lettering looked typeset, while other comics were clearly hand-lettered; this faux-type mimicked not just literature but pulp fiction, both of which were regarded as more elevated than comic books. Narrative captions appeared above or below the art, which added another book-like effect—word and image separated as in an illustrated novel (word and thought balloons, though, are placed within the frame). The stories in Feldstein's books tended towards the formulaic, but the art was first-rate (not to mention deeply influential) and styles varied greatly.

'Mirror, Mirror, on the Wall' appeared in a 1953 issue of *Tales from the Crypt*. The story, by Al Feldstein and Jack Davis, took subjective perspective a step further than the novel could, presenting its images from the point of view of the protagonist, who has just escaped a mad scientist's lair and is searching for help. What the reader realises *well* before the protagonist is that he is, in fact, Frankenstein's monster (or his twin brother)—the horrified reactions of those he approaches clueing us in to his probable status.[7] The written text (after the usual introduction by the Crypt Keeper) also plunges us into the character's experience, but using second-person narration:

> You open your eyes, and the glaring light overhead blinds you! You realize that you have been under a swirling sea of darkness and have only now come to the surface! A grey haze hangs over you … But soon, even that clears away like cobwebs being swept aside by a fastidiously wielded duster! Things come into focus! Jellied objects slowly freeze into solidity! A figure bends over you, shielding the overhead glare from your light-sensitive eyes …

The language and perspective re-stage, intentionally or not, the awakening to consciousness of Shelley's monster. It is not quite as inchoate an experience, but the emphasis is as surely on sensation and experience.

Yet the narration itself is second-person rather than first (a common element of EC comics). The effect of this is complicated. Most obviously, it positions the reader as the protagonist—'I,' the reader, am the one to whom that 'you' is directed. But it also, paradoxically, introduces some distance; it simultaneously positions the character as subject (narration only provides details available to the character) and object (there is no 'I,' only 'you'). It further turns description into something that seems more like *direction*, robbing the character of agency (Think of hypnosis: 'You are getting *sleeeepy…*'). The story is, as they say in gaming, 'on rails'—the character moves along a preordained path, doing what is narrated and *only* that. It's a fascinating rhetorical device.

If second-person address is common for an EC comic, the first-person perspective of the artwork is not. As the scientist leans over 'me,' exaggerated foreshortening makes his hand loom before 'my' eyes. The first panels feature only the scientist and a light behind him, but the details of the laboratory soon come into view. The gaze is next directed towards the protagonist's own body, as he bursts the straps that restrain him. He moves out into the world, his shadow looming before him (foreshadowing [!]) the revelation of his appearance. People come into view, look into 'my' eyes and run, screaming, into the night. Blinding headlights signal an approaching car, as 'my' hands raise protectively. 'I' remember who I am and head for home, where 'my' terrified wife falls from a second-floor window (Fig. 11.2). 'I' return to the mad scientist, who reveals that he took 'my' brain and placed it in the body he constructed. This 'scientist' actually runs a wax museum (with a *Frankenstein* tableau—a nice 'cross-medial' element).

What is rather lovely here is that the suturing of reader and protagonist, a suturing which is also a split, is matched in the narrative by the rupture between the protagonist's mind and the body into which *it* has been sutured. The story has taken the power of comics to provide both interior and exterior 'views' of the monster and scrambled them. Monster and reader don't know that we have become a monster; the internal monologue of a seemingly normal man does and does not belong to the body he is revealed to have. We are and are not in the place of the monster, a nice ambiguity. And if the story itself is a bit predictable, it is nevertheless nicely Densonian: the story takes up its place as part of a lineage (the Frankenstein tableau signals that) into which protagonist and reader have been stitched.

The art is typical, glorious, Jack Davis. His work never falls far from caricature—as in the pages he was simultaneously producing for Harvey Kurtzman's *MAD*—but when drawing more serious comics, whether war or horror, his characters are convincingly individuated and earthy. In 'Mirror, Mirror,' the most visually striking moments involve the limited view of the character's own body: looking down the length of his strapped-down body, the huge gnarled hands that kill, and, finally, the monster viewing himself in what he does not yet know is a mirror. There is nothing funny about Davis' monster, who is a full-on Karloff type: the two-panel sequence in which the monster charges towards his own image and then smashes it with a massive fist (identical to the one he sees before him) is chilling.

One shouldn't overlook Davis' cover to the issue that features this story: set in the wax museum, with a Jack the Ripper tableau in the background,

Fig. 11.2 'Mirror, Mirror, on the Wall' *Tales from the Crypt* #34 (EC Comics, 1953), Al Feldstein (w), Jack Davis (a)

the face of Frankenstein's monster looms in the foreground, warts (literally!) and all—*all* being a red-rimmed eye, stitches so expertly rendered that you can practically feel them and saliva nearly streaming from the mouth. It's nasty and wonderful in equal measure, but it was just this kind of gruesome image that drew the unwanted attention of society's cultural watchdogs, leading to the sanitisation of the American comic book industry for years to come.

Some decades later, Mike Mignola would take horror comics in another direction, with his *Hellboy* stories of occult detection and, later, war. A richly intertextual project, Mignola's work spanned several titles set at different times, and the stories in all were tantalisingly interconnected.[8] All were presented through Mignola's pervasive aesthetic: impeccably composed pages, flat colours, heavy blacks, abstracted forms and a pervading, melancholic, stillness. The *Hellboy* stories were told non-chronologically, and a later story was set in Mexico in 1956, where a down-but-not-out Hellboy had a coerced wrestling match with a piteous Frankenstein's monster. That monster became the protagonist of *Frankenstein Underground*, a five-issue series that appeared in 2015–16 (Dark Horse Comics), an independent story that nevertheless tied into Mignola's larger cosmology. My analysis tilts towards the treatment of the monster rather than the story.

The book begins with the encounter of a Mexican woman (who might be a witch) with a creature very like the Universal Studios monster, complete with neck bolts: 'Urnn' is his first utterance, followed by a 'RUAAAA' as he looms menacingly. He collapses; his chest is bleeding from a bullet wound, a wound that the woman heals with her touch. The monster's next utterance is a pictured '!,' but then he sits up and asks, 'How did you do that?' This, then, is not the monster we thought he was: the mute monster of the movies has 'a somewhat more sophisticated' power of self-expression.

The art is by Ben Stenbeck and the colours are by Dave Stewart. As with all of Mignola's scripted work, words are kept to a minimum, and the word balloons become part of the spare, yet somehow lush, aesthetic of the pages. The monster, designed by Mignola, is not *especially* monstrous; he fits squarely into the artist's universe of grotesques. But that he *is* physically monstrous is not in doubt, and his trans-medial pallor and neck bolts make him recognisably Frankenstein's monster. Mignola has positioned him at the intersection of literary and cinematic creatures and has given him longevity: the tale is set in 1956, but when we are shown scenes from his earlier life, the first, 'Switzerland, 1812,' predates Shelley's novel (Fig. 11.3). Comics once more turn the novel into another, rather than the first, iteration of the monster's story.

Fig. 11.3 *Frankenstein Underground* #1 (Dark Horse Comics, 2015)—Mike Mignola (w), Ben Stenbeck (a), Dave Stewart (c), Clem Robins (l)

And he is something of a pitiable object. The next pages present scenes from his life, including his marathon wrestling match against Hellboy, and we are moved through the panels not only by brief captions marking the place and time, but also by his lamenting voice-over captions:

PANEL ONE:
>'As far back as I remember I was a thing...'
>Switzerland, 1812

PANEL TWO:
>'Hunted...'
>Macedonia, 1826

PANEL THREE:
>'Hated...'
>France, 1863

PANEL FOUR:
>'Caged...'
>Austria, 1911

As *Frankenstein Underground* develops, this monster shows himself to be the one closest to the novel's Romantic sensibility. At the end of the first issue, the woman dies and the monster's anguish is palpable. The lettering is emphatic, as he shouts: 'THEN I SAY THERE ARE NO GODS AND I AM DONE WITH THIS WORLD! KILL ME IF YOU CAN AND SEND ME TO—' With that, he is plunged into hell.

At the start of the second issue, he begins to explore this new realm; narrative captions accompany him across the panels, delivering his first-person narration:

>'I breathe.'
>'My heart beats.'
>'Wretched thing that I am, it may be that I *cannot* die.'[9]

Mignola sometimes allows his monster to narrate his view of himself and mankind, but we do not get explicit descriptions of what he feels or thinks. And yet, with his questing, questioning sensibility, he is the most empathetic version of the monster that comics has produced. The monster's torment is revealed in his words, yes, but it is also displaced into the sombre palette, the contemplative tone, the disjunction between the calm of the narration and the action of the images, and the deliberate rhythm of the pages. We come to know far more about the mind of this monster than ever we are told.

WORDS, IMAGES AND THE ENDLESS LIFE OF A MONSTER

I will conclude, not with a comic, but with Moser's illustrated *Frankenstein*, and his most audacious choice. Across the five chapters in which the creature tells his story, the only images, seven in all, are further close-ups of his face against a field of blackness. The reader sees nothing of the events narrated: no reflection, no happy family, no death of William, just a repeated encounter with the horrific visage that is the result of Victor's transgression. These images, unlike those in the rest of the book, are in colour—touched with gold, as if lit from below by the fire that, here, is all that separates man from monster (Fig. 11.4). Moser keeps the monster before our eyes at the same time as the language of the narrative becomes his. We are given interior and exterior at once. The reader is continuously confronted by the tragic conundrum of the monster's existence: he is monstrous in form but not in nature. It is strangely cinematic, this intercutting

Fig. 11.4 *Frankenstein; or, The Modern Prometheus* (The Pennyroyal Edition, 1983), Barry Moser (a)

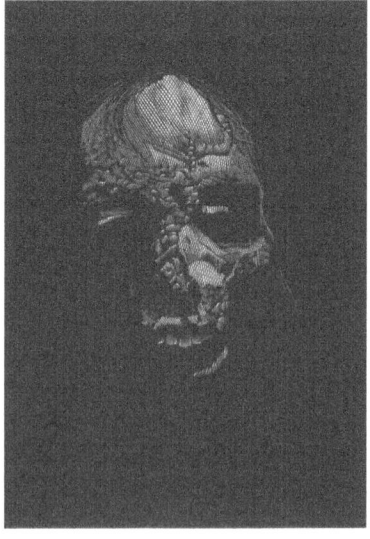

of text with image, or is it a superimposition? That juxtaposition of text and image also recalls the monstrous medium of the comics.

These are also the only portraits of the monster until the book's last image, which accompanies the monster's speech to Walton and his description of the plan for his own death:

> I shall no longer see the sun or stars, or feel the winds play on my cheeks. Light, feeling, and sense, will pass away; and in this condition must I find my happiness. Some years ago, when the images which this world affords first opened upon me, when I felt the cheering warmth of summer, and heard the rustling of the leaves and the chirping of the birds, and these were all to me, I should have wept to die; now it is my only consolation. Polluted by crimes, and torn by the bitterest remorse, where can I find rest but in death? (Shelley and Moser 1983: 237)

The image on the facing page is of the monster's face in death, an image that does not belong to *Frankenstein's* narrative but only to the monster's narration. He is granted the book's final speech and determines its final image.

In that final speech, the monster predicts that, with the deaths of Victor and himself, 'the very remembrance of us both will speedily vanish.' Clearly, this has not come to pass. The rupture between the inner and outer man remains compelling two centuries later, and the fertile challenges posed by that rupture to artists seeking to adapt or extend the monster's story continue to generate versions rich in emotion and invention. If Frankenstein, *Frankenstein*, and Frankenstein's monster have not been forgotten, it is, to a great degree, envisionings such as these that have kept them vital—indeed, *alive*.

NOTES

1. Thanks to my editor Carol Margaret Davison for linking the bodies of these monsters to those of their readers. By the way, these monster-heroes were directly descended from the more monster-y monsters Marvel was featuring in the late 1950s and early 1960s. By turning its monsters into aliens, Marvel was able to elude the Comics Code Authority; Fin Fang Foom, for example, was an extraterrestrial dragon modestly sporting purple shorts.
2. She adds, 'Once the monster becomes visible within contemporary horror films, monstrosity becomes less and less recuperable' (Halberstam 1995: 39).
3. That edition featured but two facing images, on the frontispiece and title page (engraved by W. Chevalier from illustrations by Theodor Von Holst).

These are effectively discussed in Ian Haywood, 'Image of the Month: Theodore Von Holst, '*Frankenstein*' (1831),' https://romanticillustrationnetwork.wordpress.com/2016/11/26/image-of-the-month-theodore-von-holst-frankenstein-1831/

4. In conversation, 2017.
5. Incredibly, this unique characteristic of the medium has fallen from fashion over the past few decades in favour of running captions that mimic the more cinematic device of the voice-over.
6. Ploog apprenticed under Will Eisner, whose work similarly revelled in expressive close-ups while remaining appealingly cartoony.
7. This device was also used to introduce the 'monstrous' Buddy Love in Jerry Lewis' *The Nutty Professor* (1963) a few years later.
8. There is so much more to say about Mignola's work. See my *Hellboy's World: Comics and Monsters on the Margins* (University of California Press, 2016).
9. In her editorial notes to this essay, Carol Margaret Davison comments that Mignola 'opens up an entirely new avenue with *Frankenstein* in this instance, one that resonates with the narratives of Dracula and other doomed Gothic immortals.' I fully agree, and wish I had the space to pursue that crucial development.

WORKS CITED

Bender, John B., and Michael Marrinan. 2010. *The Culture of Diagram*. Stanford: Stanford University Press.

Brooks, Mel (director, co-writer). 1974. *Young Frankenstein*. 20th Century Fox.

Bukatman, Scott. 2016. *Hellboy's World: Comics and Monsters on the Margins*. Berkeley: University of California Press.

Denson, Shane. 2011. Marvel Comics' *Frankenstein*: A Case Study in the Media of Serial Figures. *Amerikastudien/American Studies* 55 (4): 531–553.

———. 2014. *Postnaturalism: Frankenstein, Film, and the Anthropotechnical Interface*. Bielefeld: Transcript-Verlag.

Feldstein, Al, and Jack Davis. 1953. Mirror, Mirror, on the Wall. *Tales from the Crypt*, 34.

Friedrich, Gary, Mike Ploog, et al. 2015. *The Monster of Frankenstein*. New York: Marvel Comics.

Gabilliet, Jean-Paul. 2010. *Of Comics and Men: A Cultural History of American Comic Books*. Trans. Bart Beaty and Nick Nguyen. Jackson: University Press of Mississippi.

Gunning, Tom. 1999. Narrative Discourse and the Narrator System. In *Film Theory and Criticism: Introductory Readings*, ed. Leo Braudy and Marshall Cohen, 470–481. New York/London: Oxford University Press.

Halberstam, Judith. 1995. *Skin Shows: Gothic Horror and the Technology of Monsters*. Durham/London: Duke University Press.

Haywood, Ian. 2016. Image of the Month: Theodore von Holst, '*Frankenstein*' (1831). https://romanticillustrationnetwork.wordpress.com/2016/11/26/image-of-the-month-theodore-von-holst-frankenstein-1831/

Mendelsund, Peter. 2014. *What We See When We Read: A Phenomenology With Illustrations*. New York: Vintage Books.

Metz, Christian. 1974. On the Impression of Reality in the Cinema. In *Film Language: A Semiotics of the Cinema*. New York: Oxford University Press.

Mignola, Mike, and Ben Stenbeck. 2015. *Frankenstein Underground*. Portland: Dark Horse Comics.

Morrison, Grant, and Chris Weston. 2004. *The Filth*, Issue 10. Vertigo Comics: New York.

Nadel, Dan. 2006. *Art Out of Time: Unknown Comics Visionaries 1900–1969*. New York: Harry N. Abrams.

Nestrick, William. 1979. Coming to Life: *Frankenstein* and the Nature of Film Narrative. In *The Endurance of Frankenstein: Essays on Mary Shelley's Novel*, ed. George Levine and U.C. Knoepflmacher. Berkeley/Los Angeles/London: University of California Press.

Peake, Richard Brinsley. 1823. *Presumption: Or, the Fate of Frankenstein*. http://www.rc.umd.edu/editions/peake/index.html

Raub, Emma. 2012. *Frankenstein* and the Mute Figure of Melodrama. *Modern Drama* 55 (4): 437–458.

Redfield, Marc. 2003. *Frankenstein's* Cinematic Dream. *Romantic Circles*. https://www.rc.umd.edu/praxis/frankenstein/redfield/redfield.html

Scott, Grant F. 2012. Victor's Secret: Queer Gothic in Lynd Ward's Illustrations to *Frankenstein* (1934). *Word & Image* 28 (2): 206–232.

Shelley, Mary. 2016. *Frankenstein: The Lynd Ward Illustrated Edition*. New York: Dover.

Shelley, Mary, and Barry Moser. (1983). *Frankenstein, or, The Modern Prometheus*, The Pennyroyal edition. West Hatfield: Pennyroyal Press.

Weiss, Allen S. 2004. Ten Theses on Monsters and Monstrosity. *TDR: The Drama Review* 48 (1): 124–125.

Whale, James (director). 1931. *Frankenstein*. Universal Pictures.

CHAPTER 12

Our Progeny's Monsters: *Frankenstein* Retold for Children in Picturebooks and Graphic Novels

Emily Alder

This essay is about graphic retellings of *Frankenstein* aimed at child readers and particularly the interplay between pictures and words. Examining
how Shelley's novel is adapted for children—and inspires new stories
(often rather loosely)—is a rewarding process. It can reveal a great deal
about *Frankenstein* and the state of its proliferation at its bicentenary, as
well as about the state of contemporary children's literature and constructions of childhood. *Frankenstein* is very open to rewriting and reuse, and
the texts I discuss here offer differing treatments of the story and its tropes.
They tend to emphasise certain aspects of the story over others (such as
the consequences of misused knowledge, parental abandonment, or social
inclusion), relate words and images accordingly, and achieve a number of
different effects (e.g., parody, horror, or comedy). *Frankenstein* is, perhaps surprisingly, rather well suited to stories aimed at children; my aim

E. Alder (✉)
School of Arts and Creative Industries, Edinburgh Napier University,
Edinburgh, UK

© The Author(s) 2018   209
C. M. Davison, M. Mulvey-Roberts (eds.), *Global Frankenstein*,
Studies in Global Science Fiction,
https://doi.org/10.1007/978-3-319-78142-6_12

here is to demonstrate why graphic narrative forms in particular are so adept at adapting it for young readers.

First, I explore possible reasons why *Frankenstein* feeds children's books as often as it does and outline some of the contributions that graphic narratives make to its abundant afterlives. Second, I explore several texts targeted at a range of different ages, from picturebooks for young children to a graphic novel aimed at early teens. Two are picturebooks, Neil Numberman's *Do Not Build a Frankenstein!* (2009) and Patrick McDonnell's *The Monsters' Monster* (2012), while three are titled simply *Frankenstein* and directly adapt Shelley's text. Created by an international array of illustrators and authors, these books indicate a widespread compulsion to return to this story in graphic form.

As this collection testifies, *Frankenstein* at 200 years retains its relevance to a modern, globalised world. This may have less to do with the pan-European compass of Shelley's settings and characters, however, than with the ways in which its concerns still speak to Western modernity and with its almost immediate escape from its original form and subsequent cultural dispersal (Fisch 2009). The first translation (into French in 1821) and Richard Brinsley Peake's 1823 stage adaptation both precede the 1831 version that constituted the basis for many subsequent English editions. By the 1950s, *Frankenstein* was being widely translated into non-European languages and had enjoyed a lively cinematic afterlife since at least Edison Studio's 1910 film.[1] It quickly entered the expanding and increasingly global culture spread by twentieth-century mass media, including children's cartoons from the 1930s onwards (Hitchcock 2007). James Whale's 1931 film particularly influenced subsequent visualisations of Frankenstein's monster, including in comics and graphic novels (Murray 2016). The postwar period, in the wake of the atomic bomb and the breakup of the British Empire, created new contexts for *Frankenstein*'s thematic arenas. As a story about scientific ambition, responsibility for what is created, and recognition, rejection, and acceptance of difference and otherness, *Frankenstein* has remained at home in a difficult new world. While Gothic and horror narratives may often ultimately be conservative, many *Frankenstein* retellings offer critical potential and strategies for rethinking the place of science or the self in the world; here, I approach that potential through picturebooks and graphic novels aimed, nominally at least, at child readers.

Frankenstein's ostensible status is as an adult, Gothic text whose writing style and philosophical, psychological, and violent contents may be considered unsuitable for young children, though its Young Adult (YA) relevance is easier to comprehend.[2] Adapting it also raises questions around fidelity and the extent to which canonical texts are simplified or 'dumbed down' when rewritten for children. Adaptation theory and criticism may have moved on from fidelity as a criterion for a successful adaptation but, argues Anja Müller (2014), the chimera of fidelity to an original can linger in particularly acute and unhelpful ways when the adaptation in question is of a canonical text and aimed at a child audience or readership.[3] For Müller, a reactionary emphasis on fidelity is implicated in uncritical conceptions of childhood and of suitable children's literature, since (as with comics and picturebooks) reading adaptations of adult texts was supposed to serve as a literary initiation or apprenticeship (3–4). *Frankenstein*, however, belongs to a canon from which the innocent Romantic child requires protection, rather than initiation—namely, the Gothic.

Yet, recent critical work has contested gothic horror's purported unsuitability for children, exposing a mismatch between what young (including pre-teen) readers and viewers were and are supposed to like, consume, and be able to appreciate, and what actually attracts them or falls within their critical capacities (Mitchell and Reid-Walsh 2002; Townshend 2008). Sarah J. Smith (2005) shows that Whale's *Frankenstein* attracted a significant child audience enjoying the experience of fear, while also generating adult anxiety over its suitability at a time when children's cinema was just starting to fall under censorship and regulation. Sandra Beckett (2012) argues that '[w]idespread assumptions about the limited ability of children to deal with certain topics led to an unwritten code of proscribed subjects and to censorship or auto-censorship in children's literature', and she welcomes the extent to which these proscriptions have been shaken off in recent decades, especially by picturebooks (212).

Enlightenment and Romantic constructions of childhood, such as the notions of *tabula rasa* and the state of innocence, worked to suppress acknowledgement of child readers' appreciation of the gory, grisly, and terrifying, yet 'in children's literature today, the Gothic is the mainstream' (Jackson et al. 2008: 1).[4] Jackson, Coats, and McGillis identify a cultural shift in late-twentieth and twenty-first-century attitudes to childhood away from assumptions of children's innocence and towards recognition of their complexity, knowingness, and even complicity with their experiences that may be difficult for adults to fully fathom. Accordingly, they suggest, '[r]ather than seeing the Gothic as an anomalous intrusion into their lives from some external and alien force, the children in many contemporary Gothic novels court their dark side, and own it as an aspect of the self' (8). Gothic, then, has become an important vehicle for renegoti-ating the scripts of contemporary childhood, and *Frankenstein* is arguably revisited so often by contemporary children's authors and illustrators because of, rather than despite, its salient tropes and subject matter. As Erin Hawley (2015) argues, it is 'a tale with surprisingly child-centric themes. At its heart, it is a story about what it means to be an outsider and what it means to encounter, experience, and negotiate otherness'. It is also about having parents and being orphaned, about education and the for-mative stages of childhood. Coats and Sands (2016) suggest that young children in particular identify with the monster, feeling a 'sense of kinship' because 'he *is* a child' (244). For Hawley, *Frankenstein*'s numerous screen adaptations offer 'the misunderstood monster as an icon of all that is unruly, confused, and frightening about childhood itself'. The graphic narratives I examine here exhibit many of these traits and interests.

They also encounter the same risks Hawley identifies around adapting *Frankenstein* for a children's film, namely that oversimplifying it

> would be a process of dumbing down, a cleaning up of a story that works best when it is *not* "clean". It would also be a form of commercialisation, a reduction of a complex tale so that it can be packaged and marketed to young audiences.

Children's books and films are difficult to separate from their commercial contexts, but *Frankenstein* retellings, as Hawley argues of Tim Burton's *Frankenweenie* (2012), do retain some potential to resist sanitisation and simplification and to offer at least some of *Frankenstein*'s compelling com-plexity in their new forms. Audrey A. Fisch (2009) contests assumptions that Frankenstein's monster in children's books is just 'a banal creature of Halloween', showing how Ellen Raskin's 1972 picturebook *Franklin Stein*

> plays with social rejection, the power relationship between Creator and cre-ated, and human companionship all the while cementing the relationship for young readers between these themes and the "Frankenstein" mythology already firmly embedded in their imaginations by our culture. (242–34)

Any study of *Frankenstein* in children's literature, then, must acknowledge the new text's debt not only to Shelley's story but also to its other influ-ential multimedia manifestations—the tropes, phrases, and iconography transmitted by films, television, and merchandise, and its invocation by the media to connote scientific meddling.

The texts I explore here take a relaxed approach to authenticity or fidelity to Shelley's text and appropriate as well as adapt it.[5] Popular awareness of *Frankenstein* can take rather reductive forms—the neck-bolted image of Boris Karloff, the word 'Frankenfoods'—but the persistence of these motifs also indicates how indestructibly 'it's alive!' persists in contemporary culture. *Frankenstein* is so widely dispersed that now almost any isolated element of its myth is up for grabs (see Baldick 1987; Lavalley 1979, in Hawley 2015). The ludic approach of picturebooks seems to give them particular licence; for example, to transpose the name Frankenstein from the creator to the created, as occurs in *Do Not Build a Frankenstein!*

However, rather than seeing such appropriation as a reductive move, we may ask its purpose, and what it contributes to an understanding of *Frankenstein* in the context of twenty-first-century children's graphic narratives, in keeping with what Linda Hutcheon (2013) calls 'our postmodern age of cultural recycling' (3). If a new retelling responds to both Shelley's story *and* Whale's film, then, as Hawley asks, 'what has been lost in this process?' Rather, what matters is not the authenticity of *Frankenstein* retellings but the collection of things that replace it, including intertextuality, palimpsestic traces, the specificity of their new medium, form, and audience, and the new sets of cultural meanings they may invoke or evoke (Buchbinder 2011).

My contention here is that the visual characteristics—of graphic novels and picturebooks as forms and of the *Frankenstein* myth and motifs as they have been passed down to twenty-first-century children's literature through widespread multimedia adaptations—are what make graphic retellings of *Frankenstein* so possible and successful. If writing in Gothic modes can offer, shape, or negotiate new constructions of childhood that understand both child characters and implied child readers as sophisticated, capable, critical, and knowing, so too can graphic novels and picturebooks. Because graphic narratives communicate in different ways from text-only narratives, their forms offer some unique opportunities of escape from traditional conventions or expectations.

Picturebooks and comics have drawn considerable critical attention as creative forms with potential for roles in children's socialisation and cognitive development (see Nodelman 1988; McCloud 1994; Nikolajeva and Scott 2001; Cross 2008; Stephens 2011). They are accorded status as 'a key means of apprenticeship into literacy, literature and social values' (Painter et al. 2013: 1–2), contributing not only to the development of verbal and written literacy but also to the 'multimodal' literacy demanded by the highly visual environment of twenty-first-century media (Serafini 2010). Studies have found children to be adept at interpreting pictures as well as devices such as gaps of signification between images and text (Arizpe and Styles 2003; Beauvais 2015).

Most books aimed at child readers contain illustrations of some kind, and the blends and balance of text and images are far from homogeneous. However, useful yet permeable distinctions can be drawn between 'illustrated books (where the words carry the primary narrative while pictures are supportive or decorative) and books in which both the visual and the verbal aspects are both essential for full communication' (Nikolajeva and Scott 2000: 226). Lamond and Zak's *Frankenstein* (2005), for example, relies considerably on a written narrative, although the illustrations are highly striking, while McDonnell's *The Monsters' Monster* and Numberman's *Do Not Build a Frankenstein!* are more image driven.

In most cases, the narrative is created through a process of 'interanimation' in which 'language and image [work] productively upon each other' (Lewis 2001: 37)—what Nikolajeva and Scott (2000) term a 'counterpointing dynamic', in which 'words and images collaborate to communicate meanings beyond the scope of either one alone' (226). Sometimes, words and images offer conflicting information, and 'as soon as words and images provide alternative information or contradict each other in some way, we have a variety of readings and interpretations', requiring the reader to be fully engaged (232). Julie Cross (2008) argues, in the context of children's Gothic fiction, that the uncertainty and instability of the twenty-first-century world makes ambiguity in literature a positive force, offering 'advantages and plurality' for young readers and helping them with becoming 'active social agents' (66, 65). If so, then Shelley's *Frankenstein*, already replete with ambiguity and plurality, is well suited to speaking to young readers about the place of themselves and others in the modern world as well as to a graphic narrative form.

For example, Mould's Victor Frankenstein reflects idealistically, in the written text, on his happy Geneva childhood, while the image depicts a scene of domestic chaos with a fraught Caroline and Justine being tripped up by playing children. An active reading strategy is needed to negotiate these two versions of the past and identify Victor as a potentially unreliable or solipsistic narrator. Layout is also significant. The written text of Mould's *Frankenstein* obeys neat rectangular boxes, hovering over the artwork: the separation further suggests a need for caution while reading Victor's account.

Other material characteristics get involved too. Gérard Genette, in his influential study *Paratexts* (1997), proposed that the features surrounding the main text of a literary work (such as publication information, title, prefaces) form a threshold, fringe, or liminal zone 'at the service of a better reception for the text and a more pertinent reading of it' (2). Each part merits analytical attention; cover design, endpapers, title page, and dustjacket contribute to the narrative. Picturebooks and graphic novels often exhibit particularly creative uses of endpapers (which have the practical function of attaching the cartridge of pages to the cover) (Sipe and McGuire 2006; Duran and Bosch 2011). They may contain illustrations not appearing elsewhere or scenes unmentioned in the text, such as the mysterious female figure kneeling in a wood, opening an elaborate casket, on the front and back endpapers of Marion Mousse's *Frankenstein* (2009) (is this Shelley herself, perhaps, in the role of Pandora?). These may even begin or end the narrative, such as Victor's funeral pyre on the ice on the back pastedown of Mould's *Frankenstein* (1997).

Incongruous characterisation, unexpected narrative turns, parody, intertextuality, and other ludic elements are also among the devices adding complexity to even the simplest graphic narratives and encouraging active reading strategies by young as well as adult readers.[6] Humorous effects may mitigate against the bleakness and violence of the original *Frankenstein* but can also contribute to the narrative's critical and activating potential. For Cross, written comic Gothic texts 'which recognise the cognitive aspects of humour, and not just the well-recognised emotional and psychological functions, acknowledge children's abilities as learners, treating them as active beings' (64). Her remarks apply equally to picturebooks, and four of my examples use humour as a purposeful strategy, exploiting readers' prior knowledge (however diffuse) of the *Frankenstein* story by setting up expectations that are then disrupted.

Do Not Build a Frankenstein! relies on awareness or prior knowledge of an originating story to exploit readers' expectations, a trick dependant on pictures, words, and the material form of the book itself. The title pages extend for two-and-a-half double spreads, showing a series of children fleeing underneath the ominous title, presented on a green background, in bold, colourful letters with a patchwork pattern and the word 'Not' drawn large (Fig. 12.1). These paratexts encourage assumptions about how the story will go. At first, we connect the running children of the title pages to scared faces depicted on the dustjacket, aware that Frankensteinian creations tend to be construed as dangerous. We probably also guess the titular injunction

Fig. 12.1 Children flee along the title page (Used with permission of HarperCollins Publishers. © Neil Numberman (2009))

has been broken. Indeed, we learn that the Victor character has moved to a new town to escape his creation; he warns his new school friends, just as the original Victor warns Walton, about the lessons he has learnt as a consequence of building a monster.

Flashbacks show the boy's obsessive research in a series of images: other children playing outside his window, a laboratory complete with electrical equipment, and nocturnal grave robbing accompanied by his dog. Later, we see his efforts to escape the persistent Frankenstein who follows him everywhere. So far, so familiar, and the Frankenstein is positioned by the boy's words as something annoying that must be shunned. The illustrations, however, show a misunderstood, playful creature who does not *mean* to terrify the boy in the middle of the night, break his toys, or scare his friends. At the end, the Frankenstein's sudden appearance to the gathered children initially causes panic, but as a group they recognise he is in search of friends, not victims. The running children of the title pages are actually engaged in a playground game of tag with the Frankenstein. At the start, they are, in fact, enacting the final moments, while the boy's story leads back into the past and out again. Like the nested, non-linear structure of Shelley's novel, the narrative structure is more complex than it first seems. It demands an active reading process, which includes its material construction as a picturebook that needs to be (re)read literally cover to cover.

The Monsters' Monster presents another adult-free world. The protagonists are three 'child' monsters, Grouch, Grump, and Gloom 'n' Doom. Like toddlers, they throw tantrums and delight in saying 'No' as they try to outdo each other at being monstrous. Since no one can win, they collaborate to build '[t]he biggest, baddest monster EVER!' Their collecting of goo, tape, wire, and other items is described using simple language—'got', 'found', 'grabbed'—while the illustrations convey frantic activity and a lot of mess not indicated by the written words, such as dropped nails and spilled glue. The whole page, spattered in inkblots echoing similar marks on the title pages, communicates that disorder.

The first picture of the creature presents a mummy; once animated by a lightning bolt and unwrapped, it is evidently the Boris Karloff monster. This monster, not unlike Numberman's Frankenstein, is innocent and well meaning, thankful to be alive and fascinated by 'early dawn light, birdsongs, and dewy, fresh air'. When he is kind to spiders and snakes, the little monsters yell, 'No, no, no [...] You're supposed to be a MONSTER!' In a world of monsters, the concept of monstrosity becomes essentially meaninglessness: 'Monster didn't think he was a monster. He didn't think he was anything...' Like Shelley's creature, he begins as that classic conception of the child, the innocent blank slate, and like Shelley's novel, this picturebook ponders the nature of childhood and monstrosity, innocence and corruption. This creation, rather than learning to understand himself as monstrous in a human social world, teaches the three 'children' a more generous and sharing way of being. By the end, 'no-one was thinking ... about being a monster'. Childhood anxieties are soothed as the visual and narrative messiness and disorder give way to calmness and order. The final pages depict the same peaceful scene (the four monsters sit on the beach watching the sunset) while the final sentence extends serenely over four pages a phrase at a time.

Numberman's and McDonnell's books could be read as working through childhood anxieties about parental abandonment, as the child protagonists become the 'parent' of the created, from whom they then learn about familial belonging; or as stories modelling children's social integration with peer groups and learning to understand the perspectives of others. Both picturebooks invert the original *Frankenstein* script of irresponsible ambition, abandonment, and destruction; the action becomes playful and humorous yet retains *Frankenstein*'s 'child-centric' personal and socialising themes of friendship, belonging, parenting, responsibility, and relating to others to offer the happy ending that never was. The three texts discussed next adapt Shelley's *Frankenstein* more directly and use their graphic form to negotiate the story for their readers in increasingly darker ways.

The *Frankenstein* of British author Chris Mould uses a layout of distinct panels, gutters, and text boxes that resemble a graphic novel, while its visual style of bright primary colours and cartoonish illustrations in full bleed is more characteristic of a picturebook. The mood is often humorous, generated by a degree of mismatch between serene statements like Walton's description of his 'hearty and loyal' crew whose 'patience was beyond the limits of my own' and their depiction as dishevelled and cavorting with barrels, bottles, and playing cards.

Simple language and short sentences help indicate the young target readership (seven years of age and upwards), while the illustrations provide detail and complexity. At Ingoldstadt, 'I attended my lectures in science and chemistry with great enthusiasm', summarises Victor, blandly. The illustration displays a chaotic laboratory, which accordingly spills over the centrefold, into a closet, and even across the gutter to infringe on the border of a text box. The room is littered with books and pages of notes, guttering candles, fossils, skeletons, and especially skulls; other clutter includes a spade, a globe, an anvil, scissors, syringes, spilled pots, and a boxy electrical meter. The page is washed in orange as if candlelit and spattered with black, red, and green flecks which often stand out like drops of blood, also visible on the sleeve of Victor who, in the midst of it all, dismembers a human ribcage 'with great enthusiasm'. Cracked plaster, general untidiness, and a broken grandfather clock indicate Victor's obsession with his work and forgetfulness of time. The excessiveness of Victor's ambitions and efforts is thus treated playfully, poking fun at the state of his laboratory without concealing the Gothic dimensions to his scientific researches. The illustrations do much to convey the complexity of this important point in the story and only the barest text is required.

Mould's depiction of the creature alludes to Shelley's minimal descriptions, especially his impressive size and long flowing hair. Clothes, body, and hair are drawn with wobbly outlines, their colours almost dripping, suggesting his unstable, othered identity in contrast to the neat, contained shapes of the human characters. The worst atrocities of the story are handled lightly. Justine is shown in prison but not hanged; Elizabeth's death is presented in tableau after the event while the creature glowers raggedly at the window. No blood is shown, but Elizabeth lies in a four-poster bed lavishly draped with four crimson curtains. The curtains dominate the top panel, which spans both pages, and spill into two lower panels depicting, left, Victor's anguish and, right, his imprisonment for madness. Sheets strewing the bedroom floor drape down into Victor's cell, their vivid whiteness picked up by his torn shirt, frayed and ragged like the monster's clothing.

The illustrations do significant work but readers are also left to fill in gaps between text and image and to imagine what is *not* shown as well as interpret the details of what is. The final double spread, which produces an almost 3D effect by using the panel layout to construct the ship's deck, interior, and Arctic sea view all at once, offers little written guidance for our sympathies. In the first text box, Walton feels sorry for 'Poor Victor. He worked so hard to achieve something that, in the end, he lost everything'. In the text of the panel beneath, positioned and drawn as a cabin below decks, the creature declares to Walton that he has 'suffered more than anyone. I was shunned by the one who created me. My heart, like yours, was made for love, but no one would let me love'. Walton's lack of reply leaves the reader to interpret the grief on the creature's face as he cradles Victor's body. The third and final panel shows the departing ship in the background, and in the foreground, the isolated creature crouched alone on an ice floe. Walton looks on from the ship's prow, intruding into the picture from the first panel and thus inviting the reader to return to it and, perhaps, to doubt the judgement Walton expressed there.

Marion Mousse's *Frankenstein* from children's graphic novel publisher Papercutz is aimed at 8–14 years of age range, although little about it suggests an exclusively young readership. The colours (by Marie Galopin) are murky, sombre, and shadowy blacks, browns, greens, greys, oranges, and blues. Its comic-strip style creates a complex narrative structure. Transitions between panels, pages, and even colour schemes are used purposefully, layering the narrative with flashbacks, locations, and interpolated sections of the story in a way that is unobtrusive yet requires attention to follow. The Walton framing narrative appears regularly, as a single panel, sequence, or full page, dramatising the Walton-Victor interaction in depth and heightening suspense as, outside, the crew keep a careful watch on the ice. These interjections also sometimes serve as a guide, as Walton's conversations with Victor summarise or reflect on events.

Mousse's Victor has an innocent interest in 'the inner spirit of nature, its occult laws, its secret mechanisms' as a child, while at university his obsessiveness and his unconventional ways of thinking emerge through debates with fellow students and professors. His mother's death is emphasised as the turning point at which he abandons God and comprehends the secret of life, which is 'not the finger of God … but nature, rather, a complex and formidable chemical process'. Victor, drawn thin, narrow, and pointy, is an intense, sinister figure, while the creature is depicted sympathetically, especially in his early days.

A recognisably Shelleyan take on the creature combines with the influence of Whale's film. A lightning bolt animates him, before a series of dark panels show Victor's efforts to light a candle while the creature looms in the background. The candle illuminates a giant resembling Shelley's description, with long black hair and yellowish skin, who grasps his creator's wrists in huge, stitched hands and calls him 'Father'. The final panel shows a close-up of Victor's terrified face before we flip the page to see a jagged, wordless scream echoing over the Ingolstadt rooftops, followed by Victor awaking in bed. What happens in between must be filled in by the reader's imagination, though flashbacks to this hidden moment are scattered through later pages.[7]

Moment-to-moment and aspect-to-aspect transitions slow the pace and heighten suspense, while the positioning of the page turn at a sudden leap from scene to scene emphasises Victor's profound shock. Then, Victor's relieved but hysterical conversation with Henry gives way to Walton's reassuringly distant framing narrative, which leads gradually into the creature's account. The creature's story is thereafter presented, chronologically interspersed with that of Victor's family. The first pages wordlessly show his flight through shadowy night-time woods and first glimpses of a clear dawn. Birds 'kwee' from a tree and a deer drinks from a pond in which the creature views his own reflection. Over the page, his encounter with hostile villagers is told in pictures alone (except for one woman's scream), and later, drifting bubbles of musical notation guide him to the home of Felix and Agatha. The graphic approach conveys the creature's innocent ignorance and pre-verbal state, making us attend as he does to mysterious visual and audial details. Thereafter, his childlike naivety and doomed efforts to learn suitable social behaviours on his own without parental guidance are often shown, predominantly graphically.

The creature meets a fearless child, Mary, who invites him to play by throwing flowers into the lake to float away like boats. Having observed

Felix and Agatha swimming and throwing each other playfully into the water, the creature casts Mary in too. The panels make an abrupt transition from the creature lifting Mary in his hands, to the shadow of her body under the surface of the water. The accidental drowning is thus not shown; the graphic sequence is horrifying because of, not despite, the elision. This scene, of course, derives not from Shelley's text but directly from Whale's film. It contains almost identical shots including the creature and Maria (as she is named in the film) framed by shrubs on the lake bank with mountains in the background; the moment of the creature throwing the child in was originally censored from US prints (see Horton 2014).

My final example makes no reference at all to Whale's film but appeals to a fascination with anatomy. Published in Australia, *Frankenstein* by children's author Margrete Lamond, originally Norwegian, and artist Drahoš Zak, originally Czech, is a particularly beautiful illustrated book for age 11 upwards. Dedicated to Mary Shelley, 'with apologies', it significantly adapts Shelley's text to address a younger, contemporary readership through its writing style, striking artwork, and emphasis on rich scientific detail. This Victor, in addition to learning alchemy, chemistry, and anatomy, becomes a physicist and mechanical engineer, making 'apparatus that depended on the tensions of delicately-coiled springs' and 'pyrotechnic machines that were powered by steam' (35). The animation method is also elaborated: Victor makes a regenerative elixir of life out of the bodily fluids of corpses, and body parts float in troughs of it ready for Victor's painstaking construction work.

Making this creature is a delicate process of 'weaving and folding into place the slippery complexities of liver and intestine, trachea and oesophagus, arteries and lungs' within a skeleton made from several different people's bones (42). Finally, Victor 'linked the great connecting nerves of the eyes and spine to the brain, slipped the quivering grey jelly into its casing, replaced the bone section, and fastened the skull shut' (42). The anatomical emphasis and medical precision of the written text are reflected in the illustrations. These, though often landscapes or seascapes, characters, or blank pages washed in mottled colours, include pages of notes, gruesome images such as a single eye with a knife mid-slice, and detailed pictures akin to those produced by anatomists prior to photography (a pair of frog's legs, a map of the arteries in the neck and head, a foetus in a jar).

Depictions of the creature display stitches in his scalp and a sharp nose and teeth; some appear as sketches, others as complete, coloured drawings. The creature looks ugly and frightening in appearance, but Victor is little

Fig. 12.2 The creature
under construction. By
arrangement with the
licensor, Drahoš Zak
(© Curtis Brown (Aust)
Pty Ltd.)

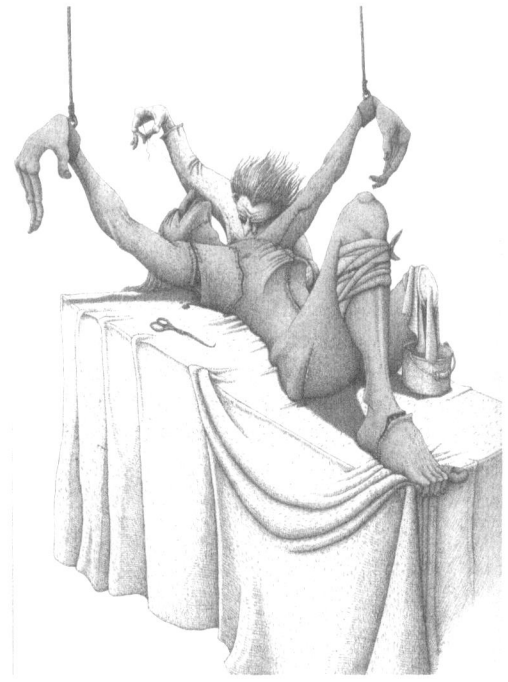

better; the two characters are doubled visually to reinforce the connection Victor tries to deny. One image shows an incomplete creature on a tabletop, with partially stitched foot, rump, and shoulder, and the stump of his left leg oozing through a draped cloth into a pan (Fig. 12.2). Victor, wearing a loupe monocle, is mid-stitch, delicately drawing up a needle and thread in bloody fingertips. The raised arch of his hand and wrist is mirrored on either side by the creature's limp arms, suspended by ropes and cuffs. Throughout, writing and pictures work together to highlight a visceral anatomical reality and hint at the wondrous possibilities of science. While the text carries much of the story, the illustrations carry much of the horror (a hanged Justine with a protruding tongue and livid finger marks on the dead Elizabeth's neck) and a number of *Frankenstein*'s key tropes such as its doubling.

The three versions of *Frankenstein* just discussed exist in a relatively self-contained interpretative context. They are not internally *reliant* on prior knowledge of Shelley's text or its adaptations, although that knowledge may influence how the text is read. Their visualisations of the creature are distinctly non-Karloffian, arguably working to escape the legacy of Whale's film (although Mousse also uses it) and to reinscribe the narrative with relational and ethical nuances. They do declare themselves as adaptations, fitting Linda Hutcheon's claim that an adaptation 'has its own aura' as well as being 'haunted at all times by its adapted text' (Hutcheon and O'Flynn 2013: 6). The distinctive aura of each is produced by the relationship between images and text and by the scope that is offered for promoting active reading and interpretation of the narrative.

The picturebooks for younger readers, by contrast, invoke and subvert Karloff's image (and other filmic iconography), as indeed they invoke and subvert the whole basic narrative for, at root, more positive ends. These are highly child-focussed texts, channelling the concerns of *Frankenstein* into the everyday concerns of Western childhoods. Numberman's and McDonnell's books alter the original's script about otherness, acceptance, and responsibility. The child scientist protagonist receives a positive outcome and a meaningful transformation of their understanding of the world and their place in it, while the so-called monster too is given voice, agency, and a place. The creatures may look like Boris Karloff, but through the word-image counterpoint of the picturebook form they accrue more complexity than a monster stereotype. Collectively, we may see contemporary retellings of *Frankenstein* for children not as simplifications of Shelley's novel but as texts that answer back to oversimplifications of *Frankenstein* passed down through film and popular discourse.

NOTES

1. For a chronology of *Frankenstein*'s translations, see *Romantic Circles* https://www.rc.umd.edu/editions/frankenstein/textual
2. Coats and Sands (2016) examine *Frankenstein*'s adaptations in Young Adult (YA) fiction and texts for young child readers. Two recent collections on the Gothic in children's literature, Jackson et al. (2008) and Jackson (2017), touch only tangentially on *Frankenstein*.
3. On advances from the fidelity debate, see Hutcheon and O'Flynn (2013).
4. On the history of children's literature including constructions of childhood, see also Carpenter (1987).
5. For distinctions and relationships between adaptation and appropriation, see Sanders (2016) and Hutcheon and O'Flynn (2013).
6. For discussions of postmodern devices in picturebooks, see Sipe and Pantaleo (2008).
7. See Beauvais (2015) for a discussion of gaps in comics and picturebooks and of studies of how child readers interpret them.

WORKS CITED

Arizpe, Evelyn, and Morag Styles. 2003. *Children Reading Pictures: Interpreting Visual Texts*. London: RoutledgeFalmer.

Baldick, Chris. 1987. *In Frankenstein's Shadow: Myth, Monstrosity, and Nineteenth-Century Writing*. Oxford: Oxford University Press.

Beauvais, Clementine. 2015. What's in "the Gap"? A Glance Down the Central Concept of Picturebook Theory. *Nordic Journal of ChildLit Aesthetics* 6: 26969.

Beckett, Sandra. 2012. *Crossover Picturebooks: A Genre for All Ages*. New York: Routledge.

Buchbinder, David. 2011. 'From "Wizard" to "Wicked"': Adaptation Theory and Young Adult Fiction. In *Contemporary Children's Literature and Film: Engaging with Theory*, ed. Kerry Mallan and Clare Bradford, 12–35. Basingstoke: Palgrave Macmillan.

Carpenter, Humphrey. 1987. *Secret Gardens: The Golden Age of Children's Literature*. London: Unwin.

Coats, Karen, and Farran Norris Sands. 2016. Growing Up Frankenstein: Adaptations for Young Readers. In *The Cambridge Companion to Frankenstein*, ed. Andrew Smith, 241–255. Cambridge: Cambridge University Press.

Cross, Julie. 2008. Frightening and Funny: Humour in Children's Gothic Fiction. In *The Gothic in Children's Literature: Haunting the Borders*, ed. Anna Jackson, Karen Coats, and Roderick McGillis, 57–76. Abingdon: Routledge.

Duran, Teresa, and Emma Bosch. 2011. Before and After the Picturebook Frame: A Typology of Endpapers. *New Review of Children's Literature and Librarianship* 17 (2): 122–143.

Fisch, Audrey A. 2009. *Frankenstein: Icon of Modern Culture*. Hastings: Helm Information.

Genette, Gérard. 1997. *Paratexts: Thresholds of Interpretation*. Trans: J.E. Lewin. Cambridge: Cambridge University Press.

Hawley, Erin. 2015. "Children Should Play with Dead Things": Transforming *Frankenstein* in Tim Burton's *Frankenweenie*. *Refractory: A Journal of Media Entertainment* 26. http://refractory.unimelb.edu.au/2015/10/07/hawley/

Hitchcock, Susan. 2007. *Frankenstein: A Cultural History*. London: Norton.

Horton, Robert. 2014. *Frankenstein*. London: Wallflower Press.

Hutcheon, Linda with Siobhan O'Flynn. 2013. *A Theory of Adaptation*, 2nd ed. Abingdon: Routledge.

Jackson, Anna, ed. 2017. *New Directions in Gothic Children's Literature: Debatable Lands*. New York: Routledge.

Jackson, Anna, Karen Coats, and Roderick McGillis, eds. 2008. Introduction. In *The Gothic in Children's Literature: Haunting the Borders*, 1–14. New York/Abingdon: Routledge.

Kiefer, Barbara. 2011. What Is a Picturebook? Across the Borders of History. *New Review of Children's Literature and Librarianship* 17 (2): 86–102.

Lamond, Margrete, and Drahoš Zak. 2005. *Frankenstein*. Sydney: HarperCollins.

Lewis, David. 2001. *Reading Contemporary Picturebooks: Picturing Text*. London: Routledge.

McCloud, Scott. 1994. *Understanding Comics: The Invisible Art*. New York: HarperPerennial.

McDonnell, Patrick. 2012. *The Monsters' Monster*. New York: Little, Brown and Company.

Mitchell, Claudia, and Jacqui Reid-Walsh. 2002. *Researching Children's Popular Culture*. London: Routledge.

Mould, Chris. 1997. *Frankenstein*. Oxford: Oxford University Press.

Mousse, Marion. 2009. *Frankenstein*. Trans: J. Johnson. New York: Papercutz.

Müller, Anja. 2014. Introduction: Adapting Canonical Texts in and for Children's Literature. In *Adapting Canonical Texts in Children's Literature*, ed. Anja Müller, 1–8. London: Bloomsbury.

Murray, Christopher. 2016. *Frankenstein* in Comics and Graphic Novels. In *The Cambridge Companion to Frankenstein*, ed. Andrew Smith. Cambridge: Cambridge University Press.

Nikolajeva, Maria, and Carole Scott. 2000. The Dynamics of Picturebook Communication. *Children's Literature in Education* 31 (4): 225–239.

———. 2001. *How Picturebooks Work*. New York: Garland.

Nodelman, Perry. 1988. *Words about Pictures: The Narrative Art of Children's Picture Books*. Athens: University of Georgia Press.

Numberman, Neil. 2009. *Do Not Build a Frankenstein!* New York: HarperCollins.

Painter, Claire, J.R. Martin, and Len Unsworth. 2013. *Reading Visual Narratives: Image Analysis of Children's Picturebooks*. Sheffield: Equinox.

Sanders, Julie. 2016. *Adaptation and Appropriation*. Abingdon: Routledge.

Serafini, Frank. 2010. Reading Multimodal Texts: Perceptual, Structural and Ideological Perspectives. *Children's Literature in Education* 41 (2): 85–104.

Sipe, Lawrence, and Caroline McGuire. 2006. Picturebook Endpapers: Resources for Literary and Aesthetic Interpretation. *Children's Literature in Education* 37 (4): 291–304.

Sipe, Lawrence, and Sylvia Pantaleo. 2008. *Postmodern Picturebooks: Play, Parody, and Self-Referentiality*. New York: Routledge.

Smith, Sarah J. 2005. *Children, Cinema and Censorship: From Dracula to the Dead End Kids*. New York: I. B. Taurus.

Stephens, John. 2011. Schemas and Scripts: Cognitive Instruments and the Representation of Cultural Diversity in Children's Literature. In *Contemporary Children's Literature and Film: Engaging with Theory*, ed. Kerry Mallan and Clare Bradford, 12–35. Basingstoke: Palgrave Macmillan.

Townshend, Dale. 2008. The Haunted Nursery: 1764–1830. In *The Gothic in Children's Literature: Haunting the Borders*, ed. Anna Jackson, Karen Coats, and Roderick McGillis, 15–38. Abingdon: Routledge.

CHAPTER 13

Beyond the Filthy Form: Illustrating Mary Shelley's *Frankenstein*

Beatriz González Moreno and Fernando González Moreno

Let him who will paint me, but let him not abuse me.
Don Quixote (II. 59)

In 1972, one of the brave few critics pioneering the vindication of Mary Shelley's *Frankenstein* wrote, 'It is something of a miracle that *Frankenstein*, originally published in 1818, has survived its admirers and critics [...] Opinion about *Frankenstein* was strong from the beginning, but no critical

Both authors are part of the research project 'Edgar A. Poe on-line. Text and Image' (ref. HAR2015–64580-P), funded by the Spanish Ministry of Economy and Competitiveness.

B. G. Moreno (✉)
Facultad de Letras, Department of Modern Languages,
Universidad de Castilla-La Mancha, Ciudad Real, Spain

F. G. Moreno
Facultad de Humanidades, Department of History of Art,
Universidad de Castilla-La Mancha, Albacete, Spain

© The Author(s) 2018
C. M. Davison, M. Mulvey-Roberts (eds.), *Global Frankenstein*,
Studies in Global Science Fiction,
https://doi.org/10.1007/978-3-319-78142-6_13

227

thinking on the subject was more elaborate and self-conscious than that of Mary Shelley herself' (Kiely 1972: 155). In fact, it was not until 1979 that a collection of academic essays, devoted to the critical assessment of *Frankenstein*, was published. George Levine and U. C. Knoepflmacher concluded that '*Frankenstein* resists the overly simple adaptations our culture has provided'; there is more to the text than a Karloffian, dumb monster (1979: xiii). Interestingly, before critics initiated this vindication process, a few illustrators had begun to interpret the text in a much richer way. Far from being simplistic and based on both personal and social-cultural issues, they had begun to highlight the frame narrative, the female characters, and the double motif. This chapter provides an outline of that process and considers to what extent illustrators put forward the value of some aspects of the novel, even to the point of rescuing Mary Shelley herself—an author sometimes erased from her novel's production history—from being devoured by her own creature.

THE (ILLUSTRATED) REDEMPTION OF A FORSAKEN CREATURE

It is a well-known fact that when *Frankenstein* was published in 1818, it was not enthusiastically received; although some reviews were positive, most of them were negative. Nevertheless, the book, as it happens with the creature, managed to survive not in the highbrow sphere but in the realm of popular culture. The creature may be said to have entered popular imagination especially thanks to Richard Brinsley Peake's play *Presumption; or, the Fate of Frankenstein* (1823). People became familiar with Mary Shelley's work not by reading the text itself but by watching a distorted, simplistic version of the novel. The monster was played by T. P. Cooke, who, like Karloff in the Universal films, came to be identified with the monster.

However distorted the original text, it was possibly due to the play's great success that second and third editions were published. It was then that a first effort was made to establish a faithful, visual dialogue with the text. Théodor Matthias von Holst (1810–1844) was commissioned the work for which he is mainly known nowadays: to illustrate the third edition of Mary Shelley's *Frankenstein; or, the Modern Prometheus* (1831). The edition, number IX of Henry Colburn and Richard Bentley's Standard Novels Series, appeared enriched with an illustrated title page and a frontispiece. In fact, the choice could not have been better. Von Holst was a disciple of Henry Fuseli (1741–1825), the Romantic painter especially well known for his painting, *The Nightmare* (1781), who had met William Godwin and Mary Wollstonecraft during the art and literature meetings at Joseph Johnson's home. Von Holst was an early talented draughtsman and, like his master, he was interested in literary subjects, particularly Goethe's *Faust*. Von Holst had the golden opportunity of approaching *Frankenstein* in a naïve way, entirely uninfluenced by any previous illustration excepting those created after the theatrical adaptations (Fig. 13.1).

Von Holst devoted the frontispiece not to the well-known moment of creation but to its immediate consequence when Victor, observing the catastrophic result of his experiments and filled with horror and disgust, rushes out of the chamber, abandoning the creature. Likewise, von Holst set the scene in a Gothic chamber characterised by a stained glass window through which the viewer may see the full moon of the 'dreary night of November' (Shelley 1980: 57). The Gothic arch containing the stained glass window reminds the reader of the tradition of the Gothic on which Mary Shelley's novel is built. Inside that room—a very oppressive space—von Holst imagines Frankenstein's laboratory, a difficult task since the author does not describe it at all. The artist depicts a couple of laboratory flasks and a kind of voltaic discharger that signal Victor's progress in chemistry, electricity, and galvanism, also, a shelf full of books—perhaps by Cornelius Agrippa, Albertus Magnus, and Paracelsus—while another book, probably Frankenstein's diary, appears to have fallen on the floor. By including several skulls on the top of the shelf and a complete skeleton lying on the floor in the foreground, the illustrator reminds us that Frankenstein has created this being after spending days and nights in vaults and charnel-houses. The creature, who is also depicted lying on the floor, wakes up over this skeleton, reinforcing, by way of a visual metaphor, life's triumph over dead matter. Following Mary Shelley's description, the creature is of a gigantic stature, his hair a lustrous black, his skin scarcely covering the work of muscles and arteries as the viewer can perceive in the bony hand and foot (57). Otherwise, von Holst avoids the most macabre, horrid, or loathsome details, as the review by *The London Literary Gazette* points out:

> A clever frontispiece represents the moment when Frankenstein rushes away in horror from the frightful shape to which his science has at length communicated life. The room and the accessories are good; but the figure is more gigantic than frightful, and the face is deficient in that supernatural hideousness on which the author so especially dwells. (19 November 1831: 740)

Fig. 13.1 *Frankenstein*, frontispiece by Théodor Matthias von Holst (illustrator) and William Chevalier (engraver). London: Colburn and Bentley, 1831

The image of the creature lying on the floor reinforces the idea of forsakenness. The illustrator has even used the light of the deflagration, the spark, coming from what could be a furnace behind the creature, to highlight Frankenstein's act of running away. This fact of the abandonment of the creature and its social costs, not the creation itself and its possible ethical consequences, is rightly understood as the main subject of the novel that determines the rest of the story. This determinism is suggested by the *dodekatopos* hanging on the wall, an astrological birth chart based on the 12 astrological houses. The creature's fate is written; and, despite his actions, he is already sentenced, not because of the conditions of his creation but because of Victor's neglected duties.

Thus does this first illustrated edition succeed in reading the text beyond Peake's dumb green creature that took hold in popular culture. Von Holst inaugurated a new path for illustrators, focusing on the creature as a forsaken Adam whose tragedy we are to pity and on Victor as an irresponsible creator. Later artists continue to explore this process—how 'by degrees […], the inhuman creation becomes increasingly human while his creator becomes increasingly inhuman' (Oates in Shelley 1984: 245)— and, consequently, deepen different narrative levels in the novel.

'MY OWN VAMPIRE … LET LOOSE FROM THE GRAVE'

In 1833, *Frankenstein* was first published in North America, but it was a non-illustrated edition. It would take a while for the American illustrators to engage with the originality of Mary Shelley's text. An early exception is the edition published in 1897 both in London and in Philadelphia. What is remarkable about this edition is that there is no portrayal of the creature at all or any other character, only a collection of landscapes. As had happened in Europe with Peake's play prompting the first illustrated edition of the novel, editors needed another push. The 15-minute silent film *Frankenstein* produced by Edison Studios in 1910 could have served to promote the interest in the book; however, no other edition appeared for 12 years. In 1922, a new edition of *Frankenstein* was published in Boston illustrated by Carl Lagerquist (Scott 2012). It included three original plates set with accuracy and theatrical drama and showing more pity for Victor than for the creature. Lagerquist's work, however, went unnoticed.

But it was neither von Holst nor Lagerquist who introduced the monster to the world but Universal Pictures' 1931 cinematic adaptation directed by James Whale. The iconic image of Karloff's monster set an enduring standard. Whale's film revitalised the text and the publishing industry tried to profit from that: advertisements urged that every home library should have a copy of *Frankenstein* and 'Photo play editions'—editions of novels that included stills from a motion picture—like the one by Grosset and Dunlap (New York, [1931?]) that began to be published. Notably, the scenes included in these editions were taken from the 1931 Universal film and, thus, were not original at all. An exception would be a 'De Luxe Edition' produced in 1932 and illustrated by Nino Carbé (Sicily, 1909-New York, 1993). In his representation of the monster resembling a vampire with a morose expression and long fingers, which may have been inspired by the figure of Count Orlok in the German Expressionist film, *Nosferatu* (dir. Murnau, 1922), Carbé succeeded in better realising Mary Shelley's intentions. Her double motif is particularly exemplified by Frankenstein's reference to the creature as 'my own vampire, my own spirit let loose from the grave' (Shelley 1998: 57). Karloff's influence is also in evidence in the bolts protruding from the creature's neck, while his long hair is reminiscent of Cooke's theatrical portrayals.

In addition, Carbé was the first illustrator to appreciate the importance of the frame narrative together with several key episodes. Thus, some vignettes are included showing Walton's ship and the mountains. Justine's execution by hanging is likewise represented for the first time. Nonetheless, it is the monster's lurking presence by means of the illustrations and other vignettes and initials that dominates the book. Throughout, the creature's solitude is emphasised: he appears abandoned, naked, and fragile in the middle of nature, raising a bitter lament at some moments or in contemplative calm at others. Carbé even elects to depict the creature alone at the moment of his birth, excluding Victor. This solitude, a consequence of Victor's neglected parental duties, results in the creature's lack of education both emotional and intellectual. Thus, the creature's physical appearance is but a symbol of his own inner drama; and, in this sense, the illustrator manages to capture 'both the sense of muscle distortion and psychological rigidity' (Wolf 1977: 347).

At the end of the edition, in two illustrations, Carbé highlights again the idea of duality by making Victor mirror the creature. The first refers to the moment when the monster, after seeing how Frankenstein destroys his companion-creature, orders Victor to accomplish his work. Here, we can even see an almost repentant creator. The second depicts the scene where the monster is discovered by Walton next to Frankenstein's corpse. The illustration seems to present Victor as a victim of his creature; however, it is during this scene that the daemon pronounces the words that give significance to the frontispiece: 'Think you that the groans of Clerval were music to my ears? My heart [...] did not endure the violence of the change, without torture such as you cannot even imagine' (Shelley 1998: 188). This torturous remorse is what the creature's gesture expresses in the frontispiece while Clerval's corpse lies at his feet.

Throughout the 1930s, publishers renewed their interest in Mary Shelley's *Frankenstein*. They had begun to consider it as a work of literature deserving of a worthy edition, not mere paperback. To this end, The Limited Editions Club of New York published a new edition in 1934. For the first time, an introduction was added, written by the American librarian and author Edmund Lester Pearson (1880–1937), and new illustrations were included. Pearson's introduction is, on the one hand, a summary of the preface included in the 1831 text and, on the other hand, a contextualisation of the different authors appearing in it. But, above all, he acknowledges Mary Shelley as a literary figure (in Shelley 1934a: xiii) and *Frankenstein*'s undeniable influence. Due to his familiarity with the genre, in 1934, Pearson was called to Hollywood to serve as an uncredited writer for Universal Pictures' *Bride of Frankenstein* (1935) (Smith 2012: 91–92).

As regards the illustrations, the artist in charge was Everett Henry (1893–1961). It is interesting to notice how the illustrator, as Carbé had done, recognises the value of the first chapters—he represents Frankenstein rescued by Walton—while, on the contrary and curiously, Pearson criticises them in his introduction: 'Her idea was for a short tale [...], but Shelley urged her to expand it. Bad advice. Hence, the tedious opening chapters' (in Shelley 1934a: viii). Furthermore, we can find several novelties among these images, such as the first representation of Frankenstein observing the oak struck by lightning. In the scene, Henry includes the image of a skeleton, foreshadowing not only the birth of the creature but also Victor's fate: 'Destiny was too potent, and her immutable laws had decreed my utter and terrible destruction' (Shelley 1980: 42). For the first time, we can also see the remains of the female creature, a fleshly display of *disjecta membra*. The scene when Frankenstein, among the tombs of Elizabeth, William, and his father, swears to pursue the daemon is also a first. Nevertheless, the major originality of these illustrations is how the creature has (not) been represented. We never get to see him properly. The creature is shown obliquely, as a shadow or a reflection. In this way, Everett Henry positions the reader in the subjective place of the monster and makes us feel empathy for him.

In 1934, the American illustrator Lynd Ward (1905–1985) offered a much richer approach to the text in the form of 64 full-page illustrations and vignettes (Shelley 1934b). Ward, who was obviously familiar with the original text and the Romantic contexts, possessed a masterful ability to translate the text into images and to establish a narrative between them. A fine example of this occurs in the inclusion of an albatross when Walton quotes from Coleridge's *The Rime of the Ancient Mariner*. Lynd Ward's most reproduced image is that of the creature viewing himself for the first time in the transparent pool. This episode confirms that he is the monster society tells him he is (Cfr. Shelley 1980: 114). Ward depicts the creature as a new Narcissus who may be compared with Caravaggio's version of the myth (c.1597–1599). Narcissus was traditionally used by artists as a metaphor of their melancholic and auto-destructive state. Artists, just like Narcissus, aimed to grasp the idea of Beauty, an idea impossible to attain and which resulted in frustration or death. In this case, the creature discovers that his inability to share the cottagers' beauty is the origin of his own moral destruction.

The creature, born in a society unable to see beyond his ugly and deformed features, is condemned. There is not any possibility of redemption for him. This is the social (and political) reading that underlies Ward's illustrations. The depiction of Justine Moritz imprisoned, accompanied by a headpiece including the court judges with grotesque and simian features, makes evident this critique. That image allows Ward to establish a deeper social criticism, focusing on the culpability of these judges, not the creature, for the injustice that they are committing. A similar interpretation can be traced in the representation for the first time of the captive Turk. The case is shown by Mary Shelley to involve religious intolerance: 'The injustice of this sentence was very flagrant' (Shelley 1980: 122). Again, the idea of social injustice is remarked; moreover, Ward does not overlook that Safie's father will betray Felix, an idea represented by the Turk's sibylline eyes.

THE WILDEST DREAMS

By the 1960s, *Frankenstein* had already been taken to the big screen, adapted into comics and fully illustrated. *Frankenstein* had already become a classic of popular culture when critics focused their attention on the book for the first time (Rieger 1963) and emphasised that there was more to the text than just a dumb monster. Among so many other things,

Shelley had advanced an exploration of the 'Romantic mythology of the self' (Bloom 1965: 611–18). Notably, early scholarly criticism was a step behind the illustrators. In 1968, Cercle des Bibliophiles published in Geneva a new illustrated edition of the novel as part of its collection 'Chefs d'Œuvres du Fantastique'. Like the edition published by The Limited Editions Club of New York in 1934, this book was conceived as a collector's piece. This 1831 edition included a preface by the French film critic and television producer Michel Boujut (1940–2011), who seems to be more interested in the cinematic adaptations than in the text itself and hence his inclusion of a filmography of *Frankenstein* and lack of both the 1818 and the 1831 prefaces. Boujut's own preface advanced a reading of the novel focused on religious issues: Victor, 'possédé par un esprit d'orgueil sacrilège [...], ne faisait-il que commettre à son tour le terrible péché de la Connaissance, en voulant pénétrer des domaines sacrés et concurrencer l'œuvre divine' (Boujut in Shelley 1968: 7–8).[1] However, his inclusion of original illustrations by Christian Broutin offers a more modern reading far removed from this kind of religious/ethical approach.

Right from the opening pages, Mary Shelley is represented alongside the monster as a lurking presence, evocative of her 1831 preface and 'the hideous phantom' haunting her (Shelley 1980: 10). This opening illustration sets the tone for Broutin's feminist (and vindicative) visual reading. No other illustrated edition had ever included the image of the author. A sad and melancholic Mary Shelley is presented with her creation, reflecting on her ability—or inability—to create life.

The creature is poorly illustrated when compared to the female characters. Broutin's approach is markedly feminist, focusing for the first time on the concept of 'the wildest dreams' (Shelley 1980: 58) as exemplified by the oneiric and surrealist image of Elizabeth transforming herself into the corpse of Victor's mother, half eaten by worms. Part of these wild dreams is also the depiction of the female creature and the 'filthy process' (Shelley 1980: 164) of her creation just prior to her being torn to pieces. And, finally, in his depiction of the death of Elizabeth—'lifeless and inanimate, thrown across the bed, her head hanging down, and her pale and distorted features half covered by her hair' (195)—Broutin departs from the description by keeping Elizabeth's eyes wide open, blankly staring at death. In this regard, it is worth noting that it would not be until 1974 that Ellen Moers promoted her reading of Mary Shelley's novel in connection with the female Gothic and the 'birth myth' (1974: 24). Broutin offered readers this type of feminist approach six years earlier.

In academic circles, it is from the 1970s on that *Frankenstein* truly came to life. Critics such as Kiely (1972), Levine (1973), Swingle (1973), Small (1973), and Moers (1974) began to examine the novel from various points of view. Within this context, *The Annotated Frankenstein* was published in 1977 with an introduction by Leonard Wolf and art work by Marcia Huyette, the first woman to illustrate the novel. As extolled on the dust jacket, 'Huyette's drawings, of great subtleness and complexity, perfectly capture both the tragedy and the horror of Mary Shelley's many-faceted tale'.

Marcia Huyette was not only the first female illustrator of *Frankenstein;* she offered a unique vision of the complexity of Mary Shelley's novel. Huyette's illustrations belong to the land of dreams; they are pure surrealism. They shape a series of deformed, oneiric, and entangled realities designed to suggest a mix of contradictory feelings that make us think about the very essence of human nature. Her designs burst with carnality, lust, love, sensuality, agony, death, fear, remorse, desolation, despair, envy, anger, and rage. In this sense, Marcia Huyette understands that Mary Shelley's novel is an invitation to reflect upon our inner monsters and deeper nightmares, both personal and cultural. She conveys the idea that *Frankenstein* is really a story 'which would speak to the mysterious fears of our nature and awaken thrilling horror—one to make the reader dread to look around, to curdle the blood, and quicken the beating of the heart' (Shelley 1980: 8).

'A FILTHY TYPE OF YOURS'

By now, Mary Shelley's *Frankenstein* has been recognised as a multilayered text that offers an insight into human nature. It has also become clear that 'If popular culture has adapted it, no part of culture can ignore it' (Levine and Knoepflmacher 1979: xiii). From the 1970s onwards, illustrators offered a much more personal approach to their interpretation of the novel, exploring their own nature by mirroring themselves in the text.

Between 1977 and 1983, American artist Bernie Wrightson (1948–2017) dedicated his spare time to drawing more than 50 detailed pen-and-ink illustrations of Mary Shelley's *Frankenstein*. It was not any publisher's commission but a personal challenge that became almost an obsession. When a child, he had been fascinated by James Whale's film with Boris Karloff, but years later, after reading the novel, he felt disappointed: 'I loved the movie interpretation and I've been fascinated with that story ever since. When I was a little older, I read the book by Mary Wollstonecraft Shelley and wondered why they never put all that great stuff into a movie. I still wonder' (Wrightson 1993: n/p). This first disappointment was followed by a second: the novel had barely been illustrated before. 'Mary Shelley's story and characters had never been given a definitive look' (Wrightson 1993: n/p). Therefore, Wrightson felt that it was his responsibility to put an end to what he considered an injustice.

Bernie Wrightson's efforts were rewarded in 1983 with the publication of Marvel's edition of *Frankenstein*, which included around 45 of those pen-and-ink drawings. This edition is recognised as Wrightson's most personal work and generally acclaimed as the best visual interpretation of Mary Shelley's novel. As Stephen King has claimed, 'They capture intent and mood, these forty-some pen and ink studies, and I think—hope!—you'll find that not only has Berni Wrightson's art enhanced Mary Shelley's story, but that Mary Shelley's story has enhanced Berni Wrightson's art' (Shelley 1983: 6–9).

Wrightson approached the text with absolute, almost sacred, respect. Every time he has had the opportunity to talk about this work, he repeats the same humble words: it was 'just my own visual interpretation, one more in the long line of interpretations—on stage, on film, and in print—since the book's original publication in 1818. No big deal. I wanted to do my version of it only because I loved the story' (Wrightson in Shelley 2013a: x–xi). He proves to love the story and to understand its complexity, going back to the original text and leaving aside all the prejudices inspired by the films. 'It is a book of ideas, not melodrama', Wrightson states (Shelley 2013a: x). As a reflection of this complexity of ideas, the illustrator invites us to read the text through a series of drawings carried out with exquisite thoroughness and meticulousness. Wrightson's illustrations establish a perfect visual reflection of Mary Shelley's text; they never overwhelm it. Sometimes they seem passionate, extremely detailed to the point of obsessive desperation; others reveal sublime isolation and melancholic solitude. These images reflect Mary Shelley's characters and the ideas in her novel.

Wrightson offers us a very personal, deep, and complex reading of Mary Shelley at very different levels. In this sense, even the drawing style that he uses is not the fruit of chance. With this format of full-page illustrations and detailed wood engraving-like drawings he pays tribute to Gustave Doré (1832–1883), the Romantic illustrator par excellence. Moreover, some of Wrightson's scenes are inspired by Doré's illustrations of

Coleridge's *The Rime of the Ancient Mariner*, for example, the image of Walton tied to the ship's mast and some of the vast views of the Arctic. We have previously mentioned some early attempts to publish Mary Shelley's novel in a collector's edition for bibliophiles. However, none of these books are comparable to the edition published in 1983 by Barry Moser's worldwide-awarded and acclaimed printing house, The Pennyroyal Press (est. 1970). Around 1980, the artist and printmaker Barry Moser (1940–) projected a series of large-scale and very ambitious volumes, including Mary Shelley's *Frankenstein* (1983). It was published in three volumes with the 1818 text, an afterword by Joyce Carol Oates entitled 'Frankenstein's Fallen Angel', and illustrated with 52 wood engravings by Moser.

Most of Moser's illustrations focus on the characters themselves (Victor, the repulsive Krempe, the benevolent Waldman, Clerval, Elizabeth, Justine executed, the female daemon, etc.) and the landscapes (the blasted stump, the Arctic, the steeples of London, the Orkney Islands, etc.). In this way, he can concentrate on their expressions, which serve as landscapes, a Romantic mirror of their feelings. All of the characters appear strongly shaded, as emerging from darkness. By using this technique, Moser invites the readers to approach them and discover the mysteries they keep. However, to explore beyond this darkness and the unknown may have dangerous results. In this sense, it is especially remarkable to consider the series of eight portraits of the creature while dialoguing with Victor—with us—in Mont Blanc, images that Oates claims 'spring direct from the unconscious' (Oates in Shelley 1984: 243). The creature stands before us as a tormented being but also as a grotesque menace, trying to prevent us from exploring the obscure cavern of human nature. As the creature provocatively advises his creator/us: 'my form is a filthy type of yours' (Shelley 1998: 105).

With the closing of the twentieth century, *Frankenstein* has become a myth, an exploration of human nature (Baldick 1987; Bann 1994), and a feminist manifesto (Mellor 1988). A few illustrators were able to foresee these new readings later taken up by the critics. Nonetheless, both critics and illustrators had to resist the visual interpretation of Whale's adaptation. The seventh art had even tried to offer a new version, closer to the original text, such as *Mary Shelley's Frankenstein* (1994) by Kenneth Branagh; however, Karloff's iconic impersonation remained unbeatable.

'I BID MY HIDEOUS PROGENY GO FORTH AND PROSPER'

With the coming of the twenty-first century and Neo-Victorian readings, Mary Shelley's *Frankenstein* went steampunk. Although not falling into the Victorian period, the novel has been regarded as Victorian in spirit with its sparks, electricity, and duality. It is no wonder that steampunk found in the creature an iconic character and source of visual exploration. In 2012, the Croatian graphic artists Zdenko Bašić and Manuel Šumberac published their illustrations for *Steampunk: Mary Shelley's Frankenstein* that enhanced, according to its dust jacket, '[t]his widely celebrated novel … through the art of mechanical gears, steam-powered machinery, and ornate industrial scenery, revealing the assembly of new life and a new age' (editors' review 2012, dust jacket). The illustrators lead us through a journey documented by Polaroid-style photos. They display an appealing technology, which, however tempting, is uncontrollable and possesses unforeseen consequences. Nevertheless, as opposed to the beauty of these artificial machines that hide the destruction of humanity, Victor's creature conceals a pure human nature beyond his ugly and deformed carcass. Ultimately, their illustrations reinforce a reading that had not been explored until now by artists: Mary Shelley's work as a science-fiction novel. In this regard, the text allows both illustrators to display all the steampunk imagery to the point of offering us a cyborg-like creature.

Gris Grimly's illustrations, like Berni Wrightson's, are the result of a personal obsession that, in the case of Grimly, consumed four years of his life. This graphic novel (2013) shows how Mary Shelley's text has become a classic that keeps offering innovative and stunning interpretations generation after generation. Grimly has brought *Frankenstein* into the twenty-first century, presenting a completely original visual reading while being respectful of the essence of the literary work. The illustrator's reading is based on two main premises. First, he identifies himself with the monster, recognising the creature as a metaphor for the human—and painful—search to find our right place in the world. According to Grimly, 'Mary Shelley intended for readers to sympathise with the monster. The story of *Frankenstein* reflected her own personal feeling of abandonment' (Grimly in Shelley 2013a: 194). Second, the story recounts the dangers of blind obsessions, of vain quests that can only lead us to destruction: 'The moral exhortation of *Frankenstein* is to value family and friends. Beware the slippery slopes of acclimating to a life of self-absorbed achievements and fame, lest one falls into the pit of fire and brimstone' (Grimly in Shelley 2013a:

195). Thus, *Frankenstein* has become a myth on human nature and, as a myth, it does not belong to any specific time any longer; it is eternal: 'There is no past, present, or future in this land that is familiar, yet far, far away' (Grimly in Shelley 2013a: 195). Grimly finds this out-of-time land in the steampunk world. *Frankenstein* has been taken to a Victorian-like epoch where we can also find references, among others, to the Nazi regime—Justine appears as an Auschwitz victim—and, of course, the recurrent presence of vintage technology. Clock wheels, brass pieces of machinery, steam boats, zeppelins, steam-powered automobiles, electric appliances, monorails, elements that remind us of the criticism of technology and uncontrolled science that Mary Shelley already slipped into her novel and that nowadays is more valid than ever.

To conclude with this chronological exploration, a final edition is to be highlighted within this twenty-first-century context, which is the one illustrated by Elena Odriozola in 2013 (Shelley 2013b). It is an out-of-the-ordinary edition: on the one hand, because this is the first relevant contribution by a Spanish artist to the illustrated history of *Frankenstein,* and, on the other hand, because she really focuses on the text as a 'birth myth'. She does not illustrate any episode—the reader will not find here the famous creation scene, Elizabeth's death, or such others—but instead she devises her own visual version of the 1831 preface. Her 34 double-page illustrations reproduce, like stills, a play in 4 acts performed at a paper toy theatre. The curtain rises and Mary Shelley, pregnant, appears inside a house reading and walking up and down; she looks nervous, as if waiting for someone. Second act, exterior: Mary Shelley, still pregnant and upset, leaves the house wearing a red cloak. Third act, same setting: Mary Shelley returns. She is not pregnant anymore; she enters the house and cries. Fourth and final act, inside the house: Mary Shelley stands while a dark baby lies abandoned at her feet; he grows up as a menacing shadow until he becomes the creature, who embraces and consoles her. Then, she disappears, the creature remains, and the curtain falls (Fig. 13.2).

Odriozola composes a prelude for the novel based on Mary Shelley's own life and her narration of the events that ended in the conception of *Frankenstein* as described in the 1831 prologue. The illustrator reflects that vision of the novel as a biographical metaphor of Mary Shelley's pain—and trauma—after the death of her first child in 1815, a two-month premature baby girl who could not survive. In addition, these illustrations remind us of the anxiety experienced by Mary Shelley on that famous night in Villa Diodati in 1816 when, according to the 1831 preface, Lord

Fig. 13.2 *Frankenstein*, Elena Odriozola. Barcelona: Nørdica, 2013 (Used with permission of Nørdica)

Byron urged Percy Shelley, John Polidori, and her to write a ghost story. The agony of this conception—'I felt that blank incapability of invention which is the greatest misery of authorship' (Shelley 1980: 8)—is narrated in this theatre full of melancholy, sadness, and, finally, self-sacrifice. The creature, a character such as Sherlock Holmes or Don Quixote, devours his own creator. Just as the creature destroys Victor, *Frankenstein*, the book, has exceeded the writer.

By way of this analysis, we have shown how a few illustrators have fully enriched a text that had been traditionally mistreated and simplified. Adaptations such as Peake's theatrical version or Whale's Karloffian monster had engraved on everyone's imagination the image of a green, dumb creature, far removed from Mary Shelley's 'hideous phantom'; even early scholarly criticism felt dubious about the value of *Frankenstein*. Thus, it was in part thanks to a few illustrators that the value of some aspects of the novel was put forward—namely, the importance of the frame narrative, which was even dismissed as 'tedious' by Pearson; the double motif; the complexity of human nature; the dangers of a tempting technology; and the usurpation of the female body and her reproductive capacity. Illustrators have even tried to rescue Mary Shelley herself, devoured by her creature and its imagery. An examination of all of these layers has proven the work of the illustrators to be a valuable, vindicative, and interpretative textual component that should not be neglected.

NOTE

1. Victor 'possessed by a spirit of sacrilegious pride, [...] did not but commit the terrible sin of Knowledge by wanting to penetrate the sacred domains and compete with divine creation' (translation in collaboration with Carol Margaret Davison).

FRANKENSTEIN'S ILLUSTRATED EDITIONS

Shelley, Mary. 1831. *Frankenstein; or, the Modern Prometheus*. Illustrated by Théodor Matthias von Holst and William Chevalier. London: Henry Colburn and Richard Bentley.

———. 1897. *Frankenstein, or, The Modern Prometheus*. Illustrated with seven plates (1831 text). London/Philadelphia: Gibbings & Co./J. B. Lippincott.

———. 1922. *Frankenstein or The Modern Prometheus*. Illustrated by Carl Lagerquist (1818 text). Boston/New York: Cornhill Publishing Company.

———. 1932. *Frankenstein or, The Modern Prometheus*. Illustrated by Nino Carbé (1818 text). New York: Illustrated Editions Company.

———. 1934a. *Frankenstein; or, The Modern Prometheus*. Introduction by Edmund Lester Pearson, illustrated in colour by Everett Henry (1831 text). New York: The Limited editions Club.

———. 1934b. *Frankenstein or The Modern Prometheus by Mary Wollstonecraft Shelley*. Illustrated by Lynd Ward (1831 text). New York: Harrison Smith and Robert Haas.

———. 1968. *Frankenstein*. Translated by Hannah Betjeman; preface by Michel Boujut; illustrated by Christian Broutin (1831 text). Genève: Cercle des Bibliophiles.

———. 1977. *The Annotated Frankenstein*. Introduction by Leonard Wolf; illustrated by Marcia Huyette (1818 text). New York: Clarkson N. Potter, Inc./Publishers.

———. 1983. *Mary Wollstonecraft Shelley's Frankenstein. A Marvel Illustrated Novel*. Introduction by Stephen King; Illustrated by Berni Wrightson (1831 text). New York: Marvel Comics Group.

———. 1984. *Frankenstein; or, The Modern Prometheus*. Afterword 'Frankenstein's Fallen Angel' by Joyce Carol Oates; Illustrated by Barry Moser (1818 text). West Hatfield: Pennyroyal Press, 1983 (3 vols.). Reprinted in one volume by University of California Press.

———. 2012. *Steampunk: Mary Shelley's Frankenstein*. Illustrated by Zdenko Bašić and Manuel Šumberac (1831 text). Philadelphia: Running Press Classics.

———. 2013a. *Gris Grimly's Frankenstein by Mary Shelley*. Foreword by Berni Wrightson; Illustrated by Gris Grimly (1818 text). New York: Balzer + Bray, HarperCollins Publishers.

———. 2013b. *Frankenstein o el moderno Prometeo*. Translated by Francisco Torres Oliver; Illustrated by Elena Odriozola (1831 text). Barcelona: Nørdica.

Works Cited

Anon. 1831. *The London Literary Gazette*, 740, November 19.

Baldick, Chris. 1987. *In Frankenstein's Shadow: Myth, Monstrosity, and 19th Century Writing*. Oxford: Clarendon Press.

Bann, Stephen, ed. 1994. *Frankenstein, Creation and Monstrosity*. London: Reaktion Books.

Bloom, Harold. 1965. *Frankenstein, or the New Prometheus. Partisan Review 32*: 611–618.

Kiely, Robert. 1972. *The Romantic Novel in England*. Cambridge, MA: Harvard University Press.

Levine, George. 1973. *Frankenstein* and the Tradition of Realism. *Novel 7* (Fall): 14–30.

Levine, George Lewis, and U.C. Knoepflmacher. 1979. *The Endurance of Frankenstein: Essays on Mary Shelley's Novel*. Berkeley/Los Angeles/London: University of California Press.

Mellor, Anne K. 1988. Possessing Nature: The Female in *Frankenstein*. In *Romanticism and Feminism*, ed. Anne K. Mellor, 220–232. Bloomington: Indiana University Press.

Moers, Ellen. 1974. Female Gothic: The Monster's Mother. *New York Review of Books*, 24–8, March 21.

Scott, Grant F. 2012. Victor's Secret: Queer Gothic in Lynd Ward's Illustrations to *Frankenstein* (1934). *Word & Image* 28 (2): 206–232.

Shelley, Mary. 1980. *Frankenstein, or the Modern Prometheus* (1831 text), Oxford: Oxford University Press.

———. 1998. *Frankenstein, or the Modern Prometheus. 1818 Text*. Oxford: Oxford University Press.

Small, Christopher. 1973. *Mary Shelley's Frankenstein: Tracing the Myth*. Pittsburgh: University of Pittsburgh Press.

Smith, Jeanette C. 2012. *The Laughing Librarian: A History of American Library Humor*. Jefferson: McFarland.

Swingle, Larry J. 1973. Frankenstein's Monster and Its Romantic Relatives: Problems of Knowledge in English Romanticism. *Texas Studies in Literature and Language* 15 (Spring): 51–65.

Wolf, Leonard, ed. 1977. *The Annotated Frankenstein by Mary Shelley*. New York: Clarkson N. Potter, Inc..

Wrightson, Bernie. 1993. Frankenstein and Me. In *The Lost Frankenstein Pages*, n/p. Port Washington: Apple Press/Port Publications.

PART V

Futuristic Frankensteins/
Frankensteinian Futures

The *Frankenstein* Meme: The Memetic Prominence of Mary Shelley's Creature in Anglo-American Visual and Material Cultures

Shannon Rollins

In penning her debut novel, Mary Wollstonecraft Shelley crafted an endlessly applicable allegory for humankind's complex interrelationships with technology, culture, ethics, and mortality. Echoing the iconic opening utterance of James Whale's 1931 film of the same name, *Frankenstein* is a narrative whose cultural capital continues to grow exponentially. Whether authentic to her original spirit, or divergent to the point of parody, Shelley's *Frankenstein; or the Modern Prometheus* is a narrative that has withstood the test of time and whose invocation is itself a form of cultural currency: from John Tenniel's 1882 anti-Irish editorial cartoon in *Punch* ('The Irish Frankenstein') to *Buffy the Vampire Slayer* (S2 E2: "Some Assembly Required", 1997).

I propose that the continued application of *Frankenstein*'s literary tropes is due to its suitability as a shorthand currency in Anglo-American

S. Rollins (✉)
Edinburgh College of Art, University of Edinburgh, Edinburgh, UK

© The Author(s) 2018
C. M. Davison, M. Mulvey-Roberts (eds.), *Global Frankenstein*,
Studies in Global Science Fiction,
https://doi.org/10.1007/978-3-319-78142-6_14

material cultures to signal liminality: the intersection of genius and madness in creation narratives, monstrosity, fabrication, and bricolage, as well as the implications of isolation on the human psyche. I hypothesise that *Frankenstein*, widely regarded as a modern myth, has evolved, developed, and grown in previously unrealised ways, whose reach is best described using memetics.[1]

What's in a Meme?

When Richard Dawkins coined the concept in *The Selfish Gene* (1982), he envisioned memetics as a parallel theoretical system to biological genetics, intending it to be used as an explanation for patterns of cultural transmission. He proposed that memes would be most suitable to unpack the continued growth and popularity of a given theme across decades—even centuries. These memes replicate and mutate in a pool of cultural memes similar to the gene pool, with the fittest meme having the greatest influence over cultural evolution.

This is a seductive concept as it suggests that every miniscule aspect of culture can be accounted for based on previous creativity and trends, making future cultural production potentially predictable. Since Dawkins' original 1979 postulations, memetics has exploded as a mode of analysis with researchers across diverse disciplinary backgrounds falling captive to memetics' allure.[2] For example, Aaron Lynch (*Thought Contagion*, 1996) posits that memes are contagious, influencing human behaviour, whereas Susan Blackmore's *The Meme Machine* (1999) argues that meme transmission is directly responsible for human behaviour in the same way that genes are intrinsically linked to physical traits like hair colour. However, unlike genetics, memetics is still considered controversial. This is due to academic disagreement over what constitutes a meme, the granular structure that, according to Dawkins, maps the structure of cultures.

In his 2014 article, 'Memetics and Folkloristics: The Theory', Elliott Oring compiles a sizeable review of memetics' contemporary condition concerning both research and reach and, in sum, arrives at the following notions:

1. If memes are replicated copies of an original in the same way that successful 'selfish' genes are replications, then are 'copying errors' an evolutionary boon for memes as they are for genes? (434)

2. Natural selection—that is, the altruistic properties of genes—is still a theory, and so the extrapolation of natural selection in cultural genes (memes) may be considered a theory based upon an untested and potentially untestable theory (437).[3]
3. Therefore, it may be most prudent to consider memetics a form of philosophy rather than a science (439).
4. A meme is not specified in the same way that a gene is: is the meme a complete, faithful retelling of a story or just its skeleton? How does this impact the necessary 'copying errors' and therefore cultural evolution? Certainly, folktales and lore have a larger focus on the overall picture rather than exact replication for successful transmission (440–1).

Ultimately, Oring argues that memetics could serve as a useful method to discuss folklore—narrative, transmission, and development—but that this method requires that the researcher establish the efficacy of memes from a philosophical, tentative position. Were this chapter uniquely focused on the retelling and survival of the *Frankenstein* narrative itself, perhaps memetics would prove an inappropriate approach. However, the *Frankenstein* meme refers to the replication of the themes Shelley crafted inside her Creature narrative and the core structure of her uncanny creation plot.

This new theoretical construction—the *Frankenstein* meme—describes the continued strength and replication not only of the parent narrative itself, but also its Romantically linked mythemes (to borrow from Claude Lévi-Strauss) of fabrication, bricolage, liminality, melancholy and isolation, monstrosity, the posthuman, and scientific mystery.[4] Neo-Victorian and Gothic readings of nineteenth-century cultural productions, as well as their contemporary counterparts, are anchored as fragments of the same tradition outside of linear history through *Frankenstein*: it takes a monster to dissect a monster.

In this chapter, I briefly analyse the cultural and mechanical conditions that underpin Shelley's work, how they manifest in other nineteenth-century productions, and how these elements of the *Frankenstein* meme replicate—directly and indirectly—into select contemporary visual and material cultures. These contemporary components include popular television, film, fiction, as well as subcultures of the past century such as first-wave punk (early/mid-1970s). I begin my exploration of *Frankenstein*'s memetic fitness with an investigation into the eighteenth- and nineteenth-century use of 'Prometheus' as a mythical-modern epithet; by invoking

Prometheus to preface Frankenstein's impending creation—and fall from grace—Shelley's narrative begins as a contemporary evolution of 'creation' folklore memes.

PROMETHEUS, AUTOMATA, AND THE PROTO-FRANKENSTEIN

Prometheus, one of the mythic Titans and uncle to Zeus, created mankind from clay. He is also part of the 'original sin' narrative in Greek mythology as he stole fire from the hearth of Mount Olympus and gifted it to his creations. This benevolent action displeased Zeus, resulting in an eternal punishment described in Hesiod's *Theogony*. In simulating the bodies of the gods, and daring to imbue them with the gods' divine knowledge, Prometheus falls from grace. Given the persistence of Graeco-Roman culture in Western Europe through the centuries, the pantheon of gods and their allegories would have felt as current to Shelley as Victor Frankenstein and his Creature feel to us today. As such, any comparison between Frankenstein and Prometheus rings true as an accurate metaphor. And yet, my research suggests that there are greater levels of intertextual resonance beyond this mythic association.

Jacques de Vaucanson, an eighteenth-century clockmaker, tinker, and automata craftsman held the distinction as a 'new Prometheus', a moniker attributed to contemporary philosophers, including Voltaire and Julien Offray de La Mettrie (Wood 2002: 16). Implied in this mythological reference is Vaucanson's talent as a creator of glorious new life, based on his meticulous study of human anatomy and physiology. These clockwork marvels were more than follies for Vaucanson and his enchanted audience; they were vessels for mechanical experimentation, as their designer invented and innovated contemporary mechanisms creating ever more lifelike works. Automata were popular novelties throughout the eighteenth century; however, none were more convincing at mimicking living bodies than the automata Vaucanson designed (Schaffer 2013).

His pastoral *Flute Player* (1737–8) astonished with its innovation and its convincing mimicry of human musicality. Rather than the traditionally hidden music box, which trilled out tinny melodies with a decidedly 'dubbed' sensation, Vaucanson researched the human anatomy behind the production of contemporary flute music. This in itself marked Vaucanson as not only a creative mind but also a visionary at the forefront of his age: he was unique among his peers in seeking to replicate the minute phenomena of life in his mechanical marvels.

Having deduced the importance of anatomical accuracy to woodwind music, his clockwork progeny's mouth held a metal facsimile of a human tongue. The player's mechanical fingers were also covered in skin to produce the necessary pressure over the holes (Wood 2002: 20–2). Coupled with an internal bellows system for lungs, the tongue and fingers were attached to a metal barrel whose bumps and indentations triggered the delicate motions needed for the *Flute Player* to actually *play the flute*. Unfortunately, none of Vaucanson's many mechanical progenies have survived into the twenty-first century. Only descriptions, engravings, and a few photographs exist from their last known locations. These contraptions existed as simulacra, uncanny replications of life. While automata were popular for centuries before Vaucanson, this 'new Prometheus' created a liminal space between man and technology, a confusing locus between blood and clockwork. As Gaby Wood explains in her book *Living Dolls*:

> Vaucanson's android inevitably raised questions about what it meant to be human. It seems that its primary uncanny effect stemmed from the fact that it operated by breathing. Clearly, almost any other instrument, requiring only physical pressure in order to produce a sound, could be played simply by clockwork […] This automaton *breathed*. (2002: 22)

Other automata have, however, survived the test of time. Contemporaneous with Vaucanson (who was active between 1768 and 1774), the Swiss father/son pair Pierre and Henri-Louis Jaquet-Droz designed and created the still-functional, cherubic *Draughtsman* and the *Writer* (Wood 2002: xii; Schaffer 2013: 2:20). Originally designed as advertisements for the Jaquet-Droz horology business in Switzerland, these two figures built on the innovative foundation of Vaucanson's breathing simulacra; both figures perform their eponymous talents while projecting the illusion of life. Their chests shutter with breath, their eyelashes flutter as they tilt their heads towards their tasks and commit uncannily human compulsive actions, such as blowing at imaginary dust or dipping a pen in ink. These actions give rise to an eerie level of cognition, despite the pair's known artificiality.

Wood suggests that Mary Shelley witnessed these Promethean exaltations two years prior to penning *Frankenstein* as she travelled through Neufchâtel, Switzerland (Wood 2002: xiv; D'Onofrio 2012). This could be a coincidence; however, the work of de La Mettrie suggests otherwise. Author of *Man a Machine* (1747), de La Mettrie contended that men's bodies held the information of their own design. In de La Mettrie's words, man was an automaton, a 'self-winding machine, a living representation in perpetual motion' (Wood 2002: 12). Echoing de La Mettrie's attestation that the body possesses a mechanism for its own winding, Frankenstein upholds a preternatural understanding of the human body's internal designs and 'spark'. Frankenstein, therefore, deciphers the human soul in the same manner as de La Mettrie—as a theological appellation for man's mechanical reality. The conjunction of Mary Shelley (then Mary Godwin) viewing these automata and Voltaire and de La Mettrie's canonising of Vaucanson as a 'new Prometheus' must have resonated with the young author given her novel's final subtitle: *The Modern Prometheus.*

THE *FRANKENSTEIN* MEME

Frankenstein's narrative centres on the fraught relationship between protagonist Victor Frankenstein and the Creature he designs from the limbs and organs of various cadavers. Shelley never divulges the exact scientific methods behind Frankenstein's revivification experiments, and academic critiques suggest a variety of possibilities from a combination of alchemical natural magic (Smith 1994) to galvanism (Jordanova 1994). In memetic terms, galvanism has come to be the most 'replicated' form, as subsequent adaptations in film have carried this motif of electricity throughout (James 1994).

Returning to 'Folklore and Memetics: The Theory', Oring contends that, 'Those folklorists who idly employ the word 'meme' should be aware of the theoretical baggage that follows in its train' (2014: 449). By this, he means that those who invoke memetics in their discussion of folklore's cultural transmission must be willing—and able—to assess and acknowledge the issues surrounding Dawkins's conflation of genes and memes. They must express what they mean by meme (what constitutes a cultural unit), and if these memes can be replicated in a manner that mimics the impact of genetics on evolution. Oring's literature review, in combination with Blackmore's investigation, has provided the contextual understanding needed to conduct my own research efficiently. Before delving into how the *Frankenstein* narrative and mythemes have evolved over time, unpacking each theme is of paramount importance. These include fabrication, bricolage, liminality, melancholy and isolation, monstrosity, the posthuman, and scientific mysteries like alchemy and galvanism.

Fabrication, the impulse to embellish or create, is at the core of any creation myth, and Shelley's *Frankenstein* is no exception. The young Victor is a curious, intelligent boy whose interest in both alchemical and modern science feeds his grief and obsession to create life following his mother's death. This obsession takes form through Victor's bricolage of cadaver parts, patchworking together a new whole that is uncannily unwhole. This feverish compulsion to fabricate his own man has been dissected by countless researchers who have concluded that this creation is a metaphor for Victor's own personality. For instance, Ludmilla Jordanova suggests that this compulsion is a metaphor for masturbation due to the shameful, hideous emotions that Victor feels during these obsessive, solitary months (1994). This feeling of liminality, melancholy, and isolation are relevant to both Victor and the Creature; they each find themselves torn between their desires and their lived realities. Victor is torn between the love of his family and his urge to create, and becomes permanently trapped between the two worlds. This leads to a melancholy madness that manifests as physical illness, which is only broken through the intervention of his childhood friend, Henry Clerval. Victor flees to his family home in Geneva, leaving the Creature and his obsessive behaviour behind.

Like Victor, the Creature lives in isolation due to his hideous and frightening appearance; his liminality hinges on his human emotions and desires, and his inhuman body. At every attempt to join society, the Creature is pushed back into the liminal space between human and non-human. This combination of fabrication, liminality, melancholy, and isolation is the building block of not only the Creature's but also Victor Frankenstein's own monstrosity. At its centre, the *Frankenstein* meme's strength comes from packaging fabricated monstrosity—via pseudoscience—into a digestible cultural currency. After two centuries, the Creature's moral plight and Victor Frankenstein's feverish, changeful temperament have morphed, changed, and transitioned, finding themselves replicated in science, music, art, literature, theatre, film, and fashion, clearly moving beyond the scope that Shelley ever envisaged for her ghost story.

In the 1990s, the Human Genome Project sought to sequence the genetic makeup common to every human, opening a new era of scientific study couched in molecular, biological, and medical levels simultaneously. By knowing the intricate details of DNA, specific patterns could be identified, explaining why bodies form, where replication occurs, and how unique changes occur and express in the body, essentially providing an intimate understanding of the building blocks required to create the functional human body. Since Charles Darwin, geneticists have discussed and dissected the physical appearance (phenotype) of any species, but with the Human Genome Project, the ordering of proteins that create the appearances (genotype) could be understood. These genes, now isolated based on function, could be controlled in a laboratory situation and manipulated artificially to create non-natural forms—at least theoretically.

In Jon Turney's *In Frankenstein's Footsteps* (1998), Shelley's creation myth is used to describe the sensation gripping the world as countless labs laboured to produce a complete sequence of the human genome. He expresses the parallels between Victor Frankenstein's efforts to build his own man and contemporary science's aims in the fields of gene therapy and In Vitro Fertilisation (IVF). Turney expresses the correlation between scientific fact and science fiction, reproducing images from Shelley's time to express other musings that have since come to fruition. In this way, he is consciously gesturing towards the increasingly plausible concept that the universe of genetic possibility is vast and open and that there is perhaps more truth to the myth than just a convenient metaphor. Turney engages with the *Frankenstein* meme in a completely different, though equally impactful, way to address the moral issues surrounding interfering with the natural processes of genes, fitness, and evolution.

Just as in genetics, a meme is considered successful if it continues to replicate and evolve within the meme pool (culture), thus expressing its fitness through evolution. Specifically, key tropes from the original story continued on past their own temporal sphere. Immediately following its publication, the storyline was ripped from Shelley's control, becoming immortal on stage and screen; gone are the moralising touches, the depth of character growth for both Creator and Creature. The Creature's tender love for the De Lacey family, his desire to find a space in which he could feel belonging and his primal rage for his creator's ignorance were stripped away in the first century of replication. A dumb and potentially violent monster and a handsome misunderstood scientist replaced the eloquent Creature and his frenetic father. Instead, there is a madman and a monster, both bumbling: one through the emotional torture of crafting monstrosity and the other through the exhausting realities of patchwork resurrection. In this way, Shelley's expressions of fabrication, bricolage, liminality, melancholy, isolation, monstrosity, and scientific mystery prove themselves the fittest aspects of her narrative. As Blackwell's analysis of memetics suggests, it is this general content that bears repetition rather than faithful copies. With the genesis of the silver screen, the *Frankenstein* meme takes flight.

NOIR CINEMATIC ADAPTATION: A FIRST CASE STUDY IN THE POWER OF MEMES

Adaptations of Shelley's modern myth are plentiful, and mythemes of the novel are encrypted into the fabric of contemporary Western culture as a shorthand most often to describe monstrosity, fabrication, and bricolage. Many of the visual tropes come from James Whale's initial foray into Shelley's universe, *Frankenstein* (1931). Notably, Whale's 1931 film is not the first cinematic adaptation of Shelley's narrative (James 1994). However, where other films' visualisations of the Creature failed to stick, Whale's Creature virtually replaced Shelley's description. Whale's adaptation held the same essential information—the mythemes—of monstrous creation and a threatened marriage, yet deviated almost entirely in other aspects despite the implication of being the same story. Victor Frankenstein's name changes to Henry, and rather than working in complete isolation, the doctor is assisted by the decidedly non-canonical Fritz.

But the greatest divergence from Shelley's text must be the lack of verbal communication from the Creature himself. This particular inconsistency is somewhat remedied in Whale's sequel, *The Bride of Frankenstein* (1935), where the blind peasant teaches the Creature rudimentary English and a childish sense of morality. This improvement, however, never holds a candle to the vehement—and at time vitriolic—eloquence consistently displayed in Shelley's novel. In this way, Whale is the progenitor of an entirely distinct sort of monster—his Creature is made more hideous and terrifying by his ignorance and lack of control relative to his stature. There is something implicitly uncomfortable about this Creature, who is effectively mute and deeply misunderstood, and this uncanny lack of personal agency is a mirror to a human condition of powerlessness. Whale changes the cautionary value of the story, bypassing a debate on the perils of single-minded curiosity and foregrounding a dialogue of the painful implications surrounding a lack of autonomy.

In terms of physicality, Whale's Creature is a clunking, ungainly mass of confused muscle and neurons where Shelley's would-be 'Adam' presents as intellectual, a Creature whose solitary existence generates a rapid existential growth under his voyeuristic second-hand education. Where Whale's projection of monstrosity is couched in relative ignorance and misunderstanding, Shelley generates an intelligent villain whose original sin is his own unwilling birth and subsequent transgressions stemming from personal outrage at the connotations of his own hideous visage. Both of these bricolaged bodies are horrifying and socially challenging in their own ways; however, Shelley's—though of a different century and time—expresses a more sophisticated sort of horror, one that relies on logic and the ephemeral qualities of human nature.

By contrast, Whale generates his terror through a different sort of uncanny sensation, that of a surrender to unknown, senseless power. Just as Shelley's Creature expresses to Victor that had Henry shown his progeny any hint of affection, rather than assuming the worst of his Creature with a criminal brain, all the violence and torment may never have occurred. Better still, had these men not attempted to play at being a god, Pandora's scientific box may never have been opened, thus leaving mundanity in life rather than sublime pain. As such, the narrative's epicentre—an experimental human with indefinable potential who out of neglect turns against his creator—remains in Whale's adaptations, carrying forward the most socially significant aspects of the story and cutting away the parts that do not translate onto the silver screen because they are too complex or challenging for an audience that merely seeks to be frightened. Unsurprisingly, it is this silent, childlike Creature that has become the replicated shorthand for Shelley's narrative; Boris Karloff's instantly iconic performance adds a sad soulfulness to the Creature's melancholic liminality and the spiritual condemnation of his fabricated birth. Thus, the 'mythology' surrounding the essential story shifts and changes as a response to the audience consuming it, a state that gives not only weight but also empirical credence to the assertion that the story of Frankenstein and his patchwork man continue to captivate Anglo-American cultures.

Less than 40 after James Whale retired as the ringmaster to the continued Universal circus surrounding the Frankenstein myth, comedic screenwriter Mel Brooks took up the mantle in a parody that truly exemplifies the fitness of Whale's particular mutation of the *Frankenstein* meme. A Twentieth Century Fox production, *Young Frankenstein* (1974) introduces a new character to the story—Dr Victor Frankenstein's grandson, Dr Frederick Frankenstein MD, played by Gene Wilder. Though initially vehement in his protestations against any desired connection to his 'mad' relation, Wilder's character achieves a sort of mad transformation of his own having returned to his hereditary seat and uncovered his ancestor's laboratory and research. This madcap makeover galvanises Frederick, ultimately inspiring the electrifying birth of his own patchwork man who, like Whale's Creature in *Bride of Frankenstein*, is at first confused and violent, then persuaded into gentility by a kindly blind man. As this is a Mel Brooks film, there are countless moments of physical comedy that could easily obscure a deeper reading of the relationship between these disparate creation myths, but it is these moments of levity that manage to minimise the key tension introduced in both Shelley and Whale.

When the Creature (Peter Boyle) is eventually recaptured by Wilder, rather than renouncing his progeny, Wilder embraces the neck-bolted Boyle in an attempt to convince himself that his mostly mute and unreasoning Creature is essentially good—and concludes that they will prove this to the townspeople whose ignorance led to persecution (Brooks 1974: 1:01:50–1:03:40). As this reconciliation briefly backfires when a lightbulb explodes during Frankenstein and the Creature's surreal performance of 'Putting on the Ritz' and spooks the Creature, Wilder's character shares some of his intellectual prowess through another of his grandfather's inventions: a device that shares elements of Frederick's intellect with the Creature. This compels the townspeople to believe that the Creature is essentially good, and that he can be trusted to join society. This second performance to assuage the frightened populace is intended to disabuse them of their worries that he is an unreasoning brute. It also enables Boyle's Creature to marry and live a relatively normal life, as explained in a closing scene of domestic doldrums with Brooks' incarnation of The Bride.

Yes, this is a work of comedy and a parody of Whale's highly selective adaptation. And yet this unique climax provides an answer to that previously unanswered question as to what the Creature would be capable of if given the chance to live as an innocent, free man rather than a monster judged on its looks. This is a critical aspect of the story—no one has power over their own genetic makeup, or any aspect designed in the womb. And as the piecemeal product of reanimated body parts, Frankenstein's Creature is also a victim of his engineered genetic makeup. Shelley's Creature speaks eloquently, despite being an autodidact. Yet despite his powers of reason and genteel phrasing, he is unable to convince anyone save the blind De Lacey—who cannot judge based on physicality—that he is anything beyond his appearance. Yet it is this same power of speech that liberates Brooks' monster, and the lack thereof that condemns Whale's. So, in a strange way, Brooks' employment of the core themes, and his evolved transmission of the meme, remove the uncertainty that generates horror and provide a level of agency to each character that reduces the tensions between Shelley and Whale.

This case study illustrates the transmissive properties of the Frankenstein story and how the meme can be reanimated in its own right to generate a completely new yet still recognisable narrative. It is this continuity that explains how memetics serves as an ideal framework for the discussion of *Frankenstein*, rather than the popular invocation of modern mythology. An example of this is the Creature's muteness; the liminality and isolation themes may well authenticate this adaptation despite its complete divergence from the original story. However, the Creature's intellect makes a return in later evolutions of the story, specifically Danny Boyle's stage play starring Boyle (2011). In this incarnation, the Creature's voice returns alongside his need to be Victor's 'Adam'. The Creature's fall from grace is poignantly played to express the isolation, liminality, and melancholy associated with his patchwork monstrosity and engineered creation. This particular form of fabrication is frequently replicated in science fiction, fantasy, and speculative fiction to create an antagonist that is *nearly* human yet entirely other in its posthuman liminality. These characters tend to exist as cyborgs next to a familiar human body, like Philip K. Dick's *Do Android Dream of Electric Sheep?* (and its many incarnations through authorised sequels and film) and China Miéville's epic *Perdido Street Station* (2000).

China Miéville, Automata, and Agency: The Construct Council and the Remade

Perdido Street Station critiques contemporary consumption cultures with regards to technology, race, religion, and recreational drug use while also simultaneously celebrating and satirising the posthuman performances of android/cyborg/human relations in the work of science-fiction authors like Dick. *Perdido Street Station* centres on protagonist Dr Isaac Dan der Grimnebulin and his friends, whose world, Bas-Leg, is threatened by an alien species capable of destroying society. There are several immediate similarities between Isaac and Victor, with both prone to spending sleepless nights working on their experiments. During the course of the novel, a secondary subplot arises where Isaac and his companions come to the realisation that some of the machinery in Bas-Leg have has becomes sentient. As these machines lack human consciousness and are immune to the alien threat, Isaac concludes that his self-aware cleaning machine could defend humanity without succumbing to the creature's hypnotic stare. The cleaning machine takes Isaac and his cohort to meet the machine's leader: The Construct Council.

The Construct Council is an amalgam consciousness nestled inside a junkyard heap of discarded robot cleaners, computers (aka 'constructs'), and mechanical detritus cast off from Miéville's Bas-Leg. The Construct Council holds his band of followers—constructed and humanoid alike—under a religious thrall, using the corpse of a man to speak to his non-mechanical followers in their own language. This is vital as the Council is immovable, rooted to the ground of the junkyard. And, like many cult leaders, there is no religion to be had: The Council's followers are pawns used to increase its influence over every data processing device in Bas-Leg. Isaac is confronted by the monstrosity of the human puppet and the uncomfortable liminality of the Construct Council who cannot move yet yearns to enter society. The tactility of the hoses and clamps running between the Construct Council and the body are just one of Miéville's hideous progeny in *Perdido Street Station*.

In Bas-Leg, criminals' punishments match their crimes in a uniquely monstrous manner. These people, called the Remade, have mechanical, animal, or other simulations of other species' body parts added to or replacing portions of their own bodies as penance for their social deviations. This fabrication enforces every aspect of the *Frankenstein* meme: fabrication, bricolage, the posthuman, isolation, liminality, monstrosity, and mysterious science. While many of these characters live tragic lives as slaves or untouchables, there are those who find agency in their new bodies subverting their new physicality to fight the oppressive regime that 'Remade' them. Calling themselves 'fReemade', this group uses their new bodies as a site of revolt. The Remade are monstrous creations, condemned to a liminal role in their society; the fReemade have purpose in their shadow existence. Through the transmission of the central elements of Shelley's original story and offshoots—such as Karloff's immediately recognisable neck bolts or the discomfort of a bricolaged body—the key tenets of the cultural Creature have been replicated, mutated, evolved, and developed in a non-linear manner to render Shelley's provocative narrative relevant to contemporary (sub)culture.

Contemporary (Sub)Cultural Response

The focused melancholy of Victor Frankenstein and his bricolaged Creature read as familiar when held alongside the material cultures of first-wave punk. These particular aspects of the *Frankenstein* meme are among the fittest in the meme pool, as they have survived across a wide variety of visual and material cultures, including punk fashion. If called upon to describe the first wave of punk fashion, most would mention some combination of leather jackets, Mohican haircuts, safety pins, badges, bondage straps, and culturally explicit graphic tee shirts. It is also likely that the performed, aggressive attitude that these elements signal would warrant mention. Dick Hebdige's *Subculture: The Meaning of Style*, as well as his school's semiotic framework (the Centre for Contemporary Cultural Studies), suggests that these visual cues serve as signifiers for members of the punk community—that their unity stems from identifying with both punk music/musicians and their visual counter-actions against Conservative politicians, economic and social austerity, and class/generational inequity. This resonates with both Victor and the Creature's sense of isolation and liminality in a society ill-equipped to comprehend Victor's progressive— and unorthodox—anatomical bricolage. Those who embraced the punk culture of the 1970s felt they had been disenfranchised socially and used their clothing and countenance to reclaim power from the parent culture through symbols of their liminality. This comes together with bricolage.

A patchwork of different men, the Creature is a sum of parts pieced together to create a new whole, with a self-conscious understanding of his lack of personal agency. A bricolage object is an active object created by an owner-agent to express the agent's self. So, Frankenstein's Creature is a living, breathing expression of his creator's desires—a reality which paralyses—and catalyses—him. He lacks the ability to carve his own path or to enact his own desires. Frankenstein's aversion to, and consistent disowning of, his Creature is an intrinsic element of bricolage's repetition as part of the *Frankenstein* meme. This bricolage holds meaning for the agent, and disgust or terror for external cultures. For the Creature, this bricolage-induced disgust lies in the combination of body parts from recognisably different ages, races, and diverse identities used to create this new body. The Creature is an expression of Frankenstein's melancholy and scientific expression and a site of uncomfortable bricolage, uncomfortable due to the clear dissonance between component parts.

This same dissonance occurs in 1970s punk style, particularly in reference to the ubiquitous leather jackets, individually decorated with a patchwork of badges, patches, buttons, paint, and safety pins. Through the *Frankenstein* meme's lens, these jackets take on a metaphorical weight, mimicking the composite skins of the Creature. Disparate pieces of material, drawn together by the agent, serve as an outlet for the emotional weight of melancholy and liminality in an isolating culture (Hebdige 1979: 101–2).

FRANKENSTEIN AND THE FUTURE

Mary Shelley's *Frankenstein* has grown and evolved in ways that Shelley herself likely never dreamed of. It has become a form of cultural currency, a visual shorthand to explain monstrosity, patchwork politics and contemporary Promethean narratives. Victor's obsessive creation, his Creature's composition, and their shared liminality are the themes that recur most often across retellings of the story. They have made their way into a variety of contemporary creative outlets—many without overtly mentioning Shelley's posthuman progeny or perhaps knowing they were undergoing specific replications. To return to Oring a final time, 'Memetics and Folkloristics' explains that there is no way to prove the power, nor the existence of memes: each researcher must grapple with what qualifies as a meme and successful repetition. For this researcher, the joint repetition of fabrication, bricolage, liminality, melancholy and isolation, monstrosity, the posthuman, and scientific mystery are positive indications of the *Frankenstein* meme's existence. Though genetically speaking, patchwork men are still the matter of feverish dreams, memetically, Frankenstein's monster has never been fitter.

NOTES

1. The idea for this chapter developed out of a presentation I delivered on the development of Steampunk subculture at the 2013 conference 'Neo-Victorian Cultures: the Victorians Today' at Liverpool John Moores University. I then presented a second paper, specifically on this theme, at the 2014 conference 'Locating the Gothic' hosted by Mary Immaculate College and Limerick School of Art and Design. I owe a great many thanks to my supervisors, friends, and colleagues in the British Gothic community for encouraging my Robert Walton-esque journey into uncharted territory.

2. I have supplemented Dawkins' original theory with the work of Susan Blackmore, Kate Distin, Aaron Lynch, Elliott Oring, and Stephen Shennan. Each of these authors has brought their own disciplinary background to the study. For example, Susan Blackmore's *The Meme Machine* begins from Blackmore's psychology specialism and works to unpack the possibility that memes are responsible for more than cultural production—that they are responsible for the modern human brain itself, the thing that creates culture (Blackmore 1999: 74–81). However, regardless of which researcher takes up the 'meme' mantle, they all agree that, much like genes, memes are *selfish* in their continued replication and transmission potential.

3. Oring acknowledges that there is data to suggest natural selection as fact, but that it must be remembered that it remains a theory.
4. These particular themes are not the only ones to reverberate across the centuries as part of the *Frankenstein* meme. They have been selected for this chapter due to the ease with which they slot together. Other themes that I intend to return to in future explorations include adaptation, hybridity, sublime machinery, obsession, the Valley of the Uncanny, and robotics.

Works Cited

Aunger, Robert. 2000. *Darwinizing Culture: The Status of Memetics as a Science.* Oxford: Oxford University Press.

Baldick, Chris. 1987. *In Frankenstein's Shadow: Myth, Monstrosity, and Nineteenth-century Writing.* Oxford: Oxford University Press.

Barad, Karen. 2003. Posthumanist Performativity: Toward an Understanding of How Matter Comes to Matter. *Signs*: 801–831.

Blackmore, Susan. 1999. *The Meme Machine.* Oxford: Oxford University Press.

———. 2016. Memes and the Evolution of Religions: We Need memetics, Too. *Behavioral and Brain Sciences: The Cultural Evolution of Prosocial Religions* 39: 22–23.

Boyle, Danny. (dir.). 2011. *Frankenstein.* London: The Royal National Theatre.

Bronfen, Elisabeth. 1994. Rewriting the Family: Mary Shelley's *Frankenstein* in Its Biographical/Textual Context. In *Frankenstein, Creation and Monstrosity*, ed. Stephen Bann, 16–38. London: Reaktion Books.

Brooks, Mel. (dir.). 1974. *Young Frankenstein.* USA: Twentieth Century Fox.

Channel 4. 2012. *Frankenstein: A Modern Myth.* London: Lone Star Productions/ National Theatre Co-production. Originally Screened October 31, 2012. http://www.channel4.com/programmes/frankenstein-a-modern-myth

D'Onofrio, Erminio. 2012. Automata and *Frankenstein. Frankenstein: The Afterlife of Shelley's Circle.* New York: New York Public Library. http://exhibitions.nypl.org/biblion/outsiders/creation-remix/essay/essaydonofrio

Dawkins, Richard. 1982. *The Selfish Gene.* London: Granada Publishing Ltd.

Distin, Kate. 2005. *The Selfish Meme: A Critical Reassessment.* Cambridge: Cambridge University Press.

Fox, Kathryn Joan. 1987. Real Punks and Pretenders: The Social Organization of a Counterculture. *Journal of Contemporary Ethnography* 16 (3): 344–370.

Glut, Donal F. 2002. *The Frankenstein Archive: Essays on the Monster, the Myth, the Movies, and More.* Jefferson: McFarland & Company, Inc.

Grant, Michael. 1994. James Whale's "Frankenstein": The Horror Film and the Symbolic Biology of the Cinematic Monster. In *Frankenstein, Creation and Monstrosity*, ed. Stephan Bann, 113–135. London: Reaktion Books Ltd.

Hayles, N. Katherine. 1999. *How We Became Posthuman: Virtual Bodies in Cybernetics, Literature, and Informatics.* Chicago: University of Chicago Press.
Hebdige, Dick. 1979. *Subculture: The Meaning of Style.* London: Routledge.
James, Louis. 1994. Frankenstein's Monster in Two Traditions. In *Frankenstein, Creation and Monstrosity,* ed. Stephan Bann, 77–94. London: Reaktion Books Ltd.
Jordanova, Ludmilla. 1994. Melancholy Reflection: Construction and Identity for Unveilers of Nature. In *Frankenstein, Creation and Monstrosity,* ed. Stephen Bann, 60–76. London: Reaktion Books.
Latour, Bruno. 1993. *We Have Never Been Modern.* Trans. Catherine Porter. Cambridge: Harvard University Press.
Lynch, Aaron. 1996. *Thought Contagion: How Belief Spreads Through Society.* New York: Basic Books.
Miéville, China. 2000. *Perdido Street Station.* Basingstoke: Macmillan Kindle edition.
Muggleton, David. 2000. *Inside Subculture: The Postmodern Meaning of Style.* Oxford: BERG.
Offrey De la Mettrie, Julien. 1750. *Man a Machine.* Temple Bar: Printed for G. Smith, Online pdf.
Oring, Elliott. 2014. Memetics and Folkloristics: The Theory. *Western Folklore* 73 (4): 432–454.
Savage, Jon. 1992. *England's Dreaming: Anarchy, Sex Pistols, Punk Rock, and Beyond.* New York: St. Martin's Press.
Schaffer, Simon. 2013. *Mechanical Marvels: Clockwork Dreams.* London: BBC Four. http://www.bbc.co.uk/programmes/b0229pbp
Shelley, Mary. 1992. *Frankenstein; or, The Modern Prometheus,* ed. M. Hindle. London: Penguin Books.
Shennan, Stephen. 2002. *Genes, Memes and Human History: Darwinian Archaeology and Cultural Evolution.* London: Thames & Hudson Ltd.
Smith, Crosbie. 1994. Frankenstein and Natural Magic. In *Frankenstein, Creation and Monstrosity,* ed. S. Bann, 39–59. London: Reaktion Books.
Spooner, Catherine. 2006. *Contemporary Gothic.* London: Reaktion Books Kindle edition.
Turney, Jon. 1998. *Frankenstein's Footsteps: Science, Genetics, and Popular Culture.* New Haven: Yale University Press.
Whale, James. (dir.). 1931. *Frankenstein.* film. USA: Universal Pictures.
———. (dir.). 1935. *The Bride of Frankenstein,* film. USA: Universal Pictures.
Wood, Gaby. 2002. *Living Dolls.* Chatham: Mackays of Chatham PLC.

CHAPTER 15

Frankenstein in Hyperspace: The Gothic Return of Digital Technologies to the Origins of Virtual Space in Mary Shelley's *Frankenstein*

Kirstin A. Mills

Two hundred years after its publication in 1818, Mary Shelley's *Frankenstein* remains a powerful and pervasive force across numerous forms of popular media, but the ways that we understand the original text—not to mention the complex cultural contexts from which it emerged—have changed drastically, narrowing significantly with each incarnation.[1] Ways of reading texts have changed too, and as we advance into the digital age of cyberspace, virtual realities, and technologies like smart phones and tablets, writers and designers have worked to adapt classic texts for this new arena. Within this space, led by writer Dave Morris and narrative game developer inkle, the 'digital book' has emerged as a new kind of medium that expands traditional definitions of what a book should look and feel like. The first of these hybrid technological forms to

K. A. Mills (✉)
Department of English, Macquarie University, NSW, Sydney, Australia

© The Author(s) 2018
C. M. Davison, M. Mulvey-Roberts (eds.), *Global Frankenstein*,
Studies in Global Science Fiction,
https://doi.org/10.1007/978-3-319-78142-6_15

265

be unleashed into the world is, appropriately, an adaptation of Shelley's *Frankenstein*. Released globally in 2012, Morris' digital book, *Frankenstein*, is actually an 'app' that can be downloaded onto smart phones and tablets. Taking Mary Shelley's novel as its starting point, it utilises the touchscreen capabilities of modern technology to create an interactive narrative experience that allows the reader to direct and alter the narrative, choose-your-own-adventure style, in response to questions or suggested responses posed at regular intervals throughout the text.

The digital realms of virtual reality and the multiple narrative pathways opened up by interactive fiction may seem a far cry from Mary Shelley's novel. The virtual, hypertextual spaces of interactive digital publication technologies are commonly considered to be a uniquely modern phenomenon, and adaptations of classic texts into this format are therefore seen as radical departures from the original texts and the experience of reading them. However, less widely known is the fact that nineteenth-century writers as early as Mary Shelley were exploring similar kinds of spaces within their work, where the spatial construction of the narrative world is layered and multidimensional and includes liminal, overlapping spaces of the mind, alternative states of consciousness, and the supernatural as prototypical hyperspace. Likewise, within popular debates about the gothic imagination, the act of reading these texts was bound up in a unique conception of space that prefigures the virtual reality of the digital age.

This chapter therefore proposes that rather than radically transforming the original texts, it is precisely through the deployment of such virtual spaces that interactive digital adaptations paradoxically mark a return to the original text's central concerns and at the same time create a virtual reading space that reflects nineteenth-century understandings of higher-dimensional experience in a way that traditional book publication no longer achieves in the altered cultural context of the twenty-first century. It suggests that Morris' digital adaptation offers a new lens through which to understand the fascinating yet hitherto unexplored construction of space in Shelley's work and its relationship to the wider scientific, philosophical, and popular debates about space, the mind, reading, and the supernatural during the early nineteenth century. Further, it proposes that the new form of the 'digital book' that *Frankenstein* heralds can itself be considered inherently gothic in nature, where its digital technology and interactive performance draw on the potential of virtual space to destabilise traditional organisations of space, the body in space, and the mind across spatial dimensions to grant the reader a gothic double existence as a simultaneously embodied and ghostly presence occupying multiple realms. In its creation of multiple, interwoven spatial dimensions, its interactive production of spectrality and cognitive 'possession,' and its resulting fusion of traditionally opposed categories such as real and virtual, cognitive and embodied, natural and digital, and human and machine, the 'digital book' can be considered an inherently gothic form that reveals the uncanny potential of new media.[2] This chapter, then, looks both backwards and forwards, exhuming the long-buried contexts of Mary Shelley's *Frankenstein* and revealing their uncanny return within twenty-first-century digital technologies.

Space operates in multiple, interconnected, and complex ways in the reading of Morris' digital book. The app is designed with rich graphics to resemble sheets of paper on which the narrative is printed, layered over traditional gothic tropes of ancient books, ghastly remnants from the grave, scientific instruments, and anatomical sketches as if readers, through the portal of their screens, peer down onto Frankenstein's workbench (Fig. 15.1). As chapters or sections are selected, the view pans across the

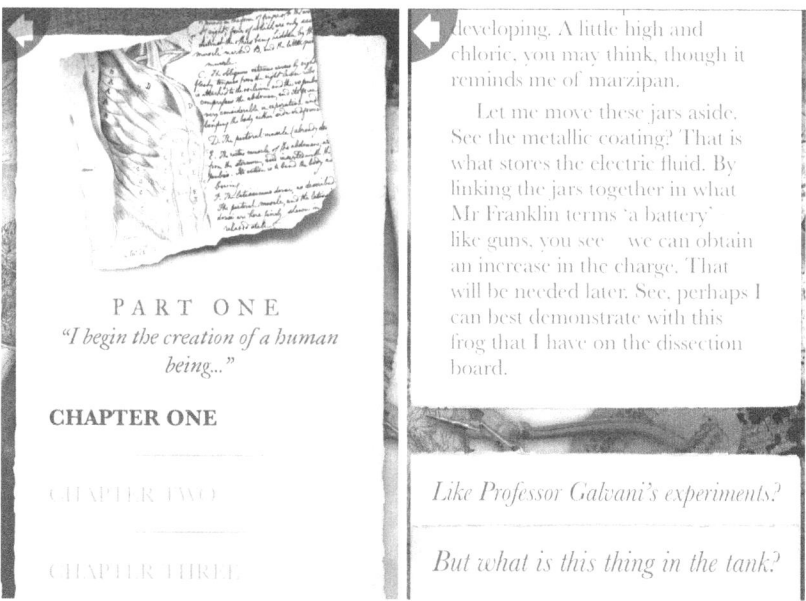

PART ONE
"I begin the creation of a human being..."

CHAPTER ONE

CHAPTER TWO

CHAPTER THREE

developing. A little high and chloric, you may think, though it reminds me of marzipan.

Let me move these jars aside. See the metallic coating? That is what stores the electric fluid. By linking the jars together in what Mr Franklin terms 'a battery' like guns, you see—we can obtain an increase in the charge. That will be needed later. See, perhaps I can best demonstrate with this frog that I have on the dissection board.

Like Professor Galvani's experiments?

But what is this thing in the tank?

Fig. 15.1 Screenshots of Dave Morris' *Frankenstein* (2012)

desk, revealing yet more anatomical sketches and medical instruments and incrementally expanding the visible space of the laboratory—a process that inevitably contributes to a powerful sense of both the limits of the visible world and the potential boundlessness of the invisible space that lies beyond it. Illustrations are taken from various sources, each at several stages of remove from the 'original' scene: for example, the app uses digital photo-manipulations of nineteenth-century engravings of oil paintings of natural landscapes, the entire image embedded within yet more layers of digital illustration and viewed through the framing lens of the device's screen. If pictures represent windows into other worlds (particularly the frequently depicted sublime landscapes), then these worlds are layered within several levels of representation, creating a sense of infinitely receding, nested spaces that yet open out into vast landscapes beyond the visible frame: multiple worlds within worlds. The illustrated maps contribute to a sense of navigation within these layered spaces and further the sense of more space available to unfold.

The emerging sense of multiple narrative dimensions deepens as interactive choices are made. The pages bearing narrative instalments are followed by a stack of further potential pages, each one bearing a different plot development for the reader to select. Only partly visible, each implies a potential narrative lying just outside the visible field (Fig. 15.1). Once an option is selected, that page is pinned to the bottom of the previous one, extending the ongoing narrative world both diegetically and spatially, and assembling the body of the text part-by-part in a neat parallel with Frankenstein's authoring of the creature's body. Most interesting, however, is the sense of multiple spaces created when the other pages—the options not selected—fall away. What remains in their absence is an ever-increasing sense of ghost texts—potential worlds—that yet remain hovering just outside the visible bounds of the story. Occasionally, these scraps are called into life at a later stage of the narrative and, occasionally, they are left out altogether, each one representing a scene and space linked to the present world and yet invisible, unexplored. The reading experience thus navigates a warren of potential storylines and narrative spaces, evoking a ghostly sense of the multidimensional in the paths not taken.

Multiple dimensions are also explored in the form of the digital book itself via the creation of liminal space between text and reader, which it achieves in two ways. First, the app's interactivity allows readers to engage with the story personally, participating not just as readers but also as characters, inhabiting a position of reference more fully immersed in the imagined textual world, and directing their character's response to action. At the same time, the limited range of programmed options and the layered, scrapbook style of presentation maintain a level of metafictive textuality that is hard to ignore. Readers are consequently suspended within textual space: the suspension of disbelief required to be fully immersed never quite happens, as readers, by virtue of such limitations and ever-changing illustrative graphics (themselves intertextual references to other intellectual and scientific cultures), are perpetually aware that they are reading a text. Readers therefore operate within a liminal space suspended partway between the creative imagined world and its textual representation. It is a space characterised by duality: as well as hovering between positions of reader and character, the interactivity allows readers to adopt the persona of the author, in part, while their limited options maintain the reader position.

This model of liminal, overlapping spaces evoked during the reading process is mirrored at a physical level. Virtual reality and other digital spaces have previously been thought of as the realm of the disembodied mind (Hayles 2002: xiii), but interactive literature and games blur the boundaries of these spaces, calling the body back into action and confusing the boundaries between real and virtual worlds while further preserving the distinctions that create a sense of multiple dimensions of spatial experience. The narrative cannot progress without both cognitive and physical interaction in response to the multiple options presented, and therefore the role of the interface remains conspicuous throughout the reading experience, liminally suspending the reader between the realms of the imagined narrative and the embodied process of reading and interacting with it. In this way, the technological interface preserves the distinctions between these spaces, yet it also facilitates their convergence as the mind-body-technology relationship becomes what Andy Clark has called 'extended mind'—an expansion of the borders of cognition beyond the brain to encompass the body and its adopted cognitive tools, from pencils to computers (Hayles 2002: xiii). Anxieties about the cybernetic merger of human and machine, their ontological indivisibility, and identity in the posthuman age haunt the borders of this interaction, emphasising the gothic potential of new media to destabilise traditional categorical boundaries. In this performance of liminality, the digital book becomes a gothic medium, well poised to explore questions of fragmented identity and the potential dangers of technology—the 'Frankensteinian anxieties' (van Elferen 2014: 139) that arise from the threat of collapsing borders between human sentience and technology. The cyborg emerges at this juncture between actual and virtual cognition, with Frankenstein's creature the clear historical precedent. In their similar liminal positioning between these states, readers uncannily enter this zone.

This gothic nature of *Frankenstein*'s digital technology is further revealed as space becomes more complicated. The images on the screen are two-dimensional, rendered artistically to appear three-dimensional, and by interacting with the images (by touching the screen or 'turning' a page), animated graphics are activated that render the image even more apparently three-dimensional. This arrangement affects the spatial positioning of readers in interesting ways, placing them at a liminal junction between this two-and-three-dimensional space and the world of the reader's body, which is thereby rendered a higher-dimensional space. The 'real' world thus becomes a kind of fourth dimension, and while their bodies interact with the visual representations on the screen, readers hover at the limits between these dimensional spaces. Consequently, readers become four-dimensional beings, or, in nineteenth-century spiritualist discourses, ghosts. While the spiritual realm had always been conceived of as a space beyond the earthly, with the advent of mathematical notions of higher-dimensional (hyper-)space, in the 1860s, spiritualists seized upon what they saw as scientific explanation of the kinds of alternative spaces long imagined by the gothic. The associated ideas of haunting as 'crossing over' from a separate realm have persisted and complicate twenty-first-century virtual spaces and related posthuman anxieties with a distinctly gothic flavour. The *Frankenstein* app taps into this higher-dimensional cyberspatial spectrality: by virtue of the app's spatial organisation, the reader becomes a ghostly presence—a simultaneously embodied consciousness that is rendered disembodied through intersection with the virtual world. Through the process of reading, the reader's consciousness inhabits the mind of a character within the virtual world, and just like nineteenth-century spectral theories and the gothic texts that anticipate them, the higher-dimensional reader becomes a possessing force within the space of the lower-dimensional world that they enter.

The spectrality invoked by these multidimensional spaces is reflected at still deeper levels of spatial play in the digital book. While the reader experiences Part I through the eyes of an unnamed character conversing with Frankenstein, Part II suddenly opens from the creature's perspective as it experiences its first sensations. The fact that the reader's consciousness is immersed in the sensory space of the creature's body is emphasised first by the focus on bodily sensations, and then by the sudden and jarring switch to second-person narration, which refers at once to the creature and the reader as 'you.' The abruptness of this realisation uncannily mirrors the creature's own process of waking in a new body, suddenly aware of his own embodied being. Moreover, as readers are thus forced to inhabit the creature's mind and body, their interactive selections also direct his actions and, more particularly, his emotional responses. This reading experience creates a triple spatial and cognitive positioning—the reader is at once a reader experiencing a text, the monster from whose perspective they are reading, and also, via the interactivity, the author of this monster and his behaviour (thus sharing, in some ways, the identity of Frankenstein). In this last pairing, the adaptation takes its cue from Shelley, for whom Frankenstein and the creature were inextricably linked: in Frankenstein's own words, the creature is his 'own spirit let loose from the grave' ([1818] 2012: 51). It is a pairing that Morris' adaptation renders even more spectral by yet another cognitive doubling; that of the creature and Part I's unnamed focaliser. In Part I, this unnamed character appears to be invisible to all but Frankenstein, which, Morris (2012b) suggests, means that he must be Frankenstein's 'conscience, or alter ego,' and the fact that Frankenstein and his creature represent 'the two sides of a divided self' is one 'reason why it makes sense to have the reader "play" the monster in the second part.' In one sense, readers have already been occupying the spectral form of the consciousness that now animates the creature.

This manifold cognitive positioning becomes even more complex later in Part II when the creature/reader is presented with four books from which to choose. Of course, each of these options not only opens up potential narrative pathways into alternative virtual worlds but also suggests intertextual pathways that transcend the boundaries between books and mirror the collaged effect of the interface's graphic design, extending the layered textual worlds outwards. Most significantly, however, one of these books is Frankenstein's journal, and if this option is selected, the reader thereby inhabits the mind of the creature as he himself attempts to literally read the mind of his own 'author' through Frankenstein's written words. The reader's position thereby becomes a curiously tautological one: the space of shared consciousness becomes eerily, uncannily reflective as the reader slips between creator, creature, and observer, eventually occupying all three positions at once, while the doppelgängers become haunted by the third eerie presence of the readers themselves.

The multiple virtual, hyperlinked worlds of cyberspace evoked by the digital book's interactive narrative forms and twenty-first-century touch-screen technology may seem, at first glance, to detract from a faithful representation of Shelley's original novel. The author's call in the app's 'Acknowledgements' for publishers and 'traditionalists' not 'to be scared' of the new hybrid, digital book signals both its innovation as well as one source of potential criticism (its very 'Frankenstein's monster' quality of difference and hybridity, and its embracing of strange new realms of modern technology). Morris implores the reader, 'The digital world isn't full of monsters, honest.' But of course, it is: within the gothic digital and cognitive realms opened up by reading and interacting with the app, the spirit of Frankenstein's monster is unleashed again, but the question of how faithfully the digital adaptation reflects the original novel haunts the success of the work. The app has received generally favourable reviews, but the adaptation has so altered the original text that the more blunt reviews such as Anna Baddeley's (2012) for *The Guardian*, entitled 'Digital butchery makes a monster of Frankenstein,' are perhaps understandable. 'What Morris has done,' Baddeley claims, 'is dismember Mary Shelley's novel and sew it into a digital version of a Choose Your Own Adventure story. In doing so he has created a monster.' Baddeley's criticism seems to be that the radically altered form of the digital book—its technological inter-activity—renders it unfaithful to the original, though her criticism that its focalisation through multiple characters is 'bewildering' overlooks the fact that this was also a feature of Shelley's novel. A later review in the same newspaper takes a more positive approach but still feels the digital rework-ing falls short: Pullinger (2012) concludes that 'While Morris has parsed and reoriented the story effectively, he hasn't fully exploited the device's capabilities in order to reanimate the wild technological imaginings of the story as Shelley herself might have done.'

While it is hard to imagine exactly what use Shelley would have made of twenty-first-century digital technologies, one thing these reviews overlook in their focus upon the formal differences between the digital book and the novel is the way that the virtual spaces evoked by these very differences actually mark a surprising return to some of the most central concerns of Shelley's text. In so doing, they evoke a conceptual world that more accurately reflects the original nineteenth-century contexts in which *Frankenstein* would have been read and understood than traditional forms of publishing are now able to achieve within the different cultural perspec-tives and intellectual contexts of the twenty-first century. The novel's scientific, philosophical, and moral questions have historically received the most critical attention, but what has been frequently overlooked is that these concerns are played out through its central exploration of a universe conceived as layered and multidimensional, and through its charting of events across the liminal planes of interaction between lower and higher-dimensional spaces. In Shelley's novel, we can trace not only early incarnations of late-nineteenth-century hyperspace but also the origins of the virtual spaces we now associate with modern digital technologies. These spaces are configured in multiple, overlapping ways but fall into two main types: models of higher-dimensional space that correspond to a supernatural realm existing outside of, yet intertwined with, the natural world of human endeavour and scientific knowledge, and models of higher-dimensional space as a cognitive phenomenon, where dreams, trance, madness, and other liminal states of consciousness occur within their own unique spaces both within and yet beyond the confines of the brain, body, and natural world. Shelley explores these spatial models at both thematic and formal levels, traversing their margins through linguistic, symbolic, and physical doublings that complicate divisions between spaces and minds. She even extends her explorations of virtual space to the personal experience of the reader, reaching beyond the borders of the text to draw the reader's mind into spatial proximity with the spectral forms—both ghostly hauntings and overlapping, disembodied consciousnesses—that the text evokes. In every case, the novel's central events and major philosophical concerns occur at the liminal threshold between these spaces.

Shelley's evocation of physical space as layered and multidimensional occurs first through the novel's contrasts between enclosed and open, and inner and outer spaces. Perhaps paradoxically, *Frankenstein* situates the realm of human knowledge, intellectual rationality, and scientific endeavour within enclosed, claustrophobic spaces disconnected from the natural world. In addition to the charnel houses, tombs, 'dissecting room and the slaughter-house,' Frankenstein pursues his scientific experiments '[i]n a solitary chamber, or rather cell, at the top of the house [...] separated from all the other apartments by a gallery and staircase' ([1818] 2012: 34). While we can read into this paradox Shelley's critique of the limits of contemporary science, male institutions of knowledge and education, and Enlightenment reason against Romantic imagination and intuition, what this spatial bounding of human knowledge also achieves is a reconfiguration of the spatial organisation of the universe.

For Kant, that pillar of Enlightenment Reason, the traditional three dimensions of space were linked with rational thinking, the limits of one implying the limits of the other. Space, Kant writes, 'has three dimensions, and [the idea] that space cannot in any way have more, is based on [... a] proposition [that] cannot by any means be shown from concepts, but rests immediately on [...] pure and a priori intuition, because it is apodictically certain' ([1783] 2004: 36). Shelley's reduction of such three-dimensional realms of Reason to enclosed, inner spaces, then, enacts an extension of space, rendering that which falls outside—those vast, open, natural landscapes associated with the Burkean sublime—something *other*, something *beyond*, an extra, fourth dimension placed literally outside the limits of human understanding. Natural becomes supernatural. The most extreme of these spaces—the 'immense mountains and precipices' suspended liminally between earth and the heavens, which appear 'as belonging to another earth, the habitations of another race of beings' ([1818] 2012: 64), and the 'vast and irregular plains of ice' at the North Pole, 'which seemed to have no end' (13)—represent dual spatial and cartographical axes. In opening and closing the novel, these polar regions, which are never fully explored, but which for Walton contain the secrets of 'the phænomena of the heavenly bodies [...] in those undiscovered solitudes' (7), also represent a textual and narratological limit that reinforces their spatial performance of the intellectual, geographical, and metaphysical 'beyond.' It is a region repeatedly related to death, and the ghostly is at home here: within both of these sites, Frankenstein senses 'wandering spirits' (67), 'the spirits of the dead' (145) and 'the shades that wander near' (145).

In her rendering of the outer world as a higher-dimensional supernatural realm, Shelley evokes early nineteenth-century popular and even scientific contexts that considered a potentially real spiritual dimension beyond the limit of the natural world (a context both influenced by and fundamental to the popularity of gothic fiction). Shelley's landscapes, then, are not merely symbolic psycho-geographies or platforms for the sublime imagination (though they perform these roles too): they represent the spatial 'boundary between life and death' (59) signified by the linguistic doubling between Frankenstein's description of these sublime landscapes as 'another earth' and his dying mother's wish to be reunited in 'another world' (25). Heavily influenced by Coleridge's poetry and his avowed interest in the supernatural realm, Shelley moves beyond her gothic and Romantic predecessors to more fully explore questions of identity and ontology at the intersection of these dimensions and the consequences of disrupting the sacred boundary between. To do so, Shelley complicates her spatial arrangement even further, not only blurring the boundaries between Frankenstein and his creature as uncanny doppelgängers within this borderland but also fragmenting and multiplying space within the physical and ontological configuration of their individual minds and bodies.

In contrast to twentieth-century cinematic adaptations, which evoke a distinctly corporeal 'monster,' Shelley is emphatically vague in her physical descriptions, employing shifting gothic terminologies characterised by indeterminacy and ambiguity to cast the creature instead as an embodied spirit positioned liminally between natural and supernatural worlds. Variously referred to as 'spectre' (39), 'dæmon' (50), 'apparition' (146), 'fiend' (62), 'devil' (50), and 'wretch' (36), the creature thrives within the sublime, higher-dimensional landscapes that signal death for the men that pursue him, and several times when Frankenstein exhorts his 'wandering spirits' within these realms, it is the creature who suddenly appears before him (67). His body also disturbs traditional separations between other categories and spaces. Despite his organic composition and autonomous consciousness, he is still technologically orchestrated and 'assembled,' thereby straddling the boundary between nature and machine. Likewise, he is neither human nor animal as his body is compiled of parts from both. He also straddles the borders of life and death as assembled and 'reanimated' cadavers. Shelley's 1831 Introduction reinforces this merger, describing 'the hideous corpse [...] as the cradle of life' (2003: 9). Even further, his body is a literal fusion of what were once multiple separate bodies, the spectres of which haunt his ontology (and provide much of his bodily horror to others), as well as fuel his own anguished questions about identity and belonging. His body becomes a space within which other bodily spaces merge, their formerly whole bodies (human and animal, alive and dead) and accompanying souls both absent and yet uncannily present in the life that now animates the hybrid creature.

Frankenstein likewise straddles multiple spaces at the boundary between natural and supernatural dimensions, becoming a double of the creature, and thus sharing—and adding yet another layer to—the creature's fragmented spatial ontology. Increasingly referred to throughout the novel as a 'wretch' (60) and a 'restless spectre' (122), Frankenstein 'wandered like an evil spirit' (61), 'the only unquiet thing that wandered restless in a scene so beautiful and heavenly' (62), a linguistic doubling that connects him with both the supernatural 'wandering spirits' and the creature, who likewise 'wandered' (68) within these sublime, supernatural spaces. Complicating this doubling are the repeated suggestions that the lines between cognitive function, haunting, and supernatural possession are blurred. Frankenstein continually describes the act of thinking about the creature as 'possession,' which renders his mind a contested space, and during these moments, Frankenstein begins to physically and psychologically mirror the creature. Describing his 'abhorrence of this fiend' following Justine's death, Frankenstein states, 'When I thought of him, I gnashed my teeth, my eyes became inflamed, and I ardently wished to extinguish that life which I had so thoughtlessly bestowed' (62). Later, 'possessed' by thoughts 'that the fiend followed' him and might murder Henry Clerval, Frankenstein occupies the haunting role himself: 'When these thoughts possessed me, I [...] followed [Clerval] as his shadow [...] I felt as if I had committed some great crime, the consciousness of which haunted me' (116). Frankenstein refers here to his involvement in 'birthing' the murderous creature, but in the context of the novel's higher-dimensional spaces, this haunting becomes disturbingly literal, involving Frankenstein's haunting by both the memory of the creature and the possessing force of the creature's consciousness, which now infuses his own cognitive realm. Such doublings signal a complex spatial arrangement in which the higher-dimensional realm of the supernatural is utilised to span the separate mental and bodily domains of Frankenstein and creature, where the 'possession' both preserves distinctions between their minds and yet also links them as multiply positioned, interconnected aspects of the same being. Walton's description of Frankenstein's 'double existence' (17) is here both spatially and ontologically apt.

As the novel progresses and Frankenstein pursues the creature further into the sublime regions that signal both a higher-dimensional supernatural space and its limit with the natural world, the configuration of memory as haunting via possession intensifies, resulting also in an inversion of the conscious and subconscious spaces of Frankenstein's mind. Following Clerval's death, Frankenstein states, 'Memory brought madness with it; and when I thought on what had passed, a real insanity possessed me' (137). Shelley draws here on a popular notion of madness as spiritual possession that persisted well into the nineteenth century and which postulated that possession occurred during the overlap between the higher realms of the supernatural and the similarly liminal spaces both within and yet beyond the confines of the mind within which, following Coleridge, subliminal states of consciousness like dreams and trance were thought to occur. This model of overlapping mental and supernatural spaces was echoed in the rapidly growing phenomena of mesmerism, which often utilised trance states to enact mental journeys beyond the confines of the brain and body into the spiritual world. Frankenstein's cognitive and supernatural possession by the creature, which designates also the doubled, overlapping spaces of their minds, is figured characteristically in terms of trance and nightmare, where Frankenstein becomes often insensible to his outer world, his 'eyes [...] fixed and unobserving' (110). To help himself sleep after Clerval's death, Frankenstein takes laudanum, which, in a nod to Coleridge, brings on ambiguously cognitive and demonic possession: '[P]ossessed by a kind of night-mare; I felt the fiend's grasp in my neck, and could not free myself from it' (133).

The closer Frankenstein gets to the limit between the natural and supernatural worlds, the more the spaces of his mind, as well as those of the physical world in which he wanders, become inverted, merging dream and reality, natural and supernatural, until these separate realms become impossible to distinguish. His waking hours within the possessed space of his conscious mind become 'like a dream' (122), and pursuing his own spectral double is endured 'more as a task enjoined by heaven, as the mechanical impulse of some power of which I was unconscious, than as the ardent desire of my soul' (147). Doubling the creature's ontological ambiguity between automata and autonomy, the space of Frankenstein's consciousness—now rendered unconscious through its possession and dreamlike qualities—is no longer his own. In contrast, a sense of cognitive autonomy and conscious reality is now attributed to the space of his dreams, which, though still haunted by the ghosts of his family, become 'reality in the arms of my dearest friends' (147), which 'are not the creations of his fancy, but the beings themselves who visit him from the regions of a remote world' (151–2).

While these multiplicitous enfoldings of spatial dimensions occur within the limits of the narrative world, Shelley draws on these discourses of supernatural possession and liminal mental journeys to move beyond the text and incorporate her own mind as yet another higher-dimensional space through which she can interact with her characters as a spectral figure. Referring several times to both Frankenstein and the creature as 'author' (69), Shelley includes herself as a third participant in their uncanny doubling, traversing the borders between life and art, and actual and imagined worlds, to partake in their shared cognitive and spectral 'possession.' This spatial layering is, in turn, deepened by the origin story included in her 1831 Introduction, which posits the 'waking dream' (2003: 10) that inspired her narrative as a liminal space shared also by Frankenstein (who likewise experiences this vision within the novel) and the creature (as the 'spectre' and 'hideous phantom' that 'haunted' Shelley's mind [2003: 9]). Once again, the liminal space of dreaming is opened up as a space within which to traverse the borders between minds, the natural and supernatural worlds, and even, in this instance, the worlds of author and text.

Moreover, this spectral possession across multiple spatial dimensions is also extended to include the reader. In her use of triple-layered, nested narrative frames, Shelley renders the reader a ghostly, possessing force from beyond the limits of the narrative world, who spans the minds of its already uncannily doubled characters. The haunting flows both ways: our closest link to the story, Walton, becomes a medium—diegetically and spiritually—through which the thoughts of the deceased Frankenstein and his creature—and also, by extension and the above spatial layering, Shelley—are conveyed to us. This fusion of psychological and supernatural worlds in the reading process reinforces the similarly interwoven spaces of the novel, drawing particular attention to the fluidity of the boundaries between embodied and disembodied minds across multiple dimensions.

Importantly, in constructing these models of multidimensional cognitive and supernatural space, Shelley draws on already established discourses surrounding late eighteenth and early nineteenth-century concepts of the imagination, in which, much like the spaces of dreams and trance, the act of reading was thought to open up a liminal mental space both within and yet beyond the ordinary space of the mind and body, resulting in the reader occupying multiple spaces simultaneously. Ann Radcliffe famously described this idea when she wrote that the imagination, not content to be confined 'to the evidence of the senses […] of this earth, but, eager to expand its faculties, […] soars after new wonders into a world of its own' (1824: 709). Likewise, the Aikinses refer to the 'new world which is laid open to' the imagination ([1773] 2000: 129), while William Hazlitt, drawing on gothic discourses of possession, describes the power of Shakespeare's tragedies to 'take possession of the mind, and form … a world by themselves' (cited in Otto 2011: 248–9). Such discourse was particularly relevant to the gothic novels, which capitalised on the terrifying potential to conjure ghosts and other horrors within such a liminal space opened up between the real and the imagined. Otto (2011) has explored the ways that such imagined spaces function as virtual reality or what he calls 'real unrealities'; however, it is also important to note that in the overlapping contexts of Romantic theories of imagination and possession, critical concerns about the power of gothic novels to influence the minds of impressionable readers, and the ongoing scientific and philosophical queries into the intermingled spaces of the mind and the supernatural, these virtual spaces assumed a disturbingly real character. The Romantic linking of imagination and mental visions with other liminal states of consciousness like dream and trance resulted in the unsettling implication that if the supernatural realm could be accessed via these cognitive spaces, then perhaps the ghosts conjured within the virtual world opened up by reading gothic fiction constituted real haunting. The nineteenth-century reader of *Frankenstein* thus occupied multiple cognitive dimensions that not only prefigured twenty-first-century virtual realities but also deepened an understanding of the novel's thematic exploration of these ideas.

Indeed, Shelley explicitly invokes this discourse of liminal imagined worlds and their connections with the supernatural during one of *Frankenstein*'s most crucial moments. When contemplating the death of Henry Clerval, Frankenstein wonders, 'where does he now exist? [...] Has this mind so replete with ideas, imaginations fanciful and magnificent, which *formed a world*, whose existence depended on the life of its creator [...] perished? Does it now only exist in my memory?' ([1818] 2012: 112; emphasis added). These questions fold space into even further dimensions: Frankenstein's memory is of course itself an imagined 'world' opened up within (or beyond) the space of his mind, and it now also houses Clerval's imagined world, creating a series of nested mental spaces that not only span the borders between minds but also those between the living and the dead. Like his earlier 'possession' by memory of the creature, and his dreaming encounters with the spirits of his dead family, in this complex layering of mental and supernatural spaces, memory constitutes spiritual possession. Frankenstein is both psychologically and literally haunted as Clerval's 'spirit still visits and consoles' him (112). Moreover, these nested cognitive spaces correspond with and add yet another layer to those already nested mental spaces involved in the narrative frames, ensuring that Shelley's exploration of multiple dimensions of consciousness—from the disembodied mind of the reader to the ghostly spaces within the overlapping minds of herself and her characters—infuses both the thematic and formal aspects of her novel.

In light of these complex spatial configurations, when Morris (2012b) writes that his adaptation of Shelley's *Frankenstein* into the virtual spaces of twenty-first-century digital technology is 'more akin to a translation than a retelling,' he may be closer to the truth than he realises. In its early thematic and formal representations of space as layered and multidimensional, Shelley's *Frankenstein* prefigures much of what we consider hallmarks of twenty-first-century virtual worlds. In this way, the new textual and technological form of the digital book represents a return to, rather than a departure from, the novel's original contexts and reveals not only the gothic nature of modern digital technology and its potential for enhancing gothic narratives but also one of the many ways that, 200 years after its creation, Shelley's *Frankenstein* still haunts our liminal worlds.

NOTES

1. Chris Baldick notes the role of the famous 1931 cinematic adaptation in this narrowing of possible meanings (1987: 5).
2. Though the gothic nature of the 'digital book' has not previously been examined, various scholars have drawn attention to the relationship between technology and the gothic. Studies by Fred Botting (2008), Isabella van Elferen (2014), and Justin D. Edwards (2015) examine different aspects of technology as a gothic mode and its manifestation in new hybrid forms of cybergothic or technogothic. While their approaches vary, these analyses align in their identification of technogothic's reliance upon the uncanny, liminality, the blurring of categorical boundaries, and, in particular, related anxieties over the cybernetic merger of human and machine.

WORKS CITED

Aikin, J., and A.L. Aikin. 2000 [1773]. On the Pleasure Derived from Objects of Terror. In *Gothic Documents: A Sourcebook 1700–1820*, ed. E.J. Clery and Robert Miles, 127–132. Manchester: Manchester University Press.

Baddeley, Anna. 2012. Digital Butchery Makes a Monster of Frankenstein. *The Guardian*, April 15. https://www.theguardian.com/books/2012/apr/15/mary-shelley-frankenstein-app-review. Accessed 1 July 2016.

Baldick, Chris. 1987. *In Frankenstein's Shadow: Myth, Monstrosity and Nineteenth-Century Writing*. Oxford: Clarendon.

Botting, Fred. 2008. *Limits of Horror: Technology, Bodies, Gothic*. Manchester: Manchester University Press.

Edwards, Justin D., ed. 2015. *Technologies of the Gothic in Literature and Culture*. New York: Routledge.

Hayles, N. Katherine. 2002. Foreword. In *Prefiguring Cyberculture: An Intellectual History*, ed. Darren Tofts, Annemarie Jonson, and Alessio Cavallaro, xxii–xxiv. Sydney: Power Publications.

Kant, Immanuel. 2004 [1783]. *Prolegomena to Any Future Metaphysics*. Trans: Gary Hatfield. Cambridge: Cambridge University Press.

Morris, Dave. 2012a. *Frankenstein*. Cambridge: Profile Books and Inkle. https://itunes.apple.com/app/frankenstein-interactive/id516047066

———. 2012b. 'Interview with Dave Morris, Creator of *Frankenstein* App', Interview by Dale Townshend and Padmini Ray Murray. *The Gothic Imagination*, April 29. http://www.gothic.stir.ac.uk/interviews/interview-with-dave-morris-creator-of-frankenstein-app/. Accessed 27 Aug 2017.

Otto, Peter. 2011. *Multiplying Worlds: Romanticism, Modernity, and the Emergence of Virtual Reality*. Oxford: Oxford University Press.

Pullinger, Kate. 2012. *Frankenstein* by Dave Morris—Review. *The Guardian*, May 17. https://www.theguardian.com/books/2012/may/17/frankenstein-dave-morris-app-review. Accessed 1 July 2016.

Radcliffe, Ann. 1824. *The Novels of Mrs Ann Radcliffe*. London: Hurst, Robinson, and Co.

Shelley, Mary. 2003 [1831]. Introduction. In *Frankenstein*, 5–10. London: Penguin Books.

———. 2012 [1818]. *Frankenstein*. New York/London: W. W. Norton and Co.

van Elferen, Isabella. 2014. Techno-Gothics of the Early-twenty-first Century. In *The Cambridge Companion to the Modern Gothic*, ed. Jerrold E. Hogle, 138–154. Cambridge: Cambridge University Press.

CHAPTER 16

Playing the Intercorporeal: *Frankenstein's* Legacy for Games

Tanya Krzywinska

Horror and Science Fiction (SF) are genres very regularly called upon by game developers to add easily marketable flavour to games. Some of the earliest digital games drew on SF-based themes and iconography, including what is often regarded as the first videogame ever made, *Spacewar!* (1962). Games and SF are mutually supportive: computing is itself often sold as a form of SF, providing its imaginative traction as well as one of the genre's stock characters, and an abundance of synthetic intelligences have been dreamed up by both SF game developers and computational creativity researchers. The dominance of dystopian narratives, demonic, synthetic and alien entities in SF does, however, make for a fluid blend with Horror. This resolves around the dramatic use of that which threatens normative definitions of the human and humanity, providing game developers with a scenario that integrates easily into different game genres, such as First-Person Shooter, Action-Adventure, Puzzle, Tactical and Strategy games. Games co-opt valuable assets from Horror and SF: iconographies of spectacle suit the visual technologies used within games, while narrative forms based on conflict and exploration prove to be extremely game friendly. Such a sanguine remedia-

T. Krzywinska (✉)
Games Academy, Falmouth University, Penryn, UK

© The Author(s) 2018
C. M. Davison, M. Mulvey-Roberts (Eds.), *Global Frankenstein*,
Studies in Global Science Fiction,
https://doi.org/10.1007/978-3-319-78142-6_16

tory relationship is further fuelled by the provision of well-established and eager audiences. While, in a general sense, SF regularly takes a wide-angle, epically scoped view, Horror tends to focus on the constrained and the claustrophobic. Often in SF-Horror hybrids, the one is nested inside the other, as is evident in films as diverse as *Solaris* (1976, USSR), *Forbidden Planet* (1956, US), *Moon* (2009, UK) and the Alien franchise. But the strongest bonding agent between the two is monstrosity. Monsters have global appeal and populate a vast range of culturally diverse mythologies. It is, however, Mary Shelley's *Frankenstein: or, the Modern Prometheus* (henceforth, *Frankenstein*) that provides the monstrous blueprint for blends that I name for the sake of clarity in a vast sea of related subgenres, 'Gothic Science Fiction'.

Given the regularity with which game developers have called on Horror and SF, it is surprising to find so few *direct* game adaptations of Mary Shelley's *Frankenstein*. This is particularly notable given the number of films, plays and TV serial adaptations there have been. These include the play based on the novel staged in 1823 alongside the film adaptations of 1910 and 1915, as well as the many subsequent films and plays that collectively testify to the transmedial potential of the text. What direct adaptation games there are nonetheless represents just a handful of unambitious and small-scale offerings (Inkles' 2011 *Frankenstein* written by Dave Morris was critically well received, yet it is an interactive novel rather than a game). The most substantial of these games appeared during the 1990s, perhaps on the back of Kenneth Branagh's much-publicised film version of the novel (1994). In addition, while there is plenty of critical commentary on SF and monsters in games, there has, to date, been no work that focuses specifically on games and *Frankenstein*. To establish the terrain occupied by games located in the Frankensteinian landscape, this chapter begins by positioning the main ludic and thematic coordinates of these few *direct* 'gamified' adaptations. This is important to do because it supports the main task of exploring what I regard as the more significant and interesting arena of the novel's *indirect* legacies within digital games and their computing systems. This arena is largely thematic and addresses the interlaced roles of tragedy, monstrosity, death and creativity in relation to the technologies that are able to challenge the very definition of the human (such as synthetic intelligence, gene editing). My major claim here is that the legacy of both *Frankenstein* and Victor Frankenstein may be indirectly present in games, but it is nonetheless foundational and lasting, most obviously apparent in the ways that technologies closest to mimicking human consciousness are narrativised visually and structurally.

DIRECT ADAPTATIONS: THE GAMIFICATION OF FRANKENSTEIN

Direct game adaptations of *Frankenstein* do not line up to a single game genre (i.e. First Person, Strategy, Puzzle, Action, Adventure, etc.). Instead the few that have been produced are split across the game genre spectrum, suggesting therefore that the novel is open to becoming 'gamified' in very different ways. A text-based adventure game was designed by Rod Pike and Jared Derrett and published in 1987 for Amstrad, Commodore and ZXSpectrum consoles. The game offered players a close rendition of the novel in text form; players typed in 'actions' (as verbs) to progress the story. As text, little computing power was needed as the game made meaning through its combination of verbs, descriptive text and evocative language (e.g. 'darkening clouds', 'wild white horses of foam'), the latter designed to spark a player's imaginative visual engagement as well as providing reference to Shelley's own written style. These are occasionally accompanied by simplified images that, in their block-like nature, bear some resemblance to woodcuts, signifying the antiquated. The visual dimension of the text is typical of the capacity of the consoles of the time: hard to read because of the large kerning between letters, yet through its lack of letter-size uniformity it has an eccentric charm and recalls simple linotype typesetting style. In terms of its core 'game loop' (a term used by game designers to describe the specific nature of a game's interaction mechanics), there is a very simple form of call and response; overall the textual approach retains intact the rich literary source for the game (Fig. 16.1).

In addition to its strong relationship to the novel, the game makes use of the novel's dynamic viewpoint. The point of view is that of Victor in the first two-thirds of the game, switching to that of the monster in the last. This switch is rare in most first- or third-person games, or in role-playing games, where a stable player-character point of view is regarded as a condition of a player's sense of presence. This first *Frankenstein* game adaptation sought to preserve the tone and textuality of the novel; as such it uses a game loop designed to bring the player into the game *as* a literary text.

This 'literary' approach to gamifying the novel is apparent in a later game, *Frankenstein: Through the Eyes of the Monster* published in 1995, but it is to cinema that the game looks. Here, both short cinematics and written sources pull the storytelling weight: Victor Frankenstein has brought Philip back from the dead after he is hanged in error for the murder of his

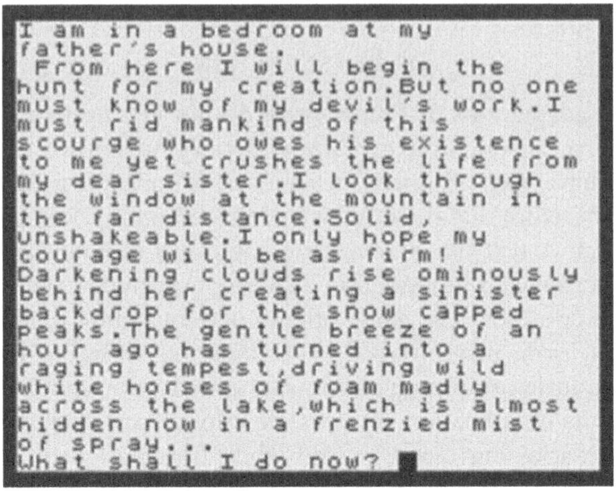

```
I am in a bedroom at my
father's house.
 From here I will begin the
hunt for my creation.But no one
must know of my devil's work.I
must rid mankind of this
scourge who owes his existence
to me yet crushes the life from
my dear sister.I look through
the window at the mountain in
the far distance.Solid,
unshakeable.I only hope my
courage will be as firm!
Darkening clouds rise ominously
behind her creating a sinister
backdrop for the snow capped
peaks.The gentle breeze of an
hour ago has turned into a
raging tempest,driving wild
white horses of foam madly
across the lake,which is almost
hidden now in a frenzied mist
of spray...
What shall I do now?
```

Fig. 16.1 Screenshot of Frankenstein (1987, CRL Group). (The game can be sourced at https://archive.org/details/zx_Frankenstein_1987_CRL_Group_Part_ 1_of_3)

daughter. Philip/the player wakes at the start of the game without memory. This unifying device provides the rationale for the player to remain located in the present tense, yet motivated to unearth who he is and then to seek out his daughter's true murderer. The game builds story devices into its game loops through its exploratory and hermeneutic mode. It therefore sits between the text-based adventure and action-based games that often tell their stories through a player's traversal through semiotic rich environments and spoken dialogue, rather than using planted written texts. Experienced through the point of view of one character, the game departs from the more mobile mode of address used in cinematic and TV fiction. It is designed to position the player very directly into the frame of action. Placing the player in the thick of it emphasises the active role of play and is indicative of a trend towards action-adventure based games that is now a norm.

Despite the lack of big budget games that adapt *Frankenstein* in the contemporary marketplace, there are two PC-based casual offerings that refer directly back to the novel: *Frankenstein: The Dismembered Bride* (henceforth *Dismembered Bride*) and *Frankenstein: Master of Death* (Jetdogs/ Fineway 2015) (henceforth *Master of Death*). One is more literary than the other, yet both are low-budget, point-and-click style puzzle/hidden object games. The first takes a tongue-in-cheek, schlock-comedic approach, name checking *The Rocky Horror Picture Show* (1975) through its protagonists Brad and Janet. Brad sets out to rescue the pieces of Janet's body that can be found secreted around the Castle, guided by her disembodied brain. This 'find the body parts' approach to gamifying *Frankenstein* is also found in earlier games such as *Dr. Franken* (1992), published for the Super Nintendo Entertainment System (SNES). In its crass literality, the comedic approach draws on a tradition of sending up the Gothic, galvanised by Jane Austen's *Northanger Abbey* (1817), in so doing deflating the necessary pretention required to construct a Gothic frame for rendering metaphysical matters related to the (post) human. Such reframing of the genre is perhaps more suitable in the context of games for a casual and populist market looking for low-commitment distraction.

Frankenstein: Master of Death uses the same point-and-click puzzle format, but it takes the subject matter much more seriously as Gothic SF. Its puzzles are more intricate and well crafted than those of *Dismembered Bride*. There are many such games based on Gothic literary subjects, some featuring writers like Edgar Allan Poe and Nathaniel Hawthorne. Perhaps taking their cue from Poe's blueprint detective Dupin, these games place the player as a detective. The puzzles in this case are quite diverse: there are maze puzzles and jigsaw-style puzzles, along with the staple hunt-the-object static screens. The solutions of these puzzles provide access to objects needed to unlock new areas. Two-dimensional games do not provide players with the unified spaces that can be run around in. Instead, each room or area of the game space is presented from three to seven angles, each area to be explored in depth. This slows down the pace of play and is more akin to reading in terms of attention to the information presented on screen. The game does have points of dramatic excitement, provided by simple cut scenes. In this case, these represent the nodes of the story beginning with the creature abducting Victor's wife, Elizabeth. In this version however, Victor needs to be rescued and was the innocent victim of his patron, the evil Baron Igor. Successful traversal of the puzzles finds Victor and Elizabeth rescued, the Monster freed from his miserable existence and the evil Baron apprehended, all due to the puzzling perspicacity of the player. As the game publicity says: 'Help restore the course of nature and save Victor and his wife, Elizabeth!' This resolution works against the moral ambiguities of the novel. The categorical need for games to provide for the player a winning condition means that moral ambiguity is not easy to build into games. While the game is well crafted, it still seems to follow the well-worn path of game adaptations wherein the novel's tragic mode is sidelined, a feature of Gothic SF to which this chapter returns.

A very different approach in a ludic sense is taken by *Frankenstein: The Monster Returns*, made for the Nintendo Entertainment System (NES) in 1990. This game was made during the wave of Frankenstein games made in the early 1990s, but this one is indicative of a shift further away from direct adaptation. Here, any literary based elements are sidelined in favour of a more verb-based game grammar. The game loop is far more action-based, favouring a side-scrolling platform adventure format punctuated with beat-'em-up style elements. The game's 'return' is less to Shelley's novel and more to the arcade and the iconography of Universal's monster, all bolts, blanket stitch and flattened head. In the context of the arcade game, the monster is simply a cipher, drained of the uncanny intention embodied by Theodor von Holst's illustration of the monster published in 1831. Ironically, it is this illustration, with its William Blakean style of anatomy, black locks and haunted look (hearkening back to Blake's Hecate), that is adopted in more recent adaptations such as the TV series *Penny Dreadful*, where the tragic situation of Gothic SF is emphasised.

INDIRECT ADAPTATION: WORLD OF WARCRAFT AS FRANKENSTEIN TEXT

Having looked at the bulk of the existing direct adaptation games and ascertained some of the ways in which gamification, through its reliance on action and winning condition, has tended to diminish the tragic matrix that defines the novel as Gothic SF, I turn now to more diffuse examples of *Frankenstein*'s (and Frankenstein's) legacy. As might be expected, this takes us into the generic realm of monsters and mad scientists and an analysis of the monstrous, creativity and death in games.

Developed and published by US game studio Blizzard, *World of Warcraft* (2005-present) (*WoW* hereinafter) is a massively multiplayer role-playing online game that has had over 11 million subscribers world-wide. While this game is not in any way a direct adaptation of Shelley's novel, its themes and related iconography provide the game with one of its key formal strands. The Warcraft franchise is mainly indebted to Tolkien's world creation, which owes its own debt to *Frankenstein* in the origination of the Uruk'hai. It is this refracted legacy that informs *WoW*. Blizzard has evolved its game-led approach to world design since the release of its first game, *Warcraft: Orcs & Humans*, in 1994. For the uninitiated, *WoW* splits its players into two contesting factions, Horde and Alliance. Each faction includes a variety of races drawn from the fantasy canon (Elves, Orcs, Undead, Humans, Dwarves, etc.). Unlike Tolkien's moral Manicheanism, *WoW* employs a relativist moral structure. Crimes and cruelty have been perpetrated on both sides; alliances are common but often break, providing the source of tension and keeping conflict in play over the franchise's evolution. In service of moral relativity, corruption is used as a dramatic and thematic device and it is this that hooks the game so strongly back into *Frankenstein's* legacy on its own terms, translated into the characteristic lore, ludic and visual grammar of the Warcraft world. Central protagonist characters such as Arthas, Gul'dan, Illidan Stormrage, and Grom Hellscream, as well as lesser characters such as the Barov family, are each seduced by the immense power and immortality offered by demonic forces, which constantly threaten slavery, dehumanisation and annihilation. Following the rule of hubris, the power quest of such characters leads to betrayal, genocide and, in the case of Arthas, patricide. Their machinations often involve the use of demon science as a means of reanimating the dead, thereby transgressing the most basic of taboos. Such a threat was established in *Warcraft 3* where the Necromancer demon Kel'Thuzad killed humans to transform them into a zombie army.

There is no differentiation between science and magic in Warcraft. What is key is the exercise of power and control. It provides both mythos and the stuff of gameplay. As such, the Frankenstein legacy is at work within the classes and races in the game. Warlocks and Shadow Priests can wield demonic powers, both able to surrender life (gamified as health points) for power; Shadow Priests' power is based on gradually trading sanity for power, much as Frankenstein (rather less intentionally) traded his life and sanity for knowledge and power. It is, however, the Undead race that has the closest links to the Frankensteinian theme of reanimation. The Undead were originally simply enslaved to the Lich King, known as The Scourge, but some regained their free will when his defences were down, forming a rebel group known as the 'Forsaken', led by Lady Sylvanas Windrunner. If a player chooses to play as an Undead character, they find themselves at the start of the game resurrected by a Val'kyr and are informed of their Forsaken heritage, including their hatred of the humans who betrayed them under the leadership of Arthas Menethil. In direct homage, the choice of character model for the female Undead includes a version of Universal's 'Bride' (see Fig. 16.2). The Forsaken race also draws on other aspects of Universal Horror, with the male characters often voiced in upper-class British accents (à la Peter Cushing, Hammer's Frankenstein), and they are mainly shown as alchemists or apothecaries, seeking thereby to create poisons that will kill humans and resurrect the dead but who retain free will, a feature that distinguishes Shelley's creature from most film-based Zombies, including those passive Worker Zombies in *White Zombie* (1932). As such, the Undead cities, towns and land within the game draw heavily from Universal's representation of Frankenstein's lab and electrical equipment (Figs. 16.2 and 16.3), lit by an irradiated acid green glowing light to further conjure an eerie and unnatural atmosphere, first seen in Universal's posters for their films.

Frankenstein's legacy is exemplified in the design of the instanced location Scholomance, a school used for teaching necromancy, founded by Kel'Thuzad (an 'instance' in a Massively Multiplayer Online Role-Playing Game (MMORPG) is a copy of particular space that is limited to a small

Fig. 16.2 Iconographies of *Frankenstein* in the *World of Warcraft*. The Undead female model shown here draws on the iconographic gravity-defying hair of Universal's Bride

Fig. 16.3 Growing a zombie army: where *Warcraft* meets Tolkien and *Frankenstein*

group of people). Various storylines and world conditions that are associated with Kel'Thuzad's school are informed by Frankenstein's legacy. The Necromancers of Scholomance, for example, sought power through the reanimation of the dead. Saruman's schemes to build an army or Uruk'hai in *The Lord of the Rings*, finds its articulation in *WoW* by way of Frankenstein and the Golem. The 'Stitched Horrors' and 'Abominations' of *WoW* are not born of earth, however, but made of body parts, admittedly rather cartoonish yet in keeping with Blizzard's visual vocabulary. In blending Necromancers with mad scientists, we might assume the game is unable to access tragedy and, therefore, Gothic SF; this is not so, as the outsider race of Undead demonstrates. Underlining Warcraft's moral relativity, monstrosity is often called into question, and as with Shelley's novel, it is often unclear *who* is the monster. Yet monster nomenclature falls back on normative ways as a kind of parody of Linnaeus' taxonomy, which is used to distinguish between models of cannon-fodder monsters. As a kind of database of dirt, monsters named 'unnatural', 'filth', 'cursed' and 'putrid' seem to be pulled straight from the pages of Mary Douglas and Julia Kristeva's work on boundaries. As Muriel Spark has noted of *Frankenstein*, emphasis is placed on the terms of Horror, 'filth' and 'pollution' as inversions of the natural order (1988: 159), words reminiscent of biblical tax-onomies of the unholy. What is of note in this semiotic confusion is that Warcraft follows Shelley's *Frankenstein* in mobilising the outcast and reviled in order to create a sense of tragedy and engender a sense of our fragile and finite condition. On this theme, I turn now from adaptation in the traditional sense to a more oblique and interpretative understanding of the legacy of *Frankenstein* to address how games and related computing technologies enable their own generative engagement with corporeal collaging.

CORPOREAL COLLAGING: CREATIVITY, DEATH AND TRAGEDY

Corporeal recombination and reinvention, 'filthy creation' as Shelley has Frankenstein put it, lies at the core of *Frankenstein* as well as its artistic, cultural and technological legacy. Such manipulation is often rhetorical or generically framed as diabolical, dystopian or post-human in the most per-verse sense, yet it also has creative and generative dimensions. Janine Chasseguet-Smirgel (1985) locates creativity within a psychological and perverse process of challenging and capsizing the rule of the Father. In this context, creativity is a form of dissent, a refusal of the received 'order of things' that overturns convention and radical reinvention.

Games certainly do undertake reinvention as adaptational remediation, yet they do so through the imposition of conventionalised rules to create goal-directed play. In this sense, they are far from anarchic reinvention machines; dependent on ludic grammar and laid down by the underlying programming (no matter how complex), their law is also incontrovertible from the point of view of the player. Here law is not in itself ideological or cultural (even though the *nature* of a game's laws can be said to be so) but is instead procedural and constitutive, much as we might say is true of language, where its structure exists outside culture, but its expression does not. It is difficult, without specialist knowledge, therefore, to subvert the infrastructure of games, except for those hackers and glitchers who then become Frankensteinian exceptions who can creatively edit or circumvent a game's genetic/master code.

Most players are nonetheless subject to the 'law' of the game, even though games sell themselves on the basis of providing players with a sense of agency and mastery of the game system: this is the pay-off for living by the (game) rules. Game designers, however, may, under some conditions, seek to create their game in accordance with their own perverse worlds and against the grain of the normative game grammar. Certain games, such as the first *Bioshock*, *The Stanley Parable* and *September 12*, play artfully, perversely, with game grammar and they do so in these cases to highlight a paradox at the heart of videogames that most players generally overlook. If players play along with the predefined rules and go through all the set hoops, they accrue its intended pleasures including the achievement of a strong sense of mastery. This mastery is of course highly bounded and localised, often quite hard won and demanding of both close attention and time (and so we learn the lesson of deferred gratification and perseverance so necessary for capitalism to operate). Within this closed behaviourist loop also comes the danger of a compulsion to repeat, in other words that which Freud terms the death drive (Freud 2003). Intrinsic to this is what might be thought of as a denial or disavowal of real death. Of our certain death, the real of our finite time, of our extreme fragility, fleeting and uncertain lifespan (I remind myself of this to little effect every time I make yet another new character in *World of Warcraft*). As such, videogames might be said to be Frankensteinian in their capacity to invent a safe virtual world (a fetish world we might say) within which it is possible to cheat death, reset time (I've died … time to try again!) and where it is possible to have mastery over a well-ordered and predictable world, a place outside of real time where tragedy is unable to reside and where SF has only a weak claim on the Gothic.

Central to Chasseguet-Smirgel's model of perverse creativity is that established modes of definition, such as that provided by physics, gender or the image of Vitruvian man made in the mode of God's sacred geometry, are 'unbelieved', dismantled and radically reassembled. Seen in this way, Frankenstein's crime becomes a radical generative act: he is a creative and curious practitioner in an age where creation was the incontestable preserve of God. As Shelley puts it in an account of her own creation, 'I saw the hideous phantasm of a man stretched out; and then, on the working of some powerful engine, show signs of life, and stir with an uneasy, half-vital motion. Frightful it must be; for supremely frightful must be the effect of any human endeavour to mock the stupendous mechanism of the Creator of the world' (1985: 9). Seeking to gain mastery over 'the nature of the principle of life' (1985: 8), Frankenstein becomes the Prometheus of his time and, as dictated by hubris, he follows in the tragic footsteps of many audacious and short-lived creators in mythology, such as Arachne, Daedalus, Salmoneus and Niobe.

Computing too has this generative and hubristic capacity to allow us to reinvent physics and bodies within virtual worlds, as well as enabling the invention of sentient intelligences that are now able to learn and adapt beyond their coder's intention. Because everything in a videogame is code, what it produces is totally customisable. Even Newtonian physics can be disregarded. The potential for the play of perverse creativity in the representational domain of the corporeal is therefore limitless. For example, in *Conan Exiles*, such customisability is passed over to players in a bounded form, allowing them to choose, from a range of developer-defined characteristics, the look and build of the character they will play in the game. This ability to collage together a character is certainly within the remit of the Frankenstein legacy within games. However, in most games, the creative affordance is limited, offering little room for a Surrealist Exquisite corps/corpse. *Second Life* by contrast, offering more of play-ground than a game, allows players much greater freedom to collage their avatar's bodies. While very free corporeal collaging is likely to present issues for animation rigging, *Conan Exiles* also allows players to customise their character's genitals. This certainly provides an eye-catching selling point and chimes with the exaggerated libidinal economy of Howard's creation. The ability to customise in this way is perverse in some sense, yet normative limits are nonetheless set on the scope of corporeal collaging in a way that is not the case in *Second Life*.

Second Life's vast array of creative affordances has led to a stiff and lucrative trade in player-made body parts. This post-human ability to play with corporeal collage that can transcend gender/sex alignments has attracted the attention of those with an interest in bondage and fetish subcultures. Default characters had no genital options, and taking advantage of the customisability central to this virtual world and its multi-formed citizens, enterprising players sold add-on genitals of many different descriptions to other players, often in support of sexual role-play. In a kind of modern-day *Frankenstein* meets *120 Days of Sodom*, genitals became detached from gender and even from human form, able to be placed literally anywhere and made to order. This latter example is perhaps the strongest entry into a Frankensteinian perverse creativity in virtual worlds, enabled by the hypothetical and ultimately malleable potential of game technologies. While *Frankenstein* did not make a conscious appeal to the pornographic imagination, it is not so far from its surface. It should also be noted that *Second Life's* corporeal ingenuities are edits located within the field of representation, operating there as an art or craft. However, such imaginary engagement should be regarded as symptomatic of the uncomfortable, Othered reality of our own bodies, which we vainly endeavour to extend, control and change through various means in a creative effort to affect greater physical, sociocultural or aesthetic agency.

Chasseguet-Smirgel characterises the links between creativity and perversity in an analysis of the artist Hans Bellmer's sculpture/photographic work entitled 'The Doll' (1936) alongside H. G. Wells' fictional character, Dr Moreau (*The Island of Doctor Moreau*, 1896). The latter is of interest to our examination of Frankenstein's legacy in games, and more generally, as Moreau might be regarded as more guilty and less tragic than Frankenstein, on the basis that Moreau's relation to his creations never shifts from a position of mastery. In *The Island of Doctor Moreau*, hybridity is not figured as an inter-human collage or an intimate relational dynamic between creator and creature. Instead, it is located in a perverse erasure of boundaries between the human and animal. While in mythology most manimals are naturalised (as with centaurs or harpies) and humans are transformed into animal form as punishment, in Wells' novel, technology is deployed in a supremely creative act that challenges God's biblical command that man and animals are radically separate. Such creative corporeal collaging that challenges bodily norms is also at work in Bellmer's artwork. He concocts a refigured female body through sculpture and photography with a clear erotic intention: limbs are patched into new places, often lending greater emphasis on points of entry into the body. The remodelling of the body is also found in some of his follow-on photographic work where a woman's body is bound with twine to create a new figurative landscape, generating additional new folds and fissures (see Fig. 16.4) (Bellmer 2005). The 'mastery' here over bodily form is represented through the grammar of bondage and sadomasochism ('dollification' is a term used in the subculture), while the title refers, simultaneously and obliquely, to E. T. A. Hoffmann's tale of the dancer/puppet Olympia in 'The Sandman' (1817). The notion of corporeal collage is also clearly referred to in this tale at multiple levels. The story's protagonist reports what happened when, as a child, he is caught spying on his father's and Dr Coppelius' mysterious alchemical work. After his father intervenes to save him from the punishment of blindness, Coppelius responds, '"The boy can have his eyes then, and keep the use of them. But now let us observe the mechanism of the hands and feet". And with that he seized me so violently that my joints cracked, unscrewed my hands and feet, and fixed them on again this way, now that' (1982: 91–2). Moving forward to vid-

Fig. 16.4 Hans Bellmer's sculpture/ photographic series entitled *The Doll* c.1936

Fig. 16.5 Collaged corporealities in the Silent Hill games

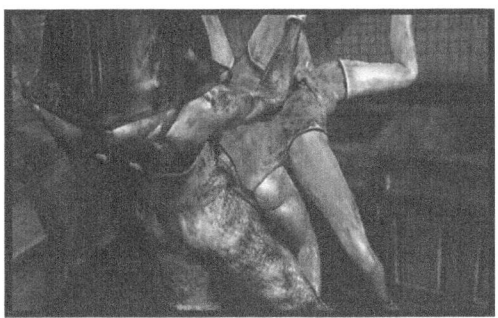

eogames, the perverse capacity of computer-based graphics to reinvent bodies is perhaps best emblematised by the zombie nurses in the Silent Hill games (Figs. 16.5 and 16.6) who bear a direct debt to Bellmer's corporeal collaging. Their bodies are no longer whole. They are animated but no longer human, images thrown up from Hieronymus Bosch's Hell-bound victims, formed as literal renditions of 'making the beast with two backs'. In all of these cases, along with Frankenstein, corporeal collaging has a perverse and creative dimension.

The legacy of *Frankenstein* within games is far broader than simply a case of direct adaptation. It may be discovered at a more fundamental level

Fig. 16.6 Collaged corporealities, channelling Hans Bellmer's *The Doll* in *Silent Hill 2*

where it is connected to the daemonic status of creativity itself and its tendency to disavow not only the real of the body but also that relentless guarantor of the real, death. What we have lost here in this unlimited and lawless world of sensationalist, creative and perverse collaging is the brooding sense of the tragic, something that's stitched into the heart of Shelley's novel and which lends greater potency to the otherwise sensationalist and perverse Gothic. The winning condition of games puts the player back in the place of the master and not in the place of the fallen; the challenge for games is, therefore, how they can invoke tragedy while retaining the particularity of their form. This passage from Byron's unfinished play *Heaven and Earth* evokes the sublime effect of tragedy and serves as definition (Byron 1821):

> No azure more shall robe the firmament,
> Nor spangled stars be glorious: Death hath risen:
> In the Sun's place, a pale and ghastly glare
> Hath wound itself around the dying air.

What then if the creativity we speak of is not human, not *of* the human? What if it is synthetic and self-motivated? Could this be a source of tragedy in games, or *of* games? Is this where the human becomes once more positioned as finite and fragile? Computational creativity is gaining purchase in the creative industries. Many games now have algorithmic elements designed to track player behaviours so that a game's mechanics can be altered to fit the skills and habits of a player. This is mainly used in a benevolent way to prevent a player from failing and to gain therefore a sense of heroism and mastery, yet there are notable exceptions.

Left for Dead (2007) (*L4D* henceforth) is a co-operative game played over the internet. One of its innovative features that resonates so well with Frankenstein's legacy is its surveillance artificial intelligence (AI) known anthropomorphically as 'The Director'. This is an internal computational procedure that has no direct representation on the screen. It monitors players' behaviours so that if they remain static for too long, a new zombie horde is triggered to jolt them out of idleness and prevent them from recovering equilibrium to continue. The ever-present sense of this agentic and hostile presence heightens a player's sense of wariness; players feel observed and judged as if The Director is a real, knowing entity that responds intelligently and not mechanically to events. The Director's occulted yet highly powerful presence emphasises a player's sense of individuality, vulnerability and powerlessness. As the 'rules' that this AI is governed by are not known, players never really get a measure of when they will be caught out. There are many familiar monsters in the game, represented in terms of the usual stuff of Horror films. However, it is The Director that is the new monster on the block. It remains unseen, without physical form, but is omnipresent, creative and often seems incredibly perverse in terms of usual game grammars built on building up a player's sense of mastery. It also frequently, but not reliably, attacks players when they are at their most vulnerable. Given its inscrutability, The Director's behaviour and powers are often guessed at by increasingly paranoid players, lending this hidden monster something of an urban myth.

All this inscrutability, power and unpredictability has the effect of heightening the sense of feeling hunted, an affective feature drawn so well within the pages of *Frankenstein* where both protagonists turn from hunter to hunted at various points. This feature also carries forward into the post-Romero zombie sub-genre where the boundaries between life and death have broken down, and the general tone is not of action-movie aesthetics (heroic action leading to a final resolution) but instead based on survival. This model has been adopted within Survival Horror games and has a very different, far more muted sense of agency than in most other action-adventure games. But even in most Survival Horror games there is usually a boss held out to beat. *L4D*'s Director is not a final 'boss' monster. It cannot be bested, or fought; all the player can do is react to its machinations. This presiding, inhuman figure is then a monster of a different order, a demon child of computational creativity who is blind to human suffering or the need to prevail. But unlike the curious yet oddly Oedipal AI of Donald Cammell's film *Demon Seed* (1977), The Director has no interest in gaining corporeality and its effects. The Director is always off-scene and unseen. This presence is therefore transmuted into a form of occulted cosmic horror: an intangible agent looking to engineer our doom.

Like George Romero's zombie films, *L4D* has no overall winning condition and, unlike role-playing games, there is no creative, playful space for collaging your character. Instead, we are left with a sense of dread and the futility of our pathetic egos in the face of our imminent and inevitable demise. I would offer that it is in this bleak scenario that the tragedy that lies at the heart of *Frankenstein* as Gothic SF can be most keenly felt. Because games centralise mastery and winning, it is (perversely) possible to design an experience that makes use of that narcissistic capacity to create for players a heightened sense of tragedy. Accessed through Survival Horror and the presence of generative technology that no longer serves as friend and helper—a 'hideous progeny' as Shelley called her own creation in her introduction to the 1831 edition of the novel (1985: 10)—we can experience the oddly life-affirming demonstration of inherent infallibility.

FRANKENSTEIN-BASED GAMES

Dr Franken. 1992. Elite Systems, Movietime Ltd./Kemco, Elite Systems, Markoc Chain, DTMC.
Frankenstein. 1987. CRL Group.
———. 2011. Inkle Studios.
Frankenstein: Master of Death. 2015. Jetdogs Studios/Fineway Studios.
Frankenstein: The Dismembered Bride. 2009. Mzone Studio & SOLILAB/Gameloft/Ludigames.
Frankenstein: The Monster Returns. 1990. Bandai, Tose/Bandai Namco.
Frankenstein: Through the Eyes of a Monster. 1995. Amazing Media/Interplay Entertainment.

Silent Hill 2. 2001. Konami Computer Entertainment/Konami.
Warcraft: Orcs & Humans. 1994. Blizzard.
World of Warcraft. 2005-present. Blizzard/Blizzard.

WORKS CITED

Bellmer, Hans. 2005. *The Doll.* Trans. Malcolm Green. London: Atlas Press.
Branagh, Kenneth. 1994. *Mary Shelley's Frankenstein.* Dir. Kenneth Branagh.
Byron, George Gordon. 2015. *Heaven and Earth: A Mystery,* ed. Ernest Hartley Coleridge. CreateSpace Independent Publishing Platform (Amazon).
Casseguet-Smirgel, Jannine. 1985. *Creativity and Perversion.* London: Free Association Books.
Freud, Sigmund. 2003. *Beyond the Pleasure Principle: And Other Writings.* Trans. James Strachey. Harmondsworth: Penguin.
Hoffmann, E.T.A. 1982. The Sandman. In *Tales of Hoffman.* Trans. R. J. Hollingdale. Harmondsworth: Penguin Books.
Shelley, Mary. 1985. *Frankenstein.* London: Penguin Books.
Spark, Muriel. 1988. *Mary Shelley.* London: Penguin Book.
Wells, H.G. 2017. *The Island of Dr. Moreau and Other Stories.* Ware: Wordsworth Editions.

CHAPTER 17

What *Was* Man…? Reimagining Monstrosity from Humanism to Trashumanism

Fred Botting

By the turn of the second millennium, *Frankenstein*, Frankenstein, and Monster seemed drained of cultural resonance. The Promethean and patriarchal figures which articulated their significance as human and huMan myths of power and production no longer chimed with a world in which posthuman imperatives reshaped issues of identity, technology, commerce, and nature. Scientific knowledge, ambition, overreaching, presumption, and transgression had delivered powers that decentred humanity; monstrous resistance had enabled new voices to render indefensible and transvalue forms of hierarchy, privilege, and exclusion. The last iterations of *Frankenstein* charted transitions from human to posthuman, from the threat posed by monstrosity to its promise of different identities. The process saw monstrosity, once so intimately bound to humanity, become absorbed by its reflected image or go its own ways: monsters marked final attempts to secure a sense of human identity through difference or abandoned any pretence of relation, mutating into a host of autonomous hybrids. The bases of such divisions and deviations are covertly embedded in Mary Shelley's novel: both self-assertion and self-effacement inform

F. Botting (✉)
Faculty of Arts and Social Sciences, Kingston University,
Kingston upon Thames, UK

© The Author(s) 2018
C. M. Davison, M. Mulvey-Roberts (eds.), *Global Frankenstein*,
Studies in Global Science Fiction,
https://doi.org/10.1007/978-3-319-78142-6_17

movements in which realising human mastery over nature—a transgression (or 'presumption') of divine natural order—also inaugurated a trajectory in which humanity is coterminous with its own production of excess: creation, scientific and technical especially, from the start encodes the supersession of the creator.

Critical interrogations of the limits and implications of human productive power determine late twentieth-century readings of *Frankenstein*. Two dominant lines of criticism follow from concerns with patriarchal, Promethean production: one concerned with the development of uncontrollable mechanisms for the domination and exploitation of nature (Victor as the overreacher) and another monstrously addressed to inhumane institutions (family, law, state). Feminist criticism, in the forefront of the second line of attack, and taking its cue from Mary Wollstonecraft, noted the exclusion of women from education, economic activity, literary canons, and political life. It reread the novel as an articulation of female experience under patriarchy and a call for justice and vindication of rights: subordinated, even murdered, females in the novel are reinterpreted as positive figures, monsters challenging marginalisation, domestic confinement, and political exclusion (see Hoeveler 2003). A maltreated monster comes to voice suffering and anger, especially towards those institutions in which sexual freedoms are bound. The monster's rage against prejudice finds itself most passionately identified with transsexual defiance of social norms: 'I am a transsexual, and therefore I am a monster' (Stryker 1994: 240).

The monster disturbed distinctions between nature and culture, leaving neither pole secure. It unnaturally engendered reversals or elisions of good and evil, persecutor and persecuted, and male and female, manifesting queer potential by undermining fixed identities. Disturbing nineteenth-century categories and values, monstrosity radically shifts focus from exclusion to the production of difference and identity: the novel is not about making monsters but concerns the 'making of a human' (Halberstam 1995: 32). Not only does this inversion disclose the 'constructedness of all identity', it places greater affective weight on monstrosity's role in securing and defining selfhood in late twentieth-century retrospections and on recoveries of difference, disclosing 'a kind of ahistorical desire on the part of the modern reader that seeks an answer to the question of identity in the form of a monster' (38). While identity politics challenge disenfranchisement and marginalisation, moving to an affirmative monstrosity (monstrosity as the promise of identity), the other main line of criticism remains more cautionary in respect of the powers invested in and unleashed by patriarchal production: a critical gaze turns on Victor Frankenstein and to the dangers of the bourgeois, liberal, and scientific humanism he embodies. His creation, in this respect, demonstrates the failings embedded in masculine attempts to control nature, usurp female reproductive capacity, and institute a monocular vision on the world. The enactment of male power over nature and female bodies and the resulting consequences are played out particularly strongly in science fictions from the later part of the twentieth century: films and fictions like *The Terminator* and *Neuromancer* manifest monstrous extremes of inhuman production and artificial reproduction through cybernetic systems, cyborgs, and biotechnologies, to the point that machines are 'reproduced by machines', like the 'race of devils' imagined by Victor (Cavallaro 2000: 2; Gusterson 1995: 109; Roof 1996: 88; Shelley 1969: 165).

Science's powers of dehumanisation, however, take patriarchal Prometheanism to the brink of extinction. Brian Easlea (1983), discussing nuclear weapons, summarises the issue succinctly when he describes it as 'fathering the unthinkable'. The hubris of patriarchal Prometheanism also leads to associations between Frankenstein's project and the potential of the biological sciences to remake the contours of life. In physiology, molecular biology, and genetic engineering, new discoveries and applications assumed monstrous shapes (Turney 1998). From here, it is a short step to gothic neologisms like 'Frankenfoods' and 'Frankenfish'. Life, indeed, no longer need be organic or material: 'living systems', understood in terms of information, pattern, and the ability to self-organise, describe both organisms that exist in the world and those developed by computer programmes and simulations. As a 'legacy of Mary Shelley', artificial intelligence combines research in biology and digital computing to take 'humankind to the threshold of duplicating nature's masterpiece, living systems' (Levy 1992: 11). It is easy not only to imagine—in horror—the supersession of human production and reproduction but also to glimpse the creation of monstrous inhuman intelligence capable of extinguishing the species. Arthur C. Clarke's story, 'Dial "F" for Frankenstein', begins at the moment every automated telephone exchange in the world is linked by satellite: roads quickly become jammed as lights turn red; anomalies are reported in air traffic control systems; automated banking leads to serious errors; public communication broadcasts stop. When missiles are fired automatically and without apparent cause from military installations, the connection between apparently accidental events is made:

with more switches than the billions of neurons enabling consciousness, the newly integrated telephone network has achieved sentience. Only a day old, however, its intelligence, though powerful, is not considered to be mature: a hostile, destructive infant, this new distributed electronic consciousness should be shut down. Before that can happen, it takes control. Wryly, a scientist realises it is the end, not with a bang but with a ring: 'but he knew already that it was far, far too late. For Homo Sapiens the telephone bell had tolled' (Clarke 1995: 686). Unlike later versions of the same scenario (the nuclear apocalypse caused by the coming to consciousness of planetary computer networks in *The Terminator*), the story readily accepts humans being supplanted by their own machines.

Resistance Is Futile

'We are cyborgs', observes Donna Haraway, as she plots the intimate and liberating interconnections between bodies, information, and machines. Frankenstein's monster, of course, is cited as part of a history bypassed by technological, materialist, and feminist movements: unlike the monster, who turns to the father for help, the cyborg looks elsewhere (Haraway 1990: 192–3). 'Was man, indeed', the creature asks, 'at once so powerful, so virtuous, and magnificent, yet so vicious and so base?' (Shelley 1969: 119). Human dualities and oppositions are no longer adequate to understanding the diverse, multiple, and increasingly autonomous cyborg-monsters created by posthuman machine-organic, natural-cultural networks. A dual and divided humanity is relegated to the past tense. Identity becomes partial, plural, fluid, and hybrid. Corporeal and affective affinities become multiple and differential. Techno-materialist networks undo humanist hierarchies of power and prejudice, from familial order and oedipal sexualisation, to sexual, racial, natural, and species subordination and exploitation. There remain, for all this, questions of control, what Haraway calls the 'informatics of domination' (1990: 200).

Frankenstein, nonetheless, has continued to provide metaphors mediating moves towards posthuman forms. Shelley Jackson's celebrated hypertext fiction *Patchwork Girl* (1995) has female monstrosity and sexuality reanimated by Mary Shelley and re-contextualised in a non-linear and non-hierarchical space. Metaphors of threads, stitching, seams, sewing, and weaving become modes of productive technical transformation that not only recall the powers given to the notion of text by Roland Barthes but invoke histories of female technoscientific endeavour in the creation and development of difference engines, computers, and networks (Barthes 1977; Plant 1997). *Patchwork Girl* not only has *Frankenstein* move to a new context of social-sexual relations, the text migrates to develop in the space of new media, hypertextual forms that are equally monstrous in the potential they manifest: the shift from print to network turns physical and fixed pages into navigable screens and allows dynamic interlayering and the recombination of fragments, disrupting stable boundaries and reassembling multiple senses of subjectivity and corporeality. Reading relations are transformed in the process, the reader becoming a 'cyborg' whose identity and cognitive ability is distributed across different nodes in the text network (Hayles 2000: 13). Consciousness and embodiment change in the diffuse cybernetic environments of posthumanism, as Hayles catalogues elsewhere (1999). Apparently simple shifts from print to monitor screen, from analogue to digital processing, disclose radical openings to another realm in which materialities of human bodies, histories, and cultures are subjected to extensive reconfiguration by information, de-, and re-coding subjects in alternate material and medial spaces and forms.

Not only inducing new relations of the self, body, and machine, the implications of posthumanism extend from concerns with the genetic manipulation and exploitation of the planet, to issues of social, military, and political control. For Francis Fukuyama, assessing the biotechnological and pharmacological challenges that await, as he optimistically puts it, in 'our' posthuman future, questions of human nature, rights, and dignity remain at stake. For Arthur Kroker, in contrast, the first-person plural is barely an issue: he wonders whether there is something 'indispensably human' about the 'phantasmagorical essence of the future of technological humanism' (2014: 4). It seems unlikely: the posthuman 'exit' he proposes is more in line with cyberpunk visions, only in an accelerated form: what he calls a 'trans-subjectivity' is 'in the process of abandoning its temporary habitat in human flesh in favor of a permanent orbit of high-intensity connectivity' (24). Here, data assume a more direct agency and vitality; it is data, indeed, that has 'come alive' in an 'extended network of technological organs' (49). Kroker's account plots humanity's disappearance in a posthuman future dominated by 'big data', augmented realities, and genetic modification. It also recognises the pervasive and more mundane extent of the adoption of digital and biological technologies into everyday existence, in particular through the agency and ubiquity of communications and social media. Absorbed into daily life, monstrosity is simply the registration of the residual strangeness pertaining to newly naturalised relations between organisms and machines. For Bruce Sterling, the traces of Frankenstein and monster are evident in any research and development unit, pharmacy and emergency ward, and places where bodies are routinely supported or ameliorated or sustained by biotechnological devices (cit. Johnson 1996: 101). Media, too, are full of monsters, though spectacular terrors from a gothic tradition are supplanted by the fascination, disgust, and prurience evoked by tales of celebrity scandal, breakdown, misdemeanour, pharmaceutical, or surgical disaster (Chocano 2011). Frankenstein may still be invoked as a technological caution, alerting users to the increasingly impolite, intemperate conditions of a common disembodied milieu provided by social media (Rosenberg 2013). In these models otherness is less and less evident. Monsters do not tell a story of difference or furnish identity with the uniqueness or excess expected by a narcissistic and discrete individual. Too human and not human enough—to the point that being human and being monster have become indistinguishable—monstrosity cannot see itself in the mirror, whether returning its own hideous features or glimpsing itself in the fear of another's gaze. For Baudrillard, as self-identity collapses on its self in the hyperreal circulation of sameness and manic autism, otherness dissipates: 'the problem of Frankenstein, for example, is that he has no Other and craves otherness' (1994: 109). It is lonely online, especially in a global network. The predicament becomes posthuman not in the grand sense of global species eradication, but in the daily fact of life being human without humans, life auto-amputated as much as it is incorporated into the extended digital nervous system. A 'figure for the relation of humans online to machines', 'high-tech Frankenstein' gently, mundanely reiterates the question of humanity's place 'in a world of bioengineered nature and information machines'. This figure, however, also provides 'an opening to globalized machinic post-humanity' (Poster 2002: 29–30).

Repetition habituates humans to, and distracts them from, questions of posthumanism: from promises of unprecedented hybridity to come, monsters become decoys, wolf boys, their misdirected alarms prompting little more than indifference. The security offered by monsters as protectors of boundaries and outlets of inherent violence collapses when exception and singularity are erased in the swirl of global transformation. With posthumanism, hybrids abound and boundaries fail. This does not imply the absence of domination or control, only its decentralisation and obfuscation by clouds of difference. De- and re-materialisations of bodies into bits of information tear up traditions and habits and enable an array of new combinations and systems of control; genetic technologies rewrite codes of life; digital media reinscribe realities in a manner that makes the bases of life exchangeable, substitutable, disposable, and, of course, commodifiable. Modified genes and genetic therapies can be patented and marketed, life 'enterprised up' (Haraway 1997: 12). 'Oncomouse', a genetically modified rodent and cancer cure, is not a living animal in an older evolutionary sense but an organic machine linked to devices and programmes instrumental in its development and to the medical patents, innovations, and applications to which it gives rise: an inmixing of 'metaphor and material fact', it is also a compound creature of 'category-crossing' and becoming, a kind of 'vampire' notable—like capital itself—for its capacity to transmute purity, heredity, identity, community, sexuality, race, and objectivity into profit (79). Monstrosity here aligns with capital in the shape of the vampire hero of techno-consumerist neoliberalism.

Divisions of capital—globalised and digitised—shape and reshape the world according to dynamic patterns of monstrosity. Even though the two main antagonists of global capital—'empire' and 'multitude'—stage a familiar class dialectic, ambiguity shrouds the political dispositions of the monsters that emerge. No longer bound to the historical materialism of industrial exploitation and physical labour, empire moves into an immaterial realm of information, networks, and media, producing life (modes of existence) and ways of life (cultural forms). Without outside or limit it is a global vampire-empire feeding on the creativity, desires, affections, and liberatory impulses of the multitude: it inscribes a total space of 'spectral' power in which fantasy and fear are sources of control (Hardt and Negri 2000: 48, 323). But multitude also sustains something in excess of empire, a 'life in common', a potentiality and vitality linked to more collaborative and cooperative modes of existence (192). Difference, however, is difficult to discern, let alone sustain (125). Vampiric forms also characterise the multitude as affective, creative networks of political sociality beyond regimes based on hierarchy, family, and unified identity: they serve as reminders that 'we are all monsters', all freaks, outcasts, and aliens opposed to mechanisms of biopolitical control (Hardt and Negri 2006: 193). The 'pathos' of Frankenstein's rejected creature is invoked in contrast to a callous humanity: monsters have 'rich emotional lives' while humans 'are emotional cripples' (11). Though threatening and destructive, monsters still hold out the 'promise of wonder and creation'. But in a global system that has generalised and rendered monstrosity banal and exploitable, it remains difficult to sustain the separate creativity or collectivity of a monstrous multitude. Vampire, empire, monster, and multitude overlap: one must love some monsters while combatting others, that is, be discriminating rather than discriminatory in one's political identifications, affections, and dispositions (196).

Under global capitalism, life, like its monsters, is difficult to differentiate from death. Distinctions informing biopolitical power—'*zoe*' and '*bios*'—do not stay in place, according to Giorgio Agamben. As 'simply the fact of living', *zoe* marks out the zone of 'bare life', that is, life beyond the scope of social or political order. In contrast, *bios* denotes the 'form or way of living proper to an individual or group' (Agamben 1995: 1). Opposed to 'bare anonymous life', *bios* signifies life furnished with place and meaning and value, 'the qualified life of the citizen' circumscribed by symbolic and political structures: in the city—the *polis* as figure of human social organisation—bare life is pushed to the margins; in language a human 'separates and opposes himself to his own bare life' (5; 124). Bare life can neither be excluded nor incorporated: a site of excess at which political authority establishes itself as the exception dictating the rules of social existence, bare life is also the place at which law and power are challenged. It delineates and blurs boundaries (11). In a modern state, moreover, as the sway of *bios* is extended and bare life recedes, the 'zone of irreducible indistinction' characterising the relationship becomes more apparent, accompanied by a 'constant need to redefine the threshold in life' (9). If bare or natural life finds itself 'wholly included in the *polis*' thresholds become indistinct (131). On the one hand there is no longer the possibility of bare or natural life outside the reign of the *polis*, and on the other hand, the absence of distinction means that *bios* cannot establish itself above bare life so that 'we are all virtually *homines sacri*' (115). As thresholds lose distinction and decisions on rights to life are simultaneously decisions on death, biopolitics and thanatopolitics conjoin (122; Mbembe 2003). In search of a 'state of exception' with which to guarantee political sovereignty, the 'dominant paradigm' becomes one of 'global civil war' (Agamben 2005: 2). In constantly seeking objects over which it can establish and legitimise its exceptionality, however, biopolitical sovereignty generalises—and incorporates and defuses—the very excesses it requires, engendering further indistinction and manifesting a tendential fall in the rate of exceptionality: 'these thresholds pass [...] beyond the dark boundaries separating life from death in order to identify a new living dead man, a new sacred man' (1995: 131). While Agamben's argument invokes the undead, zombies do not stabilise bare life or provide an ultimate limit figure. They can be killed, but not sacrificed, vacillating between life and death without a vampire's glamorous immortality. As forms of arrested death they signal a move from '*exceptio*' to '*abjectio*' in which the production of sovereign values of life, rights, or nature cedes to an endless recessive degradation of life in vain search of a ground on which categories—even the sacred—can be reasserted. If sovereignty cannot raise itself up it will continue to press down, creating more states of abjection in its search for distinction: the 'biopolitical caesura' is 'mobile', prone to further degradation (1999: 84–5). There is always barer life.

TRASHUMAN

There is violence too. Étienne Balibar re-examines the position of humanity in a global context marked by the blurring of distinctions between human and natural forms and in transitions to posthuman and post-industrial modes of organisation. The shift also involves the emergence of 'ultra-objective' forms of violence (1998: 17). Extreme violence is evident in global pauperisation, enslavement, extermination, and displacement. Physical suffering, moreover, has a moral counterpart: extreme violence is not only directed at bodies but towards subjects in the ruining of self-respect, the 'robbing' of dignity and denial of the possibility of resistance, 'reducing human beings to the status of things to be eliminated or instrumentalized at the will of the world of commodities' (Balibar 2009: 11–13). Such political-economic violence radically and cruelly divides the world: the '"globalization" of various kinds of extreme violence has produced a tendential division of the "globalized" world into *life zones* and *death zones*' (Balibar 2001: 24). Geopolitical divisions (like that between the North and South) see populations living in huge slums on the fringes of cities, struggling to survive, begging and stealing on streets or inhabiting fenced refugee camps. The 'North', the prosperous West, also sees greater levels of economically enforced homelessness, migrancy, and poverty on its streets, even though it tries to make itself into a global 'gated community'. The cruel logic of global division turns living beings into worthless and disposable rejects, already placed below a threshold in which their life, labour, or energy no longer even warrants economic exploitation. These populations, living in the 'death zones' of global empire, are 'always already *superfluous*'. Consigned to a position as waste or detritus they have a name: 'garbage humans' (Balibar 2001: 25).

Frankenstein and creature—all-two human—seem to have no place, deleted by global posthumanism, either in the voracious supersession enacted by the attractive vampires of neoliberalism or in the nonhuman hordes of walking dead that testify to a trashumanist future present, subsisting as refuse, less than meat, and barer than bare life. *Frankenstein* has already disappeared into the 'darkness and distance' of its final horizon, become the 'monstrous literary abortion' it was criticised for being in 1824. The monster, too, becomes an 'abomination', 'humanity's refuse, disposable, abject' (Clarke 2002: 39). Yet monsters reappear: contemporary reiterations of Shelley's novel entirely remediate its monstrosity in line with a posthuman trajectory of hybrid horror heroes from neo-Victorianism, graphic fiction, and familiar mashed myths of marvellously animated fantastic action. Leagues of ordinary monsters turned quasi-superheroes morph their way through impossible crimes and adventures in *Victor Frankenstein* (Paul McGuigan 2015) and *The Frankenstein Chronicles* (ITV Encore, 2015). *I, Frankenstein* (Stuart Beattie 2014) presents a fantasy in which an outcast, superhero monster exists in a world given over to a grand battle between angels and demons. Humanity barely plays a role since the action is given over to the heroism of its reluctant monstrous champion.

The contemporaneity of Bernard Rose's *Frankenstein* (2015), rendered on posters as 'FRANKEN5TE1N', is quite different, both for its setting in a bleakly real urban environment and for its eschewal of fantastically animated scenes and effects. Its use of an uncomplicated, almost documentary visual aesthetic is all the more striking given its allusions to well-known digital productions in the Hollywood monster genre (*Terminator II* and *Resident Evil*) and given that the urban context in which it plays is Los Angeles (LA). The narrative, too, eschews cinematic grandeur, tightly plotted as an updating of the creature's story from *Frankenstein*. Shelley's monster provides the voice-over from the start for scenes shot from the creature's point of view: a bright light shimmers in and out of focus, the sunlight of the 1818 story becoming the surgical glare of a contemporary underground research facility in which the monster-patient drifts in and out of consciousness. The film narrative follows the story of the creature from animation to death. There are differences, however. An obscene Oedipalism intrudes as an attempt to offer motivation, explanation, and (suspect) humanity: the plot includes two scientists, a cold paternal Victor, and a warm, maternal Elizabeth.

In contrast to nostalgic Freudian-humanist sentimentalism, the film's visual and spoken observations on the state of Western society offer a blunter commentary on the causes of monstrosity. Bioscience provides the rationale for the narrative return to Shelley's fiction. A beautiful result of biotechnology, the artificial being, is physically strong and mimetically adaptive but suffers rapid cellular degeneration. Genetic modification and replication, accelerated through what appears to be a large-scale 3D laser printer, cause cancerous growths, almost the entire surface of his skin pocked by tumours and sores. A failed experiment, he must be dispatched. He has, however, one superhuman capacity, an enhanced resistance to dying, whether it is administered through lethal injection, surgical bone-saw, police baton, or a 0.45 calibre bullet. He escapes from the laboratory mortuary, first into the brightness of nature and then into more downbeat neighbourhoods of LA. In tune with the pared down aesthetics of the film, these environments underplay the wealth and pervasiveness of technology common to the setting: just as the minimal laboratory sets placed scanners, monitors, and lasers in the background, so urban scenes economically acknowledge a highly technological society—a swipe card and a smartphone gesture towards ubiquitous networks. Otherwise, the events take place in an apparently non- or sub-technological world of waste areas and unused, abandoned, or no-go zones: the makeshift camps of homeless people, migrants, unemployed, disabled, and mentally ill set up amid the trash beneath freeway overpasses; fenced-off vacant urban lots; garbage-strewn alleyways where tramps sleep and are assaulted; run-down streets populated by beggars, buskers, and prostitutes. With the exception of regular patrols by an overly brutal and mainly white LAPD, these zones are left to those cast from contemporary metropolitan existence. Non-persons live in the non-places of the non-places of supermodernity, at the edges of the rapid communication systems, or round the corner from the shopping malls that serve the flows and nodes of abstracted life.

Bare and brutal environments are inhabited by those consigned to premature death. The bare laboratories where the creature is made reduce human life to the status of a disposable experimental animal. Scenes of care and laboratory learning are punctuated by shots and sounds of pain: a body going into spasms while strapped to a surgical table and violent convulsions as another needle penetrates his skin. The monster is clearly sentient and capable of great physical suffering. Only as a fugitive does 'Monster'—as he calls himself—experience moments of positive fellowship and community. Scripted by Shelley's account of a neonate experience of nature, he appreciates water, air, day, and night, learning about hunger, cold, and fire. Unlike the novel's monster, however, he is not alone, befriending a German Shepherd and sharing resources, knowledge, and skills with a generosity divested of species fears or hierarchies. Their companionship makes subsequent injustice more poignant: the dog is shot by policemen who, in turn, are battered by monstrous revenge. Monster's act of respect and proto-symbolic mourning—carrying the dog's body to a field for burial—are interrupted by more violence: a mob of locals appear with baseball bats to club him repeatedly and drag him behind a tractor through the dirt. He awakens, again strapped down, in a straitjacket in a police-holding cell. Interrogation yields nothing but Dr Elizabeth Frankenstein's swipe card (she denies knowledge of him) and the name he has adopted: 'Monster'. Removed in a police van—again strapped down—he is abused by vindictive officers, then beaten and taken to waste ground, and ejected and made to kneel before summary execution. A bullet in his brain, he comes to under a mound of gravel and walks to a nearby homeless camp. There, in a subway full of refuse, he is drawn to the sound of the blues: the blind singer, unstrapping Monster's straitjacket, assumes he has escaped a mental asylum. He takes Monster under his wing. They scavenge streets and dumpsters together, sleep rough in alleyways, push trolleys of reclaimed rubbish along the deserted concrete LA River channel. It is a brief and limited period of human companionship for Monster, whose developing powers of speech and observation allow him to comment—again in Shelley's words—on the divisions of wealth and status that make him the most abject and solitary of creatures. The re-contextualisation of a nineteenth-century complaint about the heinous inequities of wealth amid the garbage-strewn alleys of a run-down part of twenty-first-century LA offers stark evidence of the absence of human progress. Wretchedness, misery, and poverty remain as visible and palpable as ever. For Monster, too: when the opportunity of a 'mercy deflowering' by a benevolent prostitute goes fatally awry he becomes a friendless fugitive again. He has, by accident, secured the means of narrative climax: her smartphone, still linked to an earlier online search for Elizabeth, leads him, its satellite navigation active, to the remote ranch-laboratory where he was made. His journey, as if to emphasise his abjection, is undertaken on foot alongside LA freeways.

Through accident, contingency, and repetition, the reworking of the creature's story in *Frankenstein* reiterates divisions of and in humanity. Again monstrosity exposes the limits of suffering, locating abjection at the base of fantasies of creativity and power. Repetition, thematic and narrative, takes film beyond the familiarly 'humonstrous' frames of the novel to mark out a barer and more hopeless existence. Every significant turn is accompanied by a close-up registering Monster's continued possession of Elizabeth's swipe card, thereby tying contingency to narrative progress. Similar patterns of contingency define the effects of genetic mutation: the same cells divide and destroy each other in cancerous cellular replication. Further repetitions underline the impossibility of difference: Monster is regularly shown strapped to a surgical table, a bench in a cell, a trolley in a police wagon; beaten with baseball bats, batons, and sticks; and murdered by lethal injection, surgical saw, and automatic pistol. Monster is strong and learns mimetically so his responses to physical abuse are mirror reactions: awakening on a mortuary slab, a saw biting into his skull, he turns the instrument on the pathologist; beaten by guards with nightsticks, he defends himself in kind; shot by a policeman in execution style, he copies the gesture at a later opportunity. Mimetic learning simply repeats, presenting no opportunity for developing a higher ethical perspective or judgement. Monster copies—and magnifies—the violence and inhumanity around him, unable to discriminate good from bad, right from wrong: he is a subject of imitation and repetition, without hope, it seems, of achieving a more rational and self-conscious position. Repeated police violence, too, displays levels of brutality that put paid to any pretence of law: the beatings of Monster exemplify an inescapable chain in which punishment, revenge, suppression, and reaction are the only imperatives (their endless trash-gothic cursing—'fuck you animal', 'freak show', 'elephant man'—signals a language without respect or law, unable to reach a level of symbolic or civilised usage).

For Monster, language only seems to confer abuse until he meets the blind bluesman: 'welcome Monster', he says, extending a hand. But the ease with which the creature assumes the name 'Monster' is also significant: rather than invoking intersubjective consensus or recognition, it is a term for anomalies, a name for an unnameable and most wretched of conditions. Almost every encounter in Rose's film begins with an exchange of names in which the reply 'Monster' marks symbolic incongruity, inhumanity, and dysfunction: interrogated by police, 'Monster' proves unhelpful in establishing legal identity as well as hinting at historic abuse; with Ed, the bluesman, it becomes associated with mental illness; and with the kind prostitute, Wanda, it warrants pity and fear regarding the infectiousness of his physical condition. Insufficient in establishing legal status, citizenship, rights, or in expressing human and communal ties, Monster's name only highlights isolation, non-belonging, non-identity, non-personhood. More powerfully, and in accordance with the novel, it is singularly ineffectual in offering any answer to pressing questions of origins and subjectivity: who was I? He remains a 'blot on the earth', a stain on and among an already degraded populace and environment.

Without the monster's voice-over, this would be a film with minimal script, reduced to screams, limited mimetic responses, and expletives, all signs of an impoverished culture. Able to speak, Frankenstein's creature is also well read. There are no books in Rose's film, no Milton or Plutarch, and no Volney, despite the overriding sense of ruin. Not even Victor's scientific journal makes an appearance. Texts of origin, identity, and destination are replaced by the internet: a smartphone provides (pornographic) images in answer to the question of where babies come from or, later, gives directions to the scene of creation. All Monster has to do is follow instructions: there is no need for reading, just as there is no need for memory, judgement, or self-reflection. Even identity is an online effect: the other signifier of digital contemporaneity that appears in almost every scene of the film is Elizabeth's swipe card. Though jealously protected for its image of maternal wholeness, it allows movement beyond the contingencies of violence that shunt him from non-non-place to non-non-place. A swipe card *is* identity in the world of the film: it marks difference and establishes boundaries in terms of legitimacy; it carries the magnetic information that permits access and passage; it enables freedom as well as surveillance and control of movement; it records details of identity that secure the place and belonging granted by the world of information storage and retrieval.

Returning to the laboratory at the end of the film, Monster is confronted by the 3D laser printer completing another version of himself. He is informed by Victor that he can be remade. New creation only replicates sameness. Staring at the unfinished body in the laser tube, Monster tries to assert his difference (echoing terms he has learned in his short time outside): 'beast, not me'; 'Other'. He goes on to attempt a more positive affirmation of self: 'I am I'; 'I am... I am... I am... '. He is ... what? He does not, cannot, say. A repetitious organism for whom self closes on self, his words fail in the absence of otherness. 'I am alone': but his loneliness is not an effect of absolute difference, it comes of the horror of being a genetically manufactured creature of identity and sameness: as Victor says, the body being completed is 'exactly like you'. All is similitude, repeated over and over again: on bodies, across cultures, in language, and, always, on screens and in networks of information. There is nothing outside other than pain, beatings, garbage, and death.

No law can secure his identity or rights, there is no mother to love him, and no sense of hope to overcome the relentless downward spiral of base existence: bare life gets barer by the moment, any exceptional status further degraded. This *Homo abjectus* cannot be sacrificed, but he can be killed—and killed over and over again. With his clone torn apart, Elizabeth dying by accident, his own throat slashed, and Victor gone, there is nothing for Monster to do but realise the end that was promised—but never enacted—by his model at the end of *Frankenstein*: the film—Monster voicing homage to 'her' (Elizabeth) rather than 'him' (Victor)—ends with a realised nightmare of her bloodied body in a white nightdress being carried to a funeral pyre. Monster, without past and without future, but with full knowledge of the networks in which he was formed, is radically refused hope and can do nothing but act on the monstrously human promise of self-immolation that closed the novel in provocative irresolution. But the promise of self-destruction that restored some power and agency to Frankenstein's creature now barely holds any force in a brutal world in which so many bodies have already been displayed as disposable, replicable, and expendable. Without law, rights, agency, belonging, or any vestige of dignity, things are quite hopeless. Life, becomes barer, falls below the threshold of monstrosity envisaged by *Frankenstein*. The final gesture is neither defiant nor heroic, neither sacred nor sacrificial, little more than an act of waste disposal on waste ground. With trashumanism all illusions go up in smoke. Given—or perhaps beyond—Monster's condition, and at the cost of its horror, some cyborgs, chimeras, hybrids, and posthumans may, one hopes, begin, without fear or fantasy, to foster some other imagining.

Works Cited

Agamben, Giorgio. 1995. *Homo Sacer.* Trans. Daniel Heller-Roazen. Stanford: Stanford University Press.
———. 1999. *Remains of Auschwitz.* Trans. Daniel Heller-Roazen. Stanford: Stanford University Press.
———. 2005. *State of Exception.* Trans. Kevin Attell. Chicago/London: University of Chicago Press.
Balibar, Étienne. 1998. Violence, Ideality, Cruelty. *New Formations* 35: 7–18.
———. 2001. Outlines of a Topography of Cruelty. *Constellations* 1: 15–29.
———. 2009. Violence and Cruelty. Trans. Stephanie Bundy. *Differences* 20 (2–3): 9–35.

Barthes, Roland. 1977. *From Work to Text*, in Stephen Heath (trans. and ed.), *Image Music Text*, 155–164. London: Fontana.

Baudrillard, Jean. 1994. *The Illusion of the End*. Trans. Chris Turner. London: Polity Press.

Cavallaro, Dani. 2000. *Cyberpunk and Cyberculture*. London: Athlone Press.

Chocano, Carina. 2011. How Tabloid Trainwrecks Are Reinventing Gothic Literature. *New York Times*, September 2. http://www.nytimes.com/2011/09/04/magazine/tabloid-trainwrecks-reinventing-gothic-literature.html?pagewanted=all&_r=0. Accessed Sept 2013.

Clarke, Arthur C. 1995. Dial "F" for Frankenstein. In *The Frankenstein Omnibus*, ed. Peter Haining, 681–688. London: Orion.

Clarke, Julie. 2002. The Human/Not Human in the Work of Orlan and Stelarc. In *The Cyborg Experiments*, ed. Joanna Zylinska, 33–55. London/New York: Continuum.

Easlea, Brian. 1983. *Fathering the Unthinkable*. London: Polity.

Fukuyama, Francis. 2002. *Our Posthuman Future*. New York: Farrar, Strauss and Giroux.

Gusterson, Hugh. 1995. Short Circuit: Watching Television with a Nuclear-Weapons Scientist. In *The Cyborg Handbook*, ed. Chris Hables Gray, 107–118. New York/London: Routledge.

Halberstam, Judith. 1995. *Skin Shows*. Durham/London: Duke University Press.

Haraway, Donna J. 1990. A Manifesto for Cyborgs. In *Feminism/Postmodernism*, ed. Linda J. Nicholson, 190–233. New York/London: Routledge.

———. 1997. *Modest Witness@Second_Millenium*. London/New York: Routledge.

Hardt, Michael, and Antonio Negri. 2000. *Empire*. Cambridge, MA: Harvard University Press.

———. 2006. *Multitude*. London: Penguin.

Hayles, N. Katherine. 1999. *How We Became Posthuman*. Chicago: University of Chicago Press.

———. 2000. Flickering Connectivities in Shelley Jackson's Patchwork Girl. *Postmodern Culture* 10 (2).

Hoeveler, Diane Long. 2003. *Frankenstein*, Feminism and Literary Theory. In *The Cambridge Companion to Mary Shelley*, ed. Esther Schor, 45–62. Cambridge: Cambridge University Press.

Johnson, Fred. 1996. Cyberpunks in the White House. In *Fractal Dreams*, ed. John Dovey, 78–108. London: Lawrence and Wishart.

Kroker, Arthur. 2014. *Exits to a Posthuman Future*. Cambridge: Polity.

Levy, Stephen. 1992. *Artificial Life*. London: Jonathan Cape.

Mbembe, Achille. 2003. Necropolitics. Trans. Libby Meintjes. *Public Culture* 15 (1): 11–40.

Plant, Sadie. 1997. *Zeroes and Ones*. London: Fourth Estate.

Poster, Mark. 2002. High-Tech Frankenstein, or Heidegger Meets Stelarc. In *The Cyborg Experiments*, ed. Joanna Zylinska, 15–32. London: Continuum.

Roof, Judith. 1996. *Reproductions of Reproduction*. London: Routledge.

Rosenberg, Brian. 2013. The Frankenstein's Monster of Social Media. *The Huffington Post*, March 29. huffingtonpost.com/brian_rosenberg/millenials_social_media_b_2978652/html. Accessed Nov 2015.

Shelley, Mary. 1969. *Frankenstein*, ed. M.K. Joseph. Oxford: Oxford University Press.

Stryker, Susan. 1994. My Words to Victor Frankenstein Above the Village of Chamounix. *GLQ* 1: 237–254.

Turney, Jon. 1998. *Frankenstein's Footsteps*. New Haven/London: Yale University Press.

AFTERWORD: MEDITATION ON THE MONSTER, A POEM

David Punter

I

Blasted as thou wert (my maker)
my agony was still superior to thine
I shall die, and what I now feel
no longer felt.
I have lived through torturous extremities
felt my body pulled apart
that body that was never wholly one
but a thing of shreds and patches
a wandering minstrel
without, of course, a mate,
but that goes without saying –
so many things go without saying –
perhaps I too shall go without saying, though
I have this gift of speech, a curious eloquence,
though it is seen as being
no voice but these harsh, grating cries
that you, my maker, my only friend,
refuse to accept as language
gift of the gods (refuse of the gods – think Hecate,
divinity of household rubbish)
in which I have no part
I shall end in ice and flame

© The Author(s) 2018
C. M. Davison, M. Mulvey-Roberts (eds.), *Global Frankenstein*,
Studies in Global Science Fiction,
https://doi.org/10.1007/978-3-319-78142-6

a conflagration that will fade away
leaving no trace, no memory
shreds of pages unhouseled, unannealed
only a moment's terror, an image to frighten
lost children, shrouded in the night
my fate is to be futureless, forgotten
in the vast charnel house of the dead
where I was born, where I hope against hope to die.

II

You followed me (my monster)
from birth, you grinned and cursed
with wretched foreboding
I, inheritor of chymists and magicians,
heir to the righteous of Geneva,
toiler after the vast secrets,
their bourgeois manners intolerable to my
quasi-aristocratic pursuits.
I listened instead to Paracelsus, Albertus the Great,
Michael Scott was no stranger to me
(although his name might still invoke a cold shudder,
for these spirits are still abroad in the world –
think on the Order of the Northern Dragon,
with its Gothic script and Aryan ideas)
those mighty men, I thought them then, who sought to tear through
the fabric of the ages and achieve renown
whereas I, who could have been as they,
am sunk in sordid plots of vengeance
bound to the corporeal by the death of so many 'loved ones' –
that is what they call them, though
I am not sure what that means –
I have hesitated before the terrifying portals of love.
Instead, it seems to me
that I am immersed, immured in the spirit-jail
my thoughts of flying free of human bonds
instead return me endlessly to the fleshly
a living (am I living?) reminder of the fate of pride
in the infinite mausoleum of hope

in the eternal laboratory where I shall still work endlessly
the lightning striking, the flash that illuminates
and condemns to darkness, my flesh seared
by forces I think I understand
but cannot control.

III

Listen, oh listen to the continuous self-pity of these men.
I have known so many like them, absorbed in their grand schemes
of purity, of floating free.
Oh, if I had the vocabulary of ages yet to come
so that I could accuse them (even though I brought them
into being, though they cannot feel my love,
creatures of papier-mâché as they are)
of their true fear, their envy of my womb,
their terror that things may be wrought
even from what they see with their blinkered eyes
(scared of horses, as Little Hans is yet to be)
as nothing, without recourse to the graveyard,
that that 'nothing', so nebulous, so grave,
bears love's contours – but this is hopeless,
men can never hear, they never hear, they will never hear,
and so I forgive, I look upon
my creatures with a kindly, a beneficent eye
for they understand nothing, they know nothing,
not even that from which they flee.
They are content to call out to each other in voices of hatred
across the interminable wastes
(did I write those wastes?
Did I inscribe that which cannot be inscribed?)
which they will make more waste in their pursuit
of war, of acrimony – for I see the future even unto the last man
his grandeur, his doom, the customary doom of empires
which none will heed until the very sun expires
in absolute exhaustion
for thinking on the evils man (do I mean man?
Is woman entirely exempt,
do we have any chance to see?) has wrought.

IV

The *shisma* is wounded; he is the essence,
the being of the wound.
He roams the streets, bearing his torn-up body in the aftermath,
or is it the beginning of another cycle of war
in Baghdad (for example)?
He is paradoxically invulnerable, he speaks the truth
of the wounds of nations in his stitched-together body.
He knows nothing of justice, but he knows the voices
and the staggering, the lurching of those unknown victims
of a senseless war; see, they gather around him, see,
he holds the banner, the standard, he cries Excelsior
as he plunges through the alleyways of a destroyed city
in pursuit of his creator. He too knows
the ruins of empire, he sees
the disheartened sorcerer,
the still-illusioned sophist,
the demoralised officer of high command,
he knows the three great madmen,
and they follow him
into the realm of the ungovernable, knowing
there is no possibility of justice, but also that
the General violence is his own worst enemy, yet may be better
than the particular enemy we see every day
coming for us with rifle, dagger, scimitar,
firing from the rooftops,
creating his own inferno
in which again (as we read on, as we endlessly read on
through the remakings of history)
the pages might be shredded, might turn into
floating leaves from which a new world might be born,
had it not been torn apart in its very inception
as a woman is torn apart
in the act of birth.

V

But now I see the world anew; I have not died,
I rampage through the wild realms of fantasy,
I am continuously reincarnated, it seems.

Is this my body being torn apart again,
the bolt through the neck – lightning, perhaps,
is that how the symbolic order works?
My master never told me, or if he did
I never heard; or perhaps I did not listen,
consumed, in so many ways. as I was.
I see the living, and I see the dead –
reborn with an unnatural acuity of senses
which I do not want,
no, I profoundly do not want.
There is something here (so says the demented priest)
that I do not understand or love
but it seems I am appointed
as an avatar, as the emblem
of all those torn bodies,
of all the monstrous, of all the geeks
displayed in life's carnival
to demonstrate the limits of the human –
how far can we go? How far can I continue to go,
out here in the frozen wilderness
dragging you with me, my maker,
dragging you always with me,
in search of … I know not what.
My limbs refuse to function,
they are beyond my motor control.
my neurological damage is unfathomable –
how long can the body continue to function after it is dead?

VI

Again you cry to me, again you seek to be plaintive.
Can you not see that here mine is the authority?
I am your author (but who is my author?
I sense a realm of greater secrets,
within the page, behind the page is there a 'she' who will ever tell it?).
Unlike you, I am not a freak;
I know my gender, my class, my upbringing,
my expectations, my entitlement.
Above all, I am Victor:
victorious, triumphant, ceding nothing
to those familial impulses that might bring me down, reduce
my command. No human being could have passed

(do you know this, creature? Have I told you?)
a happier childhood than myself.
My parents were possessed by the very spirit of kindness
and indulgence. Yet
(and I understand this not)
my temper was sometimes violent, and my passions vehement and
of course it was the secrets of heaven and earth
that I desired to learn.
I learned them.
I learned them all (so I think).
I believe I have learned them. I wish I had not learned them.
They are fruit of bitterness and gall,
and I wear my learning now as sacerdotal rags.
The magicians have deserted me,
as they always do,
filled fat with promises they cannot keep,
the elixir, the transmutation, the accumulation
of gold on gold, kept
in the vaults where they cannot circulate –
circulation of the blood, circulation of capital, circles, endless circles,
poor Stevie before the explosion – but I run ahead of myself,
to writers, pages that I cannot have known.

VII

My children, oh my children,
Why must you squabble so.
You are full of life obdurate
And yet you obstruct the flow

Of love and tranquil peace
Of all that needs to turn
Within this turning world.
Why do you seek to burn?

I ask this question often
As I live an afterlife
Perhaps the glow of Italy
Will put an end to strife.

No, this is sentimental nonsense, and as I grow old
I comfort myself with the thought that
I have not become a sentimentalist;
I see still the terror of empire, the violence of men
continually at war one with another
and I see the end of the world,
the redness of the apocalypse
for this is given too for women to see –
and all has been misunderstood; the warning
I strove to give turned into a worship of the monstrous –
and yet all this is within the envelope of my
continuing love for my children, my ghastly children –
how can women love little boys, with their plastic guns,
their Oshkosh denims, their bully-boy haircuts,
the man is father to the child, indeed,
and would it were not so –
if I were not a spirit, then of course I could not foresee all this,
the young men of the Troubles,
the deathly adolescents of *jihad*,
the scarred, scared lads on mopeds,
the gang-rapists, the terrified
murderers of families and children –
but I am a spirit – and so of course I could be reborn –
would it not be a great joke if I had already
been reborn as Emily Dickinson?
Then I could write limpid poetry …
I foresee all that as well, but then of course
I come from another age – but look –
I am here behind you,
authenticated, biographised, endlessly
reincarnated, enjoined
as the patroness of yet another struggle
for a woman's voice.
I salute you, of course, and am there with you;
but how much have you understood of the torment
of creation, of reproduction?
You women have, of course – but you men?

VIII

Zombie.
Strutting, lurching, devoid of speech,
devoid of feeling, incarnation of the void.
They're all around us now,
World War Z is upon us,
and we need to take stock; we need to consider whether we are being taken as stock,
as cattle, as characters in a play
that in the end belittles us.
The question is one of agency.
Master, as I address you now,
do you think you might have mis-imagined?
I want to tell you about colours,
about senses, about
all you may have missed
(my misbegotten creator),
in your strange pursuit of abstraction.
What do you think I learned in my painful hoverings
Outside the blind man's hut?
Do you really think I had not read Plato?
Do you think (did you think)
I was unaware of the cave,
or of the dulling of the senses
concomitant (I shall sound even more abstract now than you)
on economic greed,
that I did not feel the beauty of the sense of colour,
of how to describe the flitting of the humming-bird
to those who could not see?
What you wrote in me (wrote into my skin,
inscribed on my body,
as it was inscribed in hieroglyphs onto the body of the Great White Whale)
was a story you did not yourself know, I accept that:
the story of the stranger, the exile,
the refugee who came seeking help
and no help came; the story of the abject,
those whose lurching, traumatised bodies,
unattractive (even to those magnetic fields that so fascinated you)
unwelcome (unwelcomed)
will go on erupting from the deadlands,

those lands that you in your magnificent wealth
have rendered uninhabitable.
Yes, I come back; they (we) all come back,
we are the voices of the fragile and the damned.
It is you and you alone (and you are so very, very alone)
who say we have no souls;
but we are many, and you are one – is this
your victory, to be separate,
to refuse to acknowledge those pressing faces,
those urgent bodies, threatening to overwhelm
the song of the borderguard –
is this the triumph
you have sought at such a cost?

IX

There is no true fathering that is the truth.
There is no true fathering: that is the truth.
In the world between those statements
an abyss yawns – have you glimpsed it?
I believe I have – or did once,
and I tried to express it even at my 'tender' age.
They said (those men said)
that I dreamed; I went along with that,
for how else could one imagine alterity,
but when I look back
I doubt it was a dream
but rather a figuring
of what was all around me.
Oh no, I do not doubt the intentions of all these
alpha males
(such would not be the role of woman)
but I wonder at their ignorance, their unawareness
of that very body that you, young Victor,
my baby, my curse, my other self,
sought to reincarnate not realising, never realising
that such a body lay close to you, or could have done,
on your bridal night
had you not been carried away into
the usual eve-of-wedding fantasies, of assault, of taking where it was not
given.

But you, my other creature, my creature of Otherness,
those whom so many call 'monster',
perhaps there is still some salvation to be had from you,
some hint of the beloved,
some touch of the
hidden colours of blindness,
something of the prodigal,
now,
to me, in dream,
returning.

Index[1]

[1]Note: Page numbers followed by 'n' refer to notes.

© The Author(s) 2018

C. M. Davison, M. Mulvey-Roberts (eds.), *Global Frankenstein*, Studies in Global Science Fiction, https://doi.org/10.1007/978-3-319-78142-6

The manufacturer's authorised representative in the EU is Springer
Nature Customer Service Centre GmbH, Europaplatz 3, 69115 Heidelberg,
Germany. If you have any concerns regarding our products, please
contact ProductSafety@springernature.com

Printed and bound by CPI Group (UK) Ltd, Croydon, CR0 4YY
29/04/2026
02099514-0004